The Cambridge Companion to Bartók

Béla Bartók (1881–1945) is now regarded as a key innovator of twentieth-century music. He is widely known for compositions strongly influenced by his folk music studies, and for his activities as a concert pianist, music editor and teacher.

This Companion comprises three sections: the first explores Bartók's general philosophy on life, as it evolved within the turbulent political and cultural environment in Hungary in which he grew up. Focusing on his major works the second section identifies the innovative characteristics of his musical style within the context of the diverse genres in which he composed. The third section examines the wide variety of critical and analytical responses to his compositions and his performances both during his life and after.

Cambridge Companions to Music

Composers

The Cambridge Companion to Bach
Edited by John Butt
0 521 45350 X (hardback)
0 521 58780 8 (paperback)

The Cambridge Companion to Bartók
Edited by Amanda Bayley
0 521 66010 6 (hardback)
0 521 66958 8 (paperback)

The Cambridge Companion to Berg
Edited by Anthony Pople
0 521 56374 7 (hardback)
0 521 56489 1 (paperback)

The Cambridge Companion to Berlioz
Edited by Peter Bloom
0 521 59388 3 (hardback)
0 521 59638 6 (paperback)

The Cambridge Companion to Brahms
Edited by Michael Musgrave
0 521 48129 5 (hardback)
0 521 48581 9 (paperback)

The Cambridge Companion to Benjamin Britten
Edited by Mervyn Cooke
0 521 57384 X (hardback)
0 521 57476 5 (paperback)

The Cambridge Companion to Chopin
Edited by Jim Samson
0 521 47752 2 (paperback)

The Cambridge Companion to Handel
Edited by Donald Burrows
0 521 45425 5 (hardback)
0 521 45613 4 (paperback)

The Cambridge Companion to Ravel
Edited by Deborah Mawer
0 521 64026 1 (hardback)
0 521 64856 4 (paperback)

The Cambridge Companion to Schubert
Edited by Christopher Gibbs
0 521 48229 1 (hardback)
0 521 48424 3 (paperback)

The Cambridge Companion to

BARTÓK

....

EDITED BY
Amanda Bayley

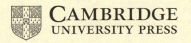

CAMBRIDGE
UNIVERSITY PRESS

PUBLISHED BY THE PRESS SYNDICATE OF THE UNIVERSITY OF CAMBRIDGE
The Pitt Building, Trumpington Street, Cambridge, United Kingdom

CAMBRIDGE UNIVERSITY PRESS
The Edinburgh Building, Cambridge CB2 2RU, UK
40 West 20th Street, New York, NY 10011–4211, USA
10 Stamford Road, Oakleigh, VIC 3166, Australia
Ruiz de Alarcón 13, 28014 Madrid, Spain
Dock House, The Waterfront, Cape Town 8001, South Africa

http://www.cambridge.org

First published 2001

Printed in the United Kingdom at the University Press, Cambridge

Typeface Minion 10.75/14 pt   *System* QuarkXPress™   [SE]

A catalogue record for this book is available from the British Library

Library of Congress Cataloguing in Publication data

The Cambridge companion to Bartók / edited by Amanda Bayley.
       p.   cm. – (Cambridge companions to music)
   Includes bibliographical references (p.   ) and index.
   Discography: p.
   Contents: Contexts: political, social, and cultural – Profiles of the music – Reception.
   ISBN 0 521 66010 6 (hardback)   0 521 66958 8 (paperback)
   1. Bartók, Béla, 1881–1945 – Criticism and interpretation.   I. Bayley, Amanda.   II.
   Series.
   ML410.B26 C35 2001
   780′.92 – dc21   00-036030

ISBN 0 521 66010 6 hardback
ISBN 0 521 66958 8 paperback

Contents

Contributors

Amanda Bayley is Senior Lecturer in Music at the University of Wolverhampton and has published on Bartók's Fourth String Quartet. Following research undertaken at the Budapest Bartók Archive she is currently preparing a book on Bartók performance studies.

Rachel Beckles Willson is Lecturer in Music at Bristol University. She has published articles on György Kurtág and is currently preparing a book on this composer.

Susan Bradshaw is a pianist and writer on music, mainly that of the twentieth century, who studied at the Royal Academy of Music with Harold Craxton and Howard Ferguson and afterwards in Paris with Pierre Boulez.

David Cooper is Senior Lecturer in Music at the University of Leeds. His publications include the Cambridge Music Handbook on Bartók's Concerto for Orchestra and a number of other essays about the composer.

Stephen Erdely is Professor Emeritus of Music at Massachusetts Institute of Technology. His field research in ethnomusicology includes the oral traditional music of central European nationality groups in the midwest and east of the United States, and more recently as an appointed 'research associate' to the Milman Parry Collection at Harvard University; his studies also include his book on the *Music of Southslavic Epics from the Bihac Region of Bosnia*.

Victoria Fischer, professional pianist, is Associate Professor of Music at Elon College, North Carolina. She is author and editor of a number of publications on Bartók's music.

Danielle Fosler-Lussier completed her doctoral dissertation entitled 'The Transition to Communism and the Legacy of Béla Bartók in Hungary, 1945–1956', at the University of California, Berkeley in 1999. She now holds a postdoctoral research and teaching fellowship at Princeton University's Society of Fellows in the Humanities.

Malcolm Gillies is Executive Dean of Humanities and Social Sciences at the University of Adelaide, and President of the Australian Academy of the Humanities. His extensive publications on Bartók include *The Bartók Companion* (1993). With Adrienne Gombocz he has edited a volume of Bartók's letters, and is the author of a forthcoming Master Musicians volume on the composer.

Lynn Hooker is completing her doctoral dissertation, entitled 'Modernism Meets Nationalism: Béla Bartók and the Musical Life of Pre-World War I Budapest', at the University of Chicago.

Peter Laki is Programme Annotator for the Cleveland Orchestra. He has lectured on Bartók at conferences in Hungary, France and the United States.

Vera Lampert holds a degree in musicology from the Liszt Ferenc Academy of

Music in Budapest. From 1969 to 1978 she was a researcher at the Budapest Bartók Archive and has published several articles on Bartók including a catalogue of all the folk melodies used in his compositions. Since 1983 she has been a music librarian at Brandeis University, Massachusetts, while continuing with her Bartók studies.

Carl Leafstedt is Assistant Professor of Music at the University of North Carolina at Greensboro. His writings on Bartók have appeared in *College Music Symposium, NOTES,* and *Studia musicologica* and he is author of *Inside Bluebeard's Castle: Music and Drama in Béla Bartók's Opera* (1998).

Nicky Losseff is Lecturer in Music at the University of York. She has written on subjects ranging from medieval polyphony through nineteenth-century literature to Kate Bush. She is also a pianist, specializing in contemporary music.

David E. Schneider is Valentine Professor of Music at Amherst College. His work has received support from the American Musicological Society (AMS 50) and the American Council of Learned Societies; he has published articles in *Bartók and His World* (1995), *Muzsika, Studia musicologica* and *repercussions.*

Ivan F. Waldbauer, musicologist and pianist, was research director of the New York Bartók Archive (1957–66) and taught music history at Brown University, Providence (1960–90). His interests, besides Bartók, are popular music of the sixteenth century and German music theory from Koch to Riemann and Schenker.

Acknowledgements

I am grateful to a number of people who have helped in the production of this book, not least of which are the contributors themselves for their enthusiasm and support. I would like to extend special thanks to Susan Bradshaw, Malcolm Gillies, László Somfai and Arnold Whittall who have offered their professional advice at various stages of the book's development. I am especially grateful to John Aubrey Richardson for the considerable time he has generously devoted to typesetting all the music examples and to the help and support offered by my friend and colleague Shirley Thompson. I am also indebted to Penny Souster at Cambridge for her guidance and patience.

Figure 1.1 has been reproduced courtesy of the Ópusztaser National Historical Memorial Park; photo by Zoltán Enyedi.

Figure 1.2 has been reproduced courtesy of the Kiscelli Photo Collection of the Budapest Historical Museum; photo by György Klösz.

Permission to reprint text, or music extracts is gratefully acknowledged to the following:

Boosey and Hawkes Music Publishers Ltd. for permission (world-wide) to reprint extracts from *Kossuth* Op. posth. © Copyright 1963 by Hawkes & Son (London) Ltd. Suite No. 2 Op. 4 Sz34 © Copyright 1921 by Hawkes & Son (London) Ltd. Violin Concerto No. 1, Sz36 © Copyright 1958 by Hawkes & Son (London) Ltd. Two Portraits, Op. 5 Sz37 © Copyright by Hawkes & Son (London) Ltd. Five Songs Op. 16, Sz63 © Copyright 1923 by Hawkes & Son (London) Ltd. Three studies, Op. 18 Sz72 © Copyright 1920 by Hawkes & Son (London) Ltd. Improvisations on Hungarian Peasant Songs, Op. 20 Sz74 © Copyright 1922 by Hawkes & Son (London) Ltd. 'From the Diary of a Fly' No. 142 from *Mikrokosmos*, Sz107 © Copyright by Hawkes & Son (London) Ltd. [Definitive corrected edition © Copyright 1987 by Hawkes & Son (London) Ltd.] *Contrasts*, Sz111 © Copyright 1942 by Hawkes & Son (London) Ltd. Violin Concerto No. 2, Sz112 © Copyright 1946 by Hawkes & Son (London) Ltd. Divertimento, Sz113 © Copyright 1940 by Hawkes & Son (London) Ltd. String Quartet No. 6, Sz114 © Copyright 1941 by Hawkes & Son (London) Ltd. Concertos for Orchestra, Sz116 © Copyright 1946 by Hawkes & Son (London) Ltd. Sonata for Solo Violin, Sz117 © Copyright 1947 by Hawkes & Son (London) Ltd. Piano Concerto No. 3, Sz119 © Copyright 1947 by Hawkes & Son (London) Ltd.

Boosey & Hawkes Music Publishers Ltd. for permission to reprint in the UK, British Commonwealth, Eire and USA, music extracts from the following work by Béla Bartók: Scherzo for Piano and Orchestra, Op. 2 Sz28 © Copyright 1961 by Zenemükiadó Vállalat, Budapest. Suite for Orchestra No. 1, Op. 3 Sz31 ©

Copyright 1905 by Editio Musica Budapest. String Quartet No. 1 in A minor, Op. 7 Sz40 © Copyright 1908 by Editio Musica Budapest. Seven Sketches, Op. 9 Sz44 © Copyright 1910 by Editio Musica Budapest.

Boosey & Hawkes Inc., USA for permission to reprint in the USA music extracts from the following works by Béla Bartók: *Village Scenes* Sz78, *Cantata profana* Sz94, Sonata for Piano Sz80, *Out of Doors* Sz81, String Quartet No. 3 Sz85, Piano Concerto No. 2 Sz95, String Quartet No. 4 Sz91, 44 Duos Sz98, String Quartet No. 5 Sz102, *Music for Strings, Percussion and Celesta* Sz106.

Dover Edition for permission to reprint the music extracts from the following works: Fourteen Bagatelles Op. 6 Z38, Ten Easy Pieces Sz39. *For Children* Sz42.

Editio Musica Budapest for kind permission (world-wide) to reprint the music extracts from the following works: Violin Sonata (1903) DD72 © 1968 by Editio Musica Budapest. Rhapsody Op. 1 Sz26 © 1955 by Editio Musica Budapest. Scherzo for Piano and Orchestra Op. 2 Sz28 © 1962 by Editio Musica Budapest. Suite for Orchestra No. 1 Op. 3 Sz31 © 1912 by Rózsavölgyi and Co., Budapest; © assigned 1950 to Editio Musica Budapest. String Quartet No. 1 in A Minor Op. 7 Sz40 © 1911 by Rózsavölgyi and Co., Budapest; © assigned 1950 to Editio Musica Budapest; revised edition © 1956 by Editio Musica Budapest. Two Elegies Op. 8b Sz41 © 1910 by Rozsnyai Károly, Budapest; © assigned 1950 to Editio Musica Budapest. Seven Sketches Op. 9b Sz44 © 1911 by Rozsnyai Károly, Budapest; © assigned 1950 to Editio Musica Budapest. Four Dirges Op. 9a Sz45 © 1912 Rózsavölgyi & Co., Budapest. Three Burlesques Op. 8c Sz47 © 1912 Rózsavölgyi & Co., Budapest; © Assigned 1950 to Editio Musica Budapest.

Faber & Faber Ltd. for permission to reprint fig. 2 from 'Dance Suite' in Malcolm Gillies (ed.), *The Bartók Companion* (London: Faber & Faber, 1993), p. 492 as Example 3.2 in this volume.

Kahn and Averill for permission to reproduce fig. 37 from Ernő Lendvai, *Béla Bartók: An Analysis of his Music* (London: Kahn and Averill, 1971), rev. edn 1979, in slightly altered form as Example 14.2a in this volume.

Pendragon Press for permission to reproduce Examples 129 and 130 in János Kárpáti, *Bartók's Chamber Music* (Pendragon Press, 1994), p. 197 as Example 14.3 in this volume.

State University of New York Press to reprint the Hungarian folksong in Example 9.8 from Benjamin Suchoff (ed.), *The Hungarian Folk Song* (Albany: State University of New York Press, 1981), p. 299, No. 299b.

Schirmer for permission to reprint music extracts from 51 Exercises, No. 7 by Johannes Brahms, and *For Children* Sz42 Vol. II, No. XXVI by Béla Bartók.

Universal Edition for permission to reprint music extracts from the following works by Béla Bartók: *Duke Bluebeard's Castle* Op. 11 Sz48, *The Wooden Prince* Op. 13 Sz60, Suite Op. 14 Sz62, String Quartet No. 2 Op. 17 Sz67, Fifteen

Hungarian Peasant Songs Sz71, *The Miraculous Mandarin* Op. 19 Sz73, *Village Scenes* Sz78, Piano Sonata Sz80, *Out of Doors* Sz81, String Quartet No. 3 Sz85, String Quartet No. 4 Sz91, Piano Concerto No. 2 Sz95, 44 Duos Sz98, String Quartet No. 5 Sz102, *Music for Strings, Percussion and Celesta* Sz106, and the Sonata for Solo Cello by Zoltán Kodály.

University of California Press to reprint Example 139 from Elliott Antokoletz, *The Music of Béla Bartók: A Study of Tonality and Progression in Twentieth-Century Music* (Berkeley: University of California Press, 1984), p. 118 as Figure 14.2 in this volume.

Chronology

DATE	FOLKSONG COLLECTING AND TRANSCRIPTIONS	COMPOSITIONS AND PERFORMING EDITIONS
1903		*Kossuth* symphonic poem. Four Piano Pieces. Sonata for violin and piano.
1903–04		Piano Quintet.
1904	First experience of folk music from Transylvania.	Rhapsody Op. 1, for piano; for piano and orchestra (1904–5); for two pianos (1905). Scherzo Op. 2, for orchestra and piano.
1904–05		Hungarian Folksongs (First Series), for voice and piano.
1905	Starts collaboration with Zoltán Kodály (–1940).	Suite No. 1 Op. 3, for orchestra. *For the little 'tót'*, for voice and piano.
1905–07		Suite No. 2 Op. 4, for orchestra (transcribed as Suite for two pianos, 1941).
1906	Annual folksong collecting expeditions using Edison phonograph. Collects Slovak songs.	Hungarian Folksongs (with Zoltán Kodály), for voice and piano. Two Hungarian folksongs, for voice and piano.
1906–07		Hungarian Folksongs (Second Series), for voice and piano.
1907	Collecting trip to Transylvania. First folksong publication, *Székely balladák* [Székely ballads].	Three Hungarian Folksongs from the Csík District (No. 3 rearranged for voice and piano as No. 3 of Eight Hungarian Folksongs, 1907/17). Two Hungarian Folksongs (unpublished). Four Slovak Folksongs, for voice and piano (No. 4, 1916).
1907–08		Violin Concerto No. 1 [op. posth.] (first movement orchestrated as the first of *Two Portraits* Op. 5, 1911).
1908	Collecting trip to Romanian villages and ethnically mixed villages, including Slovak, Ruthenian, Serbian and Croatian communities, each year (–1917). First article in the Hungarian journal, *Ethnographia*.	Performing edition of J.S. Bach's *The Well-Tempered Clavier*. Fourteen Bagatelles Op. 6, for piano (No. 14 orchestrated as the second of *Two Portraits*). Ten Easy Pieces, for piano (Nos. 5 and 10 orchestrated as Nos. 1 and 2 of *Hungarian Sketches*, 1931).
1908–09		String Quartet No. 1 Op. 7. *For Children* for piano (Vol. I, No. 40 orchestrated as No. 5 of *Hungarian Sketches*). Two Elegies Op. 8b, for piano.

DATE	FOLKSONG COLLECTING AND TRANSCRIPTIONS	COMPOSITIONS AND PERFORMING EDITIONS
1909	Collects Hungarian, Slovak and Romanian songs.	Works on an instructive edition of Beethoven Piano Sonatas (–1912).
1908–10		Seven Sketches Op. 9b, for piano.
1909–10		Two Romanian Dances Op. 8a, for piano (No. 1 orchestrated, 1911). Four Dirges Op. 9a, for piano (No. 2 orchestrated as No. 3 of *Hungarian Sketches*).
1910	The Romanian *Bihor* songs are offered to the Bucharest Academy for publication.	*Two Pictures* Op. 10, for orchestra (also transcribed for piano). Commences work on an instructive edition of twenty Mozart Piano Sonatas (–1912).
1908–11		Three Burlesques Op. 8c, for piano (No. 2 orchestrated as No. 4 of *Hungarian Sketches*).
1911		*Two Portraits*, Op. 5, for orchestra. Commences work on an instructive edition of seventeen Haydn Piano Sonatas (–1913) as well as editions of Schubert and Schumann piano pieces and the Liszt critical edition (–1917). *Duke Bluebeard's Castle* Op. 11. *Allegro barbaro*, for piano.
1910–12	Works on Slovak manuscript collection and offers it for publication.	Four Old Hungarian folksongs, for male choir.
1912	Collecting trips in Hungary.	Four Orchestral Pieces Op. 12 (originally for two pianos, orchestrated 1921). Nine Romanian Folksongs for voice and piano (unpublished).
1913	Collecting trips in north Africa. First book on folk music, *Cântece poporale românești din comitatul Bihor (Ungaria)*, appears in Romanian and French in Bucharest.	The First Term at the Piano – eighteen pieces for Sándor Reschofsky's *Piano Method*.
1913–14	Collecting trips in Romanian villages.	
1915	Collecting trips to ethnically mixed villages.	Sonatina, for piano (orchestrated as Dances from Transylvania, 1931). Romanian Folk Dances, for piano (transcribed for orchestra, 1922). Romanian Christmas Carols (*colinde*), for piano. Two Romanian Folksongs, for female choir.
1916	Collecting trips to ethnically mixed villages.	Slovak Folksong, for voice and piano. Completes instructive edition of Bach's 'Notebook for Anna

DATE	FOLKSONG COLLECTING AND TRANSCRIPTIONS	COMPOSITIONS AND PERFORMING EDITIONS
1916		Magdalena Bach'. Suite Op. 14 for piano. Five Songs Op. 15 for voice and piano. Five 'Ady' Songs Op. 16 for voice and piano.
1914–17		*The Wooden Prince* Op. 13.
1915–17		String Quartet No. 2.
1917	Collecting trip in Hungary. Article on north African folk music published in Budapest.	Four Slovak Folksongs, for mixed choir and piano. Slovak Folksongs, for male choir. Eight Hungarian Folksongs, for voice and piano (Nos. 1–5, 1907).
1918	Collecting trip in Hungary.	Three Hungarian Folksongs, for piano (No. 1, 1914). Fifteen Hungarian Peasant Songs, for piano (Nos. 7–15, 1914). (Nos. 6–12, 14, 15 transcribed for orchestra as Hungarian Peasant Songs, 1933.) Three Studies Op. 18, for piano.
1918–19		*The Miraculous Mandarin* Op. 19 (orchestrated 1923–24).
1919	Collects folksongs from Romanian soldiers.	
1920		Improvisations on Hungarian Peasant Songs Op. 20, for piano. Completes instructive edition of Chopin Waltzes. Works on editions of Couperin and Scarlatti keyboard works (–1926).
1921	Completes classification of Hungarian folk music. Completes a joint study with Kodály of 150 Transylvanian folksongs.	Sonata No.1, for violin and piano.
1922		Sonata No. 2, for violin and piano.
1923	*Erdélyi Magyarság. Népdalok* [Transylvanian Hungarians. Folksongs] (with Kodály). Volume *Volkmusik der Rumänen von Maramureş* is published in Munich.	Dance Suite, for orchestra (transcribed for piano solo, 1925).
1924	*A magyar népdal* [The Hungarian Folk Song] published in Budapest (also Berlin, 1925; London, 1931).	*Village Scenes*, for voice and piano (Nos. 3–5 for eight female voices and chamber orchestra).
1925	Preparation of study of Romanian Christmas carols (*colinde*).	

DATE	FOLKSONG COLLECTING AND TRANSCRIPTIONS	COMPOSITIONS AND PERFORMING EDITIONS
1926	Completes study of Romanian Christmas carols.	Sonata for piano. *Out of Doors*, for piano. Nine Little Piano Pieces. Piano Concerto No. 1.
1927		Three Rondos on Folk Tunes, for piano (No.1, 1916). String Quartet No. 3.
1928		Rhapsody No. 1, for violin and piano (transcribed for violin and orchestra, and for cello and piano, 1929). Rhapsody No. 2, for violin and piano (transcribed for violin and orchestra, 1929). String Quartet No. 4.
1929		Twenty Hungarian Folksongs, for voice and piano (Nos. 1, 2, 11, 14, 12 for voice and orchestra, as Five Hungarian Folksongs, 1933).
1930		Four Hungarian Folksongs, for mixed choir. *Cantata profana.*
1931		Piano Concerto No. 2. 44 Duos for two violins (Nos. 28, 38, 43, 16, 36, transcribed for piano solo as *Petite Suite*, 1936). Dances from Transylvania, for orchestra. *Hungarian Sketches*, for orchestra.
1932	Revision of Romanian collection published in 1913.	Székely Folk Songs, for male choir.
1934	Publication of comparative study, 'Hungarian Folk Music and the Folk Music of Neighboring Peoples' (in *Béla Bartók: Studies in Ethnomusicology* ed. Benjamin Suchoff (Lincoln, Nebr., and London: University of Nebraska Press, 1997)).	String Quartet No. 5.
1935	Publishes *Die Melodien der rumänischen Colinde (Weihnachtslieder)* at own expense.	*From Olden Times*, for male choir.
1935–36		Twenty-seven two- and three-part choruses, for children's or women's voices. (Seven of these appear as Seven Choruses with orchestra 1937–41).
1936	Collecting trip in Turkey.	*Petite Suite* for piano (transcription of six of 44 Duos above). *Music for Strings, Percussion and Celesta.*
1937		Sonata for Two Pianos and Percussion (transcribed as Concerto for Two Pianos, Percussion and Orchestra, 1940).

DATE	FOLKSONG COLLECTING AND TRANSCRIPTIONS	COMPOSITIONS AND PERFORMING EDITIONS
1937–38		Violin Concerto No. 2.
1938		*Contrasts* for violin, clarinet and piano.
1939		Divertimento for string orchestra. *Mikrokosmos* (1926–39). String Quartet No. 6.
1940	Completes the manuscript of *Hungarian Folk Songs: Universal Collection*, 9 vols. (vol. 1 published 1991).	Concerto for Two Pianos, Percussion and Orchestra (transcription of Sonata for Two Pianos and Percussion).
1943	Completes the manuscript of his study of Turkish folk music (published in 1976).	Concerto for Orchestra.
1944	Completes the manuscript of his study of Serbo-Croatian folksongs (published in 1951).	Sonata for Solo Violin.
1945	Completes final revisions of his study of Romanian folk music (published in 1967–75).	Three Ukrainian Folksongs for voice and piano. Piano Concerto No. 3, Viola Concerto (incomplete).

Introduction

AMANDA BAYLEY

Béla Bartók's compositional output defies straightforward categorization. He is often bracketed with Hindemith and Stravinsky as a composer of non-serial music during the first half of the twentieth century, rather than with the twelve-tone composers of the Second Viennese School. Yet what sets him apart from all these composers is his interest in folk music and the assimilation of folk- and art-music influences in his works. His lifelong commitment to folk music, not just its collection and transcription but also its analysis and systematic classification, is unsurpassed.

This book brings together many leading exponents in Bartók research and endeavours to provide a concise yet comprehensive insight into current thoughts and ideas surrounding the historical, cultural and musical appreciation of his works. Even fifty-five years after the composer's death important documents continue to be translated from Hungarian to English, some of which challenge long-standing interpretations of cultural and political issues surrounding the music. The diversity of approaches to Bartók research is demonstrated in this volume through historical, performance-orientated and analytical perspectives within the organization of material into three main sections: 'Contexts', 'Profiles of the music' and 'Reception'.

For Bartók there were a great many political and social issues that underlay his musical philosophy. Lynn Hooker opens the first section of this book with a presentation of the political, social and cultural circumstances that surrounded Bartók in Hungary from the end of the nineteenth to the beginning of the twentieth century. This extends to include the eminent musicians and literary scholars with whom the composer shared some important affinities during this rapidly changing modern world.

A major contribution to the shaping of Bartók's artistic aesthetic was his folk-music research, the extent and significance of which are explained by Stephen Erdely. A map showing the places corresponding to the years that Bartók collected folksongs is accompanied by interesting accounts of his experiences and observations that influenced his investigation of musical folklore as a scientific discipline. Since his engagement with folk music is a recurrent theme of the book his folksong-collecting expeditions and publications are listed alongside his own compositions in the

Chronology. A list of his folk-music studies, which were not all published in Bartók's lifetime, are cited as edited collections within the bibliography.

The second and largest part of the book examines Bartók's compositions grouped according to musical genre. Changing trends in his musical style are demonstrated in relation to the cultural and national issues elucidated in the first section: David Cooper pursues the contradictions and challenges that the composer faced by considering the changing emphasis of nationalist and modernist ideas throughout his orchestral music. Further conflicts are revealed in Bartók's increasingly complex development of folk material within the vocal repertoire: Rachel Beckles Willson shows how he combines the rustic nature of folksong with the Western art-music idiom.

In order that genuine folk music might reach as wide an audience as possible Bartók made many arrangements of folk melodies for instruments as well as for voice, most of which are for his own instrument, the piano. As concert pianist and piano teacher he was in an ideal position to convey the firm ideas he had about the interpretation of his own works as well as those of Classical composers, and Victoria Fischer shows how he developed his notation to support these ideas. Other contributors, including Susan Bradshaw on the piano recital repertoire and chamber music, also take Bartók's notation as a starting point to explain stylistic changes in the music and to understand the Austro-Hungarian tradition Bartók inherited in the context of other contemporary developments. Even though the piano was his own instrument it is questionable whether he adapted folk music in its most intimate or innovative way for this medium. The new ways he found for prescribing folk elements for stringed instruments, discussed in the violin works by Peter Laki and in the String Quartets and string orchestra pieces by Amanda Bayley, are arguably more adventurous than the piano works and, perhaps, come closest to the real folk sounds he was trying to imitate.

Very little help is available for understanding the composer at work since Bartók was a private man who never liked to reveal details about his compositional processes. Carl Leafstedt portrays this side of Bartók's character through his analysis of the theme of loneliness in the stage works and in relation to literary contemporaries. Two contributors, Nicky Losseff and Peter Laki, also consider the solitary figure of Bartók as composer and performer. From different perspectives they interpret the image of 'Self' and 'Other' in, respectively, the Piano Concertos, and the works for violin and piano.

Changes that have taken place in Bartók reception throughout the twentieth century are dealt with in the last section of the book. The fact that his music could not be neatly categorized by critics as atonal, serial or even entirely nationalist (since the breadth of his folksong studies made him more of an internationalist) led to a number of strong criticisms of him. The problem for many of his contemporary critics was that he was neither a modernist nor a nationalist, because he did not exploit chromaticism to the extreme of serialism, and because his fascination with the folk music of many countries was so diverse that, in their eyes, he rejected his native Hungarianness. David E. Schneider reviews the intelligentsia's thoughts on Bartók in Europe during the composer's lifetime, especially concerning the definition of nationalism, while Malcolm Gillies details Bartók's uncomfortable lifestyle and controversial reception in America from 1940 until his death in 1945.

The importance of Bartók's music as a model for future composers was hotly contested in the immediate post-war years among Hungarian composers and musicians. Danielle Fosler-Lussier assesses the influence of both Communist and non-Communist political propaganda in determining the subsequent popularity of his music, showing how international influences contributed to Bartók's eventual celebration as a national composer.

Controversy has also governed the interpretation of Bartók's music from an analytical viewpoint. As a result of his music fitting no neat, single category, predetermined analytical techniques cannot be attributed to it. Consequently a variety of analytical responses has emerged across Europe and the United States which Ivan F. Waldbauer surveys, focusing specifically on pitch organization.

Bartók's contribution to twentieth-century music has not only been in composition and ethnomusicology. The release of recordings of his own playing has more recently fuelled debates on performance practice in twentieth-century music. With consideration of advances in recording technology throughout the twentieth century, Vera Lampert evaluates performances of Bartók's instrumental music – including his own – and examines some of the issues of interpretation and performance touched upon by other contributors.

The culmination of different approaches of the individual authors together with the variety of sources examined, some hitherto unexplored, defines this book as a new synthesis of the circumstances surrounding Bartók's life, developments in his music and changes in its reception. However the composer is perceived, and regardless of labels attached to his music, his continuing status as an influential figure within twentieth-century music is assured.

PART I

Contexts: political, social and cultural

1 The political and cultural climate in Hungary at the turn of the twentieth century

LYNN HOOKER

Open an introductory music history textbook at the section on Béla Bartók and you will find references to his deep patriotism, his folk-music research, and the relationships between these interests and his compositions. What you will not usually find, despite the weight placed on Bartók's connections to his environment, are many references to the people in that environment other than fellow composer Zoltán Kodály (1882–1967) and the nebulous 'folk' – sometimes only the folk. While Schoenberg is associated with both Berg and Webern, and Stravinsky with Rimsky-Korsakov and Diaghilev, Bartók is usually depicted in English texts as an isolated naïf from the provinces. Since folk art and work influenced by it are often viewed as nostalgic, we could conclude that Bartók was a conservative longing for the past.

The historical record shows us something far more complex. After about 1904, Bartók seems to have thought of himself as much more of a radical than a reactionary. He stopped going to church, attempted to shock wealthy hosts, was called an anarchist by his friends, and railed against misconceptions of the peasantry.[1] The heritage of nineteenth-century Hungary, the political environment of early twentieth-century Budapest, the resulting polarization of intellectual and cultural groups, and the progressive musicians with whom he associated (including prominent Jewish musicians), all had an impact on his views. His symphonic poem, *Kossuth*, of 1903 was the musical culmination of the chauvinist-nationalist views he held in his conservatoire years and immediately thereafter. However, by 1906 and the publication, with Kodály, of Hungarian Folksongs, he had shifted towards a more politically radical and aesthetically cosmopolitan stance, and was interested in combining symbols of Hungarian identity with modernist approaches like those of artists in Berlin, Vienna and Paris. Bartók's provincial background was conservative in the way it looked at national and cultural issues, but the literary figures he encountered in Budapest, such as poet Endre Ady (1877–1919) and aesthetician György Lukács (1885–1971), in addition to Kodály and other musical figures, expanded his outlook. (Judit Frigyesi's recent book *Béla Bartók and Turn-of-the-Century Budapest* explores Bartók's literary connections in detail.[2]) By bringing together the political, cultural and musical issues of the day, we can paint a picture of the sphere in which Bartók and his colleagues worked and the scope of their challenge to the traditional, conservative notions of Hungarianness and Hungarian music. This portrait will also explore some of the ambiguities of Bartók's place in this sphere. What follows is a survey of issues at the fore in Hungary's political, cultural and musical life during Bartók's early career.

Turn-of-the-century Hungary: paradox and possibility

The Hungary of Bartók's youth was fraught with contradictions. After the landmark 1867 Compromise, it was both a colonial department of the Habsburg Empire, still subject to Vienna's control, and an imperial power in its own right, with broad jurisdiction in local matters over a population which was only half Magyar (ethnic Hungarian).[3] Together, the Compromise and Hungary's Nationalities Law of 1868 provided other ethnic groups (the largest groups were, in alphabetical order, Croats, Germans, Romanians, Ruthenians, Serbs and Slovaks) with civil rights guarantees before the law and in education; these laws followed the liberal principles of the ruling party and earned approval from watchful Western interests. However, these minority groups also had their own national aspirations, which were not taken into consideration in the Compromise nor in the Nationalities Law.[4] Nationality was determined by native language and not blood, so the prominent presence of Jews in society was not reflected in the census at all but was instead absorbed into other groups – mostly the German and majority Magyar categories. Furthermore, although the Liberal Party ruled the country for almost forty years after the Compromise and passed some important laws asserting legal equality for citizens, there was constant tension between the theory and practice of these laws. Some Liberal politicians, such as Ferenc Deák, the chief nego-tiator of the Compromise, and Sándor Wekerle, the first prime minister not of noble blood (1894–95), pursued civil rights issues such as freedom of religion, universal secret suffrage, and minority rights, considering them crucial to the modernization – the 'Westernization' – of the country. Other Liberal Party leaders considered issues of increasing equality and civil rights far subordinate or even counter to Hungary's more important goal of becoming a truly Magyar nation-state. This priority was due to the dominant role of the Hungarian nobility in local and national politics, from the wealthy magnates that dominated the upper echelons of govern-ment down to the middle nobility and impoverished landless gentry who made up most of the county bureaucracy.[5] The nobles considered them-selves to embody the Hungarian national ideal, and their hold on power ultimately led to further entrenchment of conservative Magyar nationalism in the government.

The Liberal ideal was overshadowed not only by nationalist ideals but also by class prejudice in an extremely hierarchical society. The government practised economic *laissez-faire* that allowed tremendous growth in some cities, but such keystones of liberalism as universal secret suffrage and freedom of religion, which might cause a loss of control over the masses, were never fully embraced. The wide latitude Hungary granted its county officials, as well as the administrative authority maintained by the Roman Catholic Church through to 1895, allowed ample opportunity for abuse. For example, the threat of legal reprisal encouraged many peasants to 'volunteer' to work for officials, just as they would have had they still been serfs. Poet and journalist Endre Ady raged against the continued poor living conditions and abuse of peasants' rights in several newspaper articles.[6] Bartók commented during his folksong collecting trips on the resentment the peasants felt for the gentry administrators.

In the sphere of religion, before the passage of the 1894–95 secularization law, the Catholic Church held a great deal of influence in its role as keeper of the official records of births, deaths and marriages. In this role it could legally decide the religion of children of mixed Protestant–Catholic or Orthodox–Catholic marriages, and it effectively banned marriages between Jews and Christians, despite the official emancipation of the Jews in 1867. A 1907 school reform law made elementary education free, greatly increasing rates of literacy in the younger generations; but to receive funding, schools had to teach a certain number of hours in Hungarian, use certain approved textbooks and implement 'programmes inculcating an "exemplary patriotic attitude"'.[7] These requirements opened the reform law to complaints from ethnic minorities within Hungary and to criticism from Western European observers as well. Furthermore, religious denominations were so often divided along ethnic lines that denomination and ethnicity were sometimes assumed to be equivalent. For this reason, oppression of religious as well as ethnic minorities was aided, indeed encouraged, by many powerful members of the Magyar Nation.

At the same time as the countryside was governed in a quasi-feudal manner, the capital city of Budapest – created by the merging of Pest, Buda and Óbuda in 1873 – was growing and modernizing at lightning pace. Large-scale milling of Hungary's grain crops, agricultural support industries and printing, among other industries, mushroomed.[8] Budapest developed an electric tram around the Körút (Ring-street) and the first underground rail system in continental Europe, going under the newly redesigned Sugár Avenue, sometimes called the 'Champs Elysées of Budapest'. By the 1890s this grand thoroughfare had been renamed

Andrássy Avenue after Count Gyula Andrássy, the first Hungarian prime minister. The new underground line began near the fashionable shopping district of Váci Street near the Danube, and its stops included the opera house, opened in 1884; the music academy at Vörösmarty Street, founded by Franz Liszt in 1875; and the splendid Heroes' Square monument celebrating the millennium of the arrival of the Magyar tribes in the Carpathian Basin. This monument also formed a gateway to the City Park (Városliget), home of a spa, a zoo and Gundel's Restaurant, where elegant visitors would come to experience the chef's famous blending of French and Hungarian cuisine. The underground line was but one sign of the city's success and modernity. Although Hungary as a whole lost about 1.2 million inhabitants to emigration (mostly to the United States) in the period 1869 to 1910, Budapest was booming faster than any city in Europe, with migrants streaming in from the depressed countryside. As World War I approached, the population of the capital was nearing one million (not counting suburbs) and Budapest was Europe's sixth largest city.

In a country that had no indigenous entrepreneurial middle class, non-Hungarians – Germans and especially Jews – were the driving force behind Hungary's economic growth of the late nineteenth century. At the turn of the century, Jews were only about 5 per cent of the population overall, but they made up 54 per cent of the country's businessmen, 43 per cent of its bankers and lenders, 12.5 per cent of its industrialists, 49 per cent of its doctors, and 45 per cent of its lawyers. In 1900, there were sixteen Jewish members of Parliament and two dozen Jewish professors at Budapest's universities. This success and the freedom that Hungary's generally liberal policies allowed in the cities inspired patriotic loyalty in this population. Hungarian Jews spoke a number of languages at the beginning of the nineteenth century, especially German and Yiddish, but as the century progressed, more and more of them adopted Hungarian as their native language. Many Magyarized their names and/or converted to Christianity. The wealthiest, such as the banker father of philosopher-aesthetician György Lukács and the physician grandfather of writer Anna Lesznai, bought – or were granted – titles and/or estates, and even adopted some of the manners of the nobility.[9] Some prominent Jewish citizens felt that 'Those who had been homeless for millennia found a home on Hungarian soil'.[10] As the father of Bartók's librettist Béla Balázs (born Herbert Bauer) said to his son on his deathbed, they felt it their duty 'to root [themselves] firmly within the soil of the Hungarian homeland'.[11] And interestingly, the high property requirements for suffrage, preserved in large part to keep out ethnic minorities, empowered the new Jewish banking barons, though not, of course, the masses of Jews; meanwhile many of the socially 'superior' Magyar gentry had civil service jobs but no voting rights.

The ironies of this situation were reflected by the physical division of Budapest. The royal castle on the hill acted as a symbol of Buda's glorious feudal and national past, and of the continuing rule of the Habsburgs. Across the river, though, Pest, formerly a German-Jewish merchants' city, looked to a more cosmopolitan future. This side of the river was growing at a much faster rate, and the manufacturing and financial sectors that provided the economic engine for the city's growth and success were in Pest. Parliament moved from an older site on Castle Hill to an ornate new building on the Pest riverbank in 1896, and the new St Stephen's Basilica was completed in Pest in 1905. By 1900, five out of six residents of Budapest lived on the Pest side of the river, along with most of the industry; 21.5 per cent of the city's population and about 40 per cent of its voters were Jewish. Though many of the city's ethnically diverse inhabitants still preferred another language (especially German), an increasing percentage spoke Hungarian.[12]

The period after the Compromise of 1867 brought great prosperity to the city and to some of the people, but towards the turn of the century and just after, tensions resulting from economic inequities and social shifts increased. The agrarian nobility spent more and more time in the Casinos (clubs), cafés and night spots of Pest because nowhere else in Hungary could one enjoy more glittering entertainments; but they were reminded everywhere of the economic success of the new capitalists. (The Casinos were an exception, since they were heavily segregated.) To a nation that so idealized its tribal roots, considered itself a unified, agrarian society, and prided itself on its ancient and nearly impenetrable Asiatic language, modern, cosmopolitan and industrial Pest still seemed uneasily 'foreign'. Bartók and Kodály perceived this 'foreignness' as a significant problem for the city's musical life. There was increasing tension in Hungary over whether it should look to an idealized Magyar past for its model, or instead should reinvent itself as a multi-ethnic, cosmopolitan society.

The 1896 Millennium Exhibition in Pest's City Park reflects this tension. The Magyar elite was especially swept up in this event, which celebrated the conquest of the Carpathian Basin by the eight Hungarian tribes migrating west from Asia in the year 896. To evoke Hungary's medieval and Baroque magnificence, those that could afford them wore elaborate 'dress Hungarian' uniforms which evoked the clothing of seventeenth- and eighteenth-century Hungarian nobility. Grand works of art were commissioned to celebrate the conquest, including the Heroes' Square monument, a centrepiece of the Exhibition, with its towering central sculpture of Árpád and the other Magyar chieftains that founded the Hungarian state. But some of these art works also show those who were conquered: the ancestors of the 'nationalities', Slavs and Romanians. Of the historical

Figure 1.1 Detail from Árpád Feszty's panoramic 'The Arrival of the Conquering Magyars' (1896). Notice not only the triumphant conquering chieftains but also the littered bodies of the conquered.

paintings featured by the Exhibition, Árpád Feszty's enormous (120 metres long and 15 metres high) panorama entitled 'The Arrival of the Conquering Magyars' shows this most spectacularly (see Fig. 1.1). The Exhibition at some level also celebrated the oppression of the 'nationalities', who were understandably not as enthusiastic about this Exhibition.

A few items from the Exhibition catalogue almost acknowledge the different meanings of the celebration to different ethnic groups. The catalogue's author praises the 'idyllic simplicity' of 'Nationality Street at the Exhibition', where each 'nationality' seems to have been represented by only one house, and states that this exhibit reflects 'the ardent desire of the nation, that the different races inhabiting this country may always live in peace and harmony side by side, united in the love of the common fatherland'.[13] Meanwhile, though, Magyar peasants are showcased by representative dwellings from several different regions in 'Exhibition Village' – the title itself a veiled reminder that the Magyars are the real centre of this nation. Here, instead of 'idyllic simplicity', the author describes how this village 'gives a lively idea of the habits, dresses, mode of living etc. of the Hungarian [Magyar] people [in different parts of the country] ... permitting to draw [sic] some favourable inferences for our future life as a nation'.[14]

In addition to a wilfully naïve and biased depiction of the 'nationality' situation and the aggrandizement of a partly mythological Magyar history, the Millennium Exhibition included monuments to Hungary's rapid modernization: pavilions of mining, milling, printing, hygiene, railways, commerce and others. The meteorological institute's pavilion, in the shape of a medieval castle but containing 'all the auxiliaries and instruments which . . . modern society demands',[15] embodied the Exhibition's schizophrenia between old and new and demonstrated the country's ambivalence about its direction.

Debates about Hungarian culture

While the Magyar establishment presented a fairly one-sided picture of the past and present of Hungary within the Exhibition, the many factions of Hungarian society – Magyar and otherwise – carried on active debates over the direction the future should take. Much of this discourse was conducted in the press. Increased literacy provided the incentive for a dramatic increase in the printing industry, which became one of the largest industries in Hungary at the time of the Millennium Exhibition. Reams of newspapers, journals, books and monographs were devoted to the questions of nationalism and the 'nationalities', the most pressing issues of the day. Contributors to this river of ink included not just professional journalists, but also politicians. Baron Dezső Bánffy, the Liberal Party prime minister from 1895 to 1899, published his views in a number of articles, plus the book *Hungarian Nationality Politics*, which came out in 1903. Bánffy was an 'iron-fisted former high *ispán*'[16] from Transylvania who shows the degree to which the label 'Liberal' was stretched. Echoing the refrain 'for the establishment of a unified Magyar nation-state' countless times, this book touches on some of the favourite issues of Bánffy's premiership, such as the Magyarization of place names and personal names and the importance of education in Hungarian that emphasizes Hungarian patriotism. Bánffy also argued for the importance of putting loyalty to the Hungarian national idea above loyalty to religious denomination and the equation of chauvinism with patriotism, in addition to claiming that it was absurd even to try to follow the equal rights provisions of the Nationalities Law of 1868.

Though Bánffy's book came out well after he left office, similar ideas continued through ensuing governments as they sought to keep the minorities, peasantry and working classes in check. Member of Parliament

Ernő Baloghy was another nobleman-politician who fumed over what he saw as the destructive effect of the petty 'nationalities' on the progress of the noble Magyar nation and its culture; he published his arguments in the monograph *Magyar Culture and the Nationalities* in 1908. He based his 'humanistic' claims for the elevation of Magyar culture and the suppression of that of the 'nationalities' on the obvious superiority of Magyars and the need for the 'brotherly protection of the Magyars' in raising the 'nationalities' to their level.[17]

After discussing the deficiencies of each 'nationality' in turn, Baloghy attacks the suspicious 'pseudo-humanism' of the progressives which would promote the development of the cultures of all the different 'nationalities', and which asserts that 'the nationalities' individuality is suppressed here in Hungary' through Hungarian government actions. Baloghy dismisses this claim as 'not only nonsensical, but also dangerous': the society would break down into various small groups with their different languages, weakening the stronger Magyar group and thereby the state as well, so that 'completely certainly, another powerful nation would gobble us up into them, together with the small groups'.[18]

Others, however, such as the social-democrat sociologist (and sometime government official) Oszkár Jászi, the radical journalist Ignotus, and firebrand poet Endre Ady, sometimes called the 'voice of his generation', railed against reactionary tracts such as these. According to progressives and leftists, chauvinism was the mask used by the powerful, especially the big landowners, to avoid basic reforms such as universal suffrage, land reform and ordinary human rights. They also published their arguments, whether in newspapers; periodicals such as the social sciences journal *Huszadik Század* [Twentieth Century], which Jászi edited beginning in 1907, and the literary journal *Nyugat* [West], founded and edited by Ignotus (born Hugo Veigelsberg); monographs like Jászi's 1908 *The Reform of Voting Rights and the Future of the Hungarians*; or literary works, such as Ady's collections of poems and stories.

While *Nyugat* was probably best known for the literature it published, including many of Ady's writings, it also included articles on cultural issues such as the nationality question and the definition of 'Hungarianness'. These tended to the radical side, which drew criticism, eventually compelling Ignotus to write a response 'About *Nyugat*'s Un-Hungariannesses'.[19] Ignotus also responded to Baloghy's 254-page diatribe in *Nyugat*:

> Each and every person has individual needs, interests and ambitions, and without the freedom and satisfaction of these they do not prosper, nor can the society prosper. The nationalities, the races and denominations ... enhance the amalgam with different contributions, from which the new Hungarian people must be created ... Unfortunately, ... industry, trade and

the accompanying urban life have been considered foreign in character ...
[According to this view,] in language, literature, art, we should experience
[only] the specifically folk-like as completely Hungarian ...

   It would be worthwhile to assemble into a mosaic some of what they have
called not Hungarian in the last ten years ... Budapest is not Hungarian. The
centralization of administration is not Hungarian. The stock exchange is not
Hungarian. Socialism is not Hungarian ... The Secession and Symbolism are
not Hungarian. It is not Hungarian to leave the [religious] denominations
out of education ... Irony is not Hungarian ... Universal suffrage is not
Hungarian. And above all: that which our conditions do not [already] grant
us is not Hungarian... Things of this sort can often be read, still more often
heard ...

   And here is the dilemma. How should we refer to the quality which gives
every happiness to our culture, if we have to brand all the terms of this
happiness as dangerous, looking at the same culture? And is this
condemnation of inevitable manifestations of assimilation a stimulation to
assimilation?[20]

The vastly different interpretations of Hungary's cultural situation led
to increasing conflict over the necessary solution to its problems. As
Ignotus illustrates, any progressive solution was liable to be labelled as
anti-Hungarian by the chauvinists. As Jews, Ignotus and Jászi were particularly vulnerable to this label. Though some assimilated Jews could be
more chauvinistically nationalist than many Magyars, radicals were
labelled Jewish just as capitalists were.

   That not all radicals were Jewish is demonstrated by Ady, who came
from a family of impoverished Magyar nobility. In addition to moody
symbolist poems, he wrote articles questioning the current atmosphere of
Hungarian society, reviews praising Jászi's works, short stories which
implicitly criticized ethnic bigotry, and political tracts in verse form, such
as 'The Magyar Jacobin Song':

Why can't a thousand faint desires
Turn into one powerful will at last?
For Hungarian, Romanian, or Slav,
Our sorrows have always been one.

For our shame, our suffering
Has been akin for over a thousand years.
Why can't we meet boldly
On the barricades of the spirit?
...

When will we unite?
When will we say something of importance,
We, the oppressed, the broken down,
Magyar and not Magyar?[21]

As Baloghy and Bánffy did, Ady urges unity; but rather than urging the assimilation of the minority nationalities into the grand successful Magyar race, Ady's tone is one of revolution: all the downtrodden, whether of the Nation or of the 'nationalities', should revolt against an oppressive power structure.

Bartók's Hungarian culture

Bartók's family reflected some of the ethnic diversity of the country. His mother, Paula Voit Bartók, was ethnically German, though she spoke Hungarian fluently; his father, Béla Sr., considered himself thoroughly Hungarian, though his mother was from a (Roman Catholic) Serbian family. Their oldest child, Béla Jr., was born on 25 March 1881, in the town of Nagyszentmiklós, on the south-eastern fringe of the Hungarian plain, an area which is now in Romania. The composer's father was a professional, the director of a school of agriculture who founded a journal on the topic. As Tibor Tallián points out, though, 'professional distinction hardly ever led to greater social prestige ... in provincial Hungary'. Tallián describes how the senior Bartók assumed some of the social airs of the petty nobility [gentry]: he 'created for himself – arbitrarily, as far as is known – a gentry rank with the title Szuhafői ... even design[ing] a coat of arms'.[22] His contradictory professional and social ambitions reflect the contradictions of the time. His composer son was also drawn at times to the family's presumed noble rank: he signed his adolescent manuscripts with the name 'Béla von Bartók', and his second marriage in 1923 was 'concluded ... under the title szuhafői Bartók Béla (Béla Bartók of Szuhafő)'.[23]

After Béla Sr. died in 1888, Paula Bartók moved the family around the fringes of the country for five years until she found a permanent job at the teacher training college in Pozsony (now Bratislava), a previous capital of Habsburg Hungary with large German and Slovak, as well as Hungarian, populations. In Pozsony, Bartók studied with László Erkel, son of the 'founder of Hungarian opera', Ferenc Erkel. He also became acquainted with composer and pianist Ernő Dohnányi, who preceded Bartók both as organist at the Pozsony grammar school and as a student at the Academy of Music in Budapest. After Bartók's years in the hinterlands, Dohnányi was the first pianist that Bartók got to know who was more proficient than he was, even at such a young age.[24] This is but one indication of how far the musical culture of Budapest and Pozsony stood above that of the small towns Bartók had lived in during the previous five years.

Although Bartók's musical upbringing was purely German, parts of his background leaned towards Hungarian nationalism. In the year of the

Millennium Exhibition, one of his uncles, Béla Voit, sent him a fragment of the sword-hilt that he had carried as a first lieutenant in the 1848 Hungarian Revolution against the Habsburgs, an event that had gathered enormous nationalist symbolism in the intervening years. Bartók and his mother travelled to Budapest to visit the Exhibition.[25] His musical world also had some nationalist flavour to it: his first public concert in Pozsony was on the occasion of the Millennium celebration of 1896, and he played in a concert in 1898 to celebrate the fiftieth anniversary of the Revolution. He turned down a scholarship to the Hochschule der Musik in Vienna to attend the Academy of Music in Budapest, probably at least in part because of his nationalist leanings.[26]

Yet Budapest also proved too German for Bartók's tastes. Bartók and Kodály, who both arrived in Budapest from the countryside just before the turn of the century, were frustrated by the extent to which German was still the language of culture, particularly musical culture. Many prominent musicians in Budapest, including many of the Academy's faculty (e.g. János Koessler (born Hans, 1853–1926), their composition teacher) barely spoke Hungarian, and German was the preferred language of most of the predominantly German and Jewish audience as well. Bartók himself was fluent in German, but as German was the language of Austria, the oppressor, it was considered a hindrance to Hungary's development and its hope for eventual independence. (Even French was more acceptable since France did not rule over Hungary, and French cultural influence was sometimes sought as an alternative to German influence.[27]) Kodály expressed his disapproval of the prevalence of German when he said in a 1932 lecture that 'Knowing German was not the prerequisite for playing classical music, but the fact that this had been entrusted to Germans had grave consequences for the development of Hungarian music'.[28]

Bartók's letters from 1901 and 1902 contain a number of complaints about the use of German at social gatherings or the prevalence of German speakers, including a substantial number of Jews, in musical circles. He had close relationships with at least two Jewish musicians: his piano teacher, former Liszt pupil István Thomán; and Emma Gruber, later Mrs. Zoltán Kodály, who was a fine pianist, a composer and a patron of musicians through her salon and her generosity. Through them, Bartók began to interact with the most prominent musicians in the city, including the Music Academy faculty and others. But still, in his zeal for things Hungarian and his ideological problems with German, he was not above an occasional anti-Semitic remark or slur against Germans who continued to speak mostly in that language.[29]

His discomfort with the predominance of German in Budapest's musical life was one factor in his sharp turn in 1903 towards chauvinist nationalism – the unapologetically reactionary style of rhetoric espoused by the opposition Independence Party of Ferenc Kossuth, the son of the leader of the 1848 Revolution, Lajos Kossuth. Bartók wrote long letters to his mother in support of the use of Hungarian command words in the Imperial army, the pet issue of the Independence Party in that year. He used stationery bearing the mottoes 'God bless the Magyars' (the first line of Hungary's national anthem) or sometimes 'Down with the Habsburgs', and he took issue with the casual attitude of friends and family towards patriotism and language. He tried to conduct a 'forced Magyarization' campaign on his family: his mother's sister Irma Voit, who had kept house for the family after Paula Bartók returned to work, hardly spoke Hungarian, but Bartók would write and speak to her only in Hungarian; he also pushed for his sister to be called Böske, the Hungarian diminutive for Elizabeth, instead of Elza, the German nickname she had always used. Thomán and Gruber tried in vain to talk Bartók out of wearing a 'dress Hungarian' suit, the chauvinists' chosen fashion symbol, for his final recital as a student.[30]

He also wore this suit for performances of *Kossuth*, his rich, Strauss-inspired symphonic poem which celebrated Lajos Kossuth's leadership of the 1848 War of Independence. The piece provoked quite a response: though some Austrian members of the Philharmonic (which premiered the piece on 13 January 1904) reportedly protested against the work's travesty of the Austrian anthem, 'Gott erhalte', Hungarian musicians and critics raved, praising the piece as filled with 'genuine Hungarianness' and hailing Bartók as 'the first really Hungarian symphonic composer'. Though many critics had problems with some harmonically adventurous aspects of the piece, put down as 'Straussisms', these were forgiven because of the nationalist programme. Most simply did not understand, or wish to understand, his more unconventional harmonies; they seem to have excused them only because the programme appealed so strongly to nationalist sentiment and the emotional sweep of the piece overall was so captivating.[31]

After *Kossuth*, as Bartók's ear drew him towards ever more daring sound combinations, his most appreciative listeners in Hungary continued to be Thomán, Gruber, and those in their circle – cosmopolitan Budapest intelligentsia, many of them German or Jewish. Though this class frequently embraced Hungarian culture, including folk and peasant culture, they distinguished between the bombast of chauvinist nationalism and what was seen as the more authentic expression that came directly from the people. Visual artists and writers found inspiration in folk materials just as Bartók, Kodály, and some of their colleagues found inspiration in the folksongs they collected among the peasantry.

Bartók and Kodály's Hungarian Folksongs, published in late 1906, presented twenty of the many tunes collected in their previous two years of research, set to their own untraditional harmonies. Though they had moral and some financial support from friends for this endeavour, the volume drew a resounding note of indifference from the general public.[32] This was one of a series of events in which Bartók's newer works were rejected by the public or by established performing organizations. Some critics attacked his increasingly radical musical tendencies not just as 'not beautiful', but also as 'not Hungarian', as they had criticized other artists who were interested in avant-garde developments from elsewhere in Europe. Bartók's sympathies shifted naturally towards those in the city who shared his enthusiasm about these developments, and about his and Kodály's way of looking at Hungarian folksong, including some colleagues at the Academy of Music and at Emma Gruber's salon. Among these progressive artists, Bartók would also find support for his growing disillusion with chauvinism.

His conversations with Budapest intellectuals would encourage the conclusions he was drawing from his own contacts with peasant musicians in the field, which gradually brought about a shift in his understanding of nationalism as well. He began collecting folksongs from non-Hungarians, the music of the Slovaks from 1906 and that of the Romanians from 1908, to better understand Hungarian songs; but soon he was collecting more songs from these nationalities than from Hungarians. His musical interactions with peasants of all ethnicities further developed his contempt for social pretensions. Where his chauvinist rants once had echoed ex-premier Bánffy, a letter to his wife, Márta Ziegler, dated Christmas Day 1916, seems to echo Ady instead: 'Is it not then a fine thing, to join with the oppressed?! . . . This is the explanation for my Slovak and Romanian sympathies; they are oppressed'.[33]

Bartók reflects on how far he has travelled in a 1907 letter to the young violinist Stefi Geyer, as he recalls the dispute over the 1894–95 secularization law requiring civil marriage and state-kept birth and death records. He remembers his fourteen-year-old self, whose 'deeply feeling heart was filled with profound sadness when a political reform . . . was introduced as an attempt to curtail the authority of the Church'.[34] With the wisdom of age (twenty-six), and in the thick of Budapest life, he could not help condescending towards his earlier point of view, which was all but inevitable for the provincial Catholic schoolboy that he once was. Attempting a precise dating of Bartók's ideological transformation would be impossible, but by the time of this letter, it is clear that he was disillusioned by the conservative nationalism of his conservatoire days. He had many

Jewish friends and associates, and he had also reconsidered his devotion to Catholicism, as he demonstrated by signing Geyer's letter as 'an atheist (who is more honest than a large number of the godly)'.[35] Of course, it is clear from the tone of Bartók's letter that he was attempting to appear even more sophisticated than he was as he wooed Geyer. But it is also clear that he had become more of a cosmopolitan: he was a touring concert pianist who made his home in the centre of Pest, for several years within a few steps of the Music Academy, and he partook of the intellectual ferment of the city (see Fig. 1.2).

From about 1905 to 1908, as Bartók struggled somewhat unsuccessfully to make his way in the Hungarian music scene, he also struggled with philosophical questions about how to transcend the everyday, whether in life or in music. Another letter to Geyer in 1907 demonstrates how he revelled in the physical discomforts of fieldwork as one of the ways to achieve the transcendence he sought: 'I am compelled to accept these many miseries because of the desire to search and discover, and it is better to fulfil this desire through hardship'.[36] This statement echoes ideas in Nietzsche's *Human, All Too Human*, which Bartók read and marked heavily, including the following:

> *He* . . . who really could participate [in others' fortunes and sufferings] would have to despair of the value of life . . . for mankind has as a whole no goal . . .
> To feel thus *squandered*, not merely as an individual but as humanity as a whole, in the way we behold the individual fruits of nature squandered, is a feeling beyond all other feeling. – But who is capable of such feeling?
> Certainly only a poet: and poets always know how to console themselves.[37]

Bartók found that he *could* 'really participate in others' fortunes and sufferings' during folksong collecting trips, which provided a way for him to 'step out from himself', another Nietzschean ideal. For Bartók, as for Nietzsche and others, these sufferings were the way to live life to the fullest extent possible.[38]

Not only Nietzsche's works but also those of Endre Ady were given to Bartók by friends in musical and intellectual circles, and Bartók presumably discussed the works with these friends as well. In 1908, Bartók's 'only friend' – Kodály – gave him a copy of Ady's collection *Blood and Gold* [Vér és Arany], which Bartók read voraciously until well after midnight. As he wrote, it was 'as if these poems had sprung from me'.[39] Ady, the lodestar for modernist Hungarian artists of the time, wrote passionately about everything, from the social injustice and prejudice that he saw all around him, whether in prose or in verse (as in the above-quoted 'Magyar Jacobin Song'), to physical and intensely personal experiences of love, with, as Frigyesi puts it, 'an almost biblical simplicity and strength'.[40] Passionate

Figure 1.2 Photograph of the Oktogon, one of Pest's major intersections, *c.* 1894. From about 1908 to 1911 Bartók had a flat on the fourth floor (European style) of the building marked with an arrow.

love between man and woman is central to many of Ady's poems, as are its corresponding difficulties; in fact 'love becomes the metaphor for life, and on a broader level for cosmic reality'.[41] Ady drew together diverse aspects of life in his poems as Bartók wanted to draw them together in his music: 'had I not been destined for music but for poetry', he wrote, 'I would have written these poems – this is what I felt'.[42]

Bartók would have been able to discuss these poems and Nietzsche's work not only with Kodály and Gruber, themselves well-read and thoughtful people, but also with writer Béla Balázs (1884–1948), Bartók's librettist for the opera *Duke Bluebeard's Castle* (1911) and the ballet *The Wooden Prince* (1914–17). As he was a close friend of both Kodály (his university room-mate) and the philosopher György Lukács, Balázs linked Bartók to wider cultural circles. Through Balázs, Bartók came into closer contact with other writers and philosophers of Lukács' circle; for example, before *The Wooden Prince* was premiered, Bartók not only attended one of their Sunday meetings but played his ballet for them on the piano.[43] Bartók was first and foremost a musician, and the esoteric philosophical debates of Lukács and Balázs' group were not his forte. But his affinity for some of the basic ideas he found through Nietzsche, Ady, Balázs and Lukács affirmed Bartók's passion for a fully lived life and his efforts to create a uniquely Hungarian modernist musical language.

In his own field of music, we find a vivid picture of how Bartók participated in the everyday cultural life of the city in the memoir of one of the
managers of the forward-looking music publisher Rózsavölgyi:

> The public would gather around the oval table, talking or studying the new
> items. In the noon hours the firm's composers and librettists often visited
> the shop – we viewed them as daily guests. Among the hundreds of names I
> mention only the most outstanding: Bartók, Kodály, . . . Antal Molnár,
> Dohnányi, . . . Pongrácz Kacsóh . . . [44]

Some of Bartók's most important musical colleagues were the
members of the Waldbauer-Kerpely String Quartet, who came together in
1909 specifically to perform Bartók's and Kodály's first string quartets, and
the composers and musicians of the New Hungarian Music Society [Új
Magyar Zeneegyesület, abbreviated UMZE] of 1911–12. Bartók was the
first president of this Society. The viola player of the Waldbauer Quartet,
Antal Molnár, was also a member of UMZE who wrote enthusiastic commentaries on new Hungarian music for various journals, undertook
extensive folksong collecting trips, and composed. Another member of the
Society was composer Pongrácz Kacsóh, who, as a critic, was one of few
who had applauded the harmonic interest in Bartók's *Kossuth*. When
established Hungarian orchestras were both unwilling and unable to play
avant-garde scores by Hungarians, the New Hungarian Music Society set
out to form their own ensemble that would be committed to performing
them well, educating the country about music, and broadening the way
Budapest audiences thought about music – Hungarian music in particular. Although UMZE was not successful in the long term, the way that
Bartók and other musicians rallied around the project is an important
instance of Bartók's involvement in Budapest's musical and intellectual
activities. [45]

The city of Budapest was a place about which he was somewhat ambivalent. When he was on a collecting trip, he sometimes romanticized the
rural life at the expense of the city: from a letter to Emma Gruber, dated 25
November 1906, Bartók writes: 'The smell of the city – I loathe it! I am
spending happy hours among my dear peasants'. [46] He often stayed with
friends on the outskirts of town, sometimes in the suburb of
Rákoskeresztur where he and his family lived after 1911. Yet even after
moving he still spent a great deal of time in the city. His rural collecting
trips and family life in the suburbs were only part of a way of life: equally
important was the intellectual energy he absorbed from the cultural
ferment of Budapest, including its ongoing debates on Hungarian culture.
His and Kodály's folk-music research speak to these debates, as do such
writings as Bartók's 'On Hungarian Music' (1911), among others. Though

on the surface Bartók often writes from a very 'scientific' point of view, his polemical 'On Hungarian Music' shows not only his zeal to convince the public of the value of the 'oldest layer of Hungarian folksong' which he, Kodály and others had been setting to music. It also demonstrates how the class and ethnic tensions of the time pervaded this project:

> We can discover among the songs adapted by the gypsies many melodies borrowed from some Slavonic neighbour, which slipped by chance into Hungarian folk music. The supercilious Magyar lords pay tribute to these songs with the compulsory national enthusiasm. But then they face the recently unearthed, valuable ancient Magyar melodies from Transylvania as strangers, uncomprehending . . . They neither love nor understand this truly Magyar folk music.[47]

This brief passage touches on several of the flash-points of the period: the extent to which Hungarian culture is indebted to that of other ethnicities, the entrenched hypocrisy of 'compulsory' national enthusiasm, and the dismissal of lower classes – in this case Transylvanian peasants – by upper classes.

In the charged context of early twentieth-century Hungary, it seems almost inevitable that Bartók should seize on the national idea as central to his work – it was the language through which everything else was discussed during the period. From his family and social connections to the radical statement of his folksong research, all his work was coloured by or spoke to this environment. Understanding the language of this environment gives us insight into both the music and writings of Bartók's early career.

2 Bartók and folk music

STEPHEN ERDELY

Early impressions, the *verbunkos*

At the turn of the nineteenth century a growing national consciousness permeated the political and cultural life of Hungary. Men of letters envisaged programmes which included the creation of national art built upon the foundations of national customs and folklore. The call went out to members of literary and scientific societies asking them to collect folk tales and folksongs, and the response was so great that by mid-century the material gathered was large enough to fill several volumes.[1] As good as the intentions of these early collectors may have been, they saw the literary value alone in folksongs and printed only their texts without the music. This unfortunate omission was partly remedied by folksong collectors of the second half of the century. Not knowing, however, the difference between the songs in oral circulation, they uncritically took up in their collections popular tunes, patriotic songs and school songs intermingled with folksongs. Not even the most important publication of the century, István Bartalus's seven-volume collection, *Magyar Népdalok, Egyetemes Gyüjtemény* [Hungarian Folksongs, Universal Collection], was free of its predecessor's mistakes.[2]

Misconceptions about folksongs during the nineteenth century were also strengthened by the popularity of two rapidly growing musical trends: the *verbunkos*, or recruiting dance – a tempestuous, flexible, appealing, sentimental type of instrumental music which took its origin from folk music, before becoming transformed in the hands of gypsy musicians; and the popular art song – a pseudo-folksong product of dilettante composers, flooding the urban musical scene during the second half of the nineteenth century.

The *verbunkos* (a Magyarized form of the German word, *Werbung*), a soldier's dance, became part of the recruitment into the imperial Austrian army between the years of 1715 and 1867. Soldiers skilled in fancy dance steps, even acrobatic movements, were specially assigned to lure young men into the service. The music was provided by gypsy bands which were always available for such events. Historians are of the opinion that the gypsies used folk tunes known to the people, giving the local Hungarian tradition primary emphasis. But throughout the development of this dance music many foreign features were also absorbed. The oldest musical elements may have been carried over from the *Heiducken* dance – a heroic dance of sixteenth-century mercenary soldiers – indicated by the motivic construction and the trumpet-like fourth jumps in the tunes. In the hands of the gypsies, however, the folk melodies were overlaid with ornamentation, scalic flourishes, augmented seconds and Phrygian cadences – the Balkan or Eastern heritage of the gypsies – and were set into a harmonic texture by the use of the cimbalom, a probable influence of Western practices. Nevertheless 'the clicking of the heels' and certain stereotype cadential formulae, triplet figures and other rhythmical features made the *verbunkos* unmistakably Hungarian. By the beginning of the nineteenth century the national characteristics of the dance were well developed and every layer of society could identify with them.

While the term *verbunkos* is hardly mentioned in the documents before 1800, the dance named *Magyar* appears in the order of ballroom dances among the *Allemandes, Françaises, Polonaises,* and *Anglaises*. Hungarian poets of the period describe the *Magyar* as a slow dance with a gradual increase of tempo without ever changing its serious, stately nature, thus fitting the dignity of the noble men who danced it. The fast part, *friss*, was regarded as a distortion, an element from folk tradition that did not suit the ballroom style. The slow, stately dance was also called *palotás* (palace dance) and the fast dance, *csárdás* (tavern dance).[3]

The *verbunkos* was diffused throughout the country in numerous forms. It grew from dance music into a musical style, reaching its zenith between 1810 and 1840. During this great period of national awakening it was elevated in the hands of brilliant and inspired violin virtuosos (such as János Bihari (1764–1827), János Lavotta (1764–1820) and Márk Rozsavölgyi (1789–1848)) into art forms, which include fantasies, rêveries, rhapsodies and fancies, and was further popularized in numerous publications noted by minor German composers. In its final stage of development, mixed with Italian and German melodies, the *verbunkos* style was taken up by Ferenc Erkel (1810–93), in his historical operas, by Mihály Mosonyi (1815–70), in his orchestral and choir works, and by Franz Liszt (1810–86) in his symphonic and piano compositions, and it became known in the West through Hector Berlioz's *Rákoczy March* and Johannes Brahms's Hungarian Dances.[4]

Popular art songs were coming into vogue from the middle of the nineteenth century. Their composers were dilettante musicians whose aim was to provide the growing urban population with songs resembling folksongs but 'on a higher level'. This was a society that had already outgrown folk culture but did not yet reach the standards of higher culture. The songs were circulated orally and were spread by folk theatres and gypsy bands on the lips of those fond of singing. They also penetrated the villages where they endured smaller or larger changes stimulating the development of newer, so far unknown, forms.[5]

At the end of the nineteenth century Hungarian music echoed the heritage of the *verbunkos* in both its art and oral traditional forms. *Csárdás* tunes and popular art songs reverberated throughout the country, overshadowing folk tradition. The general public regarded the sentimental urban song, the *Magyar Nóta* (Hungarian tune), as being the true Hungarian tune, and gypsy music the tradition. But in fact both were folkloristic products of an age that did not learn the true meaning of folksongs.

The turn of the twentieth century, which marks the beginning of Béla Bartók's musical career, witnessed a Hungarian society divided from the point of view of its musical taste into three distinct layers: the upper classes (which included the nobility, the urban financiers, industrialists and bourgeoisie) turned to the West for their musical needs; the gentry and the urban middle class found satisfaction in the music of gypsy bands and in popular art songs; it was only the agrarian folk who lived with its folksongs and musical customs, isolated from the rest of society.

Bartók obtained his childhood impressions of Hungarian music from his provincial urban environment. His mother recalls those special occasions 'when the gypsy bands were in town and the sound of music reached his ears, he nodded that we should take him there, and he listened to the music with amazing attention. At the age of four he could play with one finger on the piano the folktunes familiar to him: he knew forty of them'.[6] When Bartók entered the Academy of Music in Budapest in 1899, he had no better knowledge of his country's folksongs than that of the general public. But the early impressions struck deep roots in his memory. Music of the nineteenth century became his first musical mother tongue. In his compositions of the period between 1902 and 1907 he expressed his Hungarianness unconsciously, continuing in the Magyar idiom of Liszt's late creative period. And when he relinquished the Romantic Hungarian style, the *verbunkos* spirit continued to surface in his music throughout his life.

It should be remembered that the *verbunkos* was a performance art during most of its history. It had heroic roots, evolving the national characteristics in dance and music; it had its dignified, noble side as well as its joyous tempestuous forms; it lived in the slow, stately *palotás*, and in the fast *csárdás*; it was echoed in brilliant fantasies and rhapsodies of inspired fiddlers and rose into operatic, church and instrumental music of composers at home and abroad. By the end of the nineteenth century, however, the style showed its limitations.

In Bartók's music the *verbunkos* element becomes a symbol of the nation, of its moods and expressions, at times in passionate outburst, other times in calm reflecting mood, and at yet other times with a dignified pose or echoing the historical spirit. It is never how it was, but how it could have been if, in those promising times of national awakening, Hungarian music had evolved out of the roots of folk tradition.

Fieldwork

The early years of Bartók's career fall into a period of Hungarian history filled with political tension and unrest. The 1848–49 War of Independence and the years of oppression that followed were still vivid in the memory of the Hungarian people. Although the Compromise pact with Vienna in 1867 granted many of the demands of the Independence Movement it remained a confirmation of the Dual Monarchy. The Hungarian Parliament was divided over the Compromise; the Liberal Party was in support of it, but the Independent Party viewed the pact as an acceptance of Vienna's domination in the Dual Monarchy.[7] Amidst raging debates the Independence Movement gained strength, calling for the display of the Hungarian coat of arms, for the Hungarian hymn, in place of the Austrian national anthem 'Gott erhalte', and most emphatically, for the use of Hungarian language commands in the Austro-Hungarian army. And when the emperor denied this last demand the Movement reached revolutionary pitch.

Bartók supported the aspirations of the Independence Movement. He wrote to his mother, 'Every man, reaching maturity, has to set himself a goal and must direct all his work actions toward it. For my part, I shall pursue one objective all my life, in every sphere and in every way: the good of Hungary and the Hungarian nation'.[8] He wanted to be progressive as well as Hungarian in his art. The *verbunkos* and the post-Romantic musical idiom were not compatible.[9] 'I recognized that the Hungarian tunes mistakenly known as folksongs – which are in fact more or less trivial folkloristic art songs – offer little attraction, and so in 1905 I began to search for the music of agrarian peasantry which was up till then completely unexplored', Bartók wrote in his autobiography (1921).[10]

The incident marking the turning point in Bartók's career and motivating him to take up folksong collection occurred in the summer of 1904 at Gerlice puszta, where he heard for the first time an authentic Transylvanian folk tune sung by a young maid. He wrote to his sister, 'I have now a new plan: I shall collect the most beautiful Hungarian folksongs and raise them to the level of art songs by providing them with the best possible piano accompaniment'.[11] And with this idea in mind Bartók applied for a grant to study the music of the Székely people for which he received 1,000 crowns.

Bartók gained further support for his plans from Zoltán Kodály, whom he first met in the home of Mrs Emma Gruber in 1905. Kodály, a composition student at the Music Academy, was also a doctoral candidate in linguistics with a special interest in folklore at the University of Budapest. At this meeting, Kodály recalls, Bartók was intensely interested in his first published folksong collection and in his dissertation on the *Strophic Structure of Hungarian Folksong*, and questioned him about the way contact was made with the folk, and how the collecting was done.[12]

In the summer of 1906 Bartók set out on his field trips. At first he was looking for beautiful songs which he could use in his compositions. Scientific questions pertaining to folksong research did not enter his mind. He toured the counties of Pest, Fejér, Tolna, Zala, Vas, Csongrád, Békés, Csanád, Hajdu and Maros Torda (see Fig. 2.1 on p. 30), eager to gain an overview of his country's folk music.[13] The two composers planned their trips in a complementary way, dividing the field to cover the widest possible territory.

Folk-music tradition in the villages was competing with urban pseudo-folksongs which were popularized throughout town and country by travelling theatre troupes and gypsy bands. A valuable part of the musical folklore repertoire was heard only from an older village generation and the danger that the songs would die out with them was real. Facing the possible loss of this musical treasure, Bartók and Kodály appealed to the public and to the government for support of their plans to collect and preserve the folksongs in the interest of national culture.

Contemporary politicians and cultural leaders did not take folk-music research seriously, nor did they understand what musicians could possibly contribute to the cause of folklore. The applications of Bartók and Kodály remained unanswered. Cultural prejudice against a semi-educated agrarian peasantry and chauvinistic political attitudes against nationalities were impeding their projects.[14] Indifference and, frequently, even a hostile attitude on the part of government and cultural institutions stood in Bartók's way of attaining the success or recognition for his folksong research throughout his lifetime.

Bartók's prime objective was the recovery of old Hungarian folksongs before they faded into extinction: 'in our search for the new, the unusual, the outstanding we are not only advancing our times but we direct our steps into long passed centuries . . . And true peasant music is nothing else than the portrait of a musical culture that has been long time forgotten'.[15]

Villages on the periphery of the country, which were least influenced by urban life, held the promise of finding the survivals of an older musical tradition. But to reach these places Bartók had to face many discomforts, for such communities were as much as 60–70 kilometres away from the

closest railway station, accessible only by peasant carts, through mountains, gravel roads, or no roads at all. And then they were often in a medieval state, without a school, a priest or even a tavern. He had to make his
headquarters in peasant huts, live with the whole family in one room, and
sleep, in place of a bed, on a straw-sack or a bench.[16] On a postcard from
Bánffy Hunyad, one of such villages in Kolozs county, Transylvania,
Bartók reports: 'Daily rain storms, hardly bearable heat, astonishing folk
costumes. Moroccan dirt, and disorder on the streets, and the comfort for
the pleasure of Europeans is missing.'[17] But Bartók's difficulties did not
end with those bumpy trips to the villages; the real problem came when he
had to tell the people why he wanted their tunes. In general, the peasants
behaved with suspicion towards city folk; they were worried that their
tunes would be 'taxed' or used for commercial purposes. When, a few years
later, Bartók was interviewed on the radio, he described his task:

> The nature of collection required that I turn to older people, mainly peasant
> women, because they were the ones who knew the old songs. They had to
> sing into the phonograph and I transcribed the music. The Hungarians and
> Székelys understood quickly what the collection was all about. They smelled
> some money but did not ask for it out of modesty or gentlemanliness. But
> how difficult it is to bring an old woman to sing! That she should decorate
> her tune with the usual fiorituras so that the men should not make fun of
> her. Everybody had some strange idea that there was a trap set and nobody
> wanted to fall into it. We had to be shrewd and talk and talk . . . Finally the
> old woman comes around and starts to sing, then stops suddenly . . . Why? A
> new approach of persuasion had to be used, now from another angle . . .
> finally the woman gives in and the recording can be completed.[18]

Bartók's letters contain many pleasant field incidents as well. One of his
funniest stories – and worst field experiences – is reported from Darázs, a
small community in Nyitra county:

> This dear, naive, primitive folk! The way they stand around the phonograph,
> the way they strive to put more songs into that machine! Of course they are
> not interested in the results of the collection, only in the big 'tuba' . . . And
> how inexhaustible they are in songs! [. . . even though] Darázs is a small
> community, about 1,000 inhabitants . . . I stay and collect here in a small
> peasant hut, Tuesday was a holiday; around 4 o'clock the people began to
> march in, the small ones and the big ones. And the songs began to pour. A
> charming episode occurred as I placed a good hunk of a man in front of the
> phonograph: he respectfully donned his hat in front of the horn. The people
> broke out in laughter! Then a young girl began to sing a love song about
> Hansel. I did not quite get the name, but the others did and shouted: Martin,
> Martin should be in the song! It was her sweetheart's name . . . From the
> thirty people exhaling in that small room, the walls, the floor, my bed were
> dripping wet. I began to congratulate myself: cold room, soaking floor, wet

Figure 2.1 Counties of Hungary before 1919 and dialect areas.

walls and, on top of it, wet sheets! . . . I put my winter coat on the bed and
slept with my clothes on, covering myself with my blanket. This is the way
the first day ended in the village of Darázs. And I must say, I endured all that
and many other hardships.[19]

Bartók used the term 'peasant music' as an antonym to urban popular
art songs although Kodály was never completely comfortable with that
term; in his view every layer of society participated at one time or another
in the creation of folk music. Kodály's experiences of field collection
revealed that folksong does not have a 'genuine' form of the kind that
amateur collectors hoped to discover in perfect, most beautiful shape; for
the genre lives and spreads in variant forms which may show greater or
lesser similarity. The tune or poetry may remain stable in one village and
appear in diverse forms in the next. Melody, rhythm and structure may
endure or show unusual diversity, for folksong is basically an idea which is
re-created anew in each performance and by each performer.

Székely folk tunes collected in Csík county in 1907 were Bartók's first
proofs of the survival of an ancient musical tradition. Kodály writes: 'He
came back with such a pile of pentatonic melodies that, in conjunction
with my own simultaneous findings in the north, the fundamental importance of this hitherto unnoticed scale suddenly became obvious. Yet we
waited ten years, collecting and examining further data, before we considered it time to publish this discovery'.[20]

From the outset of his fieldwork, Bartók showed an interest in the music of nationality groups living within the geographical boundaries of pre-World War I Hungary (see Fig. 2.1[21]). Although chauvinistic politics claimed superiority for Hungarian culture and oppressed any attempt at national expression by minority groups, Bartók remained unaffected by these short-sighted political attitudes. He had already collected folksongs in Slovak-inhabited villages neighbouring Gerlice puszta, in Gömör, in 1906. We read in one of his letters: 'I have transcribed 120 songs, of which one third are definitely Hungarian melodies with Slovak texts . . . this is such an interesting question that it requires further investigation on the localities near the language border'.[22]

Bartók encountered a similar phenomenon among the Romanians in the Belényes-Vaskoh area of Bihor county a few years later. He writes to Jan Buşiţia, his Romanian guide and friend:

> I checked again the collected material, and I must say there are unusually interesting things in them . . . it is unbelievable that out of the same text rhythm (which consists exclusively of seven- or eight-syllable lines) such marvellous rhythmic variations are created . . . Having said that, you may not take it as an offense if I single out twenty to twenty-five melodies which were taken over from the Hungarians, presumably already in olden times. Such melodic borrowings are inevitable among neighbouring people. Naturally, a way out of such chaos can only be found by a scholar who has studied both people's musical folklore.[23]

From these and similar comments one can understand that Bartók found the study of neighbouring people's musical folklore imperative not only for the study of mutual influences, but also for his purpose of sifting out the indigenous features in Hungarian folk music and identifying the borrowed forms. He was an astute student of languages, learning Slovakian, Romanian, Bulgarian, Arabic, and some Russian beside, of course, German, French, Spanish and English; even if he did not speak them fluently, he mastered them well enough to be able to transcribe the folksong texts.

Bartók's folksong collecting years were between 1906 and 1918. However, amidst his concert tours, teaching and composing activities the time he was able to devote to fieldwork was limited and sporadic (see Fig. 2.2). After 1907, when he became full-time professor of piano at the Academy of Music in Budapest, he could only take time off during periods of academic recess. Christmas and Easter vacations were usually spent under adverse conditions in remote and primitive villages as the dates and places of his letters clearly indicate. Although the Hungarian Ethnographic Museum and the Romanian Academy of Sciences paid for the phonograph cylinders and his trips during 1913–14 when he was collecting in Romanian villages, his expenses were never fully reimbursed.

The dates of Bartók's field tours in Figure 2.2 are compiled from Béla Bartók Jr.'s account of his father's life, and from János Demény's excellent and detailed biographical studies.[24] The dates tell us the history of his collecting trips: he visited the counties of current Hungary in 1906–07 and then again during the war years when his travels in Transylvania were curtailed; he collected in the northern counties over a period of twelve years; and in Transylvania and the southern counties between 1909 and 1914. Within these counties Hungary's nationality groups were living in the same neighbourhoods as Hungarians. Villages and towns were often of mixed ethnicity, but some eventually became completely Romanian or Slovak, even if they were only a couple of kilometres apart. Fascinated with the music of Transylvanian Romanians, Bartók returned to their villages some twenty-five to thirty times, covering over 130 communities of this nationality group alone. In 1913 he made an expedition into Biskra and the vicinity of Algeria, recording Arabic folk and instrumental music.[25] During World War I Bartók had to alter, and even drop, some of his field plans, and after 1918 he stopped collecting altogether. In 1936, upon the invitation of the Turkish government, he went once more into the field in Anatolia, in search of tune types related to Hungarian songs.[26]

Bartók questioned his informants about how, where and from whom they obtained their tunes in order to acquire data about the music and knowledge of its association with folk customs and practices. But his primary interest was the music, instrumental or vocal, and, ultimately, its precise documentation by transcription. Example 2.1 is just one example of many that shows how, by the 1930s, his sophisticated notation turned his transcriptions into musical portraits of the singer or instrumentalist. No note, however slight, no vocal slide, pitch inflection, rhythmic nuance, tempo or articulative detail escaped his attention.

Yet, with all the skills at his command, Bartók firmly believed the phonograph to be an essential prerequisite for musical folklore work. He developed the technique for quickly noting the melody during the singer's performance while also recording it and later compared his own notes with the recorded version. According to Bartók himself, financial considerations forced him to devise such procedures. In America, as he began to study the four- to five-hour-long recordings of Southslavic epics, which the Harvard professor, Milman Parry, made in 1935, he recollected with regret the technical limitations of his own times:

> We poor scholars of those Eastern countries had to economize on time, on blanks, on expenses, on everything. So we generally had to confine ourselves to the recording of the first three or four stanzas, even of ballads as long as forty to fifty stanzas, although we knew quite well that every piece ought to be

	1906	1907	1908	1909	1910	1911	1912	1913	1914	1915	1916	1917	1918
East of the Danube													
Pest	1906	1907							1914	1915			1918
Jász - Nagykun		1907											1918
Csongrád	1906												
Csanád	1906												
Békés	1906											1917	1918
Hajdu	1906												
Transdanubia													
Fejér	1906												
Tolna	1906	1907											
Somogy	1906												
Zala	1906												
Vas	1906												
Komárom					1910								
Northern counties													
Gömör	1906												
Nyitra		1907											
Hont					1910			1913	1914				
Zolyom										1915	1916		
Bars													1918
Transylvania													
Csík		1907											
Maros Torda	1906			1909			1912		1914		1916		
Bihar				1909	1910	1911	1912		1914				
Bereg							1912						
Ugocsa						1911	1912						
Szatmár							1912						
Máramaros						1911		1913					
Szolnok Doboka				1909	1910								
Kolozs			1908		1910						1916		
Torda Aranyos				1909	1910	1911							
Also Fehér					1910	1911							
Arad												1917	
Southern counties													
Torontál					1910		1912	1913					
Temes							1912	1913					
Hunyad								1913	1914				
Krasso-Szörény												1917	
Africa													
Biskra and vicinity								1913					
Turkey													...1936

Figure 2.2 List of counties Bartók visited in different regions, with dates.

recorded from beginning to end ... I have some melancholy recollections of our worries and troubles, when after each two-and-a-half minutes of singing the business had to be stopped, the ready record taken off, then a new blank put on, and in the meantime, the singer generally forgot where he left off.[27]

In his study 'Why and How do We Collect Folk Music?'(1936), Bartók summarizes his field experiences:

The ideal musical folklorist must be indeed a polihistor. He must have the knowledge of language and phonetics in order to observe and note the smallest nuances of the dialect; he must be a choreographer, to be able to indicate the interrelations between folk music and folk dance; only a general

Example 2.1 Turkish folksong transcribed in 1936

knowledge of folklore enables the collector to ascertain the connections
between folksongs and folk customs; he must be trained in sociology, to
observe the changes disturbing the collective life of the village and its
influence on folk music. And if he wants to make final inferences he needs
historical information, primarily about the settlements ... But above all it is
indispensable that he should be an observing musician with an excellent ear.

Then he adds, 'To my knowledge there has never been and perhaps
never will be a collector who embodies all those qualities, understandings,
and experiences. Therefore folk music research cannot be carried out by
one person at a level that would satisfy, by our current standards, all
scientific demands'.[28]

With these remarks Bartók opened the gates for other disciplines to
take folk music into their domain, and investigate it with their own
methods. He also devised his own rigorous system of classification,
thereby elevating the study of folk music into a scholarly discipline.

Method of order, classification and synthesis

During the years of intense fieldwork Bartók collected an astonishing
variety of folksongs among Hungarian, Slovakian and Romanian peoples.
As he began to prepare some of the collections for publication, his attention turned towards the organization of the material. Bartók's objective
was to prove which of the songs were indigenous forms, and which were
borrowed, old or new formations in the traditions. Such questions could
only be answered by analysing and assorting the folksongs according to
their musical characteristics. The search for a system, which would
provide the tools for both the analysis and classification of tunes,
prompted Bartók and Kodály to study existing folksong collections. After
experimenting with several systems of order they found the Finnish folksong publication, *Suomen Kansan Sävelmia* (vols. II–IV, 1904–28), introduced by Ilmari Krohn, best suited for classifying Hungarian folksongs.[29]

Krohn classified the Finnish melodies by variants. The relationship of
variants was determined by the similarity of their melodic contour, syllabic rhythm and overall structure. An interesting new principle, previously unknown in methods of classification, grew out of Krohn's
observation that the ending note of a melody line is equally important in
determining its character – at least to the same degree as the opening
melodic formula. The innovation of Krohn, however, was the double
system of classification based on the syllable order, or 'quantitative property', and the cadential order, or 'qualitative property', of melody lines.

The possibilities embodied in these musical principles enriched

Bartók's and Kodály's imagination and they adopted the Finnish system
with certain modifications. Their version reads as follows: 'the arrangement of the song collection must be solely a musical one, made purely
from the point of view of the characteristics of the melody, and of a dictio-
nary-like order, so that the related songs, when placed next to another,
show the main species clearly.' The gist of the system was described as
follows:

> every tune is reduced to a common final to end on g′. As the number of
> melody lines is mostly four, only three of the line endings are considered
> here. Of the three the most important is the second one . . . All those songs to
> which this note is common are placed together. Within the groups
> originating in this way, sub-groups are formed according to the final note of
> the first line and, within the latter, according to the final note of the third line.
>   Traversing this classification is the order of rhythmic groups: each
> category starting with the shortest tunes followed by the longest ones.
>   And finally, the tunes are aligned according to their ambit, headed by the
> ones with narrow range and followed by those with wider range.[30]

The collection of Hungarian folksongs was then analysed in this
manner and each element of the tunes to be classified (cadential structure,
syllable numbers of the lines, melodic content and range) was indicated by
letters and number symbols. The system gave rise to two further forms of
classification, differing in method and purpose. In the 'lexicographical
order' the songs are classified by one principle – usually the cadential
structure of line-ending notes – as in a lexicon or dictionary. The advantage of this method is that the tune can easily be located; its disadvantage,
however, is that even the slightest difference in the cadential structure of
the tune will separate it from its variants and will not indicate the type or
style of the melody. The 'grammatical order' assorts the melodies which
belong in the same family, type or style, but uses a more complicated
classification, changing the priority of musical principles.

Bartók developed the grammatical method of classification with
several new melodic elements introduced into the system: (1) section
structure (a section referring to the melody and text-line); (2) metric
structure (a metric unit corresponding to two or three syllables); (3)
rhythmic character of the line (e.g. *parlando rubato*, or *tempo giusto*
method of performance); (4) cadential structure of the strophe; (5) range;
(6) scale notes of the melody; and (7) melodic content of sections.

He also altered his system more than once, changing the priority of
principles. 'In all likelihood every folklore material of specific character
requires the construction of a special system of order to suit its needs',[31]
Bartók stated. It is in the classification of folksongs that his scientific bent
of mind is best demonstrated.

The Romanian Folksongs from Bihor County[32] was Bartók's first major folksong publication. By grouping the songs according to cadential and rhythmical order rather than genre, Bartók admitted that he overlooked one of the most important features of Romanian musical folklore. In his next publication project, *Volksmusik der Rumänen von Maramureș*,[33] completed the same year but published only in 1923, he assorted the songs into four major categories (at the time of this publication he had insufficient examples to give a complete classification of *colindă* presented in category (a)):

(a) *colindă* or Christmas songs;
(b) laments or *bocete*;
(c) songs not connected with customs, *doinas*; and
(d) dance tunes.

The laments are classified further into: (a) songs for the funerals of young people, and (b) songs for older people. The former are two-line melodies, sung in recitative manner on three notes ($c\sharp''-b\flat'-g'$); the latter are four-line melodies, sung with ornaments in *parlando* tempo.

The *doinas* are divided into two sub-groups: (a) *hora lungă* melodies, and (b) newer *hora* songs. The *hora lungă* melodies have no fixed form; they are completely improvisatory. Nevertheless, one can distinguish three parts in their structure which are repeated or interchanged without any rule: (1) a sustained phrase opening on two notes (c'' and d''); (2) an improvised middle part decorated with fiorituras; and (3) a recitative type of ending on the final note, g'. Related to the *hora lungă* are the Ukrainian *dumy* songs. The newer *hora* is a four-line tune sung to a lyric or epic text in strict *tempo giusto*.

The dance music is also divided into two sub-groups: (a) tunes in free form composed of little two-bar motifs which are combined freely, and (b) tunes in closed forms, resembling stanzaic structures. Further division of sub-groups is based on the order of cadential notes and on the rhythmic and melodic content of lines. The classification brings several musical characteristics of the genres into focus: both the lament and the *hora lungă* are variants of a specific melody; the newer *hora* tunes, particularly the three- and four-line in the Maramureș tradition, resemble Hungarian and Slovakian melodies but differ in their cadential endings which indicate that they are direct borrowings. Only certain elements were taken over and restructured in the Romanian style.

The Romanian *colindă* melodies are based on a different method of classification. In the 1935 volume *Die Melodien der Rumänischen Colinde*,[34] Bartók deals with one specific genre and its many musical forms. In his introduction he describes Romanian folksongs in general as not being strophic in structure. Their lines consist of eight or six syllables divided in four or three metric units of two syllables. If the last syllable of the line is swallowed or missing, and the line contains seven or five text syllables respectively, the singer adds a non-essential vowel which may differ from region to region. The *colindă* are assorted into three major groups: Class A, six- or five-syllable lines, Class B, eight- or seven-syllable forms, and Class C, indistinct forms. Sub-groups of Classes A and B are determined by the number of lines of the songs and each sub-group is further divided according to cadential endings, rhythm and range of lines. Tables of scales, range and melodic content offer further overview of the *colindă*. The tunes in this genre have no uniform characteristics as Bartók's tables indicate. Individually they show certain influences of peasant, religious or neighbouring people's music, and similarities with folksongs of a particular musical dialect region.

The experiences gained by changing the priority of musical principles and by using multi-level classification led Bartók to one of his most successful methods: the classification of Hungarian folksongs by style. In his book, *Hungarian Folk Music*, he applies his hypothesis of primitivity and complexity as a basis for chronology in the evolution of folk music, to (a) melodic construction, (b) rhythmic structure, (c) syllabic structure, (d) range, (e) scale system, and (f) function of folksongs.[35]

(a) Stages in the evolution may be melodies composed of small one- or two-bar motifs (children's game songs and certain forms of instrumental folk music, like bagpipe tunes, fall into this category); single lines, as in laments, or stichic formations, as in epics; closed three- or four-line tunes without architectonic structure; and finally closed stanzas (for example, ABBA or AABA forms) as found in the majority of Hungarian folksongs.

(b) Stages in the evolution of rhythmic forms may be *tempo giusto* patterns in rigid, equal time values that turn into *parlando rubato* rhythms, and then again into *tempo giusto* formation of a more complex nature as frozen forms of *parlando rubato* rhythms.

(c) Melodic lines with few syllables are assumed to be earlier structures than the ones with many syllables; the division of lines into symmetrical sections is believed to have occurred prior to the division of asymmetrical divisions, and strophes formed of isorhythmic or isometric lines indicate older formations than those formed of heterorhythmic or heterometric lines.

(d) Melodies with a narrow range are considered more primitive than those with a wide range.

(e) Scales with missing degrees (for example, pentatonic) point to an older developmental stage than heptatonic scales, and the latter are an earlier form than scales with chromatic notes.

(f) The stages of development are also manifested by the separation of melodies into different functions. In an ancient state probably all songs represented one category. The separation of songs into customs – such as ritual songs, calendar-day songs, funeral, wedding, work songs and folk-songs – occurred later with the division of social functions.

The Hungarian folk-music repertoire is assorted into three style categories: Class A represents the 'old'-style tunes, Class B the 'new'-style tunes, and Class C the 'mixed genera'. Each style has its own musical characteristics. Folksongs in the 'old' style comprise melodies with isosyllabic lines, pentatonic tonality and gradually descending melodic construction. Other characteristics are *parlando rubato* method of performance, and rich ornamentation. Subclasses are four-line stanzas of six- to twelve-syllable lines which are further classified by their cadential structure, melodic content and range of lines. 'New'-style melodies have closed 'architectonic' forms, equisyllabic lines of six to twenty-five syllables; their method of performance is *tempo giusto*, adjusting to the quantitative property of text syllables, and heptatonic tonality. Folksongs that do not fit the description of either class are placed into Class C 'mixed genera'.[36]

Comparative musicology

The division of Hungarian folksongs by style and the delineation of the 'old' and 'new' styles were the achievements of Bartók's method of classification. The changes in Hungarian folk music and the influences of the two styles could only be conjectured on the basis of comparative research. Kodály studied the musical folklore of the ethnically and linguistically related Finno-Ugric Cheremiss and Turco-Bolgar Chuvash people and compared their characteristic features with those of the 'old'-style tunes, while Bartók investigated the folksongs of the Hungarians and their neighbouring peoples in order to obtain a better understanding of the forms of borrowings and mutual influence affecting their musical tradition.

Hungarian tunes sung by young Slovakian and Romanian men, which Bartók had already discovered during the first years of his fieldwork, showed him that melodies do cross language borders. He observed that the *hora lungă* melodies of the Romanians and the *dumy* melodies of the Ukrainians belong to the same melody family, and pointed to the rhythmic relationship between the *kolomeika* tunes of the Ruthenians and the swineherd dance of the Hungarians. Closer investigation of native and borrowed forms in the music of nationality groups required the knowledge of musical traditions. Having already collected and classified Hungarian, Slovakian, Romanian and Ruthenian folksong types, Bartók was now in a position to compare their folk music. His monograph, *Folk Music of the Hungarians and Folk Music of its Neighboring People* (1934), summarizes the results of his research.[37]

The term 'comparative musicology' was already in use by Western scholars for studies of orally transmitted music, mostly from non-European, Oriental and non-literate peoples. To lend scientific credence to the field and bring it into the realm of musicology, scholars used acoustical devices for measuring pitch and scale relations without, however, organizing or classifying the material at hand according to further viewpoints. Bartók's idea of comparative musicology was based on field research and the comparison of musical traditions. His concept of methodology followed along the lines of comparative linguistics.

Whether a particular folksong type is borrowed or indigenous to a given musical tradition is based on three aspects: (a) its geographic distribution, (b) its percentile representation in the entire tradition, and (c) its musical characteristics. Following this reasoning Bartók states that the 'old'- and 'new'-style folksongs of the Hungarians are generally known throughout Hungarian-speaking territories; they represent close to 50 per cent of the entire Magyar musical folklore and have evolved in a number of variant formations. Although songs of the two styles have penetrated the musical folklore of neighbouring nationality groups their appearance remains sporadic. What accounts for the Magyar origin of the two styles and for their borrowed forms in the music of nationality groups is argued on musical grounds.

The 'old'-style songs were taken up by the Romanians in the neighbourhood of the Székely people, but mainly in their eight-syllable forms which match the form of Romanian folk poetry. For similar reasons the Croatians have taken over only the six- and eight-syllable structures. In the music of the Slovak people, however, the 'new' style took hold in surprisingly large numbers, even beyond the language borders. This fact brought into question the Hungarian origin of 'new'-style songs. Bartók's argument that the 'new'-style songs are originally Hungarian is based on the observation that they appear mostly with corrupted forms in the Slovak tradition; for instance, the typical four-line ABBA stanza is corrupted into a three-line ABA form, and the so-called 'adjusting' *tempo giusto*, a peculiarity of 'new'-style songs – adjusting the musical rhythm to the quantitative values of the text – becomes fixed and rigid in the performances of Slovak singers.

There are, however, suspect musical elements in the Hungarian musical tradition which point to Slovakian, Moravian and Czech influences. A large percentage of the 'mixed genera' suggests foreign musical borrowings. Songs of German origin reached Hungary through

Czech-Moravian mediation during the seventeenth and eighteenth centuries; their further diffusion was probably blocked by the rise of 'new'-style folksong in the nineteenth century. Surprisingly, however, no influence was detected of the music of the neighbouring Austrian people on the Magyars. Bartók also found that the *hora lungă* tunes, which Romanian folklorists of more recent times claim to be widely diffused throughout their country outside the Carpathian Basin, had no influence on Hungarian folk music. Neither did the Slovakian *valaska* tunes that Bartók unearthed – one of the indigenous types of Slovak musical folklore in Mixolydian tonality, *parlando rubato* tempo, with shepherd or outlaw subject matter – show any influence.

As a general observation, Bartók remarks that he could find the same kind of melodies and style differences in the songs of Slovakian, Ruthenian and Hungarian peoples, moving from one village to another, whereas the traditional repertoire among the Romanians differed greatly from one region to another. The diffusion of tradition seemed to be vertical among the former, and horizontal among the latter.

Folk Music of the Hungarians and Folk Music of its Neighboring People is 'a documented statement of the common and inseparable destiny of the Danubian people who had been roused one against the other'.[38] By 1934 Bartók's nationalistic aspirations towards 'the good of Hungarian people' had changed. 'My own ideas,' he writes, 'of which I have been fully conscious since I found myself as a composer, is the brotherhood of peoples, brotherhood in spite of all wars and conflicts'.[39]

His involvement with folk music changed his amateur collector's approach to that of a rigorous scientific investigator; it changed his musical thinking, his language of music; he experienced through musical folklore the human creative impulse, the 'natural force' which enriched his own musical imagination; it changed his entire world view: through his artistic intuition he has visualized unsuspected ties between past and present civilizations:

> We have arrived at the most exciting chapter in the history of folksong research, the chapter which I would call 'pragmatic musical folklore' . . . The ancient cultural relations of peoples who have been scattered far and wide, could and should be discovered. There is much to be revealed about ancient settlements and the, as yet unsolved, problems of history. It is now possible to discover what contact there was between neighbouring peoples, in what way they were linked or perhaps separated, by spiritual beliefs.[40]

Yet with all the contributions he has made to the field, Bartók never enjoyed full recognition. In his country his discoveries were viewed with scepticism and subsequent rejection, and among the nationalities, with chauvinistic attacks. His major collections – *Serbo-Croatian Folk Song,*

Slowakische Volkslieder, Rumanian Folk Music, Turkish Folk Music from Asia Minor, and his *Catalogue of Hungarian Folksong Types* – are all post-humous publications, historical references of a growing field.[41] The intellectual thought, energy and sacrifices Bartók made to raise musical folklore to a scientific discipline have yet to be recognized. He stands in this field today as a historical figure with scientific methods and artistic visions from which future musical folklore can greatly benefit.

PART II

Profiles of the music

3 Bartók's orchestral music and the modern world

DAVID COOPER

In his essay, 'Out of Hungary: Bartók, Modernism, and the Cultural Politics of Twentieth-Century Music', Leon Botstein has argued that the composer 'uniquely managed to reconcile the claims of formal musical modernism with the cultural politics of identity and subjective musical particularity'.[1] While the music Bartók wrote between the end of the First World War and around 1930 does seem to be preoccupied with issues addressed by modernist composers such as Schoenberg (and the other members of the Second Viennese School), it should be noted that he could be sceptical, if not distinctly unsympathetic, towards some 'revolutionary' modernist artists. This can be discerned in his comments about Mondrian, Haba, Hauer and others in the first of a series of lectures given at Harvard University in 1943, where he considers the synchronic appearance of 'revolutionary tendencies' in all three branches of the arts. In Mondrian's case he grudgingly admits some public success, but he observes that 'in literature there was less success, and in music no success at all'.[2]

Although his response to a modernist artistic aesthetic may at times seem ambiguous or ambivalent, Bartók *appears* to have been a firm advocate and disciple of the 'project of modernity'. Modernity, as characterized by Jonathan Rée, is concerned with an underlying epistemological contrast: 'the modern world is enlightened, scientific, and disappointed, whereas its predecessor was superstitious, gullible and magical'.[3] Bartók's creative and scholarly work was founded on many of the fundamental tenets of modernity: he was a religious sceptic, probably an atheist or at least an agnostic for most of his life, and as a young man was drawn to the rationalistic aspects of Nietzsche's philosophy; his method of collection and classification of folk material was structuralist and similar to taxonomic approaches found in the natural sciences; he made use of the products of the technological revolution, and in particular such advances as the phonograph and gramophone, as tools which could be used for the 'objective' recording of peasant material; and he was firmly convinced of the evolutionary nature both of society and of artistic production.

If Bartók's position as a modernist is somewhat problematic (and, as Rée remarks, 'in original intention, modernism appears as a rejection of the domineering epistemological optimism of modernity'), so too, it can

be argued, is his position *vis-à-vis* modernity.[4] Bartók, the sophisticated
and erudite child of the modern world, feared and disliked many aspects of
it. His preferred society was the illiterate and often poverty-stricken peasantry of rural Hungary and its neighbouring states, especially where the
lives of such people were sustained by the fruits of their own labour. His
idealization of the isolated pre-modern and pre-industrial country was
coupled with a scorn for the 'corrupt' lifestyle of the city, the consumer-
driven ethics of which he felt to be a violation of nature. Technologies such
as the gramophone, which allowed the ethnomusicologist to record and
analyse 'those infinite, minute nuances which cannot be expressed using
musical notation',[5] were being squandered on the 'garbage-music' of
urban 'song-hit-composers'. Science, reason and nature were being prosti-
tuted for profit.

Much of Bartók's music attempts simultaneously to occupy the spaces
of the modern and the pre-modern world. In it, elements derived initially
from popular semi-urban culture (as propagated by the gypsy bands) and
increasingly after 1905 from rural traditional music, coalesce with the
high-art attributes of musical modernity. Adopting the terminology of
popular musicology, one can observe a strain between the 'intensional'
formal practices of the first two categories, in which complexity arises
from localized and often improvisatory changes of melody and rhythm
within a pre-formed framework, and the 'extensional' principles of art
music, in which substantial structures can be generated from the aggrega-
tion of simple 'musical atoms'.[6] Symphonic form, according to Hans
Keller, is founded upon 'large-scale integration of contrasts' and more
especially '*the contrast between statements* (whether monothematic or
polythematic) *and developments* (whether they concern themselves with
statements or not)'.[7] One might submit that the distinction between statement and development is not easily drawn in the urban and rural traditional music, and that Bartók's modelling of thematic material on
peasant-music processes within a framework derived from nineteenth-
century art-music practice is potentially problematic given Keller's
definition of symphonism.

Kossuth

Bartók's admiration for Richard Strauss's tone poem *Ein Heldenleben*,
which he had transcribed for piano in 1902 and performed in Vienna in
January 1903, led directly to the composition of his own symphonic poem
Kossuth from April to August of that year.[8] In *Kossuth* Bartók made use of a
programme which mythologized Lajos Kossuth, the leader of the abortive

1 Kossuth
2 Why are you so grieved dear husband?
3 The fatherland is in danger!
4 Formerly we had a better life . . .
5 Then our fate changed for the worse . . .
6 Up and fight them!
7 Come, come you splendid lads, you valiant Hungarian warriors!
8 . . . [Parody of the Austrian Imperial Anthem]
9 All is over!
10 Everything is quiet, very quiet . . .

Figure 3.1 Kossuth's programme.[9]

Hungarian revolution of 1848–49 (see Fig. 3.1). This was not the first, at least implicitly, nationalistic work which Bartók composed in 1903, for the song 'Est' [Evening], to a text by Kálmán Harsányi, begins with the line 'Csóndes minden, csóndes' ('Everything is quiet, quiet'), words which reappear as the subtitle of the final part of *Kossuth*. It is possible to read 'Est' metaphorically both as a lament for Kossuth (whose body was returned to Hungary after his death in 1894 to great national mourning) and for the failure of the revolutionary nationalist process.[10]

In a letter written to his mother on 23 August 1903, Bartók passed on to her a remark of his composition teacher at the Budapest Academy of Music, Hans Koessler (an advocate and admirer of Brahms), that the orchestration of *Kossuth* was 'very good, very *modern*', a clear reference to the influence of Richard Strauss.[11] In the crudest sense, Bartók's assumption of a modern manner finds expression in *Kossuth* in the size of the ensemble employed, for the score draws on the vast palette of the post-Wagnerian orchestra, including, in the band of one hundred or so players demanded by the composer on the title page, such instruments as E♭ and bass clarinets, bass trumpet and tenor tubas, as well as the other more usual woodwind doublings of piccolo, cor anglais and contrabassoon. *Kossuth*'s thematic material, through which the programme is made manifest, is dominated by a unifying leitmotif which reappears in a number of more- or less-complex variants and which is intended to represent both Kossuth and the concept of Magyar nationalism through victory and vicissitude (Ex. 3.1). On a deeper musical level, the potential for fragmentation inherent in a programmatic work is both intensified and tempered by a tonal scheme which prioritizes A, F and C♯, key areas which lie a major third apart and thus divide the octave symmetrically into three equal parts, rather than through the asymmetrical tonal relations characteristic of nineteenth-century practice. Interestingly from the perspective of his later practices, the climax of the work, which arrives as the final crushing

Example 3.1 Kossuth's theme on its first appearance, bars 3–4

blow is dealt to the Hungarian army by the Imperial forces, is the culmination of a passage which, by means of a deformation of the Austrian anthem ('Gott erhalte unsern Kaiser'), is contrived to be entirely derived from a whole-tone collection based on a transposition of the mode from which the pitches F, A and C♯ are absent.[12]

It was clearly Bartók's intention with *Kossuth* to compose a work in the 'authentic' Hungarian national style. Before his discovery of peasant music in late 1904, the music which was most clearly identified with Hungarian nationhood in Bartók's mind was that performed by gypsy musicians, music which can loosely be described as falling into the *verbunkos* tradition. The original gypsy-performed *verbunkos* or 'recruiting dance', a hybrid of musical materials from diverse ethnic sources which originated in the eighteenth century, had an overtly political function: to attract an audience from which soldiers could be conscripted for Imperial service by the performance of elaborate dances accompanied by popular music. Thus, while its early history was associated with the legitimization of the Imperial state's apparatus, the *verbunkos* as it developed in the nineteenth century through the *csárdás* and *Magyar nótak* was also held to characterize the Hungarian nation.[13] There was an intimate connection between the process of Magyarization and the gentry's affection for the gypsy-performed music. The *verbunkos* tradition can be regarded as the Magyarized musical language, a musical symbol of the 'soul' of Hungary for the gentry, and, in particular, for the stratum which had lost its land after the abortive 1848 revolution and which operated the state apparatus through the civil service.

The *verbunkos* tradition became established in Viennese classicism and beyond through a series of musical clichés collectively described as *style hongrois*. Many of these musical devices are to be found in *Kossuth*, including:

- the so-called gypsy scale, used in the main thematic idea representing *Kossuth* (Ex. 3.2a);
- the simulation of peasant instrumentation (for example, the *shawm*-like *tárogató* imitated by the clarinet at figure 3 in the score, the oboe at the beginning of the fifth section ('then our fate changed for the worse . . .'), and the drone fifths of the bagpipe at the work's opening);

Example 3.2

(a) Gypsy scale

(b) Choriambus rhythm

(c) 'Scotch snap' rhythm

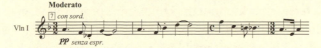

(d) Hungarian anapaest

(e) 'Kuruk' fourths

- the use of rhythmic figures such as the long–short–short–long choriambus (at the beginning of the work's fourth main section, figure 7 – Ex. 3.2b), the accented short–long 'Scotch snap' (at the start of the second section where it is associated with the hero's wife – Ex. 3.2c), and the short–short–long 'Hungarian anapaest' (widely found in the seventh and eighth sections where it is related to the Hungarian army – Ex. 3.2d);
- the *hallgató* style of florid ornamentation (the wind and string writing at figure 10);
- melodic ideas such as the '*Kuruc* fourths' involving a rhythmic rebound between dominant and upper tonic (running through from clarinet to oboe, cor anglais, horn and bass clarinet from rehearsal number 37 – Ex. 3.2e).[14]

As *Kossuth* is Bartók's only work with a fully articulated literary programme, should it be regarded as a temporary aesthetic aberration which would be redeemed by a more wholesome concern with absolute music in the subsequent years? In 1905, two years after the completion of *Kossuth*, he published an article about *Sinfonia Domestica* in the 13 February issue of the Budapest journal *Zeneközlöny* [Music Bulletin] which elaborated Strauss's terse remarks about the symphony's programme. In the final paragraph he summed up his response to the composition: 'The classical simplicity of the work is astonishing, as is the complete lack of so-called cacophony. The subject of course demands such treatment. Excepting the introduction, the entire work might pass as a performance of absolute music, in which 'unity' and 'variety' are ideally blended'.[15] Bartók thus suggests that beneath the modern surface of *Sinfonia Domestica* (and, one might infer, of *Kossuth*), with its use of an extra-musical programme to provide the structural foundations and recurrent musical motifs to act as a carrier for the narrative, more traditional characteristics lie hidden.

The two Suites

The *verbunkos* tradition remained the decisive ingredient in Bartók's construction of a Hungarian musical style in the subsequent four works: the Rhapsody Op. 1 and the Scherzo for piano and orchestra Op. 2 (both composed in 1904), and the two Suites for orchestra Op. 3 (1905) and Op. 4 (1905–1907). Like *Kossuth*, the five-movement First Suite Op. 3 has a kind of *idée fixe*, a recurring melodic idea which is so central to its integrity that in December 1915 Bartók felt compelled to write to the board of directors of the Budapest Philharmonic Society to complain about a performance of the work at a gala concert in Vienna in which it had been truncated. In this letter he notes that: 'My own composition, to which I now refer, is not only symphonic: there is such a close thematic connection between movements that certain bars of some of the movements cannot be understood unless one has already heard the preceding movements'.[16]

Malcolm Gillies has remarked that Bartók had a 'lifelong difficulty in dealing with larger forms which is quite independent of his experiences of folk music' and elsewhere he has implied that the forms of the individual movements of the Suites are not sufficiently 'organically' derived from their materials but 'present themselves as pre-arranged shells awaiting their sometimes grandiose fillings'.[17] By abandoning the use of a programme to generate or stimulate novel structures, Bartók seemingly fell back on the conventions of moribund nineteenth-century symphonic forms. Adorno, however, writing in 1925 about form in Bartók's music,

Example 3.3 Opening theme from the first movement of the First Orchestral Suite, bars 1–7 (upper staff), 'Good wine . . .' arranged Korbay (lower staff)

suggested that in later works such as the Dance Suite, the composer was well aware that these forms were worn out, and that by forcing them to cohabit with the folk-derived materials he was, in fact, performing a critique of them.[18] It can be argued his approach to form in the earlier orchestral pieces is less sophisticated and technically competent than in subsequent scores, but even so there is undoubtedly still much to be admired and enjoyed in them.

The First Suite's opening movement (Allegro vivace) provides an interesting case-study of Bartók's approach. A clear-cut sonata structure with reversed-theme recapitulation involves two strongly contrasting principal themes. The first theme, nominally in E major though without key signature, appears as a single unbroken idea spanning fifty-two bars. Although there is much sequential writing, it is not articulated as a period or sentence phrase structure with modified and extended repetition, as might be found in one of Brahms's symphonic themes, but as an extensive discrete gesture which betokens the influence of Wagner and Strauss. It is illuminating to compare it with a popular melody of the day, collected and arranged by Francis Korbay, translated as 'Good wine . . .' and described as an 'old folk song' (see Ex. 3.3).[19] The song's melody, the first two lines of which involve a similar contour to Bartók's theme, has an irregular hypermetre with two three-bar phrases followed by two two-bar phrases and rounded off with a final three-bar phrase (the latter three phrases being immediately repeated). In an analogous manner, Bartók operates by moving between four- and three-bar units, and his complete theme can be analysed as having the following grouping structure (where the numbers indicate counts of bars): 4–3–3–4–3–4–3–4–4–4–3–4–4–4–1 (with a fermata). This simultaneously propels and fragments the theme by continually frustrating expectations of a regular underlying hypermetre, even if (as has been common practice in art music for several centuries) the regularity is occasionally subverted by elision. The second subject, with its characteristic rising or falling major seventh resolving on the upper or lower octave, presents a lyrical foil to the flamboyant first theme, and has a much more regular four-bar hypermetre throughout. A large-scale tension is thus set up between regular and irregular hypermetric structures and between strategies of integration and disruption, which generates a more satisfying and coherent overall effect than Gillies's criticisms might suggest.

The second movement, Poco adagio, is the most extraordinary of the composer's early experiments with texture and form, and foreshadows the later 'night-music' pieces, including the Elegy from the Concerto for Orchestra. It is organized as a series of four 'pictures' forming a chain-like structure, and opens with a gesture which is derived from the second subject of the first movement (an example of the thematic interconnections alluded to by Bartók above), with a rising major seventh largely filled with whole-tone scale material (E–F♯–G♯–A♯–C–D–D♯) before resolving to the upper octave. This scalic motif, variously developed, acts as a kind of 'promenade' between the sections and finally rounds the movement off. It is one of the typically *verbunkos* elements identified by Judit Frigyesi, the others being the chordal accompaniment and the ornamental melody.[20] The first portrait, with its imitation of the *tárogató* by cor anglais, oboes and clarinets, use of the gypsy scale, and, in general, an emulation of the highly decorated and expressive slow (*lassú*) style of the gypsy band is also clearly (and audibly) intended as a code for Magyar identity. From the progressive point of view, however, the second portrait is the most interesting, especially in the poco agitato section where strings are multiply divided and play a mixture of muted tremolo major or minor seconds, rapid chromatic scales or arpeggios in a wash of sound which is augmented by woodwinds playing a remarkable melody in octaves.

The remaining three movements of the Suite, a scherzo with a characteristic hemiola rhythm reminiscent of the scherzo of Dvořák's Seventh Symphony, a set of variations and a bucolic finale in which ideas from the previous movements make a reappearance, indicate a composer of some technical accomplishment. Bartók's material conjoins modernist musical tendencies, developed from Strauss and Liszt in particular, with *style hongrois* mannerisms which assert a form of nationalism rooted in, and identified with, the Magyar nobility.

The commodious Second Suite Op. 4, begun in 1905 and completed in 1907, is a rather lighter work, and wears its 'national' colours less obviously. More serenade-like than symphonic, it is in four movements and evinces the turning away from Strauss which Bartók observed in a short autobiographical note published in the Viennese journal *Musikblätter des Anbruch* in March 1921.[21] Although he first became conscious of what he came to regard as an autochthonous peasant music on his visit to the village of Gerlice puszta in 1904, it had a limited impact on his compositional activities for some time. Two specific influences from peasant music can be discerned in this work, however: in the third (slow) movement

Example 3.4 (a) The falling pentatonic figure from the Second Suite for
Orchestra Op. 4, III, bars 20–21

(b) Pentatonic fragment from the finale of the Second Suite, bars 3–6

(which the composer would later subtitle 'Scena della Puszta' in his two-
piano arrangement of the work) and in the fourth movement.[22] In the
former instance, a falling idea with the pitches $F\sharp_3$–E_3–$C\sharp_3$–A_2–$F\sharp_2$ is first
announced by the bass clarinet (Ex. 3.4a) during the extended opening
solo and is developed extensively. The movement cadences on an F♯ minor
chord with an added minor seventh, a harmony which Bartók was later to
justify in 1928 by arguing that:

> in pentatonic melodies the modal diminished seventh [i.e. the minor
> seventh] takes on the character of a consonant interval. This fact, as early as
> 1905, led me to end a composition in F♯ minor with the chord: F♯ A C♯ E.
> Hence in the closing chord the seventh figures as a consonant interval. At
> that time a close of this kind was something quite out of the ordinary.
> . . .
>   The final chord of the movement . . . which is a simultaneous resonance of
> all four (or five) tones of the motive: a condensed form of the same, to a
> certain extent, a vertical projection of the previous horizontal form. This
> result is obtained by a logical process, and not, as many objectors believed,
> through sheer whimsicality. The incentive to do this was given by these
> pentatonic melodies. When the consonant form of the seventh was
> established, the ice was broken: from that moment the seventh could be
> applied as a consonance even without a necessarily logical preparation.[23]

The second 'peasant' characteristic, found in the finale, is a pentatonic
fragment played by the first bassoon (Ex. 3.4b) over open fifths in horns,
timpani, piano, lower strings and second bassoon which reappears in a
number of guises. This placid idea is juxtaposed with more chromatic, and
sometimes more aggressive, music in a structure which can feel uncomfortably fragmentary, due in part to the continual metrical alternations.
Bartók was aware of the deficiencies of this movement, remarking in 1910,
in response to a letter from Frederick Delius, that he also found the finale
to be 'the weakest, rather lacking in invention'.[24]

In his autobiographical article of 1921, Bartók noted the 'animosity' with which his works, from the Second Suite on, were greeted in Budapest. Undoubtedly, some of the animadversion Bartók's music suffered was due to the quality of performance – the orchestration of the Second Suite was somewhat more subtle than the earlier pieces, despite the slimmer forces, and required a more sympathetic and careful approach from conductor and players – but more importantly, it drew increasingly on a new musical aesthetic and politics of nationalism influenced, not by the nobility, but by the lowest stratum of society. While staying with the family of the violinist Ferenc Vecsey in Rákoskeresztúr in the autumn of 1906, he wrote to his mother that he had been discussing with Kodály a proposed collection of folksongs, and informed her that they would have 'some harsh things to say about Hungarian audiences'.[25] In the preface to the collection, the authors noted that 'the vast majority of Hungarian society is not yet sufficiently conscious of being Hungarian, is no longer sufficiently unsophisticated and yet still not educated enough, for these songs to go to its heart'.[26]

Two Portraits and *Two Pictures*

The orchestral works which Bartók composed in the years immediately following the Second Suite were on a relatively small scale. The first, *Two Portraits* Op. 5, which was consequential on the twenty-six-year-old composer's infatuation with the violinist Stefi Geyer, found its sources in two other works: the First Violin Concerto of 1907–08, whose opening movement (1907) was reused as the *First Portrait*; and the final piece from the Fourteen Bagatelles Op. 6 (1908) for piano, a grotesque waltz, formed the Second. The hyper-romantic *First Portrait*, a slow and impassioned movement for solo violin and orchestra based on a rising, arpeggiated major-seventh figure (Ex. 3.5) which Bartók associated with Stefi Geyer (and a motif which bears a striking similarity to the opening theme of the third movement of Rachmaninov's Second Symphony of 1907), exhibits a greater concern with polyphony than hitherto in the composer's oeuvre and is effectively monothematic, eschewing bold contrasts. By pairing this movement with a fast, grotesque waltz he was adopting an overall shape analogous to that of the popular art-music of the *verbunkos* tradition, and this pattern is maintained in the *Two Pictures* (or *Images*) Op. 10 of 1910.

   Two Pictures shows a development in style from *Two Portraits*. The *First Picture* (or *Image*) has a commonality with the second movement of the First Suite in its concern for texture, but it makes its point more simply and with more sophisticated orchestration. In later life Bartók noted the revolutionary effect of Debussy's music; the musical climate of Hungary had

Example 3.5 The opening theme from the first of the *Two Portraits*, bars 1–4

been dominated by German culture for three hundred years, yet the intellectual elite had always been 'oriented towards the French culture, considering it more congenial to its own character'.[27] Debussy's music offered an alternative model for an 'authentically' Hungarian music – one which was detached from the German hegemony and in which the antique and the modern were fused. His influence is apparent particularly through the use of the whole-tone scale, a mode which is not characteristic of East European traditional music, although there are some Romanian and Slovakian modes with substantial whole-tone segments. For example, the mode (expressed with D as modal final) with the pitch structure D–E–F(♯)–G–A–B–C(♯)–D (where F and C may be either sharpened, natural or between the two) has the whole-tone segment F–G–A–B–C♯ when the appropriate forms of F and C are found. Of course, Bartók had made some use of whole-tone elements before, particularly in the climactic passage of *Kossuth*.

Debussy's influence can be observed most clearly in the final eleven bars of the *First Picture*. It is not merely the persistent use of the whole-tone scale in this harmonically static moment (only the pitch E♭, which makes one brief appearance in clarinets and bassoons in the third bar of this section, is not from a whole-tone scale founded on D) that identifies this influence. Just as significant is the exquisite luminosity of the instrumentation which is redolent of *Pelléas et Mélisande* (1893–1902).

Four Orchestral Pieces

Bartók's only opera, *Duke Bluebeard's Castle* Op. 10, was completed in its first version in 1911, and is now widely regarded as one of the composer's earliest 'mature' works. It is played out on a musical canvas that draws on the *parlando rubato* style of Hungarian song in much the same way that Debussy's *Pelléas* 'reach[es] back to the declamation of the ancient French language'.[28] *Bluebeard* casts its unmistakable shadow on 'Prelude', the first of the Four Orchestral Pieces Op. 12, a work which was composed in two-piano format in 1912, but not orchestrated until 1921. Conceived as a further slow–fast pairing of two movements, Bartók added an intermezzo and funeral march to his original plan of prelude and scherzo to make yet another suite-like rather than symphonic work. The designation of the work as Four Orchestral Pieces may possibly have been a veiled tribute to Arnold Schoenberg's remarkable Five Orchestral Pieces of 1909, though Bartók's score cannot really be claimed to have the same significance, either in terms of his personal stylistic development, or of the more general evolution of contemporary art music.

Although Kodály remarked in the 1920s that the opening pair of movements was linked in mood to Bartók's one-act ballet *The Wooden Prince*, composed and orchestrated between 1914 and 1917 to a scenario by Béla Balázs, the Scherzo seems closer in temperament to the hectic and brutal opening of the pantomime *The Miraculous Mandarin*, a portrayal of the depraved city. The impact of the rather wild and fragmentary Second Orchestral Piece, which manifests Bartók's growing interest in overtly modernist composition, is all the greater because of the generally more subdued character of the other movements. If the Scherzo suggests the savagery of Stravinsky's contemporaneous ballet *The Rite of Spring* (1911–13) then the Prelude, particularly in those moments when the music appears to freeze in a trilled and arpeggiated passage, seems to have more of an affinity with Franz Schreker's opera *Der ferne Klang*, first performed in Frankfurt am Main in August 1912, the secret of whose 'distant sound' of the title lies in Nature.

Dance Suite

The Dance Suite, which was premiered in 1923, the year after the first performance of Four Orchestral Pieces, is of greater significance in the composer's development. In an essay written in 1921, Bartók clearly articulated his philosophy of aesthetic value at that time:

> At all events it is a noteworthy fact that artistic perfection can only be achieved by one of the two extremes: on the one hand by peasant folk in the mass, completely devoid of the culture of the town-dweller, on the other by creative power of an individual genius . . . When peasants or the peasant classes lose their naivety and their artless ignorance, as a result of the conventional culture, or more accurately half-culture, of the town-dwelling folk, they lose at the same time all their artistic transforming power.[29]

It is intriguing to imagine a socialist programme underlying Bartók's espousal of peasant music, particularly given his connection with the short-lived Hungarian Communist government in 1919 as a member of the Musical Directorate. However, the soviet-style regime only held power for four-and-a-half months and he was left in the awkward position of having given his public support to the losing faction, causing some discomfort for him in the ensuing counter-revolution.

It therefore seems all the more extraordinary that he should have been approached by the Budapest City Council so soon afterwards to compose a work to commemorate the fiftieth anniversary of the unification of the cities, Buda, Óbuda and Pest. The Dance Suite which resulted from the commission is scored for full orchestra, and although nominally in six movements, most of these follow each other without any break. Bartók does not make direct use of authentic folk melodies, as he does in the Romanian Folk Dances (1915), the Transylvanian Dances (an orchestration made in 1931 of the Sonatina for piano of 1915) and the *Hungarian Sketches* (another orchestration of 1931 of piano pieces written between 1908 and 1911). Instead, he composes original material which bears the clear imprint of his experience of peasant music.

Attention has already been drawn to Bartók's use of an interconnecting motif to act as a kind of promenade between the four 'pictures' of the second movement of the Second Suite for orchestra. In the Dance Suite this function is assumed by a short melody, labelled Ritornell (or ritornello) by the composer, an idea which György Kroó has described as being *verbunkos* in style. Much of the other material is derived from traditional models which render the notion of Hungarian identity problematic. The composer noted in a letter to the Romanian ethnomusicologist Octavian Beu on 10 January 1931:

> No. 1 is partly, and No. 4 entirely of an Oriental (Arab) character; the
> *ritornell* and No. 2 are of Hungarian character; in No. 3 Hungarian,
> Rumanian and even Arab influences alternate; and the theme of No. 5 is so
> primitive that one can only speak of a primitive peasant character here, and
> any classification according to nationality must be abandoned.[30]

From the post-colonial perspective (and it must be remembered that the Dance Suite is one of Bartók's earliest works to be written in a fully independent Hungary, albeit a state massively reduced in both geographical area and population) the work is of some consequence. By invoking the characteristics of North African music Bartók draws attention to 'the Other in the form of non-European cultures',[31] whilst his use of Romanian- and Hungarian-style material simultaneously suggests that his musical language (which he felt to be essentially Hungarian) can 'contain' or absorb the Other, and that these disparate cultural artefacts share some fundamental connection.

Many changes in Bartók's style can be observed over the twenty-year period since *Kossuth*. His orchestration no longer relies on late nineteenth-century conventions, but has become highly idiosyncratic, particularly in

[Bar 3]   F–A♭–B♭–C♭
[Bar 7]   F–A♭–B♭–C♭–D♭
[Bar 11]   G♯–A♯——C♯——D♯–E——F♯
[Bar 15]   B—C♯–D–D♯——E♯–F♯–G–G♯–A–B–C
[Bar 21]   A♭–B♭——D♭—E♭– F♭——G♭
[Bar 23] F–A♭–B♭–C♭–D♭
[Bar 25] F–A♭–B♭–C♭

Figure 3.2 The symmetrical pitch organization of the melodic lines of the fourth movement of the Dance Suite.[32]

the use of piano and strings. Whereas cantabile string writing is still found in the Four Orchestral Pieces, especially the third, at times Delian, Intermezzo movement, it is found in the Dance Suite only in the nostalgia of the ritornello. Elsewhere the writing tends to be rhythmic (for instance in the *martellato* down-bow figures and *col legno* of the first movement, and the minor-third-dominated low-register repeating figures in the second) or colouristic (for example, the use of glissandi and tremolos throughout, the employment of harmonics in the third movement and the multiply-divided, repeated chords in the tranquil fourth movement). Of particular interest is the use of complementary harmony and symmetrical pitch organization in the fourth movement where Arab-inspired elements come to the fore. The melodic line which is played by woodwinds is derived from the material as set out in Figure 3.2, and involves a process of expansion and contraction over the course of the movement.

Concerto for Orchestra

During the subsequent twenty years until 1943 Bartók eschewed the symphony orchestra as a major vehicle for his creativity. He did, however, complete two piano concertos (1926 and 1931), the Second Violin Concerto (1938) and *Cantata profana* (1930), all of which use the orchestra in an accompanimental role. He also composed *Music for Strings, Percussion and Celesta* (1936), one of his most successful pieces and a work which displays the fully mature Bartókian style. The events surrounding the composition of the Concerto for Orchestra in 1943 and its public reception have been well rehearsed elsewhere.[33] Suffice it to say that the work came after a period of creative inertia. A combination of alienation, fatigue and ill-health which followed his mother's death and his move to the United States in 1940, and the need to make some kind of living to support his wife and son Peter, may have sapped his compositional energy. His main musical outlet, other than a dwindling number of piano solo and duo recitals, was the transcription and analysis of material from the Milman Parry collection of audio recordings of Serbo-Croatian peasant songs.

Bartók composed his Concerto for Orchestra during a period of temporary remission from the effects of the leukaemia which would eventually kill him in 1945. It has been regarded, since its inception, as on one hand a modern yet accessible work, and on the other as a reactionary piece which compromises, even betrays, the modernist principles which have been observed in the compositions he produced in the twenties and early thirties. Undoubtedly the work displays the pluralistic and inclusive approach to musical material which he increasingly adopted in the 1930s and to which he alluded in his response to a question about his opinion on the current state of music in 1938, namely that 'in order to express our ideas and sentiments through music it is necessary to forsake all that weighs down its flight and to make use of all the means within our reach'.[34] *Verbunkos-* and peasant-modelled material fraternizes with radical modernist art music; conservative sonata structure and fugal technique commingle and coalesce with 'chain' forms; pseudo-functional diatonic progressions blend with static harmonic fields.

Bartók had previously used five-movement schemes in the First Suite and the Fourth and Fifth Quartets. In the quartets this creates a pseudo-symmetrical shape in which the final pairs of movements form distorted mirror-images of the opening pairs. This symmetry is much less apparent in the Concerto for Orchestra, for there is no large-scale link between first and fifth or second and fourth movements. Instead, a six-note germinal motif (F–G–A♭–B♭–B–C, in the form heard at the beginning of the first-movement exposition – Ex. 3.6b) is found to permeate much of the thematic material of the outer movements. This is a more condensed form of the motivic technique adopted in *Kossuth* and the First Suite. Many of the characteristics of the Concerto can be traced to earlier works as far back as the First Suite. Indeed, analysis of the first movement of the Concerto shows it to have a reversed-recapitulation sonata form like the equivalent movement of the Suite, and its second, third and fifth movements involve 'chain forms', the prototype of which can be found in the Suite's second movement. On a more detailed level of observation, the repeated chords of the Concerto's third movement (*Elegia*) find a shadowy precursor in the first 'picture' of the Suite's second movement.

If one adopts a notion of symphonic form which is premised on Keller's definition, then Bartók's use of form may well seem problematic. By coalescing reversed-recapitulation sonata and neo-Baroque ritornello forms in the first movement proper (after the slow introduction), the distinction between statement and development becomes blurred. Furthermore, Bartók's tendency to combine linear 'chain' forms with modified ternary

Example 3.6

(a) Germinal motif from the Concerto for Orchestra

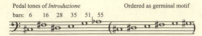

(b) The germinal motif as it appears in the first subject of the first movement, bars 76–81

(c) Pitches from the germinal motif at the start of the first section of the second movement, bars 8–12

(d) Pitches from the germinal motif at the climax of the third movement, bars 93–95

(e) Pitches from the germinal motif in the opening ideas of the fourth movement, bars 4–12

(f) Expansion of the germinal motif in the first theme of the finale, bars 8–11

structures (in the second and third movements), and his use of considerable variation when thematic material is restated, undermines listening modes which are founded on Classical symphonic practice. The mosaic-like quality of some of Bartók's large-scale movements should not be seen as a failure on the composer's part to reproduce the 'organic' forms of Viennese Classicism, however; some listeners, such as the writer Hermann

Hesse, are able to hear in them 'precisely the music of our time: an expression of our experience, our view of life, our strengths and our weaknesses'.[35]

Overall, the Concerto for Orchestra presents a balance of integrative and disruptive forces which destabilize its potential to behave as a simple chauvinistic piece of nationalist music. In a way that is resonant with many post-colonial literatures, it finds an accommodation between the languages of the colonizer and the colonized and the modern and the pre-modern worlds, but attempts no false synthesis between them. It celebrates their differences as much as their agreements, their fragmentation as much as their wholeness. Bartók's accommodation of heterogeneous material is seen at its starkest in the curious fourth movement, 'interrupted serenade', which brings together without trying to reconcile, music from three different worlds: an opening theme with a Slovak peasant-style melody and a 'Balkan' rhythm which sways between $\frac{5}{8}$ and $\frac{2}{4}$; a second idea modelled on a melody from Zsigmond Vincze's popular 1926 fairy-tale opera *The Bride of Hamburg*, harmonized by a cyclic tonal progression; and a parody of a theme from Shostakovich's Seventh Symphony. This curious movement, which combines black humour and deep pathos with a certain naivety, and whose penultimate moment is a point of repose in the natural world as encoded by a birdsong-like cadenza for solo flute, is both the antithesis and the consummation of the musical modernity expressed forty years earlier in *Kossuth*. The intermezzo, and the Concerto as whole, represents a return to the popular impulse of the earliest orchestral music, filtered through the composer's experiences of musical modernism. Bartók had discovered, perhaps, that enlightenment and magic are not mutually exclusive.

4 The stage works: portraits of loneliness

CARL LEAFSTEDT

Every portrait that is painted with feeling is a portrait of the artist, not of the sitter
OSCAR WILDE, *THE PORTRAIT OF DORIAN GRAY*

There is a moment at the end of *Duke Bluebeard's Castle* that, perhaps more than any other moment in his stage works, seems emblematic of Béla Bartók's overall career as a stage composer. It occurs when Bluebeard is placing upon Judith the crown, mantle and jewels that are to be hers in the eternity of blackness that lies ahead. 'Every night is yours now', he intones with great solemnity, his words and actions eliciting subdued expressions of protest from the woman he openly admires as 'beautiful, one hundred times beautiful'. The sombre F♯ minor theme then returns to conclude the opera. It was here, at this moment of great dramatic and symbolic significance, that Bartók, in late 1911 or early 1912, experimented by removing all Bluebeard's words in an attempt to find a more satisfactory conclusion, thereby rendering the character all but mute for the opera's final, puzzling minutes. Bluebeard, in this revised version of the ending, now sings only one line, 'Now it will be night forever', furnished to Bartók almost as an afterthought by the playwright Béla Balázs, who, separately, had also sensed that the closing needed further improvement.[1] In place of the omitted lines Bluebeard simply gestures, placing the crown, mantle and jewels upon Judith without comment or explanation, as the orchestral music wells forth around them. Bartók's experiment has never been known to the public, for six years later he restored the deleted text, modified the ending further, and shaped the conclusion into the form in which we know it today. In light of his future development as a composer, however, it bears a significance far greater than its length – some twenty bars – might otherwise suggest. For here, tentatively and quietly, the seeds of Bartók's eventual turn from opera to ballet are set forth.

Bartók was by all accounts an extraordinarily reserved man, reticent to the point of discomfort when interacting with the world around him, as numerous friends, acquaintances and fellow musicians recollect. His lack of ease in personal communication was legendary; small talk, or what Yehudi Menuhin remembered as Bartók's 'impatience with conversational exchange', was not indulged. To others he appeared 'laconic' or 'quiet' by nature.[2] Unique as these qualities were to Bartók, many of his contemporaries in early modern Hungary's artistic circles also sensed the presence of similar traits in their personalities, and, like Bartók, turned loneliness and its corollaries, among them an inability to open up completely and a tendency to shy away from close personal relationships, to productive creative ends. Gyula Krúdy, writing about his novel *The Red Mail Coach* (1914), once described its topic as 'Everything that is dear to me ... thoughts that are born in the solitude of the night of a man living a bit like a hermit'.[3] Krúdy's embrace of solitude as a source of creative inspiration was amplified in the more speculative writings of György Lukács, who, around the same time, theorized with seemingly inexhaustible energy about the intellectual's need for solitude, in such essays as 'Søren Kierkegaard and Regine Olsen' and 'My Socratic Mask'.[4] Sympathetic echoes of Bartók's experience can be encountered in the poetry of Dezső Kosztolányi and Endre Ady, in the creative writings of the dramatist philosopher Béla Balázs, who would soon write the texts for Bartók's first two stage works, or in the paintings of Tivadar Csontváry Kosztka with their small figures huddled against vibrantly colourful yet lonely landscapes.

The presentiment that a life of inescapable loneliness lay ahead of him was already well in place by 1905, when he wrote to his mother, 'there are times when I suddenly become aware of the fact that I am absolutely alone! And I prophesy, I have a foreknowledge, that this spiritual loneliness is to be my destiny'.[5] This existential sense of loneliness coloured his entire outlook on life, affecting his relationships with friends, male and female, and with society in general. Each of his stage works represents an extension of this sentiment, even, it may be argued, the coldly violent *Miraculous Mandarin* (1918–19), so outwardly different in tone from *Bluebeard's Castle* and *The Wooden Prince* (1914–17). Words, the spoken conveyors of meaning, are in these works either entirely absent, or, as in *Bluebeard*, used sparingly in halting phrases laden with ambiguity. And in each, the theme of spiritual loneliness looms large behind the characters' actions. Thus Bartók's attempt to revise the conclusion of his opera, outlined above, offers a glimpse into his fundamental personality as a composer for the stage: his text deletions find him poised, ever so briefly, between the worlds of ballet and opera, searching to express a meaning hidden behind words, and setting forth characters for whom action and deed – the visible, tangible stage play – are mere surface reflections of elusive, deeper truths.

Bluebeard's Castle, composed from February to September 1911, incorporates as its protagonists two characters, Bluebeard and his new wife Judith, who search for love and acceptance in the darkened confines of his castle, a quest that ends, futilely, with her symbolic entombment and his quiet farewell to an existence in which the soul is nourished by love.

Gloom and pessimism pervade this one-act opera; only the hope, extinguished almost as soon as it arises, that Judith will succeed in bringing light to the castle lends warmth to its plot. Like Schoenberg's *Erwartung* (1909) it is a piece utterly devoid of humour or anything approaching levity, charm, or any of the other dozens of outwardly winning qualities traditionally applauded in opera houses and therefore sought by singers as vehicles for their careers. This quality, not surprisingly, is also the source of its considerable dramatic power.

Hindsight permits us to see *Bluebeard's Castle* as an extension of sentiments that were already evident in the composer's mind three years earlier. In 1908, when he gave the manuscript of his early Violin Concerto to Stefi Geyer, Bartók copied down on its pages a poem by Balázs that summarized, in words, the feelings he had experienced in the wake of his emotionally devastating infatuation with the young violinist. 'In vain! In vain this poem too fell into my hands', Bartók wrote, and then began the poem which reads in part: 'My heart is bleeding, my soul is ill / I walked among humans / I loved with torment, with flame-love / In vain, in vain! / No two stars are as far apart / as two souls'.[6] Here, in a nutshell, is the theme of the opera he would write three years later.

On the stage appear seven large doors, barely visible at first in the icy gloom. One by one Judith will open them in the course of the opera. Behind the first she discovers a torture chamber, its walls bleeding; behind the second, a hall of weapons stained with blood. Judith has come to the castle to bring light to its walls and thus, symbolically, to the soul of a man she loves. 'I will dry off its dank walls', she proclaims towards the beginning, 'with my lips I will dry it! / I shall warm its cold stone / I shall warm it with my body / so it will be free'. Balázs describes her journey through the castle:

> When the castle's doors open forth, laboured and painfully at first, she, however, has no fear of the dangerous and, until then, hidden secrets that spring forth from the depths of the rooms; after all, more light enters the poor, dark castle. But she sees traces of blood everywhere. Where will they lead? Do they not mark the path of her own fate? She opens the doors one after the other, each with increasing restlessness and impatience. She searches for the cause of the traces of blood. She demands: 'From whence does the blood come?' And when, through the fifth door, a flood of light and warmth engulfs the castle, and Bluebeard – liberated, redeemed, luminous, grateful in his happiness – wants to embrace the woman in his arms, already the daylight is no longer visible to the woman who brought it to him. She sees only bloody shadows.[7]

Fearfully suspicious about the blood emerging from behind each door, Judith presses forward until, from behind the seventh door, three former

Example 4.1 Opening of *Bluebeard's Castle*, shown without the text spoken by the bard

wives step forward in wordless greeting. 'They are alive!' she sings, astonished. Bluebeard kneels before them, praising their beauty while Judith, sensing that her fate is to join them, eventually moves to take her place at their side. The door closes, leaving Bluebeard alone on stage to quietly disappear in the growing darkness.

Bluebeard's Castle gains its basic formal outline from the overall progression the stage lighting creates, moving from darkness at the beginning through the bright light of the fifth door scene and then back to darkness again at the end. Within this rounded structure, the numerous textual references to blood take on a weight and direction of their own, growing in import and ambiguity as the seventh door approaches. Musical processes unfold against a background tonal plan that sets the principal dramatic tension – a symbolic opposition of light and darkness – in the contrasting tonalities of F♯ and C. When the opera's opening melody rolls forth from the darkness it traces a series of pitches comprising a pentatonic scale based on F♯ (F♯–A–B–C♯–E) and reflects, in its regular four-bar phrases, Bartók's awareness of the melodic characteristics found in the oldest strata of authentic Hungarian folksong (see Ex. 4.1). This same melody, and same tonality, will return to end the work. C major is asserted as the counterweight to F♯ at the opening of the fifth door, when the brightness of the light is captured in a blaze of powerful

Example 4.2 *Bluebeard's Castle*, opening of the fifth door, before figure 75

chords set in C (see Ex. 4.2). The pitch C, however, already intrudes into the realm of F♯ in the opera's first pages, in the outlines of the menacing motif heard in the orchestra at figure 1 (Ex. 4.1) and later, suggesting that the very ability to perceive darkness presumes the existence of light; only later will enough light appear to vanquish darkness, and all that it stands for, from the castle.[8]

Bartók wrote the music to *Bluebeard's Castle* at a time when his reputation was on the rise as one of the more talented, if controversial, members of a younger generation of composers in Hungary. The founding in 1911 of UMZE, the New Hungarian Musical Society, with he and Kodály among its principal organizers, enhanced his public profile as a musician dedicated to introducing new music to Budapest audiences, even if the concerts did not draw large audiences. He was already, as Tibor Tallián writes, 'the foremost representative of the extreme avant-garde in music, and its pianist interpreter'.[9] With *Bluebeard*, abruptly, he embarked on a task whose novelty he still seemed to esteem years later when, writing about the opera, he recalled it as 'simultaneously my first stage and my first vocal work'.[10] The result was a bold attempt to invigorate Hungarian opera traditions by rethinking, in the most fundamental way, the musical language needed to accommodate the characteristic features of sung Hungarian, with its marked emphasis on the first syllables of words. In *Bluebeard* he experimented with a vocal style drawing heavily upon the *parlando rubato* he heard in Hungarian peasant music, while patterning the voice–orchestra relationships more generally after the innovative declamatory style he admired in Debussy's *Pelléas et Mélisande* (1893–1902), with its recitative-like vocal lines set in the rhythms of natural speech. Its innovative style, synthesizing, as it were, East and West, represented a departure from the Wagnerian operatic idiom, tinged with *verbunkos*-inspired Hungarianisms, then still prevalent among Hungarian opera composers. Balázs's dramatic text provided him with exactly the ingredient he needed to create a new vocal style – a malleable, concise text that reflected, like Bartók's music, the author's careful attention to Hungarian folk expression.

Bartók first met Balázs in September 1906 when Balázs, recently graduated from the University of Budapest, where he had roomed with Kodály, accompanied the composer on a week-long folksong collecting tour. A common interest in exploring the potential of Hungarian folk idioms for their creative work soon drew these two men together, initiating a relationship based on mutual admiration for the purpose and spirit of each other's work. Although they would never be close friends – 'outside of his music', Balázs wrote about his new acquaintance in his diary in 1906, 'I am able to enjoy nothing about him'[11] – their lives intersected frequently, with productive results, during subsequent years of activity in Budapest. Bartók clearly felt a deep attraction to the poetry and dramatic work of his slightly younger contemporary, with its recurrent themes of solitude and love. Balázs, once he left Hungary in 1919, would go on to earn greater renown as an early film theorist; in addition to two influential books on film, he contributed as a writer and scenarist to dozens of Austrian and German films, including Leni Riefenstahl's *Das blaue Licht* (1932) and the film version of Kurt Weill's *Die Dreigroschenoper* (1931).[12] *Bluebeard's Castle*, his third play, is the direct result of his interest in the symbolist dramas of Maurice Maeterlinck, with whose *Ariane et Barbe-bleue* (1899) it shares some common elements. It was published in the Hungarian journal *Szinját ék* [Stageplay] in its 13 June 1910 issue, where it bore a joint dedication to Bartók and Kodály.

Instead of conventional dramatic conflicts expressed through dialogue and character development, plays like *Bluebeard's Castle* eschew action for a type of drama that aims to lay bare the mysteries of life through techniques of silence, repetitions, and by setting stories in a distant time and place so as to be non-specific and, therefore, not tied to the world of external reality. For Balázs this style had strong philosophical underpinnings: true communication between souls, he felt, and the knowledge of self, could not be achieved through words alone, necessary as they were to the expression of emotions and to conveying meaning. Behind the façade of language coursed the inexpressible mysteries of life, what he once termed 'the ultimate governing force – invisible and imprecise' that permeates human existence and makes itself felt through our actions, even as we fail to truly comprehend what it is. 'Words', Balázs once stated, 'can tell little of what should be said – but it is precisely for this reason that words mean more than what they actually say'.[13] Within this basic style, the text itself is cast wholly in the eight-syllable verse patterns Bartók and Kodály had identified as among the oldest authentically Hungarian poetic forms. Referring to the play as a 'ballad', Balázs later explained:

> I created this ballad of mine in the language and rhythms of old Hungarian
> Székely folk ballads. In character these folk ballads closely resemble old
> Scottish folk ballads, but they are, perhaps, more acerbic, more simple, their
> melodic quality more mysterious, more naive, and more songlike. Thus,
> there is no 'literature' or rhetoric within them: they are constructed from
> dark, weighty, uncarved blocks of words.[14]

Frequent repetitions of lines and phrases lend an incantatory quality to the
text, a feeling enhanced by the tendency for questions and observations to
trail off into silence, unanswered.

What is the opera about? This question has no easy answer. On one
level it is a story about a man and a woman, deeply in love, struggling with
the growing awareness that true knowledge of the other's soul is impossible, for the further one penetrates into the soul – symbolized here by the
opening of doors – the more it shrinks from contact. This view becomes
complicated by our eventual realization that, as the presence of the three
former wives testifies, and as his words periodically confirm ('My castle
shall not gleam', he responds to her declaration of intent to let light into the
castle), Bluebeard *already knew* the drama's conclusion before it began: his
new wife would meet the same fate. And yet he invited her into the castle,
seeking, needing the life her presence could give. On another, perhaps
more fundamental, level, then, the entire drama thus becomes an expression of the vast spiritual loneliness engulfing humanity, final proof that
even the warming touch of love cannot, in the end, overcome the soul's
drive towards solitude, away from the object of desire. Bluebeard and
Judith end the opera as they began, separated from each other, having
learned some unspoken, inescapable truths about themselves. In Bartók's
next stage work, *The Wooden Prince*, the symbolic encounter between man
and woman would find the fulfilment, and optimism, it was denied in his
opera.

Intermittently over the next twelve years Bartók devoted a great deal of
time to *Bluebeard*'s two successor works, the ballet *The Wooden Prince*,
composed over a three-year period from 1914 to 1917, and the pantomime
The Miraculous Mandarin, whose composition occupied him from the
sketches first outlined in August 1917 to the work's eventual orchestration
in 1923–24. Once these three works were finished he would never again
write for the theatre, though he periodically contemplated projects put to
him by interested collaborators. He remained involved with them over
much of the remainder of his life, however, preparing editions and, for the
two dance works, compiling orchestral suites for concert performance.
The Wooden Prince underwent major revision in 1932, while as late as 1942
he was still attempting to arrange the first stage production of the
Mandarin.

The Wooden Prince is a tale about the triumph of love in the face of adversity. In true fairy-tale fashion, it is set in a remote time and place, far removed from the reality of everyday life, and populated with castles, forests and characters about whom nothing need be known other than that they are a prince, a princess and a wise, if somewhat possessive, fairy whose gentle presence hovers over the tale, guiding the passions of the would-be lovers as they struggle towards a love so serenely blissful no words need be said. Set as a continuous series of eight dances, the ballet tells of a handsome young prince who beholds a beautiful princess playing coquettishly among the trees, impulsively falls in love, and struggles to win her heart. In his way stand the wishes of a fairy who wishes the prince to belong, alone, in her magical nature world, and who will use all her powers to prevent him from reaching the princess. In the third dance, termed a 'grand ballet', the forest itself, and then a river, are summoned to turn the prince away from his goal, while in the distance the princess sits at her spinning wheel in the castle, oblivious to his effort. To gain her attention the prince fashions an image of himself that he can lift above the trees for her to glimpse. He takes his crown, his cloak, his sword, and, eventually, his golden hair, arranges them on a dummy, and watches as the princess instantly stops sewing and dashes down through the forest to find this handsome prince she has seen – the wooden prince of the ballet's title. Ironic developments now multiply as the princess falls in love not with the real prince, but with his external image in the shape of the wooden dummy, and the dejected prince retreats into solitude. The wooden prince is brought to life by the fairy. The rest of the ballet relates how the princess, disappointed that the dummy eventually breaks down, catches sight again of the real prince, and succeeds in regaining his heart. The prince abandons solitude for the embrace of love. As the curtain falls the lovers, now certain of their affection, stand quietly gazing into each other's eyes.

The wooden dummy or toy magically brought to life is a stock figure in the world of classical ballet; familiar examples include the toys in Tchaikovsky's *The Nutcracker*, the doll in Delibes's *Coppélia*, and, in a later example, the puppet in Stravinsky's *Petrouchka*. Balázs's innovation is to make the wooden prince a grotesque creation whose jerking, halting motions are so exaggerated that the credulity of the princess's infatuation becomes severely strained. It is almost a foregone conclusion, once the dummy is brought to life, that he will revert to his former state and that the onlookers, as in *Coppélia*, will learn from their mistakes. What is unusual and interesting about Balázs's tale is the degree to which the author's mystical philosophy guides the outcome of an outwardly unremarkable, if clever and entertaining, plot.

Bartók, clearly responsive to this element, creates music which deepens

Example 4.3 The Prince's Apotheosis, from *The Wooden Prince*, figure 120

the significance of events on stage. The prince's despair at losing the princess to an image of himself elicits from Bartók music of impassioned beauty (figures 120–26 in the score, see Ex. 4.3), anguished yet oddly beautiful in a way reminiscent of the finale of the Second String Quartet, though lacking that work's melancholy austerity.

Bartók thus extends, and makes dramatically convincing, the prince's gradual resignation and his ensuing embrace by Nature, as the fairy commands all things in the forest to pay homage to the disconsolate man. In so doing he enlarges the work's symbolism: the prince's grief is not merely a transitory grief over a lost opportunity, but a life-altering moment of realization. He sees, with a clarity never before experienced, the emptiness of humanity's pursuit of love, and in that moment of realization gains symbolic admittance into a realm lying beyond reason, beyond suffering, where man, alone, can lay down the burdens of his soul on the breast of Nature. This apotheosis forms the emotional centre of Bartók's ballet; it is surrounded on either side by the quicker, more extroverted dances of the princess and wooden prince (Fig. 4.1).

In a note published at the time of the ballet's premiere, Bartók likened the ballet's music to a 'symphonic poem for dance', and explained that the construction observed a large-scale division into three parts arranged symmetrically around the prince's apotheosis in the middle of the ballet. The inverse ordering of the action in Part 3, he stated, arose as a natural requirement because of the libretto.[15] Individual dances vary sharply in character. Highlights include the playful, scherzo-like dance of the princess in the forest, scored delicately for solo clarinet, harps and pizzicato strings (First Dance), and her vigorous comic dance with the animated wooden prince (Fourth Dance), where Bartók caricatures the dummy's lurching movements through abrupt shifts in tempo and a pulsing, repetitive rhythmic stamp. The brilliant and colourful orchestration of these dances, and of the entire score, may have resulted from Bartók's encounter with the repertoire of the *Ballets Russes*, who visited Budapest to great acclaim in December 1912.

With some of Bartók's finest nature music framing the ballet – the music of the opening is recapitulated in abbreviated form at the end – the

Part 1	[prelude before the curtain rises]	[Awakening of Nature.]
	First Dance	Dance of the princess in the forest. Prince falls in love with her.
	Second Dance	Dance of the trees. Trees, brought to life by the fairy, prevent prince from reaching her.
	Third Dance	Dance of the waves.
	Fourth Dance	Dance of the princess with wooden doll.
Part 2	[apotheosis]	[Prince alone in Nature.]
Part 3	Fifth Dance	Dance. [Princess and collapsing wooden prince.]
	Sixth Dance	Dance. [Princess and real prince.]
	Seventh Dance	Dance. [Trees prevent princess from reaching prince.]
	[conclusion]	[Prince and princess embrace. Nature returns to its former peaceful state.]

Figure 4.1 The structure of *The Wooden Prince*. Dance titles and numbering are Bartók's, as indicated in the Universal Edition score. The large-scale division into three parts represents Bartók's own clarification of the ballet's form

drama comes full circle to close in the same key, C major, with which it began. Both of Balázs's texts for Bartók feature a circular design circumscribed on the arc of the drama and reflected, perceptively, in Bartók's decision to recapitulate music heard initially at the beginning of each work. The metaphor of a circle, Judit Frigyesi writes in her analysis of *Bluebeard's Castle*, suggests both motion and inertness, simultaneously and indissolubly linked. As a geometric shape the circle 'captures motion both through its precision and through infinity; it is something dynamic and, in its ultimate result, static'.[16] It thus becomes the perfect metaphor for what Bartók expresses in *Bluebeard's Castle* and, less completely, in *The Wooden Prince*. As Frigyesi further notes, the large-scale symmetry of *Bluebeard's Castle*, in which Bluebeard returns to his initial state of loneliness, immured in the blackened confines of the castle, imposes a circular curve upon the entire drama. Every step forward Judith makes into the castle by opening doors, that is to say, every incremental step she makes towards the light of the fifth door, is also, at the same time, a step backward towards a darkness both tragic and inevitable: 'The opening of the first five doors is a movement towards light, but this movement also brings the drama closer to its unavoidable end in darkness'.[17]

Night, ebbing away from preceding nights and moving towards future nights like a never-ending circle, represents a wholeness which is Bluebeard's most natural state. In *The Wooden Prince* night is also the time of suffering and of, in Balaz's words, 'turning away from Life'.[18] As soon as

Example 4.4 *The Wooden Prince*, figure 183

the prince is rejected for the wooden image of himself, the stage becomes darker: 'the surrounding countryside becomes gloomy and grey', reads the libretto, '. . . while a heavy night is descending upon him'. Once he accepts his loneliness, and Nature comes alive around him, there is 'No more suffering, no more night'. Light, or by extension, daylight, brings freedom from suffering, a distinction that lies at the heart of the symbolism of both stage works. The light/dark dichotomy and its attendant symbolism forms the fundamental dramatic impulse of *Bluebeard's Castle*. In *The Wooden Prince* its application is more limited, and found chiefly in the central scene of the prince's apotheosis.

The ballet closes on an unexpectedly optimistic note, suggesting a return to life through love and the abeyance of that splendid *Waldeinsamkeit* the prince had discovered following his earlier rejection. The libretto, in fact, makes this symbolism explicit when it states that the prince, now holding the princess in his arms, 'has reached out his hand to grasp Life', even as the world around him, diminished by his fateful decision, returns to an 'ordinary and simple' state. Stripped of all external physical attractiveness – she has cut her hair off in despair; he has given her his mantle – the man and the woman fall in love with each other's true selves. Life, and Truth, are one. Bartók's music underlines the triumph of this moment (see Ex. 4.4) through sustained *tutti* chords moving boldly, in organ-like textures (figures 183–88), towards the eventual goal of C major. The ballet's ending, however, is not without its ambivalent points. Having gained, and now forsaken for love, a supreme awareness of the beauties of the human soul, the prince turns his back on the fairy who brought that knowledge alive for him, and stands oblivious as the trees and flowers, who had crowned him king of their world, revert to their former lifelessness. His ability to commune with the forest – to know himself – he willingly sacrifices in order to love and be loved in return, in exchange losing the rarefied clarity of vision he had briefly been privileged to experience.

Both of Bartók's first two stage works place great dramatic emphasis on the moment when the male protagonist, isolated on stage, realizes the enormity of his loneliness. It is a measure of the difference between the two that, in the ballet, this moment is dignified and acknowledged by Nature, while in *Bluebeard* there is nothing but black, existential despair. If in performance the ballet's message is more difficult to perceive, and more susceptible to interpretation as a simple fairy tale with a happy ending, that is primarily a function of the absence of language and of the varying degrees to which dancers comprehend, and successfully express in movement, the inner spiritual anxiety felt by the principal characters. In Bartók's next stage work the characterization would become sharper, the plot more energetic and vivid, the setting more realistic. And, still, the loneliness would remain, only now in new form as alienation from the cold, impersonal environment of the city.

Bartók took care, once *The Miraculous Mandarin* was written and placed in the Universal Edition catalogue in 1925, to distinguish its genre, pantomime, from the more sectional, set-piece type of dance music he had written for his ballet. The distinction, he felt, was more than academic. 'I see that U.E. is advertising Mandarin as a ballet', he wrote to his publisher in 1925; 'I have to observe that this work is less a ballet than a pantomime, since only two dances occur in it'.[19] On another occasion he urged, 'the piece must not be turned into a ballet-show; it is intended as a pantomime, after all'.[20] To Bartók, 'pantomime' meant a continuous fabric of music closely shaped to the events on stage, and not divided into a series of well-defined dances. Comparison with *The Wooden Prince* reveals the different dramaturgy quite plainly. There are not as many full-scale dance movements in *Mandarin*, and the music is written to correspond to the rapidly fluctuating demands and timing of the plot, rather like a film soundtrack. Its two larger-scale dances, not indicated as such in the score, are the waltzing seduction dance performed by the girl before the Mandarin (figures 45^{-6}–59) and the chase scene that follows (figures 62^{-3}–71, see Ex. 4.5). The latter, which ends the concert version of the work Bartók made in 1926, is a barbaric, primitivist inspiration of the sort he periodically produced throughout his life to great effect (other examples include *Allegro barbaro* and the Scherzo of the Second Quartet); it pulses with the energy of the Mandarin's determination to reach the girl. Jagged, abrupt figures bounce,

Example 4.5 *The Miraculous Mandarin*, figure 62

fugue-like, through the orchestra in literal evocation of the chase, above a pounding ostinato bass line reminiscent of the more frenzied moments in Stravinsky's *The Rite of Spring* (1913). It is characteristic of the general style of the *Mandarin* music that, even in the first of these dances, the musical flow is repeatedly interrupted by new elaborations of ideas heard earlier in the drama, as if to illustrate not only the movement on stage, but also the unfolding psychological development taking place in the girl's mind as she dances.

Melchior Lengyel's scenario, described by the author as a 'pantomime grotesque', first appeared in the literary journal *Nyugat* in January 1917. During the summer of 1918, shortly after the premiere of *Bluebeard*, Lengyel and Bartók signed a contract giving exclusive musical rights to Bartók, thus freeing him to proceed with a project he had already quietly begun.[21] The bulk of the composition was completed the following year, 1918–19, with orchestration following in 1923–24. Set in a shabby tenement in a nameless urban metropolis, Lengyel's pantomime tells the story of three thugs who force an attractive young woman, Mimi, to lure men up to their room to be robbed. The third of her prospective victims is a wealthy Chinese man of unearthly appearance and bearing. As Bartók summarized:

> The catch is good, the girl entertains him with her dance, the Mandarin's
> desire is aroused, his love flares up, but the girl recoils from him. – The thugs
> attack the Mandarin, rob him, smother him with pillows, stab him with a
> sword, all in vain, because the Mandarin continues watching the girl with
> eyes full of love and yearning. – Relying on her feminine ingenuity, the girl
> complies with the Mandarin's wish, whereupon he falls dead.[22]

Such explicit focus on human sexuality, culminating with a moment of sexual release on stage, was bound to attract the strong disapproval of audiences, yet Bartók persevered in completing a work that, by all measures, represents one of his finest compositions. He felt the plot to be 'marvellously beautiful', according to one comment made in 1919.[23] Its fate in the theatre has been mixed, despite the (by now) universal acclaim given to the music; it was not staged in Hungary until after Bartók's death, in December 1945.

At the centre of the pantomime's drama lies the character of Mimi, who is on stage the entire time. (Bartók's stage indications in the score identify her only as 'the girl'. Her name is found in the original scenario.) As a character Mimi is transformed in unexpected ways by the success of her entreaties. From the fearful, nervously flirtatious woman seen at the outset, she gains increasing confidence in her attractiveness to men, as measured in her responses to the three visitors to the apartment and in her final decision to release the Mandarin from his torment. Her 'decoy games', in which she lures passers-by up the stairs, are presented to a flickering theme in the clarinet that slides up and down in liquid cascades of tones, capturing her mercurial, hesitant personality; she is unsure of herself yet obviously alluring (see Example 4.6, and also figures 22 and 31^{-3}). Though tainted by the environment she inhabits, in dubious service to a band of thieves, she stands out as a sympathetic character once her basic humanity is revealed in the scene with the student, a young man whose admiring glances elicit from her an equally interested response. When the Mandarin enters, she is confronted with a force beyond reason, of elemental power. His desire is so strong it defies multiple deaths of his body, and rises anew, with supernatural force, after each revolting act of violence inflicted upon him by the thieves. The conflict his presence introduces – between the degraded world of the city and the raw, elemental force of life – leaves no winners save, perhaps, Mimi, whose decision to gratify his phenomenal desire completes her transformation into a strong individual. He dies in the end, a modern *Liebestod* achieved through sexual climax. She smiles triumphantly.

Lengyel, years later, reflected that 'The true message of The Miraculous Mandarin, of course, is not the excess eroticism but the apotheosis of pure, almost unearthly desire and love'.[24] Conceptualizing the difference between 'eroticism' and 'unearthly desire' is by no means a straightforward task, yet Lengyel seems to feel these are separate impulses, the one purely physical, if we read him correctly, the other allied, somehow, to love. Love, here, is replaced by sexual desire. The mutual attraction she and the student had felt for each other before the thieves forced him back out of the door had sexual undertones, but for her the response was more complicated, and involved emotional attraction as well. With the Mandarin

Example 4.6 *The Miraculous Mandarin*, figure 13

there are no such feelings; all is sexual, erotic, physical. Of matters spiritual of the sort found in Bartók's earlier stage works there seems to be very little in this drama: the pace is so rapid that little time exists for the reflection necessary to bring out a character's inner emotional states. Yet loneliness, while no longer the principal theme, remains as a sentiment all characters in the pantomime must contend with. Its presence is felt in the characters' actions, and inferred in the setting itself. Bartók's music, by repeatedly breaking into the music of the opening throughout much of the score, relentlessly shapes the environment in which the thugs ply their dangerous trade; the city itself becomes a dramatic force bearing down upon the characters on stage. The Mandarin, a man of exotic Eastern origin, clearly stands apart from society with his unusual appearance and otherworldy demeanour. The city denies him his humanity, so that any warmer side to his personality remains hidden. All the girl sees is evidence of sexual passion. Her earlier brush with genuine love, however, in the form of the student, has renewed in her a sense of compassion for the men who long for her. Wordlessly, she reaches out to the Mandarin, one soul understanding another's need, as Judith did when she came to Bluebeard's castle. In so doing she completes a symbolic chain of lonely selves populating Bartók's stage works – Bluebeard, Judith, the Prince, Mimi, the Mandarin – characters seeking, and sometimes finding, however briefly, the release from solitude and the wholeness that love can provide.

5 Vocal music: inspiration and ideology

RACHEL BECKLES WILLSON

Bartók's mature compositions for voice are spread across a range of musical genres. Aside from the opera discussed in the previous chapter, there are six works for voice and piano, six for unaccompanied choir, one for double choir and orchestra with soloists, one for choir and piano, and there are also further arrangements of these works for voice and piano, voice and orchestra, and choir and orchestra. The common thread connecting the mixture of genres is folk music: not surprisingly, Bartók's passion for folk song is even more manifest in his vocal works than in his instrumental music. He wrote only two cycles of 'art' songs and his discovery of peasant music infiltrated even these. As he pointed out in 1920, there was no other vocal tradition in Hungary from which to develop a modern vocal style: '[w]e Hungarians have nothing but our *parlando* peasant melodies . . . to solve this question',[1] he wrote.

The use of peasant materials also carried a message, however: Bartók's initial aim in arranging folksong was to clarify a contemporary misunderstanding about the omnipresent gypsy music of Budapest, which was celebrated as Hungarian folk music. As his career progressed, his use of peasant materials came to intertwine increasingly with his nationalistic and then humanistic vision: whether or not he intended them to be active 'agitators', texts from folk sources came to embody his critical view of urban society. As József Ujfalussy wrote in 1971 of Bartók's *From Olden Times* (1935), 'every word and every tone in this work was an undisguised political appeal'.[2] The presence of text leads this ideological aspect of folklorism to dominate his vocal works.

Early folksong arrangements

Hungarian Folksongs for voice and piano (1906), a volume of ten settings by Bartók and ten by Kodály, was the first major result of Bartók's encounter with folksong. The difficulties the composers faced in their first aims are made clear by Kodály's 'Foreword' to the volume:

> The . . . objective is to introduce the general public to folksongs so that they can be *taught to appreciate them* . . . The best must be selected and then to some extent *adapted to the public taste* by some form of musical

arrangement. Folksongs must be dressed to be taken from the fields to the city. In urban attire, however, they are awkward and uncomfortable. Their apparel must be cut in a fashion that will *not hinder their breathing*. Whether for chorus or for piano, the accompaniment should always be of a nature as to make up for the lost fields and village.[3]

The songs had to be presented in a way that the public would like and from which they would also learn; the folksongs' essential qualities were, moreover, not to be disturbed and in Bartók's resultant settings his compositional subservience is apparent. The accompaniments are based mainly on simple dominant–tonic relationships; the plagal cadence of the first song complements its rather hymn-like chordal texture. Bartók's desire to educate the public is clear: the melody is doubled in the right hand of the piano so that in the case of a *Hausmusik* setting with an amateur singer or no singer at all, the song would still be heard.

Bartók's subsequent four transcription publications depart from this primitive beginning to a greater or lesser extent. Eight Hungarian Folksongs for voice and piano (Nos. 1–5: 1907; Nos. 6–8: 1917) allows for a declamatory delivery of the text in sections of simpler accompaniment. The piano no longer doubles the voice. The fourth of Four Old Hungarian Folksongs for male choir (1910–12, revised *c.* 1926) introduces the first example of counterpoint. Slovak Folksongs for male choir (1917) are harmonically and textually more challenging; this is probably a response to the first song's striking opening of an augmented fourth. Four Slovak Folksongs for mixed choir and piano (1917) are the most inventive of the settings of this period. They form a rather unusual *mélange* of folksong, choir and Romantic piano writing.

This gradual increase in inventiveness is a sign that Bartók was beginning to experiment with an interaction between his own compositional voice and his original concept of folksong. With one exception, however, the works of this period show no sign of what was to come. The startling anomaly is the unpublished, incomplete, Nine Romanian Folksongs for voice and piano (*c.* 1912). This was Bartók's second attempt to set Romanian folksongs and demonstrates an adventurous experimental approach to the idiosyncrasies of the source.[4] The chromatic linear conception of the first accompaniment is provided with a jaunty chordal ostinato; the fifth heralds Bartók's later use of diminished fifths; the eighth, centred on D minor, sets a four-note melody (F–G–A–B), by extending its whole-tone line downwards in the tune's mirror image (F–E♭–D♭–C♭) in parallel root position minor triads with the third at the top.[5] This description offers only a small taste of a wealth of interesting devices. It was hardly by chance that Bartók left the collection unfinished in 1912: he had not yet formulated a rationale for maintaining this level of innovation within the self-inflicted restrictions of folksong arrangement. Nor, however, was it by chance that he returned to work on this, one of his several unfinished collections, while in America.[6] He evidently perceived its potential.

Art songs

The year 1916 might appear to be an interruption to Bartók's intense involvement with peasant music: Five Songs Op. 15 for voice and piano and Five Ady Songs Op. 16 for voice and piano set contemporary poetry. Both musical and textual links with folklorism are strong, however. Op. 15 employs folk-like pentatonic melodies in a declamatory, *parlando* style and four of the cycle's poems were written by the young Klára Gombossy who was accompanying Bartók on his ongoing collecting trips (one poem was by another young friend, Wanda Glieman). The work of Endre Ady (1877–1919), whose texts Bartók set in Op. 16, embodied a rebellion against Hungarian gentry and chauvinism – aspects of Hungarian society that Bartók's folk settings were also countering. Ady was a beacon of social criticism and also linguistic experimentation: his 1906 volume *Új versek* [New Poems], indebted to the French symbolists, produced a 'veritable explosion' in artistic circles.[7] Even though society as a whole found his metaphorical language difficult and his forthright eroticism hard to accept, Béla Reinitz (1878–1942), the cabaret pianist, composer and critic to whom Bartók dedicated his Op. 16 'in true friendship and affection' and who achieved a cult-like popularity in the second decade of the century, brought Ady to a wider public through his own settings.

Although the link with Bartók's peasant-inspired work is strong in these two cycles, there are other clear influences, including his personal circumstances and his capacity as a pianist. The relationship with Gombossy triggered a choice of morbid, intimate and at times lugubrious poems for Op. 16 that are carried forward by expansive, often dramatic, piano writing. The vocal treatment is indebted to Kodály's understanding of the natural emphases of old Hungarian and Bartók was certainly familiar with the songs of Kodály (including settings of Ady) that demonstrate simpler Debussyan (or folk) fourth-based harmonies. In Bartók's Op. 16, tonality is obscured by chains of dissonances and non-functional sonorities: the cycles are a step in the direction of his intensely chromatic works of 1918–21, in which his quartal harmony was infiltrated with elements more akin to progressive German practice. Example 5.1, for example, shows the alternation of perfect fourths a semitone apart which is characteristic of both Bartók and Schoenberg, although there is no need to

Example 5.1 'Sounds of Autumn', Op. 16 No. 2, bar 4

assume Schoenberg's influence – Bartók could have found such a chord in Liszt, of whom this expansive piano writing is also reminiscent. The piano dominates the voice throughout, unlike in the simpler, declamatory settings of Reinitz, of which Bartók was also clearly aware.[8]

The fourth song sets a poem using repetition in a way characteristic of both Ady and of folk texts, but, paradoxically, is one of the least folk-like: 'Egyedül a tengerrel' [Alone with the Sea] is in six three-line strophes, the second and third lines of each being identical; the form is thus ABB ABB ABB, and so on. Bartók explored the potential of this line-coupling with a striking manipulation of arpeggio patterns. A long rising arpeggio figure from F♯ leads to the opening word 'Tengerpart' (Sea shore): the arpeggio embodies a wave motion of the sea (see Ex. 5.2). The first strophe's repetition, 'Elment, nem látom többé már soha' (She's gone, I'll never see her again), emphasizes loneliness through an almost monotone vocal line and a still, solitary, piano chord on the second statement. The repetition in the second verse of 'Megölelem az ócska pamlagot' (I embrace the worn-out couch) is treated with the same low-register stillness in the voice, but the piano bursts out from a low G♯ with a rising arpeggiation of chromatic sonorities just as the voice stops, now as if expressing the inner, unresolved passion of the poet rather than the sea.

Bartók then omits the repetition of verse 3 and runs straight into verse 4, 'Lent zúg a tenger' (The sea is sighing below): this first line of verse is accompanied by arpeggios, clearly related to the opening pattern but based on C♯. The repetition of 'Jöjj édesem, lent a tenger dalol' (Come my sweet, the sea is singing below) is treated to a falling sequence, and the piano bursts out again immediately now from G: rising arpeggios are once again embodying the sea. The repetition in verse 5 is also omitted by Bartók: an elaboration of the arpeggio from F♯ leads rapidly into verse 6 (see Ex. 5.3). The repetition in this final verse, 'Dalol a tenger és dalol a

Example 5.2 'Alone with the Sea', Op. 16 No. 4, bars 1–4

Example 5.3 'Alone with the Sea', Op. 16 No. 4, bars 34–35 compared with bar 1

mult' (The sea sings, the past sings), is treated to a further descending sequence, the piano adding a bell-like chime to the second statement and easing into a final arpeggio passage now on E.

It is through the piano that Bartók reveals the meaning of these repetitions: the significance of the line is shifted on second hearing, allowing the piano interludes to form a remarkable dialogue with the voice, whether symbolizing the soul of the poet, or the voice of the sea. This transformation of the poem's structure ensures that the strophic setting is loosened: it falls into two short and two long parts (ABB ABB ABABB ABABB). Bartók never returned to this Romantic expressionistic vocal style, but this manipulation of the text is not unlike some of the alterations he made to folksong in his later work for voice.

Further folksong arrangements for voice and piano

Village Scenes for voice and piano (1924) was the first folksong arrangement after the 'chromatic' period and breaks out of the formal constraints of arrangement in several respects. Bartók releases himself from the restrictive dimensions of the folksong: in his third song, for example, he interleaves verses of two different folksongs; in his fourth song he uses two to create a ternary structure. He also creates dramatic shifts by transposing verses, an idea completely alien to folksong. This is especially effective in the fifth song. Bartók adds a few shrieks ('ejajajajajajaja!') to the third too: these are characteristic of Slovakian folksongs in general, but were not notated by him in his original transcription of this particular melody.[9] Bartók also broke the melody into sections that he used repetitively. His treatment of the songs was at once iconoclastic, displaying the influence of Stravinsky and in particular *Les Noces* (1922),[10] but, ironically, also brought his arrangements closer to the original, evolving, nature of their source.

As pointed out by Vera Lampert, '*Village Scenes* represents the second of two types of arrangement described by Bartók in one essay: the melody provided a '"motto" while that which is built round it is of real importance'.[11] Bartók later referred to a third level in his hierarchy: 'the added composition-treatment attains the importance of an original work, and the used folk melody is only to be regarded as a kind of motto'.[12] He gave the adventurous Eight Improvisations on Hungarian Peasant Songs Op. 20 for piano (1920) as an example, the work often considered the closest instrumental partner to *Village Scenes* in Bartók's oeuvre. These two uses of the word 'motto'[13] in the context of Improvisations and *Village Scenes* present us with the degree to which Bartók was able to treat his sources as mottoes in instrumental and vocal works respectively. In Improvisations, the folksongs are subjected to multiple transformations and form part of a rich fabric.[14] Even if complete synthesis is not achieved, there is a strong sense of what Paul Wilson describes as 'melody and setting...moving back and forth along a continuum between tension and mutual reinforcement'.[15] The folksongs in *Village Scenes*, however, are not allowed to integrate to a comparable extent. Although the accompaniment can largely be analysed from the starting point of the folksong (sections of melodies are used vertically as chords, as motifs or in counterpoint), influences in the other direction (from Bartók's pianistic ideas into the vocal line) are almost non-existent. The folksong thus retains a high degree of autonomy.

The one, exceptional, integration of the two 'realms' of accompaniment and folksong seems to have been stimulated by the shrieking idea referred to above. The stages of reflection on this part of the folksong may be charted as follows:

1   Bartók had the idea of framing the folksong with wild shrieking inspired by a generally characteristic Slovakian gesture, not by loyalty to a specific rendering of the folksong in question.
2   He then used a similarly wild ostinato figure as a piano introduction and *vivacissimo* refrain. This is related in pitch terms to the folksong, but is entirely different in rhythm and spirit. Example 5.4a shows the main *Grave* folksong melody and Example 5.4b shows the first time the shriek appears in the voice, accompanied by the piano's refrain.
3   Later still he wrote a new wild melody for the voice to set the cry of 'Heia hoiaho', superimposed upon the piano's final *vivacissimo*, using pitches derived from that *vivacissimo*. The voice's contour may be said to be derived from the original folksong, but the actual pitches and gestures are far more indebted to the piano refrain. Example 5.4c shows this final refrain of the third song.

Bartók's sketch materials bear witness to the fact that the addition of the voice to this final refrain was indeed made at a second stage in the compositional process. They also reveal that other elements that 'challenge' the folksong's autonomy were added later. The first draft of the first song, for example, reveals a more consonant concept than in the final version: diatonic and pentatonic chords were enriched with major sevenths and minor seconds in the second draft. Minor seconds are part of the folksong too, but only in an ornamental, tremolo capacity.

The formal experimentation of *Village Scenes* continued in Bartók's next period: Twenty Hungarian Folksongs (1929) form short, independent cycles within the main set, like the immediately preceding collections by Kodály.[16] The set is published in four separate volumes; in terms of form, the most interesting is the fourth, which joins five folksongs into a continuous musical texture with connecting piano passages. The fact that Bartók numbers the songs, rather than providing titles above each, reinforces the group's continuity in the score.

The most prominent motivic element running through the songs of this fourth volume is a scale passage, usually descending. Sketches reveal that Bartók carefully reinforced the songs' unity in this way. He revised the third, central song to interpolate not only a piano interlude based on a retrograde of the main scale passage of the melody, but also a descending scale over ten degrees in counterpoint with the voice's preceding verse. An organic conception for this group of songs was, however, present from the

Example 5.4 (a) 'Wedding', *Village Scenes* No. 3, folksong melody, bars 11–13

Ann-chen,   dei - ne Tru he Liegt schon auf dem Wa - gen, Der wird dei - nen Braut-schatz,
An - csur - ka, a lá - dád Már sze - kér - re rak-ták, Ván - ko-sod föl - tet - ték:
A   ty   An-ča krá-sna, Už vo vo - ze ka-šňa, Na ka-sni pe - ri - ny:
An - nie,   in your box - es, On the wag - gon car - ried,There's fine clothes and bed - ding,

Example 5.4 (b) 'Wedding', *Village Scenes* No. 3, beginning of first interlude, bars 17–21

Ei - ja - ja - ja - ja - ja - ja - ja - ja - ja - ja!
Hi - ji - ji - ji - ji - ji - ji - ji - ji - ji - ji!
Hi - ji - ji - ji - ji - ji - ji - ji - ji - ji - ji!
ai - ya - ya - ya - ya - ya - ya - ya - ya - ya - ya!

1) Shrill cry of indefinite pitch in the rhythm indicated.
2) Gradual downward glissando, duration about 5-6 quavers, going down to E.

Example 5.4 (c) 'Wedding', *Village Scenes*, No. 3, final refrain, bars 101–04

Hei - a hoi - a - ho,   juch-he, hei - a   hoi - a
He - je-hu-ja haj,   i - haj   csu-haj he - je
Hoj že ho-ja hoj,   he - ja   ho - ja hoj - že
Hey - a-hoy-a ho;   O - hey, hey - a, hoy - a

start: Twenty Hungarian Folksongs were set in an apparently random order (Nos. 7, 4, 3, 15, 13, 5, 8, 11 and so on) until 16, 17, 18, 19 and 20 were composed in one uninterrupted stretch.

The cyclic nature of the group does not signify a radical departure for Bartók: his choral collections had always been conceived in terms of cycles even if, for reasons of their difficulty, they were sometimes performed in incomplete sets. The expressly linear conception and connecting piano passages are new to his voice and piano works, however. The linear conception actually recalls Bartók's earliest collection of all, which predates even the 1906 volume: Hungarian Folksongs (First Series), for voice and piano (*c.* 1904–05). This cycle was composed with the same principle of continuity, although it was never completed. Bartók wrote no key signature in his draft, although the songs pass from C minor to A♭ major, E♭ minor and via a piano interlude into G minor.[17] Nor did he begin a new line for individual songs. At this early stage in his writing for the voice it is likely that he was influenced by Schumann's concept of the cycle; his non-folk settings would certainly imply that as well.

In terms of the Western concert aesthetic, Twenty Hungarian Folksongs represent the peak of Bartók's folksong arrangements: they demonstrate his most sophisticated handling of polyphony and harmony.[18] The concept of 'motto' can be used once again to describe them. The first song of the whole cycle, 'A tömlöcben' [In Prison], takes a group of notes from the sinking pentatonic tune as an ostinato; consistency through the song is provided by this contour and sense of tolling while it expands in range, alters in pitch and embraces a range of dissonances to reflect the text. Such a 'motto' comes to function as a centre, if not a tonal centre, in each song.

Later choral works

Twenty Hungarian Folksongs, and the uncomprehending reception they received at the Budapest premiere, mark the beginning of a new period, the most important composition of which is *Cantata profana* (1930), one of Bartók's best-loved vocal works. Thoroughly dispirited by Budapest, the composer withdrew at this point from what had been regular concert appearances in the capital and did not return to the platform between 1930 and 1934, playing his own work again only in 1937.[19] His ensuing works are coloured by his bitterness, but also by his firm conviction in the importance of folkloristic research and its synthesis with modern art. An argument in the press about the nature of folk music as opposed to popular music irritated him profoundly, and warnings about the potential manipulation of folklorism for fascist aims must have disturbed him too.[20] Four Hungarian Folksongs for mixed choir (1930) seem to offer a commentary on his view of the world around him: the text of the first song, 'The cedar tree has withered at the crest of the hill; I too have withered at the bottom of this cell', draws a parallel between pure Nature and 'I', a thought which became increasingly significant to Bartók and which surfaced powerfully in *Cantata profana*. Four Hungarian Folksongs are the most difficult and rewarding of Bartók's *a cappella* works: the folksongs move freely between the parts and there are frequent tonal shifts, the firm logic of which is enriched by complex dissonances. Dialogue effects between parts in the third movement anticipate *Cantata profana*; indeed, Bartók made sketches for the latter on a manuscript draft of Four

Hungarian Folksongs[21] which Miklós Szabó considers 'a preliminary study' to *Cantata profana*.[22]

Cantata profana stands apart from Bartók's other vocal works in terms of scale and overtly ideological statement. It is also the only work in which Bartók wrote his own text, which he adapted from two versions of a Romanian ballad he had heard sung as a *colindă*, a song connected, in Transylvania, with the winter solstice.* He planned two or three other cantatas to join the work in a cycle, probably on Hungarian and Slovakian texts: the cycle would have embodied his evolving *ars poetica*, which had moved away from Hungarian nationalism to a longing for integration of the mixed races of the Danube basin. Unfortunately, such visions of unity were unrealizable at the time.[23] Bartók's letter to his publisher in October 1932 illustrates the political intolerances and suspicions by which he was surrounded: 'My wish was only that my *Cantata profana* should not be given a performance in Hungary, for the time being, on account of its text which was drawn from Rumanian folklore'.[24] The work had to wait until 1934 for a premiere, which took place in London, and the rest of the cycle was never completed.

Nonetheless, *Cantata profana* is one of Bartók's richest and most 'complete' works in its own right: scored for double choir, tenor, baritone and orchestra, it contains several layers of structure in textual and musical terms. Five sections are clearly defined by musical tempi and character; this slow–fast–slow–fast–slow scheme is overlaid by three continuous movements delineated in the score and by seven strophes in the libretto. The libretto, narrated by the choruses, tells the story of nine sons whose father taught them nothing but how to hunt stags and who were magically turned into stags themselves while out hunting. This climactic point of metamorphosis occurs at the beginning of the central slow section following a hectic fugal hunting scene. The father goes in search of his sons but is unable to draw them back from their new, natural surroundings into stifling domesticity. The dialogue between the father (baritone) and the eldest son (tenor) forms the core of the work, leading from the central slow section into another fast one. The last strophe of the libretto in the final slow section reiterates the chain of events, completing a further level of construction with an arch-like recall of transformed musical elements.

Bartók's allusions to Baroque oratorio contribute to the sense of ritual which the work evokes. The gradually unfolding scalar opening, as shown

---

* Although Bartók consistently translates *colindă* as 'Christmas carols' it is perhaps more accurate to describe them as 'winter solstice' songs since many of the songs contain references to Pagan worship. – *Ed.*

Example 5.5 *Cantata profana*, opening bars in piano reduction

in Example 5.5, recalls the beginning of J. S. Bach's *St Matthew Passion* (1727) (although it is also reminiscent of the 'primeval' forest music with which Bartók begins *The Wooden Prince* (1914–17)). The scales in *Cantata profana* are Bartók's own inventions of folk-like, or even liturgical, modes. Such synthesis between folklore and Baroque infuses the entire work: the double chorus, for instance, another Baroque influence, also has roots in antiphonal *colindă* singing.[25] He also harnesses the difference between the Baroque and the wildness of nature: the 'coolness' of the oratorio setting is shattered when the eldest stag cries out to prevent his father from shooting him. In a high-pitched, fantastical melismatic melody, the tenor solo makes clear the impossibility of returning to human life. The idiom here is generally acknowledged to have been inspired by the Romanian *hora lungă* (literally 'long song'), although it does not quote one directly. As suggested by György Kroó, 'we are suddenly brought face to face with Nature'.[26]

This use of peasant materials is far more sophisticated than in any other vocal work. 'Natural' elements appear within a range of other symbols, and what sounds like folk melody has actually been composed by Bartók 'in the spirit of' folksong and thus has taken on a more personal dimension, rather like in the *Dance Suite* (1923). Despite the similarity of rhythmic and melodic outlines to *colindă* melodies, those in *Cantata profana* are his own.[27] By contrast Bartók's libretto is faithful to the original Romanian ballads; indeed, he seems to have been reluctant to alter them. Not unlike changes made in *Village Scenes*, Bartók's recapitulation, the most fundamental alteration to the ballad 'form', was decided upon very late.[28]

After *Cantata profana* Bartók brought only one more actual folksong arrangement to completion, this was Székely Folksongs for male choir (1932), which heralds his late, less complex harmonic language.[29] It recalls an early arrangement: the second song of the collection was also set in 1907 in the unpublished Two Hungarian Folksongs for voice and piano. The positioning of the bar lines, which are scanned differently in the two settings, alerts us to the difficulties faced by the arranger of folk music. Bartók evidently listened again to his phonograph recording and changed his mind about the emphasis of words: the 'proof' copy (*támlap*) of the collecting book with the 1907 transcription has two different sets of bar lines superimposed.[30] Interestingly, the later lines indicate emphasis in unexpected places, as we hear in Székely Folksongs: 'rózsám' (my sweetheart), for example, is quite out of kilter with Hungarian prosody. Bartók was apparently slow to pick up on this idiosyncrasy, initially assuming the familiar.

From Olden Times for male choir (1935) is a triumphantly bitter work and continues the progress towards harmonic distillation. Bartók used polarity in his texts, which he adapted from 'old folk and art songs',[31] in the outer movements of this modal, motet-like triptych, the only example of Bartókian symmetry in his vocal works. The first song laments the impoverished life of a peasant ('There's no one as unhappy as a peasant for his misery is deeper than the ocean'); the third turns this text upside down ('There's no one luckier than the peasant for his lot is happier than any profession') in an apparently ironic celebration of the vitality of peasant life.

Works for children

Although Bartók composed a considerable amount of instrumental music for children, until 1935 his writing for children's voices had been scant. He had written a set of vocal miniatures on nursery texts in 1905: Children's Songs 'For the little "tót"', for voice and piano. These were for private use, a present to Bartók's new niece (his sister's married name was Tót). He also included vocal parts for four of his *Mikrokosmos* (1926–39), two on folksongs (III/74 and V/127) and two original pieces in folk style (II/65 and III/95). From his explanation in the score we gather that he felt that all children's instrumental learning should evolve from singing exercises.

Twenty-seven Two- and Three-part Choruses for unaccompanied women's or children's choir (1935–36) is Bartók's only large-scale vocal work for children.[32] It embodies his final attempt to educate and redirect society, this time from the roots of its future. Kodály's influence is clear yet again: the genre had been established by him. Just as in *From Olden Times*, Bartók sets folk texts, rather than folksongs; and, similar to *Mikrokosmos*, he writes in a folk-like melodic idiom. Groups of these very short choral pieces form little cycles, like Twenty Hungarian Folksongs, but harmonically they are very different from that rich set. Bartók's late-period distillation of harmony is seen nowhere more clearly than in the pared-down bareness of these settings.

Bartók's sense for shifting the meaning of text is as striking as in the

Ady cycle. The polyphonic settings are an ideal medium because they create textual repetitions. In 'Keserves' [Grief] the opening 'Jaj!' (Oh!) is positioned in the central voice on an F♯, then flanked by A above and D below in the outer voices. By the end of the strophe a central 'Jaj!' appears a semitone lower and is flanked on either side by B: the tritones set up a new poignancy. At the end of the song the central part (still 'Jaj!') has returned to F♯ and the outer ones rest on B; the bareness of the perfect fourth is then abandoned for the solitary F♯ ending.

Such pristine control is evident in every single song. 'Kánon' [Canon], for example, slips from octatonic to whole-tone to pentatonic to a partial C major collection all in the first seventeen bars; each collection delineates a phrase of the text. Bartók combines a Palestrina- (and Kodály-) inspired choral simplicity with his own mature harmonic techniques. The 'inner cycles' are established through the clear tonal or modal centres of each movement, although these are not always closed in themselves. The first cycle moves from F major to F♯ minor to G major; the seventh, penultimate, cycle from G minor to C minor to E major which denies us a reassuring closure: it 'ends' on a solitary B setting the simple exclamation 'Nem!' [No].

Like his instrumental works, Bartók's vocal works display a range of compositional techniques, from arrangement (Twenty Hungarian Folksongs), emulation of idiom (Twenty-seven Two- and Three-part Choruses) to large-scale, free composition with folk-like elements and symbols (*Cantata profana*). They also mirror the process of harmonic development of the instrumental works. Nevertheless, there are some important differences between the two genres, some of which are highlighted by the marginal notes Kodály made to the manuscript of Twenty-seven Two- and Three-part Choruses,[33] which include comments relating to Hungarian prosody. Significantly, Bartók rarely took his advice, presumably hoping that performers for whom Hungarian was their mother tongue would treat the *parlando* style 'authentically' and read the score as a guide.[34] Bartók's purely musical considerations emerge from the document, in contrast with Kodály's primary interest in text and its authentic delivery, thus confirming Bartók's position as a primarily 'instrumental' composer.

Comparison of the way Bartók used peasant music in vocal and instrumental works is also revealing: he rarely allowed the rough side of peasant music to enter his vocal works. There is little of the harsh rumbustiousness of the String Quartet No. 4, for example: a major part of compositional input to vocal works involved a cleaning process. Although by 1920 he had a code of signs for notating all the nuances of the peasant singers (intonation falling between two notes, speech, clucking sounds, slides and tremo-

los, irregular metres, subtle variances in pulse, secondary stresses and relative intensity of individual notes, occasional sobs) such indications never
appeared in his vocal scores. The desired performance practice of folksong
arrangements is evident from Kodály's 'Notes' to the 1938 reissue of the
original Hungarian Folksongs: although the composers expected performers to be aware of true peasant character, they acknowledged that
opera singers could add a further dimension.[35] The singer whom Bartók
accompanied most often was the opera mezzo Mária Basilides
(1886–1946). The tenor Ferenc Székelyhidy (1885–1954) was another
partner, whose performance of song Nos. 6, 7 and 8 from Eight Hungarian
Folksongs is less 'professional' and polished than that of Basilides, yet his
declamatory style is less distant from peasant singing. Another partner for
Bartók was *diseuse* Vilma Medgyaszai (1885–1972): she was well known
for her performances of Reinitz songs, and her performance of Five
Hungarian Folksongs, an arrangement from the 1906 collection, is characteristic of the Paris-influenced Budapest cabaret style.[36]

Two non-Hungarian works, *Cantata profana* and *Village Scenes*, are the
only exceptions to this conservative vocal style, a fact which is partly
indebted to the differing musical qualities of the sources themselves, but
which also brings us back to the original aims of folksong setting. Bartók
wanted to win over Hungarians with Hungarian folksong: the taste of his
audiences must have contributed to the creation of this relatively 'tame'
style. The capabilities of the singers for whom he was writing may also
have been significant: Bartók did not trust them to, or wish them to,
extemporize or perform in a more 'naturalistic' manner, although the very
essence of folk music – its constant evolution in ornamentation and text,
its reflection of passing activity or mood and its quality as community
activity rather than performance material – was lost in his Hungarian
arrangements. Perhaps Bartók, the 'instrumental' composer, had a fundamental inhibition, a reserve about the most powerfully expressive qualities
of the human voice. And while harnessing the 'real' nature of rugged
peasant song was acceptable in a transformed, abstract instrumental work,
in a vocal work it would have seemed a mockery of the peasants whose
trust Bartók personally had gained, and whose singing he himself had
recorded.

6 Piano music: teaching pieces and folksong arrangements

VICTORIA FISCHER

Bartók worked as a piano teacher for most of his life. He began to give piano lessons as a teenager while still in Pozsony, and eventually succeeded his own teacher, István Thomán, at the Budapest Academy of Music in 1907, where he taught for nearly thirty years. During his last years in America he maintained private students. If, ironically, piano teaching was not his primary musical and creative focus, falling rather distantly behind composition, folksong study and performance, he was nevertheless a conscientious and thorough teacher. Although a few notable performers, such as György Sándor, emerged from his studio, he never established the kind of following enjoyed by his colleague at the Academy, Ernő Dohnányi. Piano teaching provided a basic source of income that enabled him to devote himself to his more compelling occupations. Bartók's greatest pedagogical contributions may be, therefore, not a pianistic legacy through his students, but the creative results of applications of his compositional work to teaching purposes. From the beginning his pedagogical ideas were bound up with folksong study, which was the primary catalyst in the development of his unique musical language. As he wrote much later, in 1940:

> Already at the very beginning of my career as a composer I had the idea to write some easy works for piano students. This idea originated in my experience as a piano teacher. I had always the feeling that the available material, especially for beginners, has no real musical value, with the exception of very few works – for instance, Bach's easiest pieces and Schumann's *Jugendalbum*. I thought these works to be insufficient, and so, more than thirty years ago I myself tried to write some easy piano pieces. At that time I thought the best thing to do would be to use folk tunes. Folk melodies, in general, have great musical value; so at least the thematical value would be secured.[1]

Bartók as teacher

Like all Hungarian pianists of the time, Bartók was thoroughly trained in traditional harmony and in the works of the Classical and Romantic masters. He had a direct link to one of the most innovative and influential nineteenth-century pianists, teachers and composers – Franz Liszt – through his teacher Thomán, who had been a Liszt student.

So what kind of teacher was Bartók? Did he enjoy teaching? And what was his playing like? Can we learn about his style and about his own compositions from his teaching and performing? His students have provided us with a number of first-hand accounts, and the testimonies are amazingly consistent. Ernő Balogh, who studied with Bartók between 1909 and 1915 at the Budapest Academy, was one of the most outstanding of his early students. He wrote:

> All his students admired and loved him for his genius, of which we were convinced, for his profound knowledge of every phase in music, for his gentle and kind manners, for his unfailing logic, for his convincing explanation of every detail. He was just and fair, but he could not conceal his annoyance with his less gifted students.
>
> The essence of his approach as a teacher was that he taught music first and piano second. Immaculate musicianship was the most important part of his guidance and influence. He clarified the structure of the compositions we played, the intentions of the composer, the basic elements of music and the fundamental knowledge of phrasing.
>
> He had unlimited patience to explain details of phrasing, rhythm, touch, pedaling. He was unforgiving for the tiniest deviation or sloppiness in rhythm. He was most meticulous about rhythmical proportion, accent and the variety of touch.[2]

According to György Sándor, one of the most successful students, Bartók was:

> an extremely original, accomplished pianist. He didn't explain or talk about technique ever, he simply said 'Practice, you have to practice'. Then I asked him *how* to practice. He said 'this is how I do it' and he sat down and played it. Absolute mastery. So he just played. I remember I played the Liszt sonata for him once. He was very polite, said 'yes, very good', and he sat down and played the whole piece, totally different, every note had to be changed.[3]

This kind of teaching approach, simply demonstrating how it should be done, is corroborated over and over again in the eye-witness accounts. According to Bartók's comments about his own teacher Thomán, this was an approach from which he had greatly benefited in his own upbringing.[4] Interesting, too, is the evident avoidance of technical instruction. Balogh said: 'Bartók insisted on first solving the musical problems and then the pianistic ones. In fact, he was not deeply interested in pianistic problems. He had a natural technique and although he was recognized in time as a virtuoso, virtuoso problems did not interest him'.[5]

It is probably true that Bartók's first musical love was not teaching.

Several students suggest that he was simply too busy with other, for him, more absorbing interests, especially folklore investigation and composing. But it is clear from his students that he was a teacher of the utmost integrity, demanding patiently and unceasingly their best efforts. Concerning repertoire, Bartók taught the classics as well as the new music of his time, especially Debussy and Kodály. But he evidently did not like to teach his own works.

The picture that emerges is of an absolute master of the keyboard with the highest musical standards; who taught mostly by demonstration, yet insisted on absolute attention to details; who preferred to address the musical dimensions with his students, leaving them to unravel the problems of technique on their own. Judging by his own account of his study with Thomán, he continued very much in the tradition in which he was taught, except his account includes quite clear references to technical instruction, the implication being that music-making is the end to which technique is only a means.[6]

A new approach to pianism and piano composition: articulatory notation

The evolution of Bartók's original musical language was sparked by his discovery of indigenous Hungarian folk music in 1904. Already an accomplished pianist and teacher, the creative innovations in his composition, brought about by the intersection of folk influences and issues of musical modernism, were often expressed in his piano works. As an element of his developing style, he was thinking in new ways about his own instrument, how it should be played, and how to communicate his new ideas. In 1927 he stated that the piano's 'inherent nature becomes really expressive only by means of the present tendency to use the piano as a percussive instrument'.[7] He probably did not intend to suggest that the pianist should bang away mercilessly at the instrument. He implied, rather, that the piano is not an instrument that lends itself to legato, cantabile lines, which are more idiomatic to a bowed or wind instrument, but one in which each tone is produced by a single stroke into the key, that the natural mechanism is of hammer striking string. The potential variety of tone colour, duration and volume of each note is enormous, and Bartók had very specific ideas about how sound should be produced.

Against the background of a thorough training and continued practice in nineteenth-century piano traditions and repertoire, Bartók's pianistic philosophy was informed by an appreciation of the new works of Debussy (the contemporary composer for whom he expressed more admiration than any other), other trends in new music of the time, and, most substantially, the folk music he was simultaneously exploring.

It is interesting that during the period when Bartók was breaking new ground in his own musical language and in musical folklore, he was also occupied with the preparation of editions of the classics such as J. S. Bach, Mozart and Beethoven. These editorial tasks were used as a testing ground for some of his new ideas about piano touch and sound. He prepared a teaching edition of Bach's *Well-Tempered Clavier* during 1907, shortly before he began the composition of the Fourteen Bagatelles Op. 6 (1908), the ground-breaking work which contains the first substantial seeds of his new folk-inspired musical language. The intention of the edition was pedagogical: he rearranged the order of the pairs of preludes and fugues to follow a sequence of increasing difficulty, and filled the score with detailed indications concerning touch. Clearly preoccupied with the same problems of articulation that he faced in his own piano compositions of 1907–08, Bartók appended an illuminating explanation of articulation and dynamic markings which can serve as a reference to his own works. By 1916 his ideas had crystallized into a specific catalogue of articulation markings included in an edition of selections from the *Notebook for Anna Magdalena Bach* (Ex. 6.1). There can be no doubt that Bartók's instructions about playing Bach should also be applied to his own music, because he described clearly and in much detail the same style of notation that he was employing in his own piano works.

Bartók's teaching and composition intersect at this point: he composed a sequence of works, some with expressly didactic purposes, and in them expressed through notation and folk elements his evolving musical language. His first simple setting of folksongs for piano, the Three Hungarian Folksongs from the Csík District (1907), was followed by the radical Bagatelles and Ten Easy Pieces of 1908, and the two series of *For Children* (1908–09). With Sándor Reschofsky he produced The First Term at the Piano (1913), a set of eighteen pieces for the absolute beginner. Although this publication does not specify which author composed the pieces in the method, Reschofsky's letters testify that all the pieces were from Bartók's pen, and therefore this 'has to be listed as a true Bartók work'.[8] A series of folksong-collecting expeditions in Romania inspired the Sonatina, Romanian Folk Dances and *Colinde* (Romanian Christmas carols) all composed in 1915.

The Bagatelles, which, according to Bartók, 'inaugurate a new trend of piano writing in my career',[9] are a remarkable set of fourteen short pieces, only two of which are settings of authentic folk tunes (No. 4, a Hungarian

Example 6.1 Catalogue of articulation indications from Bartók's 1916 edition of the *Notebook for Anna Magdalena Bach*

▼ ▼ ▼	=	sharp staccato (staccatissimo) implying a certain accentuation and stronger tone colour.
. . .	=	the regular staccato, whereby the sounding of the notes ranges from the shortest in value to half the value of the note.
͡. . .	=	portamento [portato], whereby the tones must be permitted to sound almost up to half the note value in conjunction with a certain special colouring.
⁔ ⁔ ⁔	=	the symbol for half-shortening (the tones should not sound shorter than half the note value.
— — —	=	the tenuto symbol above different notes signifies that they must be held for their entire note value; when above each note of a group, that we must permit the notes to sound throughout their entire note value if possible, without linking them to one another.
⌒	=	the well-known legato symbol, which we are also using, in the case of legato parts, for marking the phrase for lack of another symbol.
sf	=	the strongest accentuation.
∧	=	accentuation still forceful enough.
>	=	weak accentuation.
— — —	=	the tenuto symbol above the different tones of the legato parts signifies delicately emphasizing the tone by way of a different tone colouring.

tune, and No. 5, a Slovakian tune). The set as a whole represents in microcosm practically everything that was to come in Bartók's compositional style, including settings of folk tunes, syntheses of tonal, rhythmic and structural folk characteristics in non-folk settings (most of them), the 'primitive' style (No. 10), issues of tonal and formal symmetry (Nos. 2, 3, 8 and 12) and autobiographical influences (Nos. 12, 13 and 14). Each Bagatelle is experimental in at least one way, and examples of new applications of piano articulation abound. The first is a prime example for demonstrating how Bartók's ideas about piano technique, as expressed in his editing work, can be applied to his own piano composition. This small piece contains at least one articulation sign for practically every note (Ex. 6.2). Only three notes have no such embellishment.

Similarly the Ten Easy Pieces (really eleven with a 'Dedication' preceding No. 1), composed immediately after the Bagatelles (completed in

Example 6.2 Bagatelle Op. 6 No. 1, bars 1–4

1908), are just as varied, but as a whole less complex and pianistically less difficult than the Bagatelles. By contrast, however, the original 1908–09 edition of *For Children* comprises four volumes of eighty-five authentic Hungarian (vols. I and II) and Slovakian (vols. III and IV) folksong settings (six pieces were omitted in the 1945 edition). These progress from elementary to intermediate difficulty, and, as the title implies, the work has pedagogical intentions. The rich collection of forty-two Hungarian song settings in the first two volumes suggests that the articulation style for folk settings can be divided into two subsets according to the characteristic types of 'old'-style Hungarian folk melodies: one for the slower *parlando rubato* tunes, and one for the more dance-like *tempo giusto* tunes. *Tempo giusto* tunes are obviously faster, the rhythm more regular, and articulation marks can be taken to refer more to variations in touch and tone colour, as Bartók described in his editions, less for rhythmic inflection. He uses this type of notation often to imitate a folk instrument. In fact, he uses even more of these articulation marks in his folksong transcriptions when attempting to capture the character of folk instrumental playing, whereas he uses very little of this type of notation in transcriptions of vocal pieces. No. 6 from the first volume of *For Children* (Ex. 6.3) exemplifies the *tempo giusto* style, which is supported by Bartók's own recorded performance.[10]

On the one hand *tempo giusto* tends to feature the so-called 'percussive signs'[11] – staccato and the various degrees of accent – in a regularly articulated style within a fast tempo. On the other hand, *parlando rubato* often employs a more expressive 'non-percussive' style of notation – tenuto, portato, legato and half-tenuto – which Bartók described as requiring 'special colour' in his annotations to the Bach editions. No. 28 from volume I of the pieces *For Children* (Ex. 6.4) shows the *parlando rubato* style, in which the articulation marks imply rubato in performance.

Thus, rather than interpreting the notation based on an indication that the piece is *tempo giusto* or *parlando rubato*, the reverse can be true, and infinitely more useful, because Bartók does not always specify one or the other. One can often decide whether the piece is *tempo giusto* or *parlando*

Example 6.3 *For Children*, Vol.I No. 6, bars 1–14

Example 6.4 *For Children*, Vol. I No. 28, bars 1–2

Example 6.5 'Evening in the Country', bars 1–4

rubato from the articulation markings themselves. The style of notation indicates which style of interpretation is appropriate.

Perhaps the most illuminating example in understanding the message of Bartók's articulatory notation comes from Ten Easy Pieces. The sixth piece in the set, No. 5, variously translated as 'Evening in the Country' or 'Evening in Transylvania', is not based on an actual folk tune, but is rather an exact imitation of both *parlando rubato*- (see Ex. 6.5) and *tempo giusto*-style tunes. It has no actual text, so it represents the most significant challenge in achieving a Bartók style: to evoke the quality of text, of storytelling. Unlike Romantic rubato by which emotional responses to tonal, melodic, rhythmic or harmonic impulses in the music are expressed, this subtle type of rubato reflects the natural accents of language. A literal reading from the notation will differ strikingly from Bartók's own performance, which, fortunately for us, was recorded three times.[12] His own interpretation illustrates with amazing clarity the degree of rubato which the composer sanctioned.

'Evening in the Country' is a crucial example of the insight Bartók's own performance can provide in deciphering his notational language. Unfortunately, he left only a few recordings of his works, which makes it necessary to establish some interpretative principles from those that do exist. When cross-referenced with his own writings and editions, these sources can contribute to a more informed understanding of *all* his piano works.

Folksong settings for piano

In a letter to his sister Elsa, in 1904, Béla Bartók wrote: 'now I have a new plan: to collect the finest Hungarian folksongs and to raise them, adding the best possible piano accompaniments, to the level of art song'.[13] This letter was written soon after the composer had been smitten by his first encounters with authentic Hungarian folksongs. His consuming and abiding fascination with East European and other folk music was to shape and inform the entire evolution of his powerful and influential musical language. During the intermittent years from 1904 when he was free to pursue folksong expeditions, he personally collected several thousand folk tunes. In his lifetime, he studied, analysed and categorized songs in their tens of thousands including those collected by other researchers. While other forces of early twentieth-century music exerted unarguable influences on Bartók's musical style, the primary and most far-reaching factor was folk music.

Bartók's fieldwork and subsequent study of folk music resulted in two types of publication: volumes of folkloristic research (discussed in chapter 2) and original compositions. He prepared volumes of Hungarian, Romanian, Turkish, Slovakian and Serbo-Croatian folksongs which included detailed analysis and discussion of the folksong styles, as well as large numbers of carefully transcribed tunes and texts. Parallel to his immersion in folksong studies, Bartók was incorporating folk music into his own compositions. His first published collection of folksong arrangements was Hungarian Folksongs for voice and piano, published in 1906 in collaboration with Zoltán Kodály, in which the composers' objectives were clearly defined. As described by Halsey Stevens:

> The preface, signed by both composers but written by Kodály, was the
> subject of much thought; days were spent in framing it to express their
> intentions clearly and unequivocally. There they distinguished carefully
> between the two points of view in the publication of folksongs: the one

ethnological, its purpose being the scientific comparison of folk material in order to determine its origins and its relationship to its own and other cultures; the other practical, to make folksongs available to the greater public in a form suited to performance.[14]

Bartók subsequently employed folksongs in his compositions in a number of ways, ranging from the literal quotation of a melody to the capturing of the 'general spirit of the style'.[15] He wrote at length about their different settings as follows: 'they can be approximately divided into three categories. One of these categories represents transcriptions where the used folk melody is the more important part of the work . . . The added accompaniment and eventual preludes and postludes may only be considered as the mounting of a jewel'.[16] Most of the *For Children* pieces fall into this category. The second category represents transcriptions 'where the importance of the used melodies and the added parts is almost equal', such as in Fifteen Hungarian Peasant Songs (1914–18). In the third category, 'the added composition treatment attains the importance of an original work, and the used folk melody is only to be regarded as a kind of motto'.[17] Eight Improvisations on Hungarian Peasant Songs Op. 20 (1920) epitomize the third category.

Bartók composed nearly 200 settings of folksongs, many of these for piano, some of which were inspired by a particular ethnic culture. Works utilizing Hungarian melodies only include Three Hungarian Folksongs from the Csík District, *For Children* vols. I and II (1908–09), Fifteen Hungarian Peasant Songs, and Improvisations Op. 20. Compositions which use Slovak folk tunes are *For Children*, vols. III and IV, and Three Rondos on Folk Tunes (1916, 1927). Romanian-inspired folksong settings include Two Romanian Dances Op. 8a (1909–10) and the Sonatina, the two series of *Colinde* and the well-known Romanian Folk Dances, all from 1915. As one might expect, Bartók had spent profitable time during these years studying the Romanian tunes he had collected.

In addition to complete sets from one ethnic source, Bartók also included individual folksong settings in collections of other types of pieces. Fourteen Bagatelles and Ten Easy Pieces each include one Hungarian and one Slovakian setting. Seven Sketches Op. 9b (1908–10) contain a Romanian folksong. The six volumes of *Mikrokosmos* (composed between 1926 and 1939) and *Petite Suite* (1938) include a number of settings of folk tunes from various ethnic origins. Most of these were published without text of any kind, and none with translations into a more commonly used Western language.

Why did Bartók separate the texts of the melodies from the musical settings in these piano works, if they have the potential to provide insights to the performer? We can certainly make no presumption that these texts were commonly known even to Hungarian audiences. In 1911 Bartók wrote, somewhat derisively:

> Although we did not have a Hungarian art music to date, we actually had prior to the present time – and still have – a precious folk music of special character. But our compatriots who are loudly enthusiastic about national specialties do not know, research or love it. Out of the bulk of this music they know only those one to two hundred songs which our gipsy band leaders had the kindness to take over from the peasants and drum into the ears of the Hungarian gentry, and which are unimaginably jarred almost past recognition by their oriental fantasy.[18]

In the ethnological works, a folksong was always presented with text in the original language. The folksong arrangements for piano were never published with text and setting together on the same page, although a few, including the Fifteen Hungarian Peasant Songs, Eight Improvisations on Hungarian Peasant Songs and *Colinde* were provided with a frontispiece containing the original melodies and at least partial texts in the original language. In Kodály and Bartók's preface to the first edition of folksong arrangements there is an implication of compromise as the folksong is 'to some extent adapted to public taste . . . dressed to be taken from the fields to the city'.[19] Such practical issues may have been decided for marketing reasons – perhaps Bartók and/or his publishers decided that saddling the piano compositions with texts in what would have been difficult, exotic languages to consumers in Western Europe and the United States would limit their marketability. There is no question that Bartók was ambitious, and desired exposure beyond the borders of Hungary. Perhaps he simply did not find it necessary, considering the musical aspects of the setting paramount to considerations of text, or feared that text on the page might actually distract from the musical setting. He may even have enjoyed the extraction of melody from text, and abstraction of verbal elements – this is certainly illustrated in 'Evening in the Country', discussed above. Whatever his motivation, the texts remain obscure to the non-Hungarian (or Romanian, or Slovakian) speaker who would interpret these works.

And yet it may be that the understanding and interpretation of these folksong settings for piano could be significantly enhanced by reuniting the melodies with their texts. Just as the natural rhythm of the language has a great deal of impact on the inflection of the melodies, the meaning of the text may also be reflected in the setting, as when Bartók indulges in word painting. Many of these settings, especially the simpler ones such as *For Children,* do not usually seem to treat the text in any special manner, although one might still appreciate knowing about it. There are, however,

Example 6.6 Improvisations on Hungarian Folk
Songs Op. 20 No. 3, bars 15–16

Example 6.7 Fifteen Hungarian Peasant Songs,
No. 6, bars 42–43

significant instances in important works when the knowledge of the texts
will profoundly influence the interpretation.

The Eight Improvisations on Hungarian Folk Songs Op. 20, wherein
Bartók 'reached . . . the extreme limit in adding the most daring accompaniments to simple folk tunes',[20] exhibit some wonderful examples of word
painting, such as the preening gestures of the raven in No. 3 (Ex. 6.6)
whose text reads:

> See there looming a black cloud
> In which is preening his plumage a yellow-legged raven.

Fifteen Hungarian Peasant Songs also contain striking examples of
word painting, notably No. 6, which is by far the most sophisticated folksong setting of the work – its centre of gravity. Bartók was perhaps inspired
by the text of the original folksong in choosing this type of setting. Its
extraordinary length (twenty-three verses) and narrative quality (he des-
ignated the movement 'Ballade') seem appropriately set in a theme with
nine variations. The tragic story describes the death of a young woman,
whose lover leaves her after she discovers she is expecting his baby. Her
lover returns and, finding her in her tomb, kills himself with a dagger.

The mood of the musical setting is foreboding, lyrical, wistful and
above all tragic. Perhaps it is not too far-fetched to suggest that its overall
ABA form was also suggested by the text – in the song Angoli Borbála's
lover departs and returns again in the end. When he finds his beloved
already dead he drives his knife into his own heart – graphically depicted
by the harsh and dissonant chords in the last two bars (Ex. 6.7). The story

told in the folksong must not have been far from the composer's mind when he created this set of theme and variations.

Conclusion

The evolution of Bartók's musical language is best understood as a complex of simultaneous influences, interests and goals. His teaching and folksong efforts have left a valuable legacy for teachers, pianists and students of all ages and levels. As a piano pedagogue he had practical reasons for creating easy teaching pieces but he also used this medium for the exploration of folksong settings. The body of his piano music compliments the traditional repertoire by presenting a musical language evolved not from Western art music but from the folk music of Eastern Europe. The natural inflections and characteristic rhythms of folk languages held a particular fascination for Bartók. Just as important, however, are the texts themselves, the stories they tell, and the layers of meaning they hold. His general absorption into folk-music studies catapulted his musical ideas into specifically new directions, manifested in the works he composed. In particular, the expression of folksong style, modelled on the specific articulation developed in his many teaching editions of other composers' works, provides a significant contribution to the definition of twentieth-century piano styles and notation.

7 Piano music: recital repertoire and chamber music

SUSAN BRADSHAW

The sin against the spirit of the work always begins with a sin against its letter. . .

IGOR STRAVINSKY, *POETICS OF MUSIC*

Unlike Bartók, who had almost nothing to say about his own work, Stravinsky was a man of many words, both philosophical and eminently practical. Had Bartók been minded to expand on the subject of his own music vis-à-vis performance, he too might well have observed that 'The sin against the spirit of the work always begins with a sin against its letter', as well as endorsing Stravinsky's remark that 'An executant's talent lies precisely in his faculty for seeing what is actually in the score . . .'.[1] But it is at this point that Stravinsky the composer evidently parts company with himself as performer, since he too-often fails, by default, to provide the very information he trusts the talented executant to note. Not so Bartók, for whom intervallic shape and motivic phrasing is a *sine qua non* for the cut and thrust of his Beethovenian developments. It is not so much that, like Debussy, he expanded the range of classical accentuation according to the needs of his own music, but that he succeeded in devising an articulation precisely appropriate to the needs of each particular piece (see for instance Nine Little Piano Pieces, Nos. 1–4); in other words, the relative weight of phrase and of points within that phrase may be signalled by metre, dynamics, accents and, everywhere, by articulation slurs which define shape and intervallic content. Any properly articulate performance should of course take account of all these punctuating elements.

Although Bartók and Webern were born scarcely two years apart and died within eleven days of one another in September 1945, their musical eventualities could hardly have been more different. Yet both were descended from Brahms through their teachers, Hans Koessler and Arnold Schoenberg and, had the seventeen-year-old Bartók taken up the scholarship offered him by the Vienna Academy, their separate futures might have become more closely entwined; instead, he decided to follow his compatriot, Ernő Dohnányi, in electing to study in Budapest. Yet, despite the example of Liszt's interest in the gypsy mutations of Hungarian peasant tunes, it was as much that of Brahms (who also drew on folklore filtered through similarly popularizing processes in the hugely successful arrangements of four sets of Hungarian dances for piano duet) which impressed the teenage composer; Bartók's own schoolboy orchestrations (Halsey Stevens does not say which, or how many, but evidently not the three already arranged by Brahms himself[2]) were given at the Pozsony gymnasium in 1897. But it was the overwhelming experience of his initial encounter (in 1902) with the work of Richard Strauss (in a Budapest performance of the tone poem, *Also sprach Zarathustra*) that was to rekindle his dormant enthusiasm for composition. Like his earlier Brahms orchestrations, Bartók's piano transcription of *Ein Heldenleben* was a labour of love, in this case one that served immediately to unleash a notably prolific compositional outpouring, as well as more directly to influence the narrative structure of his own symphonic poem, *Kossuth* (1903), written midway through the Four Piano Pieces discussed below.

If the child be indeed the father of the man, then Bartók at the age of eleven foreshadows his adult self as a man of chords rather than melodies; for while most musical children make up little tunes, the harmonically sophisticated Béla starts and ends with chords, leaving the tune to unfold a stream-like course (of 'The Danube River') deriving from the topmost notes of each ensuing chord pattern. Such early childhood efforts aside, there are quite a few unpublished pieces dating from his later teenage years including Three Piano Pieces, a Sonata, and a Piano Quartet (all dating from 1898). Five years on and the unmistakably Brahmsian Study for the Left Hand from Four Piano Pieces (1903) is proof only of lessons well learnt. Spreading over eleven pages of printed score, it reveals an impressive compositional fluency as well as an ability to construct a large-scale sonata movement out of an arpeggiated chord and a much-used descending scale pattern which eventually turns into something approaching a second subject. Between this and the extended virtuosity of the final Scherzo (dedicated to Dohnányi who, as it happens, was to act as Bartók's repertoire coach that year of his graduation[3]) come two slow movements, Fantasias 1 and 2. Fantasia 1, ostensibly in C minor, predates the *Kossuth* Symphony, and follows the free-flowing Straussian outlines of a bass-dictated harmony which here, in the context of what seems uncannily like a song transcription, shows him master of the art of melody and accompaniment. Post-dating *Kossuth*, Fantasia 2 in A minor is much less predictable, especially in terms of writing for the instrument, and with an exploration of registral contrast linked to the tentative beginnings of a recognizably motivic development.

If the shadow of Brahms still hovers over Fantasia 2, albeit more distantly, it is now the questing, introspective Brahms of the late *Intermezzi* from Op. 116/119 rather than that of the rhetorically outspoken, occasionally bombastic composer of the Two Rhapsodies Op. 79. Different yet again, the waltz-cum-polka of the final Scherzo approaches the more flamboyantly diatonic mode of its dedicatee (Dohnányi), with an anarchic little rhythmic variant of the opening that is first heard to bridge the end of the $\frac{2}{4}$ polka from the middle section and the return of the $\frac{3}{8}$ waltz from the opening. With this, the twenty-two-year-old composer is already imagining a counterpoint of metrical emphases five years before beginning to toy with counterpoints of different keys in the first of the Fourteen Bagatelles Op. 6 (1908).

Whether or not Bartók came to regret his impulsive decision to allow the publication of several of his early works, including these Four Pieces (but not the closely contemporary Piano Quintet (1903–04), whose comparatively featureless and repetitive accomplishment Bartók revised extensively before discarding the score in pique following its third and supposedly final performance in 1921; it was eventually retrieved and later published in Hungary in 1971), will forever remain a moot point. For us, observers at the birth of a new language, they have much to tell of the stylistic problems faced by young composers in the early years of the twentieth century. In Bartók's case, a fluent keyboard technique might well have seduced him into settling for the confidently post-Lisztian expression of his own Rhapsody Op. 1 (1904). With the already long-standing popularity of *all'ongherese* and other 'exotic' musical ingredients reaching a positive frenzy of virtuoso endeavour in the second half of the nineteenth century, and with Liszt by far the best known of the Hungarian perpetrators, it was Liszt's virtuoso keyboard style that naturally lay behind the equally elaborate textures and sectional contrasts of Bartók's own Rhapsody. Composed only two years after his Straussian awakening and scored, apparently in one fell swoop, for piano, for two pianos and for piano and orchestra, this is by no means a routine student piece, nor even one sparked by a noticeably youthful ardour. There is instead much evidence of a zealous rhapsodizing in the supposedly grand manner whose expressive purpose the young Bartók must even then have begun to question. But even within the slightly alien context of an outdated rhetoric, he is already beginning to detail the intervallic shape of melodic fragments (motifs) in terms of their harmonic and rhythmic placing – that is to say, according to whether they are destined to arrive at or depart from the next shift in the series of elaborately defined tonal chords as they move in and out of the diatonic. It is moreover clear even at this stage that the directional emphasis of subsidiary chord formations may as readily be defined by dynamics as by slurs (Ex. 7.1).

It is worth emphasizing that it is the significance of intervallic definition that was to leave Bartók heir to a classical articulatory tradition that should on no account be confused with the stylistic neoclassicism espoused by Stravinsky and Schoenberg. Bartók's classicism is less a

Example 7.1 Rhapsody Op. 1, bars 30–31

matter of style than of a motivic articulation that dates back to Haydn and, in particular, to Beethoven – for whom musical punctuation (by whatever the means used to achieve it) was paramount when it came to promoting phrase structure as the outcome of the motivic connection or disconnection between one note and the next. Bartók was eventually to become past master in the art of Beethovenian development, and not only in his String Quartets. But a certain confusion was meanwhile to reign between the articulatory purpose of extended slurs as used to indicate phrase lengths and short slurs used to indicate the manner of performance, as well as the duration and articulatory emphasis of secondary clauses within the phrase. (Alban Berg's near-contemporary Sonata Op. 1 (1908) is still more confusing in this respect.)

At first glance, the eighth of the Fourteen Bagatelles Op. 6 (1908) might seem set to perpetuate a similar confusion, except that the longer slur showing the curve of a phrase is here underlaid by tenuto lines proposing a not-quite-legato articulation. Later, the thirds are shorn of their tenuto articulation and set above an expanding bass line that by implication increases in articulatory emphasis to a point where the balance of the three-part layout must allow for the extended melodic continuity of an expressive upper voice (see Ex. 7.2). The most important performance objective must be first to mark the connecting link between the descending semitones, whether separated by a major third (as here in a new context), or, later, by a semitone, then a minor ninth (in the 'recapitulation'), and then to promote the syncopated major triads with as much contrast in articulation as the dynamic rise and accented on-beat arrivals might suggest.

Example 7.2 Fourteen Bagatelles Op. 6 No. 8, bars 20–21

Example 7.3 Two Elegies Op. 8b No. 1, bars 1–6

After five sabbatical years (1904–09) consumed by the collecting and transcribing of folk music, the Two Elegies Op. 8b (1908–09, following hard on the heels of the First String Quartet Op. 7) mark Bartók's return to entirely abstract composition. Picking up where the outer sections of the Rhapsody left off, filtered through his intervening encounter with the music of Debussy, they look backwards to the rolling reiterations of an intermittently formulaic bass, as well as forwards to the suspended harmonic movement of prolonged ostinati. The first piece begins as it intends to unfold, introducing staccato elements within the two-bar slurs that shape the opening motifs (see Ex. 7.3), both so as to throw the weight of each phrase towards the rising fourth which spans the bar line and to account for the matching fall towards the triadic formations that conclude the second and sixth bars; meanwhile the separately accented arrival points include the suggestion of cadential close. It is the outcome of this motivic delineation, with its characteristic dynamic retreat from each succeeding downbeat arrival, that is in effect the rhythmic 'theme' of the piece, recognizable as such even as the intervals expand and then contract towards the close.

Dating from the same period, Four Dirges Op. 9a (1909–10), Three Burlesques Op. 8c (1908–11) and Seven Sketches Op. 9 (1908–10) seem both to presage the future of *Allegro barbaro* (in Op. 8c) and to effect a nostalgic reminiscence of octave-based chords and tolling melodies outlined in octaves (in Op. 8c and 9a respectively). The $\frac{2}{2}$ time signature and clearly marked bar-phrasing (4 + 4 + 2 + 2 + 1 + 1 + 1) of the third Dirge leave no doubt that the melodic impetus belongs to the bass, and that the synco-

Example 7.4 Four Dirges Op. 9a No. 3, bars 1–4

Example 7.5 Three Burlesques Op. 8c No.1, bars 1–5 and 9–10

pated right-hand tolling develops a melodic feature only to stop short of the bar line (Ex. 7.4), later contracting to form an inverse (rising/falling) sequential relationship with the bass on approach to the climax. In the final Dirge, chords are initially placed either side of a central melody that limps from one downbeat to the next until the rhythmic emphasis is later reversed to direct the corresponding intervallic inversions across the bar from weak to strong.

Meanwhile, the leaner, insistently semitonal relationships of the Three Burlesques make extended play with sequence (in No. 1) and with conflicting, quasi-bitonal triadic or scalic elements (Nos. 2 and 3); throughout the triple-time rhythmic pulse of No. 1 ($\frac{3}{4}$) and No. 3 ($\frac{3}{8}$) articulation depends as much on the placing of old-fashioned phrasing slurs as – for the first time – on a range of accentuation evidently set up in advance of *Allegro barbaro* (see below). Moreover, the tapered, one-in-a-bar phrasing and unison repetitions of Burlesque No. 1 only gradually begin to reveal a sequential purpose that is as much harmonic as it is linear – in other words, essentially *not* the outcome of a three-in-a-bar stress that would expose successive tritones at the expense of the intervening major third (see Ex. 7.5). This contrary phrasing is reserved for two climactic points at which the metrical emphasis becomes a duple one, paced across the bar line – both where the second tritone successively becomes a perfect fifth and, later, where the separated identity of the major third doubles to support the twofold image of an augmented triad. It is only then that the tapered phrasing of the opening bars is understood specifically to focus on the diminished fifth while deliberately delaying the mirrored outcome central to the continuity or discontinuity of the bar-phrasing overall.

Of the Seven Sketches (1908–10), four announce themselves as

Example 7.6 Seven Sketches, Op. 9
(a) No. 4, bars 29/3–30 (RH)

(b) No. 7, bars 7–9 (RH)

based on folk material, the remainder pursue more abstract concerns. Particularly interesting in the present context is the considerable refinement of a motivic argument conducted almost entirely in terms of phrase accentuation in the most substantial central piece of the seven. Here, the main subject matter is the melodic relationship that unfolds between successive major/minor thirds, expressed in terms of the slurs that connect or (mostly) separate their downbeat emphases, no matter what the metrical placing (Ex. 7.6a). Likewise in the final piece, a marked emphasis on the downbeat character of the answering phrase dictates that beginnings should be heard as successive restarts, each caught up from beneath the end of the last (Ex. 7.6b).

Then, almost out of the blue, comes the explosive confidence of *Allegro barbaro*. Although dating from 1911, this was a piece that had no public performance until the composer himself played it at a concert in Budapest in February 1921. By then he had completed both the Suite Op. 14 (1916) and the Three Studies Op. 18 (1918), as well as giving the premieres of both in April 1919 (again in Budapest). Coming between *Duke Bluebeard's Castle* Op. 11 (1911) and the Four Pieces for Orchestra Op. 12 (1912), *Allegro barbaro* is one of Bartók's best-known and most successful concert pieces; yet, like increasing numbers of works dating from between 1904 and 1919, and all those written thereafter, it has no opus number. But while he seems to have decided quite early on to withhold opus numbers from works directly influenced by or even indirectly indebted to folk music, he was by no means consistent – especially as it gradually became less and less possible to draw a clear distinction between the two.

Behind the breathless pulse of its rhythmic ostinati, *Allegro barbaro* discovers a quasi-diatonic use for major/minor chords whereby the paced-out repetitions between one (generally root-position) chord and the next are in themselves indicative of phrase-creating periods. Phrasing slurs of a kind inherited from the nineteenth-century masters clearly have no function in a context defined by block chording and where supplementary motivic emphases derive from the kind of articulation scale first used in Three Burlesques No. 1; this ranges from zero (no accent at all), regardless of dynamic, to the sparingly used extreme: · − > ≳ ≳ ∧ ∧ ∧ *sf sff*. Bartók is moreover meticulous in marking the emphases appropriate only to right or left hand as well as the silences (rests) that aerate the surrounding (harmonic) continuity; it is this aerated continuity which of itself releases two, later three, notes to stamp out a coded motivic message.

Bartók was at the height of his folk-inspired creativity during the years separating the composition of *Allegro barbaro* in 1911 and the two World War I piano works, the Suite Op. 14 (1916) and Three Studies Op. 18 (1918). Perhaps not wholly coincidentally, the ending of the war in 1918 was to mark the beginning of an upturn in Bartók's musical fortunes as well as the auspicious start of his long association with Universal Edition – an arrangement that lasted until, in March 1938, he reluctantly agreed to assign all future works to Hawkes and Son (later Boosey and Hawkes) in London. Meanwhile, 1914–18 travel restrictions had meant the indefinite postponement of plans for further ethnomusicological research, a postponement which in turn led him to take a close look at his compositional purpose: just in the nick of a time which could have led him to resume the dedicated work of ethnomusicological recording and transcription, he retreated from the brink of a future that could otherwise have been devoid of three piano concertos, the Sonata for Two Pianos and Percussion, *Mikrokosmos*, *Contrasts*, and all the wealth of chamber and orchestral works that were to occupy the last twenty years or so of his life.

In any case, the folk material already to hand was more than enough to occupy the war years, especially since he additionally set to work on his one-act ballet, *The Wooden Prince* (1914–17), following this with the four-movement Suite Op. 14. The alternating-hands layout of the chord that sets the momentum for its Allegretto first movement is evidently not so remote in kind from the opening of *Allegro barbaro*. But here the three-note motif is immediately extended in melodic sequence coupled with a repeating rhythmic motif designed to throw the weight of the phrase towards the middle of each second and the downbeat of every fourth bar; meanwhile, the staccato offbeat chording shifts in line with the inflected melody while remaining dynamically independent of it.

The very different character of the one-in-a-bar Scherzo needs only the springboard arrival on/off every fourth bar for the phrasing of its descent through a sequence of augmented triads to take care of itself. The corresponding ascent has no cut-off point; instead, the dynamic rise across 4 + 4 + 2 + 2 + 2 bars serves an equally explicit purpose – just as the one-in-a-bar slurs of the ensuing section, coupled with heavy or reduced emphasis,

Example 7.7 Suite, Op. 14 No. 3, bars 29–30, 33–4

Example 7.8 Brahms, Fifty-one Exercises, No. 7, bar 1

mark the divisions of an eight-bar phrase into $1+1+2+4$ bar beats. Dynamics are used to similar effect at the start of the Allegro molto third movement, later projecting a phrase that seems momentarily to shift the bar line, then abruptly to detach the final quaver of each bar, lifting it into upbeat mode so as to draw attention to the fleeting cadential close as an outcome of the ruling ostinato (Ex. 7.7). Dynamics again take charge of phrasing in the concluding Sostenuto, where a sequence of two-note melodic rotations gradually expands its intervallic horizons to reach a small dynamic peak at each half bar.

If *Allegro barbaro* and the 1916 Suite were to point Bartók towards a more sinewy style of keyboard writing – devoid of the cimbalom-like arpeggiations so characteristic of the 1904 Rhapsody and heard still to propel an essentially fragmented melodic line even in the Elegies of 1909 – this was nonetheless a style as yet dependent on diatonic chords, even though the chords had by now assumed a role that was rhythm-provoking rather than merely decorative. Two years on, the Three Studies Op. 18 (1918) move into darkly expressionist realms of an uncompromising harmonic uniformity.

Brahms knew all about the finer points of piano-playing technique, and his Fifty-one Exercises are second to none when it comes to finding imaginative solutions to such problems as contracting the hand within the space of a minor third (Ex. 7.8) or of extending it beyond the octave; with his early admiration for Brahms, Bartók would surely have known and admired the compositorial quality of these exercises and may even have had them in mind as he came to write his own studies. To display the one in terms of the other is for instance not only to appreciate the similarities but to begin to feel the broad harmonic sweep of the underlying chromaticism and implied melodic momentum in the first of the Three Studies (Ex. 7.9).

Example 7.9 Bartók, Three Studies Op. 18 No. 1, bars 31–33

Example 7.10 Three Studies Op. 18 No. 3
(a) bars 10–11

(b) bars 41–42

Later, the dynamic accentuation of a Chopinesque cadenza ends up against the grain of both the motivic phrasing and the rhythmic groupings. In the final Study a similarly graded accentuation is expressed in terms of duration rather than dynamics, while the ongoing semiquavers reveal themselves not just as the accompanimental figure they had seemed at the outset but as a foreground thread with speech-like implications of its own (Ex. 7.10a). The motivic syncopations that emerge as an initially fragmented sostenuto eventually develop a more extended pairing, *leggierissimo*, (Ex. 7.10b), and with a skeletal harmony likewise paired in octave transposition on either side.

The Three Studies were by far the most exploratory piano pieces of a decade that had begun with the *Allegro barbaro* and ended with its first performance (along with Eight Improvisations on Hungarian Peasant Songs Op. 20) in February 1921; the Studies, premiered in April that same year, touch on quasi-Schoenbergian areas of a harmony by now inseparable from melody, bass from treble, vertical from horizontal, and vice versa. Yet it was not until eight years on – with his early pieces (Opp. 1–9, 1904–10) beginning to be overshadowed by more recent developments in other areas – heard to notable effect in the Second String Quartet Op. 17 (1915–17) – that Bartók began to think of filling the gap in his pianistic output. Scarcely pausing to draw compositional breath between June and October 1926, he wrote the Sonata, the folk-based suite *Out of Doors*, and Nine Little Piano Pieces (sketches for other works of the period, but none the less striking on their own account), then gave the premières of all three on 8 December in Budapest (although Halsey Stevens seems uncertain, since in the text he cites Baden-Baden, July 1927[4]); he had meanwhile completed his first Concerto for Piano and Orchestra, begun in August and finished in November, for performance in July the following year. (When *did* he find time to practise?)

At first sight, the Sonata appears characterized solely by a relentless rhythmic energy whose textures initially resist coherence, seeming almost wilfully to distance themselves high from low, vertical from horizontal; the richly doubled chord-voicings of *Allegro barbaro* have gone, sacrificing harmonic resonance to a punched-out rhythm whose intervallically cramped articulation often seems designed to emphasize rather than to fill the musical space between high treble and low bass. And since these rhythmic ostinati are given little opportunity to escape the unison, harmonic underpinning has to be teased out from within the ongoing pulse of a chorded linearity. In the context of a generally thematic rhythm, coupled with pedal-point insistence on block pitch repetition, octave doublings take on a quasi-harmonic role, and it soon begins to seem as if finding a balance between the non-virtuoso aspect of these various doublings may of itself serve to substantiate a harmonic continuity too often obliterated in a welter of uniform loudness. In this respect it should by now be clear that Bartók uses dynamic markings not only to increase or diminish long-term sound levels, but as short-term indicators of an expressive surging (see Exx. 7.11a and 7.11b below, and also Ex. 7.5 from the opening of Burlesque No. 1). Such instances of successive falls or rises in dynamic energy are evidently no more cumulative than are the isolated *sforzandi* (Ex. 7.11c) here attached to single notes or chords, particularly since these *sf* (seldom *sff*) accents are placed well clear of the dynamically independent central ostinati.

After finishing the Sonata in a few short weeks during the early summer of 1926, Bartók carried straight on with the suite of five pieces which, for obviously rustic reasons, he called *Out of Doors*. The largely one-dimensional settings of these five technically daunting pieces are obsessively close-positioned even when reaching beyond the octave; yet the sound must evidently escape constraint, especially in the nocturnal surroundings of the fourth piece. Here, unfolding clusters, whether on or before the beat, are placed and articulated with the same exquisite precision as in an

Example 7.11 Sonata, I

(a) bars 1–4

(b) bars 7–11

(c) four-part layout of opening (compressed)

* enharmonic notation

earlier and less complex incarnation as the 'tonic' (opening and closing) chord of Improvisations Op. 20 No. 3 (see Exx. 7.12a and 7.12b); later, the simplest diatonic contours of the middle section (of *Out of Doors*, No. 4) are minutely varied not only in pitch and rhythm, but in a range of motivic articulation on a par with the most sophisticated of developmental techniques, whether classically notated or folk-improvised.

Compared to the generally unyielding percussiveness of the suite, the unmistakeably harmonic underpinning of the Sonata gives it an almost indigestible richness, so that Constant Lambert's oft-quoted disapprobation reads all the more peculiarly. The 'dangerous split' he observes 'between melody and harmony'[5] undoubtedly stems from diatonic expectations that would have us seek out consonant verticalities from within the linear cast of a movement which is in effect a series of unresolved harmonic suspensions. It may be interesting to ponder upon the ease with which Lambert's perceived objections could be overcome, if only by the somewhat negative expedient of transposing the topmost pitches of the

Example 7.12

(a) Improvisations Op. 20 No. 3, opening (non-chronological example)

(b) *Out of Doors* No. 3, bars 1–2

right-hand part (those attached to up-facing stems) a degree or so in either direction in the search for a harmonic consequence sufficiently bland to have satisfied Lambert, but which would at a stroke have obliterated Bartók's compellingly semitonal argument. Simplistic maybe, but because it focuses on vertical relationships, this little experiment could prove significant in alerting the ear to the fact that the linear progress from point to point within each ostinato phrase is supported by the harmonic concerns of a bass line (the down-facing stems) which, if heard to connect through the rests, serves equally to suggest a lighter, essentially propulsive purpose for the intervening (alto/tenor register) middleground (see Ex. 7.11c).

The mostly contrapuntal focus of Nine Little Piano Pieces (1926) offers rewards of a gentler kind with regard to stylistic emphasis. The first four are particularly revealing of Bartók's simpler, if no less subtle, approach to articulation both as a means of indicating character and of circumscribing motivic events, each one being punctuated by means which serve to enhance its own particular style; the fourth, without a single slur in sight, relies entirely on metre (whether variable bar lengths or note groupings) and dynamics (including just two different accents) for its phrasing.[6]

Twelve years on from the spate of piano music characteristic of the essentially 'percussive' 1920s, a commission from Benny Goodman and Joseph Szigeti was to result in *Contrasts* for violin, clarinet and piano; unique in Bartók's output as his only piece of chamber music to include a wind instrument, the piano is here allocated an intermediary role between two more evidently virtuoso contrasts. Drawing throughout on the particular rhythmic character of much Hungarian folk music, all three movements project the resolutely downbeat emphasis of motivic beginnings,

Example 7.13 *Contrasts*, I, bars 3–13

regardless of their placing within the metrical bar – which, conversely, is often correspondingly de-accented (see Ex. 7.13). As if to risk no mis-understanding in such contexts, the vertical stroke observed in the first of Nine Little Piano Pieces to indicate the release of one sequential element prior to the start of another recurs here but, oddly, only in the clarinet part: had Bartók by then discovered that wind players were especially prone to overlook the structural implications of such motivic articulation? (Or were they in this instance inserted by Goodman himself as a form of aide-memoire, later to be perpetuated in the Hawkes and Son copyright score of 1942?)

In any case, since these marks serve only to reinforce the punctuating purpose of the printed slurs, they are no more 'optional' than is an articu-lation designed to emphasize departure; to disregard a downbeat succes-sion responsible for the remarkable buoyancy of a phrasing devoid of cumulative arrival points would indeed be (*pace* Stravinsky) to 'sin against the spirit of the work'.

8 The Piano Concertos and Sonata for Two Pianos and Percussion

NICKY LOSSEFF

In M. C. Escher's drawing *Three Worlds*,[1] water acts as the medium for an encounter between phenomena which otherwise could not meet. Images of tree silhouettes are shown as a reflection, existing in conceptual terms at the same distance below the surface as the real branches above it, though neither the real tree nor its reflection is truly in contact with the water. Dead leaves float on the water: on it but not of it, since only their undersides touch the surface. Under the water, or rather in it, is the hazy vision of a swimming fish, the only physical object represented which is truly in its element. We cannot 'see' the water since the only framing device is the physical edge of the picture, but we understand it thus from the manner in which the three worlds interrelate through it.

Somehow, aspects of this drawing put one in mind of that part of Bartók's activity concerned with the forms and structures of Western art music. These act in the same way as Escher's water, in that they form the interface between ideas and phenomena from worlds as different as the fallen leaves, the silhouette and the fish. Some belong themselves firmly within the Western art tradition, most notably that of thematic process: the unfolding of motifs, their transformation through rhythmic and decorative variation, and their subjection to different musical techniques such as ostinato or polyphonic treatment. Other ideas – those we associate with the concept of 'nature' music – are designed to evoke atmospheres or, as stylized noises, represent the actual sonorities of birdsong or night creatures. The third of Bartók's worlds is that of the folk music to which he devoted a lifetime's work; this can manifest itself as real quotation of pitched material, *parlando rubato* and asymmetrical rhythms, or by the evocation of textures and colours of peasant bands.

Although these concepts are broadly applicable to all his music, the works for piano and orchestra represent something special: firstly, Bartók never otherwise, in purely instrumental terms, worked with such a broad palette of sounds; secondly, they are (mostly) composer-pianist vehicles in which Bartók was one musical agent within a large body of others; many of the conflicts and dualities he would take the opportunity to explore are unique to the piano concerto, the genre above all able to showcase the lone soloist's privatized subjectivity against the 'external world' as exemplified by the orchestra. The Sonata for Two Pianos and Percussion, essentially a work of equilibrium, symbolizes the opposite of that type of duality. Bartók insisted that the pianists and percussionists were all of equal importance;[2] the players within the quartet work together, in synthesis, and the conflicts are in the processes of the musical ideas, rather than the nature of the instrumental groups themselves.

Works for piano and orchestra frame Bartók's mature output. The Rhapsody Op. 1 and Scherzo Op. 2, dating from 1904, are based in the Romantic tradition, with the kind of highly idiomatic characteristics of the *verbunkos* style which Bartók was to reject shortly after their composition. Nevertheless, despite their allegiance to Liszt on the one hand and Strauss on the other, these works do provide the glimmerings of a transition into a more mature style. Since Bartók continued to perform the Rhapsody until 1939 we can assume that he felt at least a sincere affection for the work. (The Scherzo he never performed.) The First and Second Piano Concertos, written in 1926 and 1931, are among the most important works from the 'years of flowering'. Written for himself as soloist, they exploit the virtuoso potential of the instrument to the full, and even though their tonal language is far removed from that of the great Romantic piano concertos, they do belong firmly in the composer-pianist tradition. The Third Piano Concerto was in effect the last work he composed, wanting only seventeen bars of orchestration plus performance indications at the time of his death. Bartók's idea had been to provide his wife Ditta Pásztory with something new for her own pianistic career after he had died; understandably, though, she was too upset to play in public for many years, and the concerto was premiered by György Sándor in 1946. Of the works under discussion here, only the Sonata for Two Pianos and Percussion was written in response to a commission, though Bartók admitted he had for some time been harbouring the intention to compose a work for that combination of instruments. It was requested in 1937 by the Basle section of the International Society for Contemporary Music. Like the *Music for Strings, Percussion and Celesta*, another Basle commission written the year previously, it represents Bartók at the height of his powers; a year later, the threat of fascism would engulf Hungary, and the consequent decline of his material prospects became inevitable.

Form

When writing about his own compositions, Bartók is frustratingly coy about their real concerns. The reader turns eagerly to the composer's own 'analyses', only to find him pointing out little more than the barest bones of their structure.³ Moreover, the information he gives is most likely to be of the sort readily available from a brief acquaintance with the scores themselves. It is probably only to be expected that that part of Bartók's somewhat intractable nature which refused to teach composition would also manifest itself thus – in a similar refusal to divulge in print the secrets of the real moment of creativity – but perhaps it is also symptomatic of his insistence that all should be rooted in tradition (an ideal saturating his writings) that he wished to stress the classical forms of works rather than their more innovatory aspects. In what way can this be linked to his statement that compositional 'plans were concerned with the spirit of the new work and with technical problems (for instance, formal structures involved by the spirit of the work)'?⁴ Sonata form, ABA song form and sonata-rondo are the frameworks around which all three Concertos and the Sonata are built, not to speak of Bartók's other large, 'public' works. The forms themselves were therefore clearly not chosen because of the demands of the work's spirit; he undoubtedly turned to them because of their long association with large-scale pieces, because so much life still remained to be breathed into them and, not least, because their intelligibility meant that other, less derivative aspects of his style could always be understood within a recognizable context. For Bartók, the real meaning of a composition lay not in its structure but in its extra-musical message; in a letter to his first wife, Márta, of 1909, he admitted that autobiographical events fed directly into his works.⁵ And as he expressed in frustration to Ditta in 1926:

> To be frank, recently I have felt so stupid, so dazed, so empty-headed that I have truly doubted whether I am able to write anything new anymore. All the tangled chaos that the musical periodicals vomit thick and fast about the music of today has come to weigh heavily upon one: the watchwords linear, horizontal, vertical, objective, impersonal, polyphonic, homophonic, tonal, polytonal, atonal, and the rest; even if one does not concern oneself with all of it, one still becomes quite dazed when they shout it in our ears so much. As a matter of fact it is best not to read anything at all, and just to write, regardless of these slogans.⁶

Thus, the ubiquity and transparence of sonata form allowed both composer and listener 'direct access' to the work's discourse of ideas and to its 'message'.

Two interlocking concepts are necessary for sonata form to operate in conventional functional harmony: a narrative structure and a tonal trajectory which begins as conflict (exposition: first and second themes in contrasting keys) and is finally grounded (recapitulation: reconciliation) after a series of 'adventures' (development). Bartók was able to utilize such a scheme because his music is not atonal but works in ways either closely allied to tonality or, as Ernő Lendvai has shown, through harmonic 'axes'.[7] Bartók is tied to nothing more than a tonal centre in the case of the Concertos and Sonata: both the First and Third Concertos centre on E; the Second, on G; and the Sonata, on the 'pole-counterpole' F♯–C. Furthermore, the conflict-development-reconciliation is not in the transformation and grounding of tonalities but in the thematic processes themselves.

Let us examine these. In the First Concerto, no theme is stated by the solo instrument which has not already been lurking in the orchestral texture. The 'chaos' introduction contains both a proto-rhythm (the 'hammer' motto, on timpani and piano) and a proto-theme (which endlessly circles around itself, on horns and bassoons). These are the seeds from which the entire movement grows. A change of speed articulates the point at which the first subject appears (the Allegro after figure 3 in the score), which is itself a worked-out version of the 'hammer' motto. While this is unfolding, its imminent transformation into a hammer-ostinato plus descending thirds is already being prefigured by an accompanimental passage in thirds on clarinets, oboes and bassoons. The transformed first subject finally appears at figure 7. At figure 9, sited within the unfolding of the transformed subject, the original proto-rhythm of the horns (from figure 1) is extended into a scalic passage whose full significance is explored in the development at figure 19. Even the 'second subject', which appears at figure 12, bears a generic relationship to the proto-theme, and the accompanimental texture is replete with figures with which we are already familiar. All is theme, all is variation. Indeed, the 'exposition' acts as a miniature sonata form in itself. The two proto-ideas are stated and developed, then finally the closing passage (at figure 16) recapitulates the first subject. There is no overt reference to the proto-theme until five bars after figure 22, but the drone-sonorities which underlie this (D–D♭–E♭) have already been etched into our sonic consciousness through a series of rhapsodic cadenzas which continue, punctuated of course by little references to the hammer rhythm, the scalic passage, and fragments from the proto-theme itself. Bartók shows that these nuclei can transform themselves into anything by opening out the proto-theme first into a sunny, major-mode materialization (the Allegro after figure 27), which will eventually become a bucolic dance (figure 31). And so the process continues, sometimes infinitely subtle but always punctuated with the unmistakable signpost of a triplet scale to close off major sections (figures 11, 18, 44, then three bars before the end).

It is as if Bartók were able to pass motifs through different prisms of varying force – an ability which is also evident in the Second Concerto. The character of this work, as he pointed out, contrasts with the First, being

Example 8.1 Piano Concerto No. 2, I, opening

lighter and 'less bristling with difficulties',[8] and this also extends to the presentation of material. Rather than a 'first subject', there are three jovial mottoes, presented by the trumpet (bars 1–3 – Ex. 8.1a), the piano (Ex. 8.1b) and the oboes (Ex. 8.1c), which are then built up layer by layer to form a sophisticated polyphonic texture.[9]

Contrapuntal working is everywhere, from the fugato at bar 155 to the thematic inversion of the recapitulation (bar 180). When the thematic motifs return in the finale, clarified by the piano's octave presentation, Bartók takes the work's Baroque affiliation one step further by creating a *ripieno–concertante* dialogue – something he would return to explore in the Concerto for Orchestra. The Second Concerto is a more controlled work, subject to a greater intellectual restraint; but even though the characters of these works are so different, there are two important points of reference between the two: the stringless orchestration of the First's middle movement which would be re-explored in the opening movement of the Second, and the 'hammer' theme of the First to which reference would be made in the Rondo-subject of the Second's finale.

Like the First Concerto, the Sonata for Two Pianos and Percussion utilizes the idea of introductory 'chaos' which will present important compositional elements (again, circling melody and proto-ostinato). However, the three main themes are not derived from these and bear only a generic resemblance: the first subject, at bar 32, is assertive, open and athletic, tending to ostinato; the second (at bar 84) leans towards the more slippery, mysterious, chromatic, closed type; the third can utilize its characteristic leap of a sixth to range as freely and energetically as it wishes. And yet it is the 'wild card' proto-theme from the chaotic introduction that forms the scaffolding for the development section. In a sense, the procedure is the opposite to that found in the First Concerto, since in the Sonata there are true 'themes' with clear identities, subjected to different compositional techniques (such as counterpoint or ostinato) – rather than mottoes, which form viscous, concentrated textures out of which theme-like ideas emerge.

One feels in the Sonata that Bartók was intent upon working out principles and ideas to their absolute limit in the sparest possible way. The 'chaos' introduction does contain major compositional elements, and yet he wished to pose himself a more complicated problem by also including three separate themes. We have already glimpsed the possibilities offered by piano and percussion sonorities in both previous Piano Concertos, but here he leaves no stone unturned in the effort to explore everything within his own musical language that those instruments could offer. (Afterwards, the combination no longer seems to have held the same interest for him and is not used significantly in the Third Concerto.) As Lendvai has shown, the various systems of melodic, tonal and structural invention seem to be exemplified above all others by this piece, with its clear pole–counterpole tonal biases, its closed/chromatic first movement and open/diatonic finale, and its proportions which so closely match Golden Section and Fibonacci numbers – vexed though the latter question has now become.[10]

The use of traditional forms is allied to Bartók's constant study of other composers. The Beethovenian model of conflict–resolution only truly resolved in the coda of a finale – a model beloved also of Brahms – showed Bartók that multi-movement works with related themes could operate as one master plan. This manifests itself in such 'arch-form' works as the Second Concerto and the Fourth and Fifth Quartets, where a nucleus, the middle section of the slow movement, is placed between two related outer sections, and which in turn are placed between fast movements which are thematically related. Not only is the form satisfying in itself and in the compositional challenges it posed, it also relates to the cyclical property of Nature on which Bartók endlessly pondered. However, whereas Beethoven tends to focus on the single 'tone of anxiety', such as the C$\sharp$ introduced in bar 7 of the *Eroica* Symphony, Bartók – as we have seen – preferred a motto-based process in which true themes 'emerge' out of a sea of thick textures containing proto-mottoes and proto-themes, and which on their reappearance are varied in quite transparent ways, openly displaying the organic nature of the work. Even where he looks directly towards Beethoven – for instance, the Adagio of the Second Concerto, a tribute to the slow movement of Beethoven's G major Concerto, or the overt references in the Andante religioso of the Third to Beethoven's 'Heiliger Dankgesang' of the Op. 132 quartet[11] – it is the form itself rather than the nature of the transformative thematic process to which he is alluding.

Bartók had travelled a long way since the early Rhapsody Op. 1 and Scherzo Op. 2, brimming as they are with 'gypsy Hungarianisms' and virtuosic excesses. It would be something of a curious exercise to forecast his later development from those early works, yet they can be seen in retrospect to have been useful stages along his creative journey. At the very least,

Example 8.2 Scherzo Op. 2, bars 201–04

the composer's craft is honed through experimentation and use. Both make use of the slow–fast *verbunkos* model to which he would return in the Rhapsodies for Violin and *Contrasts*, though in the Scherzo this takes the form of a slow introduction (bars 1–89) to the first 'scherzo' section, in Hungarian style (bars 90–103, 104–497), which is then separated from its Western-style reprise by a central trio section (bars 498–596). The Scherzo, written first, is perhaps the more interesting of the two works, showing not only some surprising appearances of what would later prove characteristic scale-types – the alternating thirds and semitones in Example 8.2, for instance – but also a dark grotesqueness which prefigures aspects of *The Miraculous Mandarin* (1918–19). Notably, there is a constant exploration of ways in which themes can 'distort' both melodically and rhythmically; the four major themes more or less recur throughout the work in varied forms, which means that the two main 'scherzo' sections are essentially early experiments in the synthesizing process which became increasingly important to Bartók's compositional ideals as time went on.

Aspects of the rhapsodic form resonate in this work, particularly the dramatic affectation embodied in *verbunkos* formulae which are then transformed in the reprise of the 'scherzo'. The Rhapsody Op. 1 is, as its title suggests, overtly in the *verbunkos* style, in which a slow opening section – the *lassu* – is succeeded by a complementary, fast *friss*. Bartók's first version, without the extended introduction, was for piano solo; in the orchestral version, he not only expands the work with an opening Adagio but also extends the process of thematic development partially by altering the melodic material. The return of the Adagio in effect unites the work, although in any case *lassu* and *friss* share thematic material.

Nature

The slow movements of the three Piano Concertos and the Sonata make use of what has loosely been termed 'night' and 'nature' music: colours and textures which evoke the atmosphere as well as the concrete sounds of the night, or, in the case of the Third Piano Concerto, the evocation of birdsong within a context of naturalistic serenity.[12] 'Night music' should probably be understood within a larger category of 'nature music'; the latter would encompass not only the sonorities themselves which he clearly so loved, but also the (rather medieval) idea of a mathematically ordered nature and an intellectually perfect cosmic structure.[13] Bartók's sensitivity to tiny nocturnal sounds is a testament not only to his extraordinary sense of hearing but also to his interest in sonorities obscured by the noise of people, with their endless clatter, during the waking part of the twenty-four-hour cycle: the sounds of creatures insignificant to human consciousness and which emerge when unthreatened by human predacity.[14] Sounds also assume greater significance when the sense of sight is denied stimulation; in the absence of vision, they are wholly responsible for giving comprehensibility to the world.

Through the 'night music' it is also possible to access Bartók's music on a magical, rather than emotional or intellectual level. We first encounter the term in the fourth movement of the *Out of Doors* suite which was dedicated to Ditta (and, written so early in their marriage, the other meaning of 'the night's music' cannot altogether be disregarded). The 'night music' is never the 'dark night of the soul' of St John. Yet, as in the middle movement of the First Concerto and the opening section and slow movement of the Sonata, it can verge on the sinister. Bartók was no sentimentalist, after all, and these movements testify to his recognition of Nature's inherently ruthless laws of survival. This concern with nocturnalism is not only part of the larger philosophical question Bartók was prone habitually to ask about the relationship between man and Nature, but also impinges on his personal relationship with the urban society which in one sense he despised, yet which, he must have acknowledged, he could never feasibly leave. The dualities and oppositions inherent in the virtuoso piano concerto make it the most suitable genre in which to explore the struggle of subjectivity against the external world, since the encounter between lone soloist and orchestra is in more than one sense representative of conflict: between the single, elite individual and the group, and between a single instrumental part which yet constitutes 'half' of the music against the very large collection of colours and timbres which collectively form its complement. These dualities are perhaps most evident in the Second Concerto's Adagio, in which the alternating piano (with timpani) and orchestral sections seem to indicate not so much a dialogue as two soliloquies which simply make way for each other, as we have seen.[15] In the case of Bartók, the flamboyant virtuosity and independence of the solo piano concerto parts (excepting, in some ways, the Third) represent several aspects of his 'otherness' at once: and if these characteristics also seem antithetical to his intensely private nature, then we should remember that everything, including his predilection for solitude and seclusion, was to be subservient to his musical vision.

Example 8.3 'From the diary of a fly' in *Mikrokosmos*, Bk 6, bars 51–60

Contrasting juxtaposed 'night music' types are best exemplified by the middle movement of the Second Piano Concerto. The strings, which are silent throughout the first movement, are instructed to play their eerie, other-worldly chorale of superimposed fifths with mutes and without vibrato, creating a sound manifestation of the night itself – the canvas of darkness against which representationalized sounds will be etched. In this movement above all others, the silence which precedes the music thus has symbolic as well as functional significance, acting as a threshold of stillness which prepares the ear for the new, subdued level at which the subsequent sonorities are to be heard. Emerging from this crepuscular world, the piano's entry at bar 23 is 'prepared' by a timpani roll; the following piano and timpani duet, ornamented to soften an otherwise stark set of polyphonic octave lines, then alternates with the veiled and mysterious string fifths. Bartók could not have shown human solitude in Nature more precisely (nor, in the second Adagio, its eventual 'eco-philosophical' union with the environment). And just as the timpani roll acted as an introductory bridge to these human musings, it returns to signal the piano's departure from that state into a taut Presto chase which forms the centrepiece of the entire concerto. Here, Bartók shifts our gaze from the large-scale evocation of nocturnal signalling to the small-scale scurrying of some insect hunt. This is made explicit by reference to motifs in 'From the Diary of a Fly' (*Mikrokosmos*, No. 142 – see Ex. 8.3) which gradually emerge between bars 75 and 90 in the Concerto – a reference reinforced by the fact that not only does the fly 'free itself' from the web at the Golden Section of the *Mikrokosmos* piece (if one agrees with Lendvai), but also that the Concerto's 'reference' to the fly's release occurs at the Golden Section of the Presto. Moreover, the pianist is left to enjoy this moment on his or her own. The orchestra fades out between bars 65 and 85 to leave the piano closing in on smaller and smaller sonorities with no 'external protection' – acting, as it were, as the 'eye of the storm' after which the relentless chase starts its endless circling again. When the chorale section is recapitulated, the separate soliloquies of piano/timpani and strings have somehow, as so often in Bartók, been reconciled and now cohabit the same space.

The Third Piano Concerto's Andante religioso is also tripartite, with an initial section alternating string (now with clarinet) and piano writing, a central Nature tableau, and a recapitulation in which contrasting forces experience reconciliation – but beyond this superficial similarity, the two movements could not be more different. 'Nature', depicted in both the earlier concertos as a mysterious force, indifferent to compassion but never sinister, also represents a private, inner, twilit world. Here, however, all is subjected to a merciless brilliance which lights up an increasingly painful nostalgia and a crumbling of hopes, expressed through the use of an ever more overt late Romantic harmony. Culminating in a series of minor-seventh chords descending by thirds (bars 48–54) which reaches up briefly before its apotheosis, there is probably no other passage of his entire oeuvre in which so much anguish is spilled out. It is undoubtedly the presence of the piano which makes the emotion of this passage so overt; even the *Elegia* of the Concerto for Orchestra is more objective, less raw. We should remember that the piano was Ditta's instrument as well as Bartók's; and that through the piano they had not only met, but also had been used to expressing to each other and to the public their intimate thoughts and feelings about music. Sketched first, the second movement is in more ways than one the nucleus of the Concerto.[16]

However, the message to this work's dedicatee was more than just one of sorrow, and this is made explicit by the birdsong theme of the central section (Ex. 8.4a). This appeared among other notations of birdsong on a small piece of tissue paper found in a miscellany, where it bears the number '6' (there are five other notations, though these are unnumbered) and the legend 'Parting in peace' (see Ex. 8.4b).[17] Bartók's occasional naivety in the face of Nature's wonders notwithstanding, it would be uncharacteristic of him to anthropomorphize a bird's call to the extent of ascribing a concrete meaning; it is possible that he had already decided to utilize the tune to deliver such a message in a composition. Thus he surrenders, 'parting in peace' not only from Ditta and his own micro-cosmos, but from music itself. We read this Concerto as weak, 'one-sided' or 'feminine' at our peril: the yin–yang equilibrium is as ever there, as the energy of the finale shows, but Bartók has taken his leave through the medium of light, not dark, and through thrift and transparency rather than the sonic abundance (and indeed far greater dissonance) of the earlier concertos.

Example 8.4

(a) Piano Concerto No. 3, II, 'birdsong' theme of central section, bars 60–63

(b) 'Parting in peace': birdsong notation No. 6

Timbre

The piano-plus-percussion sounds exploited so extensively in the slow movements of the first two Concertos and the Sonata probably represent Bartók's greatest innovation in musical colour – notwithstanding the veritable catalogue of new articulations we see him devising in the string music. The 'pointing up' of piano sonorities with percussion strokes had never previously been explored so systematically, and it was partly because of the almost endless possibilities offered by this new vocabulary that the 'night music' never retrod the same path. Thus, in the First Concerto, we understand the piano entry at bar 5 to be not only in canon with the percussion sounds but also somehow to be completed by them; the small climax after figure 2 is made explicit by the side-drum roll which accompanies it. This is one sense in which we might understand Bartók's statement that '[t]he "neutral" character of the piano tone has long been recognized'. 'Yet', he goes on, 'it seems to me that its inherent nature becomes really expressive only by means of the present tendency to use [it] as a percussion instrument'.[18] The *sonic ideas* on which the 'night' musics depend are of qualities somehow inherent in the piano but needing percussion to define them precisely. On the other hand, the piano only assumes a percussive nature in certain contexts. It is often used so in ostinato – for instance at figure 9 of the First Concerto's slow movement, where it becomes a backdrop for the polyphonic workings of the winds – but when used in duet with 'real' percussion instruments, its function changes and it becomes most piano-like: the only instrument capable of carrying melody, harmony and rhythm simultaneously. Thus, Bartók displays the unending richness of his own instrument by placing it in different timbral contexts.

Folk influence

By notating the sounds of nature, Bartók also brought them under the control of his own intellect. His inclination to translate these noises into organized sounds can be understood as similar to his impulse to notate and classify folk music, and perhaps both activities were the inevitable consequence of the training of the classical musician, taught ceaselessly to develop, to forge into shape, to refine. The relationship between Bartók's experience of folk music and the composed art work was not uncomplicated, since in organizing derived material he seems to have wanted it to retain the potential to rupture the veneer of classical respectability. With stringed instruments, the way forward was to use extended techniques which actually come close to the sound of peasant fiddling; however, the piano has no folk equivalent, and in order to explore peasant 'topics' Bartók is left with re-creating the sound-world of the village bands. One example occurs in the First Concerto, during the last section of the first movement's development. Here the theme, though not itself a folk melody (it was sketched on the draft of *Out of Doors*), becomes increasingly thickly textured and is subjected to a wild increase in speed ($\flat = 100$ to $\flat = 152$). At figure 31, the music has erupted into some wild peasant revelry which is eventually dragged down to earth by a false recapitulation – back to the world of culture, as it were. Bartók even committed to print his thoughts on the limited nature of Western classical training – pointing out that the members of a 'rather good orchestra' had been 'helpless' in the face of 'Bulgarian' additive rhythms which, in contrast, 'most Bulgarian pupils have . . . in their blood'.[19]

In fact, Bartók's ethnomusicological activities acted not only as a constant inspiration but also as a kind of compositional training. His development of a genuinely new rhythmic model, based on the asymmetrical rhythms of folk music, is the most conspicuous feature of the 'Bulgarian' pieces, for instance; however, a much subtler 'processing' of rhythmic variants found fruit in the Piano Concertos. As Judit Frigyesi has shown, both first and second subjects in the First Concerto move from symmetrical to asymmetrical presentation when they recur in the recapitulation. Similarly, the second subject, which is presented in $\frac{2}{4}$ in the exposition, recurs in altered, rhythmically distorted form in the recapitulation: compare the piano passage between figures 12 and 13 with that at figure 46. And in the first movement of the Third Concerto, the first subject is notated in a kind of hardened rubato; from the basic, as it were 'dotted', motif develops a series of asymmetrical variants formed from decorating and elongating values from the original rhythm (Ex. 8.5).[20]

Example 8.5 'Hardened rubato' in Piano Concerto No. 3, I, bars 2–9 (after Frigyesi)

Performance

Bartók stressed that asymmetry was more a matter of accentuation than notation – 'my feeling is that the extension of a note value is no other than the translation of a dynamic stress into terms of duration'.[21] His recorded legacy shows that an engagement with this aspect of peasant music informed his performance practice quite dramatically, even while remaining firmly rooted in a Romantic tradition.[22] To what extent should modern pianists aim for the authentic Bartók sound? And what does the character of his pianism itself reveal about the pianistic techniques employed in the mature works? Among the wax, lacquer, decelith and x-ray foil survivals is the complete Sonata for Two Pianos and Percussion, and fragments of the Rhapsody for Piano and Orchestra and the Second Concerto;[23] while the Sonata was recorded professionally, the others were amateur home recordings taken from Hungarian radio broadcasts and there are gaps where the records had to be changed over. Despite their technical faults, these amateur recordings are highly revealing, perhaps more so since Bartók's famous remarks about the piano's essentially percussive nature could so easily – and wrongly – be taken to indicate some quality intrinsic to his own playing. The startling similarity in his approach to both the Rhapsody and the Concerto suggests that although the *language* of the early work is identifiably Romantic, he still drew on essentially similar pianistic *styles* for the Concerto written nearly thirty years later – from the bravura octaves of the opening to the slow and intimate passages of the Adagio. Although we hear very little in this recording other than the solo piano part and faint strings (owing to the curious

Example 8.6 Piano Concerto No. 2, I, bars 18–20

Dynamics and pedalling as Bartók articulated them in performance

placement of the single microphone and the notoriously poor acoustic of the Vigadó concert hall in which the recording was made), it is evident that Bartók shaped the Concerto's first subject on a local level not only through dynamic but also agogic accent, with small pushes on the quavers and – a quality of true rubato – a resultant making up of the bar's time on the semiquavers. He also treats the return of these motifs at figure 58 in a similar fashion, and in the transformed appearance of the first subject at bar 45 of the finale, phrases are shaped by means of leaning towards the *sforzandi* – the more bucolic character of the last movement notwith-standing. At bars 19 and 20 (Ex. 8.6), there are pronounced crescendi to the ends of each crotchet group, and this type of figure is habitually treated in that way. The pedalling too is surprisingly copious by comparison with the often essentially dry performances of many present-day pianists, and the character of the opening and related sections (such as its reappearance in the last movement) has a quality of grandiose, even Romantic power under Bartók's hands.

At bar 180, where the recapitulation begins, the chords are even thicker and the pedalling extended almost through to the end of each crotchet group. In the transitional passage from bars 32 to 57, the triplets are accented not with dynamic, as the score seems to indicate, but more often with dabs of pedal, and he even pedals the second subject's arpeggiated chords. Here, the recording shows that the beaming of these chordal groups is all-important, and again quasi-*parlando* agogic accentuation provides local shaping to each group. Overall, the tempo gains pace rather before the marked *tornando al mosso*. In the Adagio, melodies are empha-sized not only by voicing but also by the 'split-chord' technique so beloved of many pre-war pianists (whereby the left hand leads and the right hand comes in slightly later). The ornamental figuration can be subject to con-siderable rubato; at bar 27 of the second Adagio (Ex. 8.7) there is weight given to the first of the anacrusic demisemiquavers. Thus, the extravagant pianistic style of his performance of the Rhapsody is equally at home in the Second Concerto. This is true even of those passages in which the sound-scapes of peasant music are evoked, such as the rondo subject of the finale,

Example 8.7 Piano Concerto No. 2, II: second Adagio, bars 26–28

Bartók makes use of extravagant rubato, giving particular
weight to the first of the anacrusic demisemiquavers in bar 27

in the playing of which Bartók seems to be calling forth some wild, orien-
talized ritual dance, made more obsessive by the full, accented weight
which is given to the whole group – not just the initial note. While such
factors crept into his playing as they crept into his aural consciousness,
they never expelled the pianistic traditions in which he had been educated.

Conclusion

The works for piano and orchestra are situated at important points in
Bartók's output as a whole and demonstrate many of the changing trends
of his musical language. From the theatrical and Romantic Scherzo and
Rhapsody, so firmly based on the one hand on Liszt and on the other on
Strauss, through the 'barbaric' First Piano Concerto with its high level of
dissonance and then the tauter and lighter Second, we arrive at the classically simple, transparent Third which yet connects right back to the beginning of his activities in this genre through the *verbunkos* nature of the first
subject. In formal terms and in the treatment of the piano as a solo instrument within a concerto idiom, these works can be counted among the last
of the great Romantic composer-pianist vehicles. Although the concertos
themselves were not ostensibly innovatory, the special sub-genre of 'night'
music found in them its most varied outlet, primarily through the combination of piano and percussion, and here Bartók's idiosyncratic exploitation stands at the forefront of twentieth-century practice. In this way, the
Sonata for Two Pianos and Percussion represents the culmination of his
experiments with those sonorities and will thus always occupy a unique
place in the repertoire.

9 Violin works and the Viola Concerto

PETER LAKI

Bartók wrote more solo works for violin than for any other instrument except his own, the piano. In fact, the violin is just about the *only* instrument besides the piano for which Bartók wrote solo works at all, aside from the cello version of the First Rhapsody (1928), originally for violin, the clarinet part in *Contrasts* (1938), playing alongside the violin, and the Viola Concerto (1945, incomplete). The piano works, taken as a group, have been the subject of several extensive studies, but the solo violin works have usually been discussed individually or in small groups. As for the Viola Concerto, its incompleteness and the problems surrounding the different performing versions have understandably compelled scholars to focus on the source situation and touch on stylistic issues only tangentially.

A noteworthy difference between the respective genres of violin and piano works has to do with form. With the exception of the 44 Duos (1931), the violin works adhere exclusively to the two- or three-movement forms of sonata, concerto or rhapsody, while among the compositions for piano, one notes a large number of short character pieces (bagatelles, burlesques, dirges, sketches, or simply 'pieces') alongside works like the Suite or the Sonata. By considering all the solo violin/viola works in one integrated survey, one begins to see a distinct stylistic thread spanning Bartók's entire career, one that cuts across lines of genres and style periods as they are normally perceived. Almost all the works in this group were written for famous instrumentalists whom Bartók knew personally (a number were his close friends); in other words, many of them can be seen as 'musical offerings' for another person – as opposed to the piano music, most of which was written for the composer himself to play. Moreover, through his work in ethnomusicology Bartók became familiar with the fiddle as a folk instrument, and some of the violin works reflect an influence of village performances in ways that would not be possible in the folksong arrangements for piano. The two Rhapsodies, based on instrumental melodies collected by Bartók, are by no means the only examples of this influence.

It would not be too much of an exaggeration to say that if the piano represents the 'Self' in Bartók's oeuvre, the violin stands for the 'Other'. The relevance of this dichotomy to Bartók has recently been stressed by

Judit Frigyesi.[1] She applies the term 'Other' to the feminine principle, while in the present context it stands for Bartók's 'melodic' violin style. The two approaches converge, of course, in the person of Stefi Geyer. The important question to ask, however, is whether the distinction between the 'Self' and the 'Other' has any discernible musical consequences in the works themselves.

One of the 'founding fathers' of Hungarian musicology, Bence Szabolcsi (1899–1973), introduced the term 'warmly melodic style' (*melegen melodikus stílus*) in a now-classic 1955 survey of Bartók's life and works. He wrote: 'For the first time this new, "warmly melodic" style manifests itself in the *Second Violin Concerto* (1938) although, as every change of style, it was foreshadowed in his piano music, this time in the *Mikrokosmos* [1926–39]'.[2] The expression subsequently enjoyed a certain currency in Hungary to refer to the style of Bartók's last decade. It is true that in the easy piano pieces of *Mikrokosmos* he had found a new simplicity and concision that fed his large-scale works from the Violin Concerto (1938) onwards; yet other aspects of this style, such as the predilection for long cantabile phrases, were present in his violin writing from the start. These features have surely more than a little to do with the idiomatic possibilities of the violin – a 'melody' instrument in a sense the piano is not – and maybe also with the expectations of the performers. Long cantabile phrases are not characteristic of the piano music, which is often dominated by the 'percussive' quality of harmonic and rhythmic ostinati.[3]

Sonatas

Sonata 1903

Allegro moderato (molto rubato) – Andante – Vivace

During his student years, Bartók wrote several works for violin and piano of which only the 1903 Sonata has been published.[4] It was the first Bartók work to attract attention in the music world of Budapest: the third movement was performed at the Academy of Music in June 1903, with Bartók and one of his fellow students, Sándor Kőszegi. A few months later, the entire piece was performed by no less an artist than Jenő Hubay, the famous professor who taught all Bartók's later violin partners.

The 1903 Sonata is in three movements: an opening movement in sonata form (with a development section containing a fugue), a second movement in variation form, and a third-movement rondo that contains a near-quote from one of Brahms's Hungarian Dances.[5] As in the Piano Quintet (1903–04), Bartók's goal seems to have been to fuse Brahmsian chamber music form with Hungarian elements, which, to Bartók at the time, still

Example 9.1 Violin Sonata (1903), II

(a) bars 33–36

(b) bars 177–78

meant the nineteenth-century semi-popular style with which he had grown up. Of course, this particular fusion is already present in several of Brahms's own works. Yet it was significant that Bartók, determined to write 'Hungarian' music from the very beginning, should acknowledge and build on both of these elements. Similarly his friend and mentor, Ernő Dohnányi, also started his career with chamber music in a Brahmsian vein (Piano Quintet Op. 1, 1895) and incorporated Hungarianisms within that style, for example in his Symphony in D minor (1899), which Bartók admired.

Needless to say, as native Hungarians, Dohnányi and Bartók went far beyond Brahms by infusing the Western Romantic idiom not only with Hungarian melodies but also with a specifically 'gypsy' way of playing. Examples in Bartók's 1903 Violin Sonata include the ornamental first variation (Ex. 9.1a) or passages explicitly imitating the sound of the Hungarian cimbalom in the piano part (Ex. 9.1b). Here Bartók effectively combines two distinct violin styles – Western and 'Hungarian' – alternating between the two.

First and Second Violin Sonatas

No. 1 Allegro appassionato – Adagio – Allegro
No. 2 Molto moderato – Allegretto
The contrast between the 1903 Sonata and the two mature works written for the same medium, in 1921 and 1922, could not be greater. Yet it seems that the dichotomy underlying the earlier work – 'folk' materials embedded in a Western art form – had not fundamentally changed, even though

Bartók's ideas on folk music and his grasp of the Western art form had both evolved almost beyond recognition. The folk-dance finale of the First Sonata, with no direct folk quotes, and the Romanian *hora lungă* ('long song') echoes of the Second (see below), are mature examples of the 'third-degree' assimilation of folk music (whereby the work is 'pervaded by the atmosphere of peasant music'), replacing the Romantically inspired *style hongrois*.[6] As for the Western element, Brahmsian Romanticism has been replaced by what has been unanimously recognized as Bartók's most 'modern' harmonic style.

János Kárpáti and Paul Wilson have both recently provided detailed analyses of the two Sonatas, placing particular emphasis on issues of formal structure and pitch organization.[7] In the present survey, the discussion will be limited to the different kinds of violin and piano textures found in the two works. One of Kárpáti's observations is crucial in this respect: the violin and the piano hardly ever share any thematic material in the Sonatas.[8] This thematic independence shows that it was more important than ever for Bartók to keep the violin and piano worlds as separate from one another as possible. Yet each of the 'contrasting worlds' is extremely complex in itself and cannot be reduced to simple schemes. While the violin part is often dominated by long legato phrases and the piano part by chord progressions or angular rhythmic gestures, this is by no means always the case. Each instrument follows its own path along the two intersecting continua of 'warmly melodic' vs. 'percussive' on the one hand and Western vs. folk inspiration on the other.

The Sonatas were written for the Hungarian-British violinist Jelly Arányi, whom Bartók had known since his student days. Bartók and Arányi, who had not seen each other for years, met again after the end of World War I, and the composer was said to have fallen in love with the violinist (who, however, did not return his feelings).[9] The First Sonata opens on an emotional and textural high point: the tempo marking is Allegro appassionato, and an intense legato theme of wide melodic leaps is played *forte* by the violin, accompanied by agitated arpeggios in the piano. The piano style subsequently shifts to a languid and *espressivo* waltz beat reminiscent of the last movement of the Piano Suite Op. 14 (1916) or the first Ady song Op. 16 (1916), and then to a *risoluto marcato* idea at figure 3 in the score, while the violin continues the style of the opening. The violin's first major textural change occurs at figure 6 where the tempo slows down to Sostenuto and the violin begins to play wide arpeggios. The second theme (at figure 7: Vivo, appassionato) grows out of the earlier *risoluto* idea, shifting from the 'warmly melodic' world into the domain of angular rhythms. Much of the development section (starting at figure 10) is again in a slower tempo, as the passionate violin theme returns *piano dolce* (figure 13). The rest of the exposition's material is used to build a gradual increase in tempo and dynamic (reaching Agitato at figure 17 and *forte* at 18); but the recapitulation, surprisingly, begins Tranquillo (figure 20) as the violin begins its opening theme in the highest register and *pianissimo*. For the rest of the movement, the Allegro tempo is resumed only intermittently (as for the repeat of the second subject at figure 24); the predominant mood remains soft and subdued to the end of the movement.

The second movement begins with a long, unaccompanied violin solo whose close kinship with many other 'warmly melodic' Bartókian string themes has been noted by Kárpáti.[10] The piano answers with a countermelody harmonized with parallel triads. At figure 4, the Hungarian anapaests of the violin signal an extremely ornate new section in which the cantabile melodic line of the piano is contrasted with violin figures centred around single pitches or intervals (first C, then the D–E♭ minor ninth and the D–E major ninth, etc.). In the recapitulation (figure 10), the violin melody of the opening returns with rich ornamentation. The idea, if not its execution, was certainly derived from Bartók's studies of instrumental folk music.

Kárpáti and Wilson have shown how, in the last movement, Romanian folk-dance elements are placed within a Western sonata-rondo scheme. The thematic separation of the two instruments continues, with the piano playing *Allegro barbaro*-like ostinati against the more flexible melodic materials of the violin. The movement develops along the lines of these two intersecting pairs of oppositions.

A completely different realization of the same folkloric–Western duality is achieved in the Second Sonata (1922). Whereas in the First, the folk inspiration was saved for the last movement as a kind of final arrival, the two interconnected movements of the Second are built around a folk-derived motto and, in a way, everything in the Sonata is defined by its relationship to that motto. The folk source of the motto was identified by László Somfai in a lecture given in 1977.[11] He compares the violin's first theme to the Romanian *hora lungă*, which Bartók discussed at length in his ethnomusicological writings.[12] The two cardinal points of the piece are the exposition of the 'improvisatory' *hora lungă* theme at the beginning (Ex. 9.2a), and its transformation into a regular, strophic melody at the end of the piece (Ex. 9.2b). These passages are from two otherwise complex movements, neither of which fits classical formal categories. Although the first movement vaguely resembles a rondo and the second a sonata there are many details in both that do not fit the structures implied by these labels.

Punctuated by recurrences of the *hora lungă* theme – which belongs, emphatically, to the violin – the first movement contains two other types

Example 9.2 Violin Sonata No. 2
(a) I, bars 4–6

(b) II, figure 56

Example 9.3 Violin Sonata No. 2, I
(a) figure 5

(b) figure 13

of material: the first is more 'linear' (Ex. 9.3a), the second more 'gestural' in character (Ex. 9.3b). Both instruments play themes of both types, though – as in the First Sonata – they never borrow actual melodic fragments from one another. The 'linear' melody, transformed, will provide the main theme of the fast second movement, while the 'gestural' material, after bringing about the climax of the first movement, returns twice in the second: once as an allusion just before the recapitulation (figure 34), and a second time – in an expanded and metrically regularized form – just before the end of the piece (figure 56). The instrumental characteristics illustrated by these examples are entirely consistent with earlier manifestations of the 'violin' and 'piano' characters.

By comparing the two Sonatas, Somfai has stressed that whereas in No. 1 there is a progressive move from one character to the next, from the heightened passion of the first movement to the introspective poetry of the second and the exuberant folk dance of the third, in No. 2 the boundaries are less clear-cut, with the simultaneous appearance of different characters as well as frequent flashbacks to earlier stages. For his part, discussing the sources of the folk-music inspiration in both works, Kárpáti has also pointed out that the finale of No. 1 shows the influence of Romanian folk-dances, but he identifies the fast movement of No. 2 as more Hungarian in origin.[13]

Sonata for Solo Violin

Tempo di ciaccona – Fuga – Melodia – Presto

The Sonata for Solo Violin (1944) was the only solo violin work by Bartók written for a non-Hungarian artist, and one who had never been his sonata partner. His relationship with Yehudi Menuhin was very different from the ones he had enjoyed with Zoltán Székely, Joseph Szigeti or the Arányi sisters (to say nothing of Stefi Geyer). Bartók was not closely acquainted with Menuhin (who was thirty-five years his junior) before hearing him perform the First Violin Sonata in November 1943, in a concert programme that also included J. S. Bach's unaccompanied Sonata in C major (1720). Bartók was so impressed by Menuhin's artistry that he decided to comply with the violinist's request for a new work.

The fact that Menuhin performed unaccompanied Bach at the concert attended by Bartók is important. Not only does the Sonata show many signs of Baroque inspiration, especially in the first and second movements, it is also one of the most significant compositions for unaccompanied violin since Bach's three Sonatas and three Partitas. Some of that inspiration may have come via Bartók's friend Zoltán Kodály, who (some three decades earlier) had composed his Sonata for Solo Cello Op. 8 (1915), itself the most important work of its kind since Bach. The two openings of the Bartók and Kodály Sonatas are surprisingly similar in their rhythmic shape, their chordal texture and their combination of Baroque features with pentatonic Hungarianisms (Ex. 9.4). Kodály uses *scordatura* and the notation indicates the fingered pitches (Ex. 9.4b shows the actual sounds instead). Bach's D minor Chaconne is also not far from the surface of Bartók's first movement marked Tempo di ciaccona (Ex. 9.4a). Yet the movement turns out to be in sonata form, with a second subject that is entirely Bartókian and has little to do with the Baroque. The development section is based mostly on the first theme; the recapitulation brings back both themes.

The second-movement Fuga is another case where Baroque techniques merge completely with impulses of different origins, including folk music. It has for its theme that same minor third, presented in an unadorned, almost brutal way, upon which the 'Arabic' scherzo of the Second String Quartet (1915–17) had been based, and its expanded repeat involving the chromatic upper neighbour is also rooted in a long-standing Bartókian practice derived from folk music. Furthermore, the rhythm of folk-dance is woven into the fugue theme; it briefly comes to the surface in bars 56–59,

Example 9.4

(a) Bartók, Sonata for Solo Violin, I, bars 1–4

(b) Kodály, Sonata for Solo Cello, I, bars 1–4

and then takes centre stage when repeated in diminution (bar 84, leading to the 'drumming' figure from bar 88 onwards). The movement's polyphonic intricacies have been explained by Malcolm Gillies.[14]

The third-movement Melodia leaves the Baroque models behind and is devoted entirely to a typically Bartókian chromatic melody (recalling, for instance, the second theme in the third movement of *Music for Strings, Percussion and Celesta* (1936)). The movement is in an ABA form with, as always in Bartók, an extremely free recapitulation whose articulation points are emphasized by changes in playing technique. The ending of the main theme is marked by a short tag played in harmonics. The central section, one of Bartók's mysterious 'night musics', is then distinguished by the use of the mute. The movement ends with an extension of the tag played in harmonics: instead of single pitches though, harmonic double-stops are required. (Regarding the use of the mute, Bartók indicated some alternatives in his letter to Menuhin dated 26 November 1944: 'The third movement can be played entirely with mute; and how would it be altogether without mute?'[15])

It is now widely known that Bartók originally composed the last movement in quarter-tones, and the version published by Menuhin represents a compromise that Bartók may have agreed to but that was obviously not his first choice.[16] The effect of the movement is vastly different from the microtonal version (in addition to quarter-tones, bars 58–62 contain thirds of tones as well) – not least because in this way one does not miss the contrast between microtonal and regular sections, a contrast that turns out to be a crucial structural principle in the finale.[17] The microtones affect the perpetual-motion-like opening section and then disappear in the two melodic episodes, the first pentatonic, the second diatonic/chromatic. A single passage such as bars 38–40 is sufficient to show the difference between the original and the Menuhin version (Ex. 9.5).

Example 9.5 Sonata for Solo Violin, III, bars 38–40

(a) Menuhin edition

(b) Original version

Rhapsodies

Nos. 1 and 2: 'lassú' – 'friss'

The two Rhapsodies (1928), written for Joseph Szigeti and Zoltán Székely, respectively, are Bartók's most extensive works based exclusively on folk material. In these pieces he was aiming for much more than harmonizing or arranging a folksong; his goal was to capture the whole style of East European village fiddle playing and to place it in the context of Western concert music. To this end, he insisted that Szigeti listened to original field recordings and it is advisable that every performer who plays these works today does the same.[18]

Both Rhapsodies, originally for violin and piano, were subsequently orchestrated, while the First Rhapsody also exists in a version for cello and piano. Both pieces follow the *lassú–friss* (slow–fast) format Bartók had inherited from the Hungarian Rhapsodies of Liszt. On the surface, this structure appears to be simple enough: the *lassú* sections are written in forms involving recapitulations (ternary and rondo, respectively); the *friss* sections are open sequences of dance tunes, although the first ending of No. 1 includes a recapitulation of the *lassú* melody.

The origin of the melodies, with only two exceptions, is Romanian, as identified by Vera Lampert.[19] There is a single Hungarian melody (in the middle part of the First Rhapsody's slow movement, from figure 5 in the Boosey and Hawkes edition) known as the 'Lament of Árvátfalva'. This is a Transylvanian fiddle tune recorded by Béla Vikár (the first person in Hungary to use the phonograph to record folksongs) and transcribed by Bartók. In addition, one of the episodes in the fast movement of the Second Rhapsody (from figure 18) originates from a Ruthenian fiddler.[20]

Despite their exclusive dependence on folk melodies, the two

Rhapsodies are much more than simple arrangements. Bartók lavished great care on the elaboration of the virtuoso violin parts in order to satisfy the two dedicatees. The multiple stops, artificial harmonics and other devices prepare the ground for the great Violin Concerto of 1938. That the two Rhapsodies represented a compositional problem for Bartók may be seen in their multiple endings. No. 1 has two alternative endings, both published in the score (in the piano and the orchestral versions) but No. 2 is even more complicated: according to Székely, Bartók had written 'four or five' different endings over a period of ten years;[21] having reviewed all the extant sources, Somfai writes of three different versions but identifies as many as ten different 'versions or stages in the gradual maturation of the first, second, and third endings'.[22] He adds: 'The sheer amount of work Bartók devoted to this composition already alerts us to his occasional problems with the "formal structure involved by the spirit of the work", as he formulated it in the Harvard Lectures'.[23]

Even though the two Rhapsodies are first and foremost virtuoso vehicles for the violin, the piano parts, which Bartók wrote for himself, are also highly demanding. The piano tends to behave more like a foil to the violin, complementing and imitating it, rather than being a partner with a distinct, contrasting personality. The part therefore lends itself very well to orchestration and was perhaps conceived with that possibility in mind from the start. The orchestrated version of No. 1 (1929) includes the cimbalom, and it is interesting to note that in the recital given at the Library of Congress in Washington in 1940, Bartók added some cimbalom-like effects to the piano part that are not found in the published score.

There are some interesting differences between the piano and orchestral versions of the Second Rhapsody (orchestrated in 1929) aside from the issue of their endings. Several passages played by the violin in the version with piano were subsequently given to the orchestra. Bartók evidently considered these melodies violinistic and not consistent with his 'piano style'; in the orchestral version he was able to keep the string sound while giving the soloist a brief respite (figure 28). A fascinating colouristic change occurs at figure 14 in the *friss* section of the Second Rhapsody, where the piano's tone clusters are replaced by harp glissandi, rapid scalar passages in the orchestral piano, *sul ponticello* tremolos in the violas, and soft tremolos in the muted violins.

44 Duos

The 44 Duos (1931), written with an educational intent at the request of German violin pedagogue Erich Doflein, are among the last works of

Example 9.6
(a) *For Children*, Vol. II, No. XXVI (original version, 1909), bars 1–9

(b) 44 Duos, No. 19, bars 1–3

Bartók to consist almost exclusively of folksong arrangements. (*Mikrokosmos* for piano, written between 1926 and 1939, contain only a few such arrangements.) Lampert's catalogue reveals that only two of the Duos (Nos. 35 and 36) were not based on authentic folk melodies, even though they are titled 'Ruthenian Dance' and 'The Bagpipe', respectively. In the case of No. 8, no single melody could be identified as Bartók's source. Most of the melodies were originally vocal, sung to Hungarian, Romanian or Slovak texts. Only Nos. 38, 39, 42 and 44 are instrumental melodies. Of these, Nos. 38 and 44 were fiddle tunes (both Romanian); Nos. 39 and 42 represent two additional cultures with which Bartók came into contact, Serbia and Arabia, respectively.

Like *Mikrokosmos*, the Duos serve instructive purposes in more ways than one. In addition to being a collection of easy works (arranged in order of difficulty) for young instrumentalists, the Duos are equally valuable as a composition primer. Through relatively simple examples, Bartók demonstrated how a folk melody ought to be harmonized and contrapuntally elaborated. His ideas on phrase structure and thematic development are formulated with the utmost clarity in these pedagogical anthologies. It is significant that Bartók arranged five of the Duos for piano solo and published them as *Petite Suite* in 1936. In transferring the material to his personal performance medium, he considerably increased the level of technical difficulty, thus indicating that the pieces were of greater importance to him than merely serving an educational purpose.

One of the Duos (No. 19) is based on a folksong which Bartók had also arranged for piano in the second volume of *For Children*. The two arrangements are remarkably different, reflecting not only the difference between the string and the keyboard mediums but also approaching the melody from a whole new angle the second time (Ex. 9.6).

Concertos

First Violin Concerto

Andante sostenuto – Allegro giocoso

The contrast between Bartók's cantabile violin material and his more angular pianistic idiom is epitomized in an early work for orchestra, *Two Portraits* (1907–11). Both movements of this work ('the ideal' and 'the grotesque', respectively) were derived from the Violin Concerto (1907–08) written for Stefi Geyer, with whom Bartók was deeply in love at the time. The Concerto, whose manuscript remained in Geyer's possession after she had broken off the relationship, was never performed or published during Bartók's (or Geyer's) lifetime. It is understandable, then, that Bartók wanted to reuse some of the material in other works: the first movement of the Violin Concerto was eventually published as the *First Portrait* in 1911 (see chapter 3, Ex. 3.5, p. 55 in this volume).

In a study of the 1907 Violin Concerto, Günter Weiss-Aigner notes, 'Geyer later recognized in the first movement "the young girl whom she had loved", and in the second movement "the violinist whom he had admired".[24] Obviously, the amorous portrait in the first movement depends on a rich legato tone and an even rhythmic flow – in fact, Szabolcsi's 'warmly melodic style' is already 'in full bloom' here (if one is allowed to borrow the title of another early Bartók work here, the first of the two orchestral *Pictures*, or *Images*).

In the second movement Bartók confronted the problem of following a 'warmly melodic' portrait with contrasting material just as he did in *Two Portraits*, though in this case he was thinking entirely within the violinistic realm.[25] The contrast is therefore less extreme. It even disappears totally ten bars after figure 12 (and again at figure 28) where the tempo becomes slow and the mood, if not the actual musical material, reverts to the world of the first movement.

This Allegro giocoso has received less attention than it deserves, perhaps because (unlike the first movement, salvaged as the first *Portrait*) it remained suppressed for many years. Yet it is in many ways a pivotal piece whose connections with other Bartók movements say a great deal about the evolution of certain stylistic elements we have come to recognize as typical of the composer. The four-note opening theme can be seen as a 'polymodal chromatic' variant of the 'Stefi Geyer leitmotif' from the first movement (Ex. 9.7).[26] The same theme, in turn, was used again to open the First String Quartet of 1908 (see Ex. 10.1, p. 154), as Bartók himself pointed out to Geyer, calling this motif his 'death song'.[27]

Yet in the Concerto, the *giocoso* character of the 'death song' is combined with the *verbunkos*-derived dotted rhythm that relates it to one of

Example 9.7 Violin Concerto (1907–08)
(a) I, bars 1–2

(b) II, bars 1–2

the young Bartók's most frequently used musical types. Another typical Bartókian gesture appearing here is the rhythm of the Hungarian 'swineherd's dance' (related to the Ukrainian *kolomeika*) at figure 10 and then, transformed, at figure 17 – a figure also echoed in the finale of the First String Quartet (figure 17). The little tune six bars after figure 30, with quotation marks above the staff, has been identified as the German song 'Der Esel ist ein dummes Tier' (The donkey is a stupid animal),[28] and the footnote in the manuscript, 'Jászberény, June 28th, 1907', reveals that this tune had a personal meaning for Bartók and Geyer. More important, perhaps, is the inclusion of an intentionally vulgar melody and its placement as the penultimate event – a procedure to which Bartók was to return many years later in the *Allegretto con indifferenza* passage of the Fifth String Quartet (1934) and the Lehár/Shostakovich episode from the Concerto for Orchestra (1943).

Second Violin Concerto

Allegro non troppo – Andante tranquillo – Allegro molto
The genesis and structure of the Second Violin Concerto (1938) have been discussed in great detail in the literature.[29] It is well known, for instance, that Bartók originally wanted to write a large-scale set of variations but the work's dedicatee, Zoltán Székely, insisted on a traditional concerto. Bartók finally managed to have it both ways: not only is the second movement in variation form, but the first and third movements are also variations of each other. All the principal melodies of the first movement return in modified form in the finale.

As mentioned above, it is in the 1938 Violin Concerto that Bartók's 'warmly melodic style' was first 'officially' acknowledged by Szabolcsi. It is certainly true that here the style takes centre stage as never before. This time Bartók emphasized the continuity with the great concerto tradition of Beethoven and Brahms in a way he had not done in Stefi Geyer's Concerto. This is evident from the three-movement structure and the breadth of the entire symphonic conception. Therefore, numbering the two Concertos as First and Second does not only go against Bartók's intentions, it also obscures the basic difference between the two works.

His intention to write a 'classical' concerto was much less clearly pronounced in the First and Second Piano Concertos (1926 and 1931) than in the Violin Concerto – thus making the separation between piano and violin idioms as clear as ever. Bartók turned to Baroque music and Stravinsky in the First and Second Piano Concertos as his primary sources of inspiration while in the Violin Concerto he built on the concerto tradition as he inherited it directly from the nineteenth century.* The Violin Concerto, however, dates from a decade that saw the birth of many of the greatest twentieth-century violin concertos, from Stravinsky to Prokofiev (No. 2), from Schoenberg to Berg, from Szymanowski to Walton. It appears as if most of these composers were more likely to introduce quasi-Romantic cantabile materials ('warmly melodic' styles, as it were) in their violin concertos than they were in other works.[30]

In Bartók's Violin Concerto, elements learned from folk music are inseparable from features inherited from Western music of the eighteenth and nineteenth centuries – unlike his writing in the two Sonatas, where 'East' and 'West' were treated more like opposite poles. The opening of the Violin Concerto, on the other hand, with its harp chords moving in equal crotchets, can be interpreted as simultaneously 'Eastern' and 'Western' in origin. David E. Schneider sees it as an allusion to the *dűvő* accompaniment of Hungarian instrumental folk music;[31] but it could just as easily be taken as a reference to the opening timpani strokes from Beethoven's Violin Concerto. These various derivations are by no means mutually exclusive; in his last period Bartók had reached a vantage point from which he could see his Eastern and Western sources of inspiration, previously so separate, converge in a single source – a large treasure-house of tradition that served as a frame of reference with many possible meanings.

The opening melody (marked Tempo di Verbunkos in an early copy of the beginning of the solo part) was clearly modelled on the structure of 'new-style' Hungarian folksongs (Ex. 9.8). In addition, its third phrase contains Hungarian echoes of a different kind: Schneider found a striking parallel between this passage and Ferenc Erkel's Hungarian Romantic

* Here the reader will notice a different emphasis of influence from the previous chapter which drew on Beethovenian connections and romantic styles in the Piano Concertos. Space precludes more in-depth treatment of this interesting debate. – *Ed.*

Example 9.8
(a) Hungarian folksong collected by Bartók in 1907[32]; (b) Violin Concerto No. 2, I, bars 6–23

opera *Bánk bán* (1861) which itself strongly builds on the *verbunkos* style. Yet the transition after the statement of the main theme, and many other points in this fairly regular sonata movement, uses classical Western techniques. The alternation of tutti and solo passages and the repeat of the opening harp chords in the development section are clear classical attributes, while the inversion of the themes in the recapitulation places a Baroque procedure in a new context. Bartók's interest in melodic inversion may have been stimulated by the use of inversion in twelve-tone music. After all, there is also a famous twelve-tone theme in the movement, though there is nothing Schoenbergian in the way Bartók employed either of these devices.

His original idea about a concert piece in variation form was realized in the slow movement of the Concerto, as Somfai has demonstrated in an important essay analysing Bartók's different 'variation strategies' on the levels of tonal system, phrase structure, orchestration, register and tempo.[33] He emphasizes the simultaneous presence, in the theme, of classical periodic structure and the strophic principle derived from Hungarian and Slovak folk music. He also shows how Bartók (for whom the variation procedures of folk music had become second nature) approached the classical theme-and-variation form in a completely unique manner and with an 'encyclopaedic' intent – encyclopaedic both in the scope of the variation procedures used and in the way the different variations are organized into a 'super-structure', characterized by a complex web of internal symmetries.

Although most of the third movement's material is a variation on themes from the first movement, the new features (among them, dance rhythms and new orchestrational ideas) make the themes sound as fresh as the first time. The twelve-tone theme is separated from the rest of the movement by a slower tempo, Quasi lento, that places special emphasis on the particular structure of this theme. A new motif, made up entirely of perfect fourths, appears in the coda (bar 527) as if to remind us of the importance of that interval – a principal ingredient in Hungarian folk-songs of all styles – in almost all the Concerto's themes.

The Viola Concerto

Many surveys of Bartók's music omit discussion of the Viola Concerto on the grounds that, in the form that it has become known, as completed by Tibor Serly, it cannot be considered a work by Bartók. It is true that with only fourteen pages of manuscript, too many questions are left unanswered for us to be certain of his intentions. Serly's work has received a great deal of criticism and has now been followed (though probably not superseded) by another published alternative version (by Peter Bartók and Nelson Dellamaggiore) and (at least) two more unpublished versions (by Csaba Erdélyi and Donald Maurice, respectively).[34] It is understandable that so much attention has been focused on how to complete the Viola Concerto. Yet the question as to what the surviving notes tell us, as they are, is equally worth asking.[35]

To be sure, the sketches leave many important points about the overall form undecided. There are only a few hints at the orchestration. In fact, we know little more than the solo viola part (fully worked out by Bartók) and the thematic segments of the orchestral accompaniment. On the basis of this information, however, it is possible to make a few concrete observations on the Concerto as the composer envisioned it. In particular, the themes and their development, to the extent that they were notated, suggest at least something about the general character of the Concerto as it must have existed in Bartók's mind.

The fact that Bartók worked on the Viola Concerto concurrently with the Third Piano Concerto has naturally caused commentators to look for parallels between the two. Such parallels do in fact exist as both works share a certain intimate, inward-looking character that is not present (at least, not to the same extent) in his earlier Concertos. In the case of the Piano Concerto – written for Bartók's wife Ditta Pásztory – this character markedly contrasts with that of the first two Concertos, written for the composer himself, along the lines of the duality between 'Self' and 'Other' seen above and discussed in chapter eight. The Viola Concerto, on the other hand, seems to have been intended as a more direct continuation of the style of the Violin Concerto of 1937–38 and other examples of Bartók's earlier string writing.[36] After all, the lyrical, 'warmly melodic' style, which characterizes much of the Viola Concerto, had been present in the violin works from the start, whereas in the piano medium, it took a special circumstance (writing for Ditta rather than for himself) to bring it about.

The Viola Concerto opens with a solo that is unaccompanied except for a few timpani strokes. It recalls the unaccompanied opening of Stefi Geyer's Violin Concerto: in each case, there are two metrically identical phrases, one ascending and one descending, with the major seventh/diminished octave emphasized. Of course, the Andante movement of the Geyer Concerto is devoted almost entirely to the elaboration of this one melodic idea and its derivatives. It completely lacks the contrasts that are clearly recognizable in the draft of the Viola Concerto, between solo passages and sketched tutti episodes, between melodic writing and virtuoso passage-work within the solo part, and between primary and secondary thematic areas in general. These aspects of the Viola Concerto relate more closely to the Violin Concerto of 1938. For example, in the development section of the Viola Concerto's first movement Bartók places a variant of the opening melody in the orchestra (instrumentation unspecified), while the soloist plays semiquaver passages.[37] This can be compared with an analogous moment from the first movement of the 1938 Violin Concerto (bars 169–70).

In his performing version of the Viola Concerto, Tibor Serly chose to designate the second movement as 'Adagio religioso' after the slow movement of the Third Piano Concerto. He clearly thought of the two movements as being similar in content, a perception that, no doubt, is at the root of his elaboration of the second section, where he added woodwind figures that resemble the nocturnal sounds from the analogous section in the Piano Concerto. Yet, aside from the tremolo markings in the single system that represents the orchestra, there is nothing in Bartók's sketch to suggest that he intended the section to sound this way. Even the opening melody, which prompted Serly's tempo marking, is not really reminiscent of the Piano Concerto. Instead of a chorale, whose chordal texture is idiomatic of Bartók's piano writing, there is a string melody (*Facsimile Edition*, p. 60, first system) whose real antecedent may be found, once again, in the second movement of the 1938 Violin Concerto (bars 6–7). Moreover, later in the movement (*Facsimile Edition*, p. 60, last system), over the orchestral tremolos, unfolds the same emphatically repeated minor-third motif that had haunted Bartók for years, most recently in the Fugue of the Sonata for Solo Violin. The use of the motif here, however, more closely recalls the climax of the second movement of the Divertimento.

In the third movement, Bartók revisited, one last time, the 'folk-dance' type to which so many of his earlier finales had adhered. Evidence from the sketches shows the finale to be a relatively uncomplicated ABA design. Sándor Kovács refers to its folk background as Romanian, although there are of course no original melodies used.[38]

This spirited dance movement turned out to be the last music Bartók wrote for a stringed instrument, and also his very last composition. Works for stringed instruments (first and foremost, the violin) were not only present in Bartók's oeuvre from the earliest student essays to (literally) the day of his death; they also form a coherent strand in his music. Factors of different kinds – such as the creative transformation of folk music, the inspiration received from performers who were often personal friends, and the desire to establish a second main instrumental medium besides Bartók's own instrument – worked together to give rise to a body of work that contains some of the greatest masterpieces of twentieth-century string literature.

10 The String Quartets and works for chamber orchestra

AMANDA BAYLEY

The Six String Quartets offer a fascinating insight into the chronology of Bartók's musical style, as they span some thirty years of his compositional career. Their stylistic development is such that each Quartet is the culmination of a different phase of his artistic growth, focusing almost all his creative ideas and compositional techniques into a single genre. On the one hand they represent the continuation of a Classical tradition through an intensity of motivic writing that parallels Beethoven's, while on the other they reflect developments in musical language and a changing aesthetic during the first half of the twentieth century.

Unlike his Austro-German contemporary Arnold Schoenberg, Bartók did not consciously seek to champion the cause of atonality. Rather, his interest lay in the fusion of folk and art music, the synthesis of East and West Europe: his inspiration from the folk music of different nationalities uniquely influenced the melodic, harmonic and rhythmic structures of his own music. Furthermore, developments within the realm of his string music – the String Quartets, *Music for Strings, Percussion and Celesta* and the Divertimento for string orchestra – include the many imaginative ways in which he exploited the timbral properties of stringed instruments, devising techniques new to the idiom in order to achieve a whole new range of sonorities within the context of an extended tonality.

Background

The First Quartet (1908–09), written within the early period of Bartók's mature style, reveals Romantic qualities with influences in its chromaticism that could be identified as Liszt, Strauss or Wagner. Some of the individual sonorities and overlapping textures reflect Bartók's acquaintance with the music of Debussy, while references to folk music emanate from his relatively recent interest in collecting folksongs. His absorption in the folk idiom was already leading him to incorporate some of its characteristics into his music.

Bartók began the Second String Quartet in 1915 although it was not completed until 1917, after a surge of compositional creativity which included *The Wooden Prince*, several piano pieces and the Opp. 15 and 16 songs. He dedicated the work to the Waldbauer-Kerpely Quartet following their successful premiere of the First Quartet.[1] Following his increasing involvement in the collection and study of folk music, the Second Quartet shows a more direct use of folksong than the First. The discovery of unusual scale structures provided him with new melodic and harmonic formations to explore in response to the general weakening of tonality at the beginning of the twentieth century, although his use of folk music is not yet all-encompassing. The piece contains the seeds for the full germination of Bartók's compositional style in the Third and Fourth Quartets, completed in 1927 and 1928 respectively.

The ten years that separate the Third Quartet from the Second represent Bartók's development towards an intense, expressionist style during which time he wrote such radical works as *The Miraculous Mandarin* (1918–19), the two Violin Sonatas (1921 and 1922), the Piano Sonata (1926) and the First Piano Concerto (1926). The Third Quartet won him joint first prize in a competition run by the Musical Fund Society of Philadelphia, although it was again the Waldbauer-Kerpely Quartet who gave the first public performance.

The 1920s have sometimes been labelled Bartók's experimental period and, although his music could never be described as atonal, extremes in his style are reached in the Third and Fourth Quartets where all twelve notes of the chromatic scale are kept in play, with individual pitch centres functioning as focal points. In these Quartets he creates unusual sound effects and fully explores the different ways of incorporating folk music into new formal structures.

The Fifth Quartet was completed in 1934 as a result of a commission from the Elizabeth Sprague Coolidge Foundation and was premiered in America by the Kolisch Quartet. Prior to this, apart from numerous folksong settings and arrangements, Bartók had written only two major works since the Fourth Quartet in 1928. After 1934, however, he proceeded to write a series of large-scale works in fairly quick succession. He was encouraged by the commissions he received from the Swiss conductor, Paul Sacher, which resulted in the unique *Music for Strings, Percussion and Celesta* (1936) and the Divertimento (1939), both written for the Basle Chamber Orchestra. These pieces are more accurately described as orchestral rather than chamber works but they are discussed here in the context of the String Quartets with which they have much in common, especially regarding thematic integration.

The Divertimento for string orchestra was written as a result of the seclusion Paul Sacher offered Bartók and his wife away from the increasingly depressing political situation in Hungary. Before Bartók left for the

USA he composed the Sixth String Quartet in 1939 for his long-time duo partner Zoltán Székely, leader of the New Hungarian Quartet, although the work was eventually dedicated to the Kolisch Quartet who gave its premiere in New York in 1941. Bartók started writing it in the same month that he completed the Divertimento: both these pieces relate to established traditions whereas *Music for Strings, Percussion and Celesta*, where the combination of instruments enabled him to explore a more unfamiliar sound-world, reflects his most innovative writing.

This chapter will focus on some of the ways in which Bartók developed his variation technique within an extended tonality expressed in terms of degrees of chromaticism. As he himself said: 'You have probably noticed that I lay great emphasis on the work of technical development, that I do not like to repeat a musical thought identically and that I never bring back a single detail exactly as it was the first time. This treatment stems from my inclination towards variation and transformation of themes.'[2] The technique of variation developed throughout the chamber works can be attributed to two sources: the Austro-German tradition he inherited, and the experience of studying and notating folksongs. In addition to pitch, harmony, rhythm and metre, details of accentuation, articulation, dynamics, timbre and tempo become increasingly important in outlining structure. Such a change in emphasis is typical of twentieth-century works in general, but for Bartók the roles of such seemingly small-scale details are to become of crucial importance in motivic, thematic and textural definition.

String Quartet No. 1

Lento – Allegretto – (Allegro) Allegro vivace

The First Quartet (1909) immediately indicates a break with tradition by starting with a slow movement. The sections of the short Lento define a simple rondo ABA form whose middle section portrays a heightened expressivity: the succession of sighing motifs in the viola's cadenza-like passage, coupled with a slightly increased tempo, creates a sense of urgency as it introduces the new lyrical theme of the B section in the first violin at bar 36. The accompanying pedal, C–G, temporarily alludes to a stable tonal area, rare for this movement. More common throughout the Quartet is the emphasis on a linear movement whose chromatic outlines are immediately more apparent than any tonal harmonic foundation. For example, the opening suggestion of F minor followed by an E♭ minor seventh is attributable to the interaction of melody lines (Ex. 10.1), with further harmonic progressions similarly resulting from the vertical coincidence of pitches.

Example 10.1 String Quartet No. 1, I, bars 1–4

Elements of Classical tonality are restricted to specific structural points such as the first movement recapitulation (bar 53) which momentarily returns to the identical pitches of the opening. At the end of the movement, however, instead of the expected arrival at a 'tonic', a harmonic clouding is achieved via an unconventional succession of chromatic chords which finally end on an Ab–Cb minor third. This is yet another momentary resolution, as the melody lines shift to the major third (A–C♯) that begins the second movement. In the introduction to the sonata-form Allegretto the parallel thirds of a new melodic material point to a more consonant harmony but the establishment of a tonal centre is still avoided until the final arrival on a B major chord. In the absence of conventional harmonic techniques, tonal stability can only be achieved in a relative sense from the repetition of pitches rather than from functional harmonic relationships.

The increase in tempo from movement to movement coupled with the progressive increase in rhythmic repetition drives the piece forward to the concluding sonata-form Allegro vivace, preceded by an introductory Allegro. Rhythmic unisons (from bar 1 of the Allegro vivace) and repetition of motifs (for example bar 20) contribute to the movement's Classical qualities, even though it ultimately ends on a harmonically neutral chord of superimposed fifths (or superimposed fourths as described by Bartók): A–E–B. Bartók's placing of this seemingly dissonant chord at such an important strategic position at the end of a piece gives it a new stability. He seldom wrote about his compositional processes, but a glance at his writing on folk music can help us to understand his tonal thinking more clearly. Just as he attributes his use of a seventh chord as a consonance in its own right to Hungarian pentatonic melodies (as in his Suite No. 2 for orchestra Op. 4 (1905–07)), so too he describes the fourth chord from the end of the First Quartet – A_4–B_4–E_5–A_5 – as a consonance, 'derived thematically' from an old Hungarian melody which contains 'frequent occurrence[s] of the skip of a perfect fourth'.[3]

Further instances of Bartók's then recent folk-music research are evident in the contrasting characters of a spirited *tempo giusto* (upper strings) with an expressive *parlando rubato* (cello) in the introduction to the finale. The movement's persistent rhythmic momentum is twice

Example 10.2 String Quartet No. 1
(a) II, bars 1–2, and 18–19

(b) III, bars 5–7 and 20

interrupted by an Adagio melody which features the accented short–long rhythm of the Hungarian *verbunkos*, while upbeat ornaments and triplet figures dominate the fugal passage of the development section (bar 162). These are only short-lived examples of a folk idiom which was later to infiltrate Bartók's works more widely. Additional percussive qualities also hint at his later style, such as the accompanying quaver chords and the pizzicato triple and quadruple stopping (bar 159).

At this point, in 1909, he was still working within a tradition based on predominantly Classical and Romantic techniques: following Beethoven's example, the motivic content of this Quartet, as in the later Quartets, is derived from the minimum of material. An examination of the melodic articulation illustrates, for example, how the insistent semitonal relationships in the second and third movements (Ex. 10.2) emerge as significant variants of the opening (Ex. 10.1). Here and elsewhere, articulation slurs are allotted the same structural significance as in Beethoven – that is, to confirm or to alter emphasis and to define or redefine motivic material.

String Quartet No. 2

Moderato – Allegro molto capriccioso – Lento
The structure of this Quartet (1915–17) is again unusual, ending as it does with a slow movement. However, a symmetry is created from the outer movements, loosely based on sonata form, framing the central rondo form of the dance-like Allegro. The Allegro is the focal point of a piece whose lively, often violent folk-like character is portrayed by accented dissonances, rhythmic repetition and percussive pizzicati.

It is clear from the outset that Bartók's harmonic idiom has advanced to extend vertically the linear chromaticism and semitonal relationships of the First Quartet. Nevertheless chromatic elements still feature in the

Example 10.3 String Quartet No. 2, I
(a) bar 2

(b) end of the recapitulation, bars 156–57

linear dimension, as seen in the opening melody which also includes a
tritone, emphasized by its metric placement (see Ex. 10.3a). The tritone
interval plays an important part in the move away from tonality, especially
in the second and third movements: according to Bartók, it is another
example of 'many similar harmonic inspirations we owe to the latent harmonies contained in the peasant songs of ours'.[4] His examples show how
the tritone derives from the modes used in Romanian and Slovak folksongs, as well as his awareness of how 'many different chords are obtained
and with them the freest melodic as well as harmonic treatment of the
twelve tones of our present-day harmonic system'.[5] He also acknowledges
parallel developments in the music of other composers. But for him the
especial significance of the tritone lay in the fact that it was 'created
through Nature: the peasant's art is a phenomenon of Nature'.[6]

Whilst the Second Quartet shares imitative qualities with the First, its
motivic content is more highly integrated. Whether or not the melodic
material is identified as thematic or motivic is perhaps a matter for debate.
Ernő Lendvai's analysis (at the front of the Philharmonia pocket score)
identifies three themes in the first and last movements, whereas Halsey
Stevens states that 'in the Second Quartet . . . there are no "themes"; there
are only motives, and the process of development is continuous from
beginning to end'.[7] The point is that while such continuous working out of
thematic material is still strongly rooted in the Austro-German tradition,
the reliance on intervallic fragments within the process of development
challenges the very structure of conventional sonata form. Bartók is not
the only composer to have extended the thematic procedures of variation

Example 10.4 String Quartet, No. 2, III
(a) bars 11–12

(b) bars 18–20

and transformation he inherited. Schoenberg (among others) had already been extending them, for example in his Second String Quartet which pre-dates Bartók's by eight years, although there is no evidence to suggest that he influenced Bartók in any direct way.[8]

One major difference between Bartók and Schoenberg is the extent to which Bartók explores the folk idiom in his works – which is why his music sometimes shows a greater affinity with that of Stravinsky.[9] For example, the opening movement of the Second Quartet hints at a bimodality directly related to the folk music to which Bartók refers in the Harvard Lectures of 1943 (see the A minor/A major juxtaposition at the end of the recapitulation, Ex. 10.3b): 'It is very interesting to note that we can observe the simultaneous use of major and minor thirds even in instrumental folk music'.[10] He gave an example of two violins playing dance music, one playing the melody, the other playing 'queer-sounding' chords. Even though the influence of folk music in the Second Quartet is by no means all-encompassing, the vigorous Allegro molto capriccioso is driven by rhythmic drumming patterns accompanying an Arab-like melody which continues to explore the major/minor third conflict from the first movement, this time between D–F and D–F♯.

A greater contrast between the fiery outburst of the central Allegro and the expansive, pensive lyricism of the final Lento could hardly be imagined. The atonal tendency in parts of the Lento is perhaps the most forward-looking aspect of this Quartet which pre-empts the more intense phase of chromatic writing that Bartók was to pursue next, its mysterious quality defined by creatively scored dissonances marked *con sord.* Despite its opening atonal allusions there are nevertheless distinct motivic and thematic connections with the first movement, such as the contour of the melodic motif after figure 1 (compare Ex. 10.4a with 10.3a). Less obvious is the three-note bass line motif, C♯–F–B, seven bars later (Ex. 10.4b), which Lendvai identifies both as a leitmotiv and as a variant of the upbeat semiquaver motif from the first movement. It is also interesting to note that this motif now harmonizes each of the ascending notes A–B–C from the recapitulation of 'Theme 3' in the first movement (compare with Ex. 10.3b). Harmonic, as well as motivic, coherence guarantees the unity of the piece, with the final chord of the phrase in Example 10.4b anticipating the Quartet's final resolution on to the A tonality which was the dominating pitch region of the first movement.

String Quartet No. 3

Prima parte – Seconda parte – Recapitulazione della prima parte – Coda

By 1920 Bartók was already conscious that '[t]he music of our time strives decidedly toward atonality', yet he also recognized that 'the time to establish a system in our atonal music is not at all here as yet'.[11] Within the context of the Third Quartet (1927), it is enlightening to identify some of Bartók's short-term solutions to 'The Problem of the New Music'.

The single-movement form (in four sections) both advances and condenses Bartók's compositional techniques: a heightened intensity of expression is achieved by the melodic, harmonic and rhythmic contrasts being more tightly compacted than in any other of his works. In spite of the headings, appropriate for identifying the thematic content of different sections, there is little in the way of pitch centricity which would seem to support a sonata structure. Instead, one or more of a chromatic group (C♯–D–D♯–E) functions as a tonal reference point throughout, the C♯ extending this group further where it pairs with its lower neighbour note, C. Such semitonal juxtapositions now have a more prolonged functional purpose than in the Second Quartet.

A possible influence on Bartók's harmonic development at this time could have been his meeting with the American composer Henry Cowell in 1923. Although Bartók had already been piling up notes into dissonant chord formations, their use was intensified after he had encountered Cowell's harmonic tone clusters.[12] In any case, the significance of overlapping thirds which dominate the motivic material of the Third Quartet may be understood to emerge from the C♯–E bounding the opening cluster chord (Ex. 10.5).

In addition to sustained or repeated notes identifying longer-term pitch centres, the melody itself is used to generate harmony in the short term. For example, while the opening bars (Ex. 10.5) comprise the main motivic material for the entire work – not only is motif b itself a variant of motif a, but so too is the whole of the first phrase – their melodic outline

Example 10.5 String Quartet No. 3, I, bars 1–6

Example 10.6 String Quartet No. 3, I,
summary of harmonic structure, bars 2–6

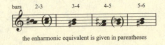

the enharmonic equivalent is given in parentheses

provides the underlying harmonic contour (summarized in Ex. 10.6). As
in the Second Quartet, Bartók's technique of developing variation shows
how themes are the outcome of the combination and recombination of
motifs – a technique that is continued throughout the piece so that the
Recapitulazione della prima parte is not a literal recapitulation but is based
upon condensed redefinitions of earlier motivic and thematic material.

Shifting away from the C/C♯ tonality of the *Prima parte*, the faster
Seconda parte is orientated around two other notes from the opening
cluster chord – D/E♭. An extended modal variation of motif b from the
Prima parte (played pizzicato) now adopts an introductory role. The subsequent E♭ minor theme (figure 3 in the score) then takes up the whole-
tone/minor third emphasis from the *Prima parte*. The C/C♯ antithesis is
soon taken over by the energetic Coda – itself a transformed recapitulation
of the *Seconda parte* – to resolve finally on C♯.

Within a predominantly chromatic background, diatonic references
are reserved for specific places; for instance, tonal harmonies are often
employed at cadence points in the *Prima parte* (such as the crotchet chords
built on fifths two bars before figure 4). Conversely, in the context of the
diatonic theme of the *Seconda parte*, it is more often the cluster chords that
provide cadential definition (for example, on approach to figure 23). What
these and other cadence points have in common is the unison and
repeated rhythmic articulation that defines their function, usually reinforced by specific performance directions, such as *col legno*.

Since pitch formations themselves do not necessarily distinguish
between melody and harmony, it follows that rhythm and texture take on
greater importance as a means of structural definition. Throughout the

Quartet, changes in rhythmic articulation are responsible for emphasizing changes in texture. In the *Seconda parte* different kinds of articulation identify relatively large sections of the music, particularly towards the climax. Compare, for example, the largely detached articulation of the fugato section (figure 31) with the wholly legato passage of rising/falling chromatic scales at figure 40. Even though there was a single instance of a string glissando in the 1903–04 Piano Quintet, the use of accompanying glissandi to blur pitch definition – from figure 41, and later, in the Coda (figure 10) – can be interpreted as a temporary solution to Bartók's 1920 prediction (in his essay 'The Problem of the New Music') that 'a further splitting of the semitone (perhaps infinitely?) will ultimately come'.[13]

String Quartet No. 4

Allegro – Prestissimo, con sordino – Non troppo lento – Allegretto pizzicato – Allegro molto

Even though the Fourth Quartet (1928) was written only a year after the Third, it immediately reveals differences of both form and content. Uncharacteristically, Bartók provided his own structural outline of the piece:

> the slow movement is the kernel of the work; the other movements are, as it were, arranged in layers around it. Movement IV. is a free variation of II., and I. and V. have the same thematic material; that is, around the kernel (Movement III.), metaphorically speaking, I. and V. are the outer, II. and IV. are the inner layers.[14]

This arch form was likewise to be the basis of the Fifth Quartet, and Bartók was also to use it for individual movements, such as the third movement of *Music for Strings, Percussion and Celesta*.

Whereas in the Third Quartet the thematic material is developmentally fragmented from the very start, the Fourth Quartet presents an identifiable motif as early as the cadential conclusion to the opening phrase in bar 7 (Ex. 10.7). This motif is the outcome of the vertical interaction of melodic lines which open the piece – a different relationship between melody and harmony than that observed at the beginning of the Third Quartet. Here harmonic orientation depends upon the outcome of the horizontal lines in the polyphonic texture, as explained by Halsey Stevens: 'the harmonic idiom of the Fourth Quartet can hardly be called harmonic at all. The coincidence of sounds at any point is so completely dependent upon the horizontal motion of the voices that it seems illogical to analyze them vertically'.[15]

Example 10.7   String Quartet No. 4, I, bar 7

Example 10.8   String Quartet No. 4
(a) I, bar 16

(b) V, bars 16–17

Although it undergoes various transformations, this principal motif – now the underlying feature of the piece – retains its articulation throughout, returning in its original form, and with its characteristic half-tenuto/legato identity, in the very last bar of the piece. The distinctive character of each movement is achieved through Bartók's extended range of developmental procedures. For example, changes in rhythm, metre, articulation, dynamics and tempo are all used to vary the character of the otherwise similar themes of the first and last movements (Ex. 10.8). The second movement is likewise based on the principal motif of the first by extending the rising/falling chromatic line in a new *prestissimo* tempo to create a joyful scherzo played *pianissimo* (see Ex. 10.9a). Intervallic compression and expansion are also to be found among Bartók's repertoire of transformational techniques, and are responsible for changing the emphasis of chromaticism to diatonicism and vice versa: the transitional theme from the first movement (Ex. 10.8a) is already a diatonic expansion of the chromatic motif in Example 10.7. Similarly, the thematic material of the lively fourth movement (Ex. 10.9b) is an expanded diatonic version of that of the second (Ex. 10.9a).

Further exploitation of instrumental techniques increases Bartók's rich palette of timbral qualities for stringed instruments. The middle section of the scherzo-like Prestissimo already develops the glissando to an even greater extreme than in the Third Quartet, while the first instance of the percussive 'snap' pizzicato for which Bartók is widely known (whereby the string is plucked between two fingers to rebound on the fingerboard)

Example 10.9   String Quartet No. 4
(a) II, chromatic melody, bars 1–4

(b) IV, diatonic melody, bars 6–9

occurs in the penultimate Allegretto pizzicato. In the central Non troppo lento the unusual changes from non-vibrato to vibrato take on a unique form-defining role, demarcating each section.[16] László Somfai comments on this technique as 'a stylized and sublime version of the *dűvő* accompaniment in instrumental folk music'.[17]

In the Fourth Quartet, Bartók's solution to the problem of the new music is different from the Third: his inspiration is derived specifically from folk music, even though he avoids direct quotations. One of his recommendations to composers was 'not [to] make use of a real peasant melody' but to 'invent [an] imitation' of it: for the most part it was less important for Bartók to copy an exact folk melody than to let the music be 'pervaded by the atmosphere of peasant music'.[18] For instance, an immediately striking feature of the cello's rhapsodic *parlando rubato* melody in the third movement is the downbeat semiquaver/dotted-quaver rhythm intrinsic to Hungarian prosody: the strong-beat start to the phrase is indigenous to 'old'-style Hungarian melodies. This type of melody, whose 'long notes are encircled by shorter ornamental notes', is identified by Judit Frigyesi as 'a lament or slow *verbunkos* belonging to the Hungarian tradition'.[19] Yet the construction of the melody throughout the movement also fits Bartók's description of the Romanian *hora lungă*: 'a single melody in numerous variants. Its features are strong, instrumental character, very ornamented, and indeterminate content structure'.[20]

bars		
6–13	A^1B^1	
14–21	A^2B^2	exposition
22–33	A^3B^3	
34–54	$A^4B^4A^5$	development
55–71	B^5A^6	recapitulation (coda)

Figure 10.1 Three-part structure of String Quartet No. 4, III, showing the construction of verses.

The folksong characteristics are moulded into a Classical art-song structure. Bartók's own brief analysis identifies three sections and a Coda,[21] although closer examination of the melody reveals a sentence structure based on verses. Figure 10.1 shows how these verses fit into Bartók's three-part structure.

The 'numerous variants' Bartók describes in Romanian folk music are here coloured by changes in register, timbre and specific techniques, such as the dramatic use of tremolo, and the use of harmonics in the representation of 'night' music (bars 47–49, itself a development of bars 35–40). The 'development' section contains the first examples of 'night' music in the quartet genre with the depiction of birdsong heard from the upbeat to bar 35. The ethereal quality of the birdsong section continues as the accompaniment changes from tremolo to *sul ponticello* in alternation with *ordinario*. The distribution of such instrumental techniques in the third movement contributes to its arch form as well as to the overall shape of the work.

String Quartet No. 5

Allegro – Adagio molto – Scherzo – Andante – Finale: Allegro vivace
Following the composition of the Third and Fourth Quartets, Bartók's 1931 essay 'On the Significance of Folk Music'[22] concludes that it is not possible to reconcile folk music with either atonal, or with twelve-tone music. He was evidently aware of concurrent developments in atonal music, just as he was aware of those who criticized modern music based on folk ingredients as being a simplistic compromise. Yet his strong humanistic commitment to saving genuine peasant music and transforming it into a 'higher' art form remained with him to the end of his life. He was not prepared to sacrifice his own aesthetic principles for the sake of appeasing critical opinion by writing music that would follow broader European trends. Neither, however, did he fall back on neoclassical principles in order to accommodate his predominantly tonal language.[23]

Bartók gives a plan of the Fifth Quartet (1934) showing that it follows

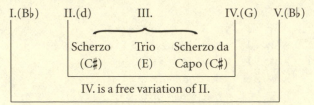

I. and V. have common features concerning tonality.

Figure 10.2 String Quartet No. 5: Plan of tonalities and structure of the work.[24]

an arch-form structure similar to that of the Fourth (see Fig. 10.2). However, the character of the respective movements is now reversed, with the fastest movements framing the slower ones, which in turn frame the quick central movement again based on folk music. This time Bartók depicts dance music from Bulgaria with its characteristically asymmetrical rhythms (earlier heard as the basis of a background ostinato in the fifth movement of the Fourth Quartet). Rather than using accents to define the rhythm, the grouping of quaver beats is shown by the $4 + 2 + 3$ metre of the Scherzo, changing to $3 + 2 + 2 + 3$ in the Trio.

Although the impact of its rhythmic momentum is perhaps the most striking feature of the work as a whole, the Fifth Quartet immediately identifies the tonal centre of its opening and closing movements as an unambiguous B♭, while the remaining movements complete the diminished triad indicated in the composer's plan of tonalities. It is in this Quartet that Bartók begins to distinguish more clearly between chromatic and diatonic regions – a duality that is further dramatized in his subsequent string music – although it is the work's chromaticism that remains uppermost here. As in the Second Quartet, he uses the tritone (B♭–E) to replace the traditional tonic–dominant relationship, heard for example at the beginning of the development section in the first movement (bar 59). There is one tonal reference that intentionally sounds out of place; that is in the Finale (bars 699–720) where Bartók includes the parody of a banal tune, all the more memorable for the clashing dissonances of the melody in B♭ major against an accompaniment in A major (from bar 711).

Different melodic contexts throughout the piece are characterized by ostinati, repeated-note rhythms, and punctuating cluster chords, all familiar from previous Quartets, while short melodic fragments from the exposition of the sonata form Allegro (Ex. 10.10) recur as extended melodic variants in the recapitulation (Ex. 10.11). These melodic fragments function in a new guise in the slow movements, where Bartók evokes the sonorities of a more mystical atmosphere: the introductory trills of the Adagio molto, combined with motivic fragments, lead to chromatic gestures sounding against a diatonic background in conjunction with novel string

Example 10.10 String Quartet No. 5, melodic fragments from the exposition of the first movement

Example 10.11 String Quartet No. 5, I, recapitulation, bars 132–33 and 136–37

techniques (the slurred pizzicato of bar 26ff and the left-hand fingernail pizzicato of bars 32–33). The corresponding Andante initially features repeated notes (from the first movement), melodic fragments, glissandi and arpeggiated chords, all played pizzicato. The repeated-note idea is varied (from bar 7) by alternating the sonority of a stopped string with the same note on an open string on successive quavers. Although this technique can be traced back at least as far as the first movement of the Solo Cello Suite No. 6 (1717–23) by J. S. Bach, its unusual appearance in a string quartet is indicative of the numerous ways in which Bartók was exploring variations in timbral quality. The gradual move towards *arco* playing in the fourth movement is introduced by short trills (from bar 9) in dialogue with slurred pizzicato fragments. Subsequent integrative processes within the movement stem from Bartók's inexhaustible resources for the generation of new rhythmic, articulatory and textural variants.

The continual change of melodic emphasis indicated by slurs and accents reaches its most advanced stage yet in the Finale. Bartók's careful placing of slurs in his prescriptive notation is akin to those differences of articulation he was fastidiously detailing in his descriptive notation: during the 1930s he revised his folksong transcriptions from recordings and from his own earlier versions in order to represent even more precisely the instrumental and vocal nuances he heard in folk melodies – even if it entailed slowing the recording to half speed. The striking ways in which

Example 10.12 String Quartet No. 5, V, melodic statements
of the first violin thematic material

Bartók makes apparently similar melodic ideas turn out so differently in
different compositional contexts is similarly due to the way he articulates
them. Example 10.12 shows different melodic statements from the theme
of the Finale (closely related to the first movement – see Ex. 10.11) whose
subtle variations are not necessarily apparent until placed one above the
other.

String Quartet No. 6

(Mesto) Vivace – (Mesto) Marcia – (Mesto) Burletta – Mesto

That 1939 was a most depressing time for the composer is expressed most
overtly in the melancholy, even mournful, character of the opening Mesto
whose theme, uncharacteristically for Bartók, pervades the entire piece
and becomes the actual material of the finale. The well-defined thematic
opening lacks a clear tonality and is unique among the Quartets (having
been added at a relatively late stage in the compositional process[25]) in that
it serves to ensure the cyclic structure of the whole. Typical of Bartók's
variation technique, subsequent occurrences of the Mesto theme are given

Example 10.13 String Quartet No. 6

(a) Mesto introduction showing derivation of motifs in the Vivace and Marcia, bars 1–13

(b) Vivace first subject group, bars 24–25

different harmonizations and textures: the muted, tremolo accompaniment to the cello melody introducing the Marcia spans three octaves in unison, while the Mesto preceding the Burletta has a contrasting legato accompaniment harmonized in thirds before being extended polyphonically. This legato polyphonic texture later presides in the finale where additional colours – *sul tasto* (bars 72–74) and *sul ponticello* (bars 75 and 76) – vary the tremolo chords accompanying the penultimate statement of the Mesto at a *pianissimo* dynamic.

The idea of a motto repeated as the introduction to each movement establishes a continuity from which the organic integration of the work evolves. This is a different kind of integration from the previous Quartets because in the *Vivace* Bartók's repetition of motivic material and similar phrase lengths identifies the sections of a sonata structure quite clearly (see the development section at bar 158 and the recapitulation at bar 287). By comparison, the processes of fragmentation in the earlier Quartets reach such minute proportions and complex recombinations that formal definition is more effectively concealed. Regarding continuity, János Kárpáti observes that 'the material of individual movements is connected to various elements of the ritornello theme by motivic threads'.[26] For example, the link between the opening Mesto (Ex. 10.13a) and the Vivace (Ex. 10.13b) identifies the three-note motif from the Mesto as the basis of the first subject group. This thematic material is clearly based on the tonality of D (sometimes major, sometimes minor) in contrast with the C tonality of the second subject group (stated at bar 81). Both groups of motivic material are in a state of flux throughout the movement, which eventually settles on D major.

The persistently dotted rhythm of the highly contrasted Marcia is

Example 10.14

(a) String Quartet No. 2, II, bars 384–90

(b) String Quartet No. 6, II, bars 115–17

developed from a fragment of the fifth bar of the Mesto theme (Ex. 10.13a) in the character of a *tempo giusto*, while the contrasting rubato tempo of the passionate cello melody of the Trio is vigorously portrayed by accompanying agitated tremolos and fast strummed chords. Bartók's aggressive writing is taken a stage further in the Burletta by an articulation designed specifically to imitate the grotesque nature of the 'bear-dance', with different modes of attack (including playing at the heel of the bow) and rough quarter-tone slides (denoted by a downwards arrow). The occurrence of quarter-tones in *The Miraculous Mandarin* is another of Bartók's experiments in the 'splitting of the semitone', but here he had learnt to notate their direction as a result of his experience of transcribing folksongs. In the context of the Burletta the clash of quarter-tone glissandi emphasizes the comic aspect of the dance.

Another example of the sophisticated development of Bartók's descriptive folksong notation influencing the way in which he continued to refine the articulation of his melodic ideas can be seen by comparing a transitional passage from the second movement of the Second Quartet (Ex. 10.14a) with a similar passage in the second movement of the Sixth Quartet (Ex. 10.14b). These extracts show how articulation is expressive of structural sense: although both examples are slurred within rather than across the beat, it is evidently important that, for textural as well as motivic reasons, each part in the Sixth Quartet should be independently punctuated within each beat. If the composer had not intended slurs to indicate separations of any kind, he would have had no reason to be so meticulous about their placement. As is always the case with Bartók, it is the differences in articulation that give such vivid life to his textures.

Music for Strings, Percussion and Celesta

Andante tranquillo – Allegro – Adagio – Allegro molto

The commission received from Paul Sacher in 1936 gave Bartók the opportunity to explore an unusual combination of instruments (double string orchestra with celesta, harp, piano, xylophone, timpani and percussion) and to reconsider their traditional roles. The antiphonal use of two string orchestras justifies Bartók's symmetrical layout in which he divides the strings into two groups on each side of the central group of piano, celesta, harp and percussion. Placing the piano within the percussion team means that the work fits the orchestral rather than the concerto repertoire, although even in the First and Second Piano Concertos (1926 and 1931, respectively) and the Sonata for Two Pianos and Percussion (1937) the piano has a percussive as well as a soloistic role. This is just one example of the many overlaps between the styles of different genres in Bartók's music.

Like the Fourth Quartet, *Music for Strings, Percussion and Celesta* derives its dissonant harmony from the vertical coincidence of the pitches of individual lines. However, underlying the chromatic foreground of the opening fugue is a surprisingly tonal construction based on the cycle of fifths. The composer explained that:

> The second entry appears a fifth higher; the 4th again a fifth higher than the 2nd; the 6th, 8th, and so on, again a fifth higher than the preceding one. The 3rd, 5th, 7th, and so on, on the other hand, each enter a fifth lower. After the remotest key – *E flat* – has been reached (the climax of the movement) the following entries render the theme in contrary motion until the fundamental key – *A* – is again reached, after which a short coda follows.[27]

The superimposition of chromatic and diatonic elements in the first movement is just one example which shows Bartók extending tonality beyond the extreme dissonance of the Fourth Quartet while stopping short of total chromaticism. Another is the way in which he contrasts chromatic and diatonic elements across the time-span of the entire piece

Example 10.15 chromatic and diatonic melodies of similar contour

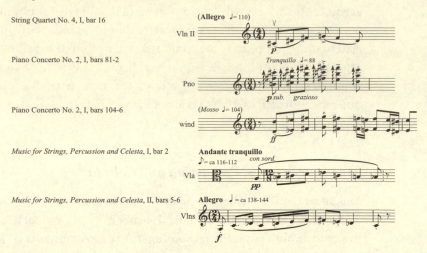

so that their alternation on a large scale outlines the harmonic orientation of each of the four movements. On a smaller scale the function of intervallic expansion and compression in changing the emphasis of chromaticism and diatonicism has already been identified in the Fourth Quartet. In the Harvard lectures of 1943 Bartók explained this apparently new device, which he called 'extension in range', by which the chromatic form of a melody could be turned into a diatonic one: 'such an extension will considerably change the character of the melody, sometimes to such a degree that its relation to the original, non-extended form will be scarcely recognizable'.[28] Examples of the altered character of the chromatic and diatonic melodies of the first and second movements of *Music for Strings, Percussion and Celesta* are shown in Example 10.15; above these are further examples of melodic contours from the Fourth String Quartet and Second Piano Concerto whose shapes can also be regarded as variants of each other. (The respective tempo indications of these phrases are given, although their different harmonic contexts obviously require reference to the scores.) Comparing the diatonic theme of the Allegro with the chromatic theme of the Andante tranquillo it will be seen that the metre has shifted, the phrase has been extended, and its character transformed by a new rhythmic definition highlighted by changes in dynamics, articulation and tempo.

In the chromatic context of the two slow movements the timbral qualities of instruments are fully exploited. Following the fugal entries of the opening Andante based on the cycle of fifths, Bartók marks the arrival point of the final melodic statement beginning on A (bar 77) by introducing contrasting 'night music' timbres. Supported by tremolo muted strings, shimmering arpeggiations in the celesta juxtapose a quasi-dominant cluster (E–E♭–D–C♯) prior to the final 'tonic' resolution.

The 'tonic' harmony of the Adagio third movement in rondo form is provided by a C–F♯ tritone, and again it is the timbral characteristics, combined with changes in rhythmic and melodic articulation, that define the sections of the arch form identified by Bartók.[29] The prosodic nature of the folk-like melody is strongly reminiscent of that in the third movement of the Fourth Quartet, as are its 'night music' qualities, although here they persist throughout the movement as an introduction and accompaniment to the melody rather than as a development of it. Extremes of register and timbre play an important part in depicting the different sounds of Nature within each section, while melodic connections are ensured by a return of thematic material from the Andante.

Bartók's varied use of instruments helps to project the opposing characters of successive movements. From its first entrance in the second movement it is the piano that immediately adopts a percussive, quasi-soloistic role before engaging in a melodic dialogue with the strings. The strings, harp and timpani also have dual roles and it is the way these percussive/melodic elements are integrated and varied that makes for such striking contrasts. For example, during the development section of the Allegro Bartók gives all the strings a strong rhythmic identity, using punctuating unison chords to define a forceful cadence in bars 177–82. Following a brief canon between the two orchestras he then proceeds to divide their roles so that one has more of a rhythmic function while the other has a melodic one (bars 199–220). Despite the different structures of the Allegro movements – the sonata form of the second and the rondo-like structure of the fourth – Bartók makes full use of changes in sonority to mark each section, such as the distinctive *staccatissimo* piano combined with pizzicato strings at bar 28 in the fourth movement (compare a similar sonority in the second movement at bar 200).

The A major tonality of the Allegro molto is an unexpected yet powerful conclusion to a piece whose rhythmic vitality is occasionally reminiscent of Stravinsky. The sharpened fourth degree of the scale relates to the tritonal harmony of the preceding Adagio and contributes to the exuberant character of the movement. Following the model of a conventional finale the Allegro molto restates material from previous movements: the chromatic theme of the first (bar 203), followed by the 'night music' elements of the third (bar 232), are now incorporated into a diatonic background where the new slower tempi help to reinstate their original characters.

Divertimento

Allegro non troppo – Molto adagio – Allegro assai

The term 'divertimento' has historically been used to evoke music of a light, entertaining character, either for solo instruments or groups of instruments. It is significant that at this point in his career (1939) Bartók turned to such an early genre as the Baroque *concerto grosso*, characterized by alternating *concertante* and *ripieno* sections. It could be argued that his intention was to develop the divertimento in a way comparable to the string quartet, yet the adoption of a loosely tonal idiom within a Baroque structure suggests a marked attempt to remain conventional, even to be consciously neoclassical.

Bartók's conventional approach does not, however, recall early works such as the First String Quartet: the pulsating rhythmic accompaniment to the theme of the first movement of the Divertimento reveals a modal diatonicism that is as different from the chromatic lyricism of the First Quartet as it is from the intense chromaticism of the Third and Fourth. Nor is the harmonic language of the Divertimento even remotely comparable with that of the Sixth Quartet written immediately after it. Instead, it shares more of the characteristics of *Music for Strings, Percussion and Celesta*, especially with its movement-to-movement alternations from the diatonic to the chromatic and back again. The Divertimento's relative tonal simplicity is closely linked to the diatonic second and fourth movements of *Music for Strings, Percussion and Celesta*, the tonalities of each movement – F–C♯–F – being made even more explicit due to their underlying pedal notes (as in the finale of *Music for Strings, Percussion and Celesta*).

The Divertimento's first movement incorporates markedly Classical features in the style of its flowing melody and accompaniment based on unison repeated-note rhythms. However repetitive the ostinato feels, internal changes supplied by accents and changing time signatures give an extra dimension to the harmonically static accompaniment. The melody of the second subject (from bar 25) is also Classical in shape and structure, with a Viennese lilt characterized by changes in time signature and tempo, and accompanied by light pizzicato arpeggios.

Compared with the gradual development of thematic material noted throughout the first five String Quartets, the announcement of an entire theme at the outset of a piece, as in the Sixth String Quartet, is exceptional. Similarly, in the first movement of the Divertimento Bartók reverses his established process of arriving at a theme through motivic transformations: he here begins with a theme which he later fragments.

Example 10.16
(a) Divertimento, I, bars 40–42

(b) Divertimento, I, bars 125–27

The alternation of repeated-note rhythmic fragments with melodic interludes enhances the variety in texture already suggested by the alternating solo/tutti passages of the *concerto grosso*. Extremes of dynamic and register, combined with the brevity of successive dynamic and rhythmic changes, reinforce the dramatic impact of these textural changes. The first such dramatic interjection is at bar 40 (see Ex. 10.16a), by implication repeated just before the recapitulation at bar 132 (Ex. 10.16b).

The more characteristically chromatic side of Bartók, at first reserved for the development section of the first movement, dominates the entire Molto adagio second movement. The furtive character of this *adagio* is portrayed by slow, *pianissimo* quavers moving by semitone, accompanying a chromatic melody of ascending and descending tones and semitones. In many respects this movement acts as a summation of Bartók's various structural techniques, falling into small sections which rework familiar elements of both folk music (*verbunkos* rhythms) and 'night music' (such as grace notes leading to trills). Even here, without the added effects of different instrumental sonorities, timbre, rhythm and texture create dramatic and colourful contrasts similar to those in *Music for Strings, Percussion and Celesta.*

The vigorously downbeat tread of the Allegro assai completes the fast–slow–fast symmetry of the piece. Its typically folk character is texturally enhanced by trills, by a brief fugato (from bar 192) and by a bird-like violin cadenza (bar 256). As in the rest of the piece, there is much imitation within the various sections, especially between *concertante* and *ripieno*, as well as more evidence of unison and homophonic writing than anywhere else in Bartók's output. The rhythmic energy penultimately ebbs, to arrive at a briefly satirical pizzicato Grazioso, cut off by a wild Vivacissimo ending.

The Divertimento suggests that Bartók may have been intent on reviving aspects of a Classical idiom that would provide him with a new source of inspiration for the future. The Sixth Quartet is also a more traditional form than the previous five, so it is perhaps surprising that he did not continue the diatonic emphasis begun in the Divertimento. As it is, any similarity between the two pieces lies in their thematic beginnings alone. A stronger connection can, however, be made between the chromatic outlines of the Mesto theme in the Quartet and in *Music for Strings, Percussion and Celesta.* More notable still is the difference in character between the two string orchestral pieces and the Sixth Quartet, differences which seem to reflect Bartók's own circumstances, especially in the subjectively persistent Mesto motto which pervades the whole piece. This turns the Quartet into a statement of profound disquiet – both his personal sorrow following the death of his mother, and the anguish of preparing to leave Hungary for good.

PART III

Reception

11 Hungarian nationalism and the reception of Bartók's music, 1904–1940

DAVID E. SCHNEIDER

Mixed reception: an introduction

With the premiere of his ambitious symphonic poem *Kossuth* (1903) in Budapest on 13 January 1904, twenty-two-year-old Béla Bartók seemed to have instantly achieved the status of a national icon. For weeks to come critics in no less than seventeen publications would echo the applause that had brought Bartók to the stage some dozen times.

Yet such unbridled enthusiasm hardly typified Bartók's reception in Hungary during his lifetime. For most of his career he was as frequently castigated by Hungarians as embraced. Even more painfully, Hungary's most prestigious musical organizations, the Opera and the Philharmonic Society, often simply ignored him. As was the case with a number of composers of his generation, a troubled relationship with the public was almost guaranteed by Bartók's allegiance to the difficult aesthetics of modernism. In Hungary, however, where musical style was often explicitly bound to the expression of *magyarság* (Hungarianness), the progressive (hence implicitly cosmopolitan) political stance Bartók's music was taken to represent erected further barriers to acceptance. Accordingly, reactions to Bartók's music in Hungary during his lifetime were heavily laced with social criticism, while his reception in Western Europe reflected more generic concerns about modern music. Bartók's Hungarian reception serves to remind us that not only his music, but modernist art in general – despite its appeals to abstraction and universality – carried culturally specific social messages that depended for their decoding on the contexts in which they were received.

1904: patriot

Bartók's success with *Kossuth* is easy to understand given the strongly nationalistic and anti-Austrian mood of turn-of-the-century Budapest. Replete with a caricature of the Austrian national anthem 'Gott erhalte' to represent the invasion of the Austrian army, Bartók's depiction of the suppressed Hungarian War of Independence (1848–49) and its leader Lajos Kossuth served as a battle cry for the Hungarian audience. On that evening, applauding Bartók's musical re-enactment of the events of 1848–49 was tantamount to joining a rally for Hungarian independence from Habsburg rule.

The Hungarian reception of *Kossuth* was a glorious windfall; Bartók's mother was so overcome by the raves in the press that in her euphoria she could barely teach her classes.[1] But this success would burden Bartók with the expectation that he continue as a 'national' composer. With the benefit of hindsight one can discern tendencies in the Hungarian reaction to *Kossuth* that would become a pattern: listeners judged the artistic value of Bartók's music largely by its perceived political stance; they recognized his work only after it had been accepted abroad; and they resisted the complexity of his musical style.

Most Hungarian critics valued *Kossuth* for its relationship with an established nationalist tradition. When the critic of *Zenevilág* [Music-World] wrote that 'the *Kossuth* Symphony is the greatest cultural achievement in the history of Hungarian music since *Bánk Bán*',[2] he recognized Bartók as the inheritor of the nationalist tradition of Ferenc Erkel (1810–93), the most important composer to have voiced Hungarian national sentiments in opera. In *Bánk Bán* (first performance 1861) Erkel had resorted to the familiar operatic ploy of expressing outrage over a contemporary political condition – the mid-nineteenth-century oppression of Hungary by Austria – through the foil of a similar injustice several centuries earlier. In *Kossuth* Bartók employed an analogous strategy to align himself with the latest clamour for independence.

Kossuth and *Bánk Bán* carried the same revolutionary message, which explains why the first performance of Erkel's work was delayed by the censor, and why several Austrians occupying key positions in the Philharmonic had boycotted rehearsals for *Kossuth* and nearly sabotaged its premiere. But, for all the incendiary bluster, by focusing on the Hungarian Independence Movement in his first publicly performed orchestral work, Bartók had adopted a tried and true formula for success in Hungary.

Moreover, in *Kossuth* Bartók continued his country's musical tradition of combining stock figures from Hungarian-style fiddling or *verbunkos* within a West European harmonic idiom – in this case an idiom identified with the tone poems of Richard Strauss. On the one hand, Strauss, whom Hungarian critics labelled 'ultramodern'[3] and 'the modernest of the moderns',[4] was a controversial choice for Bartók because Budapest remained a conservative bastion of Brahmsian aesthetics. On the other hand, Bartók continued the genre of the symphonic poem from Liszt, while following Brahms or any other composer so closely associated with

Vienna might have compromised his anti-Austrian stance. Nor would anything less daring have served to distinguish the young composer from Ernő Dohnányi (1877–1960) whose Brahmsian D minor Symphony had caused a sensation at its Budapest premiere the previous year.[5]

Despite Bartók's clear indebtedness to Strauss, the fact that in Hungary the symphonic poem was considered less characteristically Germanic than the symphony allowed the critic of the *Budapesti Hírlap* [Budapest News] to read national expression into Bartók's use of form:

> [I]n Bartók there is something deliberate and wilful that springs from the depths of artistic conviction. Dohnányi proceeds in the footsteps and forms of the German masters Beethoven and Brahms, in these he produces perhaps a more refined and mature art, but [Bartók] creates form according to Hungarian feeling: wild, luxuriant, rhapsodic, not so sober and symmetrical that it requires the rules of the German symphony.[6]

More important than form in *Kossuth* was Bartók's reliance on widely recognized *verbunkos* figures: front-accented *short*–long rhythms, dotted figures and quick ornaments at ends of beats. These expressions of *magyarság* as well as Bartók's parody of Austria prompted even critics who bemoaned Strauss's modern influence to overlook it in the name of patriotism. While describing *Kossuth* as 'garish cacophony and an endless series of musical atrocities', the critic of *Magyarország* [Hungary] nevertheless concluded his review with a show of forgiveness:

> Patriotic feeling and a strong affection for one's own race radiates from this work and that is why Béla Bartók's patriotic artistic attempt pleases us in spite of all its extravagance and exaggeration. We are living in eventful times, we must therefore doubly respect the kind of noble endeavour that has its roots in the soil of patriotism.[7]

The English reaction to the *Kossuth* premiere in Manchester some five weeks later was another story. English critics also objected to the Straussian dissonances, but for them Bartók's patriotism was no saving grace. In Budapest, Bartók's distortion of 'Gott erhalte' had been a particular hit, but in Manchester it was dismissed as cheap and 'laughable'. The work as a whole, English critics agreed, deserved its tepid reception.[8] Yet ironically enough, had it not been for Hans Richter's offer to conduct *Kossuth* in England, the Budapest Philharmonic, a conservative organization with a number of Austrian administrators, might not have given it a hearing.[9] This would not be the last time that a Hungarian audience would be able to hear a work of Bartók's only because it had been championed by someone abroad.

1905–1916: traitor

The failure of *Two Pictures* (1910) at its premiere in Budapest on 25 February 1913 demonstrated how little patience Hungarian audiences had for Bartók when he assumed a more cosmopolitan stance. Reviewing the concert for the *Budapesti Hírlap*, Emil Haraszti (1885–1958) described the composer's fall from grace:

> It's been about ten years since the Philharmonic presented Béla Bartók's *Kossuth* Symphony. At that time the audience and critics eagerly expected the patriotically dressed young man from Debrecen [*sic*] to become a great Hungarian musician. A few of his later works – for example his Hungarian Suite [Suite No. 1, Op. 3, 1905] – seemed to fulfil this expectation. But then all at once Bartók became the slave of a foreign spirit. His strong, characteristic Hungarian individuality was all but extinguished by the absorbing foreign influence.[10]

The foreign influence to which Haraszti referred was twofold, encompassing Bartók's interest both in modern composers and in the folk music of non-Magyars. According to Haraszti the first movement of *Two Pictures* was a 'pallid copy of Debussy', while the second had 'noisy dynamics that recall Strauss'.[11] Worse than Bartók's imitations of West European composers was his interest in the folk music of neighbouring peoples. How could it be, Haraszti wondered in print, that Bartók, a professor at the Royal National Hungarian Academy of Music, had absolutely no interest in Hungarian music? 'He has become the apostle of Czech, Romanian, Slovak and God knows what kind of music, only Hungarian music has been left high and dry'.[12] However inaccurate Haraszti's review, it seems to have reflected the opinion of much of the audience. Despite a claque of cheering admirers, a torrent of boos and hisses prevented Bartók from taking a bow.[13]

Haraszti's accusation that Bartók lacked interest in Hungarian music was false, but even if Bartók had restricted his inspiration exclusively to Hungarian folk music it is doubtful whether his *Two Pictures* would have received significantly more sympathy at home. While sheet-music publications of *magyar nóták* [folksy Hungarian popular songs] remained the staples of bourgeois Hungarian parlours, a run of only 500 copies of Bartók and Kodály's easy-to-play Hungarian Folksongs for voice and piano (1906) took thirty years to sell out.

This general lack of enthusiasm for Hungarian peasant music in Hungary was due in part to the social implications of Bartók's and Kodály's assertion that the music of Hungarian peasants differed fundamentally from that of urban 'gypsy' bands. By declaring that peasant music rather than the well-worn clichés of 'gypsy' music should serve as the basis for a new national style, Bartók touched a raw political nerve. Since the early nineteenth century the Hungarian nobility and gentry had claimed themselves to be the sole proprietors of the Hungarian national spirit: their music consisted of *magyar nóták* and dance music in the *verbunkos* style frequently played by gypsies. To suggest that peasants, whom the upper classes did not even consider part of the nation, could hold the key to an authentic Hungarian identity in music was for many at least as unsettling for its social as for its artistic implications.[14]

Whereas the nationalist associations of the 'gypsy'-style inflections in *Kossuth*, and other works written before 1907, had made Bartók's Straussian style acceptable in Hungary, the incorporation of peasant music in *Two Pictures* and his other works of the period did little to make his music palatable. In fact, Bartók's preference for modal or pentatonically based peasant music over 'gypsy music' with its comforting tonal harmonies and familiar rhythmic clichés was often seen as a threat to the traditional concept of the Hungarian nation.

1917–1919: a break in the clouds

On 12 May 1917 Bartók was relieved from months of worry and nearly a decade of disappointing reception of his music by the unexpected success that greeted the Hungarian Opera's premiere of his ballet *The Wooden Prince* (1914–17). According to one report, no work had been received with so much enthusiasm at the Opera since its first staging of *Madama Butterfly*.[15] Although it might seem logical to conclude that this performance signalled a significant policy change at the Opera, which had refused to stage *Duke Bluebeard's Castle* (1911), in fact it only signalled the beginning of two short seasons of grudging support for Bartók. Two factors allowed the performance to succeed: the only non-Hungarian member of the Opera's conducting staff, the Italian Egisto Tango, tirelessly supported the production by arranging for an unprecedented thirty rehearsals and refusing to be intimidated by resentful members of the orchestra; and Béla Balázs, author of the scenario, resourcefully took over the direction when the Opera's stage director left the production in protest. Thus, for the first time since *Kossuth*, Bartók's orchestral music was heard in a careful and sympathetic rendition. That under the proper conditions Bartók could gain a truly popular success in Hungary suggests the extent to which the country's most prestigious, state-funded musical organizations had been tacitly sabotaging the reception of his music.

Among the reviews of *The Wooden Prince* one could still find the accusation that in his modernity Bartók had completely abandoned any trace of *magyarság*, but this criticism was rare.[16] Perhaps inspired by the overwhelming audience reaction, even Izor Béldi, notorious for having called for aspirin after the premiere of the Suite No. 2, Op. 4 (1905–07), was moved to proclaim that 'Bartók will play a major role in Hungarian music drama with great and enduring works'.[17] More significant than Béldi's parroting of public opinion was one of Antal Molnár's (1890–1983) earliest writings on Bartók. In this thoughtful review, Molnár made a case for Bartók as a symbol of a progressive ideal to be imitated by Hungarian society.[18] This would become the leading credo of the liberal Hungarian press for years to come – from 1919 to 1935 this thought would be repeated consistently, more often than either the Philharmonic or the Opera would perform Bartók's music.

1920s: a radical vision for the nation

As a member of the alliance that had been defeated in the First World War, Hungary at once gained its independence from Austria and, at the peace treaty signed at Trianon in 1920, lost two-thirds of its territory. The thrust of Hungarian nationalism changed from separatism to irredentism, the goal of which was to regain Transylvania and the part of Slovakia that had belonged to Hungary before the war. In post-Trianon Hungary, Bartók shone as a beacon of internationalism for his openness to modern West European influences and to the folk music of all the peoples of the former Hungary. We know of the symbolic importance of Bartók's work primarily from the music criticism of Aladár Tóth (1898–1968), Antal Molnár and Sándor Jemnitz (1890–1963), three of the most respected writers on music in Hungary between the world wars. For them and for a small but significant circle of artists and intellectuals, Bartók's music came to represent an enlightened, multi-ethnic vision of a modern nation capable of holding its own among the great European cultures and even surpassing them through a synthesis of Eastern peasant culture and Western sophistication. These idealistic critics saw Bartók's music as a means of uplifting Hungarian society by teaching it about itself; and, by advocating the notion of Bartók's music as an embodiment of an idealized Hungarian culture, they hoped to help bring that culture into being.

A regular feature of Tóth's annual commentaries on the Budapest concert season for the progressive journal *Nyugat* [West] were his laments over 'popular taste' and his chastisement of the country's premiere musical organizations for their neglect of Bartók. As he put it in spring

1923: 'It is totally unacceptable that the Philharmonic Society indifferently turns its back on the greatest Hungarian composer: on Béla Bartók ... We demand that [the Philharmonic] not serve 'popular taste' in its work, but educate and direct its public'.[19] The Philharmonic Society and the Opera, the most frequent objects of Tóth's attacks, were upper-crust institutions. Accusing them of betraying their patriotic mission to 'educate and direct the public' by pandering to common taste, Tóth implicitly condemned the members of middle- and upper-class society who saw music as entertainment rather than as moral edification. More was at stake for Tóth, who believed that an understanding of Bartók's music would lead the audience out of what he saw as a superficial appreciation of art and guide them to a more modern understanding of *magyarság*.

Although the country's musical establishments were notoriously conservative, the neglect of Bartók in Hungary throughout much of the 1920s was not solely due to his status as a modernist composer. Already in the 1910s there had been years in which his orchestral music had been heard less frequently in Budapest than Stravinsky's, and this was sometimes true in the twenties as well. Thus when János Hammerschlag described *The Wooden Prince* in 1917, he compared it to the music of Stravinsky, with which he seems to have expected his Budapest audience to be familiar.[20] In 1926 the Budapest Philharmonic acknowledged Stravinsky's celebrity throughout Europe by mounting an entire evening of his works, something no Hungarian orchestra had yet done for Bartók. The tendency for the Opera and Philharmonic to promote foreign contemporaries over Bartók (the Philharmonic especially favoured Respighi in the twenties) demonstrated Hungary's sense of cultural inferiority, the assumption that imported goods, especially from the West, were superior to domestic products. But it also reflected the fact that these composers posed no particular political challenge in Hungary, while Bartók's music, for many, represented an uncomfortably novel conception of *magyarság*.

However new and uncomfortable it may have been, Bartók's *magyarság* did, nevertheless, allow Hungarian critics to hail him over Stravinsky. Reviewing the Hungarian premiere of Bartók's First Piano Concerto (1926), Tóth tied its barbarism to an expression of nationality, which also enabled a defence of Bartók against the threat of Stravinsky's 'neoclassical' style: 'Stravinsky's barbarism was merely a backdrop that he abandoned when he approached the refined concentration of French neoclassicism. The more "classical" Bartók is, however, the more ... complicated, the more "barbaric", all the more "Asia"'.[21] Here, scare quotes around the words barbaric and Asia help signal that Tóth was not merely invoking *The Rite of Spring*. For Hungarians the words 'barbaric' and 'Asia' would have conjured up images of the ancient Magyar tribes of the central Asian steppe, suggesting that Bartók's brutally percussive style was inherently Hungarian. When Antal Molnár argued that the inherent humanity of folk music 'raise[d] Bartók's Concerto above the phenomenon of fashionable "neoclassicism"',[22] he was arguing, like Tóth, that Bartók's modernism was deeply rooted in his native soil.

While Bartók's apologists in Budapest praised the First Piano Concerto for what they considered its uniquely Hungarian synthesis of the ancient and the modern, foreign critics found the same features unconvincing. Although Bartók quoted no folk music in the work, Frankfurt reviewer Theodor W. Adorno dismissed the First Concerto as a throwback to 'naive folklorism' in which 'national themes are adorned with dissonances'.[23] A Dutch critic blamed its lukewarm reception in Rotterdam on what he regarded an unsuccessful combination of aesthetics:

> We cannot condemn the audience in its judgement . . . In his Piano Concerto [Bartók] made use of lessons from Stravinsky's *Rite of Spring* and even *Petrushka* but his mentality is different; his tools are not in agreement with his temperament, which is still Romantic. So there is a gulf between the mode of expression and the content; for this reason the piece is not convincing.[24]

Tóth's and Molnár's criticism notwithstanding, most of the Hungarian audience appears to have shared the negative opinion of the foreign critics. According to a report in the *Budapesti Hírlap*: 'The public at tonight's premiere [of Bartók's First Piano Concerto] was perplexed. They did not understand the piece, they scolded, belittled, mocked it . . . With few exceptions, even [Bartók's] supporters voiced only banal commonplaces'.[25]

The 1920s saw the emergence of Bartók as a major international force in contemporary music, with performances of his First Violin Sonata (1921) in France and England in 1921, and the Dance Suite (1923) at the ISCM concert in Prague in 1925 and throughout Germany during the 1925–26 season. In 1928 Philadelphia's Musical Fund Society awarded its first prize to the Third String Quartet (1927). Yet Bartók was increasingly frustrated by his treatment at home, typified by the Hungarian Opera's refusal to produce *The Miraculous Mandarin* (1918–19) or to revive his other dramatic works.

1930s: homecoming

By 6 May 1930 Bartók had grown so weary of his shabby reception in Hungary that he refused to give concerts in Budapest for nearly four years:[26]

> I do not, I cannot play my own works in Budapest ... Of course, neither is
> there any sense in my playing my own works abroad, but I do it regardless of
> how people behave towards us [me]. I have nothing to do with them. But in
> Budapest I expect something different from what I receive – and I am not
> able to endure this in any other way than by withdrawing completely.[27]

While Bartók maintained that he was received equally poorly in Budapest
and abroad, in the first half of the 1930s the Hungarian 'indifference' to his
achievements was so pointed as to border on official censorship. Even
Bartók's return to the Budapest concert stage in January 1934 marked only
a partial recovery from his disillusionment earlier in the decade for he continued to refuse to play his own recent compositions in public there until
May 1937.

A telling example of the gap between Bartók's high world renown (not
necessarily equated with popularity) and his relative neglect in Hungary in
the early 1930s was the occasion of his fiftieth birthday, 25 March 1931.
While the French government awarded Bartók the Legion of Honour, the
Hungarian government let the occasion pass. The Hungarian Opera,
however, did offer a greeting of sorts – two days after Bartók's birthday it
announced the cancellation of what was to have been the Hungarian premiere of *The Miraculous Mandarin*.[28] Appalled by the official neglect and
mistreatment Bartók had been suffering, Sándor Jemnitz published a long
tribute to the composer in the leftist paper *Népszava* [People's Word].
Jemnitz claimed that Bartók was ignored in Hungary for political reasons
– more specifically, because he refused to pander to public sentiment by
exploiting the power of 'pathetico-patriotic terminology' (read: 'gypsy'
music) to stir up irredentist nationalism.[29]

Oblivious to the political implications of Bartók's preference for
peasant music over Hungarian 'gypsy'-style music, foreign critics in the
1930s were often simply relieved that the folk elements in Bartók's music
sometimes made him more accessible than other modernists. An all-
Bartók concert on 29 February 1932 in Glasgow featuring a number of
folk-music transcriptions garnered three rave reviews all reporting an
enthusiastic public. The critic Montague Smith wrote that Bartók's use of
folk music made him 'less abstract than Schönberg [*sic*] and less dry and
cunning than Stravinsky; [and] more human than either one'.[30]

So, while Bartók could wryly observe that instead of being awarded
the Legion of Honour he would have preferred more performances of his
music in Paris, his relation to foreign musical institutions never hit the
low point it had reached in Hungary by the early thirties.[31] 'I unfortunately have no influence' at home, he grumbled to a German acquaintance in spring 1934: 'my relations with our Opera are very bad, with
Hubay [director of the Music Academy] utterly bad, with Dohnányi

[conductor of the Philharmonic] very chilly, with the government quite bad, and I am on the verge of having a quarrel with the Radio, though we have never been on particularly friendly terms'.[32]

Although it would take several years for Bartók to recover from the blows dealt his pride by Hungarian indifference, his position did begin to improve slowly a few months after he penned this unhappy letter. The first sign was the government's approval, dated 27 July 1934, of his petition to transfer from his position of professor of piano at the Music Academy to that of folk-music researcher at the Academy of Sciences. While his solitary work transcribing Hungarian folk music might at first seem to be a symbol of withdrawal, it was in fact a harbinger of other forms of government funding that soon followed. In January 1935 the Opera unveiled a new production of *The Wooden Prince,* in which the choreography was informed by Hungarian folk dance;[33] and on 16 May 1935 Bartók was elected to the Hungarian Academy of Sciences – the first musician ever admitted to that select body. The 1936–37 season saw a new production of *Bluebeard's Castle,* which, after a conspicuous absence of seventeen years, joined *The Wooden Prince* in a double-bill. Autumn 1936 also saw the belated but well-received Hungarian premiere of *Cantata profana* (1930), and on 10 December of that year, a Hungarian orchestra finally presented an all-Bartók programme in Pest. At this concert, Bartók ended his moratorium on playing his own works in Budapest with a performance of the Rhapsody for Piano and Orchestra Op. 1 (1904). By spring 1937 the sense that he was better appreciated even wooed Bartók back to performing his more recent compositions. Aladár Tóth, always quick to blame Hungarians for neglecting Bartók, was forced to admit: 'We have perhaps never felt the power of Bartók's music to be so redeeming, so liberating as this year, when our great composer's works have been performed by ever greater numbers of our singers and musicians'.[34]

Beyond the sheer increase in the number of performances, there was a change in the attitude of the Hungarian audience towards Bartók's music. Reviewing the all-Bartók orchestral programme, Tóth observed:

The biggest, epoch-making achievement of Thursday's Bartók concert is that Bartók's voice was understood by the portion of the Hungarian middle class whose politics, school, societal upbringing and 'social' taste had until now artificially kept it away from the truly life-providing geniuses of living *magyarság* – from Ady, Babits, Móricz, Kodály and most importantly . . . from Bartók . . . This programme did not only include Bartók's 'more easily understood' youthful works . . . but the *Two Pictures* and Bartók's 'most revolutionary', most difficult, dense masterwork, the *Cantata profana.* And lo! the first hearing of this masterwork immediately, deeply and completely captivated Hungarian ears and hearts that had been nurtured for so long only by gypsy music, [*magyar*] *nóták* and hit tunes from operettas . . .[35]

What had changed? For one thing, Hungarian nationalism had. Throughout the 1930s Hungarians were developing new expressions for their cultural identity in response to growing nationalism in Germany. Ironically for Bartók, a government initiative begun by fascist Prime Minister Gyula Gömbös in 1934 led to increased budgetary support of projects related to folk culture, ranging from the scientifically oriented research of Bartók and Kodály and a group of sociologists known as *falukutatók* [village researchers], to an organization of tourist-oriented 'folk ensembles' called the *Gyöngyösbokréta* [Pearly Bouquet]. While so-called gypsy music never lost its patriotic associations, peasant music was now officially allocated a place in the nationalist scheme. Although Bartók always distanced himself from right-wing politics, under these conditions, as both a well-known expert in folk music and the only widely recognized composer representing Hungary abroad, Bartók himself emerged as an emblem of *magyarság* for a larger segment of society at home.

Perhaps the most important by-product of Bartók's reconciliation with Hungary in the late 1930s was a slight softening and renewed 'magyarization' of his compositional style. The clearest example of this change is the Violin Concerto (1937–38), which Bartók wrote for his friend Zoltán Székely, a Hungarian violinist living in Holland. In this work, Bartók returns not only to *verbunkos* gestures, the mainstay of Hungarian Romanticism, but also to a more Romantic approach to tonality. Although Székely was unable to play the work in Hungary before the war, he did give six performances of it in Holland (1939–40). At the premiere Dutch critics familiar with such gritty works as the two Piano Concertos, Sonatas for Violin and Piano, and Fourth and Fifth String Quartets, made the Violin Concerto's surprising accessibility the subject of their reviews. While they consistently praised the work, they also wondered out loud whether Bartók's new style should be judged as progress or regression, strength or weakness.[36] Camouflaged in these reviews are the first hints of the charge of artistic compromise that would for a time dominate the discourse about Bartók after World War II.[37]

To those unaware of its Hungarian subtext, Bartók's rapprochement with the society he had struggled within and against could indeed sound like a retreat from the ideals that had both made his work difficult for most audiences to love and secured a place for him among the highest echelon of modernist composers. But inside Hungary the notion of compromise in connection with Bartók's life and work was unthinkable in the late 1930s.

Even Béla Bangha, a Jesuit priest who in 1937 accused Bartók and Kodály of corrupting the nation's youth with their dissonant folksong arrangements, never invoked the idea of artistic compromise.[38]

1940: farewell

Certainly the most potent symbol of Bartók's moral integrity was his decision to leave Hungary for the United States in 1940. Writing about Bartók's farewell concert to a standing-room-only crowd of the country's leading musicians and intellectuals at the Music Academy on 8 October 1940, Sándor Jemnitz, instead of commenting on either the quality of Bartók's playing or his compositions, addressed the question: 'what does it mean that a great master *lives among us . . .*'. He concludes: 'This is not the time for details, when with tearful eyes we bid farewell to the whole thing – to Béla Bartók living among us. Those who ardently applauded him took a stand next to these symbols: the crystalline purity of human and artistic character'.[39] Had Aladár Tóth not already fled to Sweden to protect his Jewish wife, pianist Annie Fischer, he might have expressed the symbolism of Bartók's last appearance in Hungary even more eloquently. But it is clear that while Jemnitz's review is an extreme case befitting an extreme circumstance, ever since *Kossuth* Bartók's reception in Hungary was governed as much by what he was seen to represent as it was by the sound of his music.

It is ironic that Bartók's late-found peace with Hungary, his spiritual homecoming as it were, should have come so soon before his physical departure. Grimmer still was the fact that his belated reconciliation was due in part to the same government policies that ultimately forced him to leave. In addition to all the horrors that came with being allied to Nazi Germany, the Hungarian government, whose recognition of folk culture had seemed a positive step only a few years before, had quickly learned to exploit it. By 1940, folk music had begun to be enlisted in the propaganda war that supported Hungarian irredentism and helped propel Hungary into World War II.[40] In the past, Bartók had faced adversity at home by withdrawing from the public arena; now his symbolic power had become too great to allow him the anonymity he would have needed to survive in a hostile environment.

Despite his many successes and failures throughout Europe, only in Hungary was Bartók's reception so deeply and consistently tied to social questions often considered beyond the scope of abstract artistic expression. It is a testimony to the strength of Hungary's need for symbols of *magyarság* that Bartók, who for much of his life aggressively challenged his country's self-image, should have become, in his countrymen's eyes, a reflection of it as well.

12 Bartók in America

MALCOLM GILLIES

Ever since his Academy graduation in 1903 Bartók had looked forward to visiting America. His piano teacher István Thomán had encouraged him to attend the Louisiana Purchase Exposition in St Louis in 1904, but this plan fell by the wayside as Bartók failed to develop the same international following as a pianist that his model, Dohnányi, had done.

It would be another quarter of a century before Bartók finally visited the United States. For ten weeks in the winter of 1927–28 he undertook a successful coast-to-coast tour, sometimes in association with such Hungarian colleagues as the violinists Joseph Szigeti and Jelly Arányi, and the conductor Fritz Reiner. He hoped to return soon as he liked the people and concert fees were comparatively high. Moreover, Hungarian-American friends persuaded him in 1928 to enter his Third String Quartet in a competition of the Musical Fund Society of Philadelphia, for which he subsequently won joint first prize of $3,000. But the Depression put an end to his plans for an American return. The Philadelphia prize money instead helped to maintain something of his standard of living in the early 1930s. Bartók's second visit, of April–May 1940, was altogether more purposeful. Although performing in numerous concerts, including a prestigious appearance with Szigeti at the Library of Congress and recording his recent *Contrasts* (1938) with Benny Goodman and Szigeti, Bartók's aim was to determine if he should move to the United States. That brief visit provided him with a strong, and unexpected, reason to do so. In response to an ethnomusicological lecture which he gave at Harvard University he received information about a large collection of Serbo-Croatian field recordings undertaken in the mid-1930s by a Harvard professor of classics, the late Milman Parry. While promises of concert engagements and professional positions were given during Bartók's visit (most of which later turned out to be unrealistic), it was the chance of working on the Parry collection which finally persuaded Bartók and his wife to leave Hungary in October 1940.

The essential facts of Bartók's five American years are now well established. Already having worked for six years as a full-time researcher at the Hungarian Academy of Sciences – with occasional breaks for concerts, and the writing of one or two compositions each year, normally during summer vacations – Bartók became even more intensively occupied with folk-music analysis and categorization during his American years. For

1941 and 1942 he held the modest position of Associate in Music at Columbia University in New York, where he worked most productively on Parry's materials. During 1943–45, when illness made full-time research impractical, he continued to work, as best he could, and managed to finalize not just a Serbo-Croatian study, co-authored with Parry's associate Albert B. Lord, but also a Turkish and a voluminous Romanian collection. Performance, which Bartók had hoped would be a major income support in America, soon became incidental, as he and his wife failed to gain frequent or lucrative concert offers. Composition, too, continued its occasional pattern of engagement in Bartók's American years. During 1941 and 1942 he found neither time nor inspiration for sustained composition, even during the summers, but then during 1943–45 he did start to compose again when on rest cures for his failing health. During these stays away from New York he wrote the Concerto for Orchestra (1943), Sonata for Solo Violin (1944), and the twin offerings of his final year, the all-but-complete Third Piano Concerto and the Viola Concerto, left incomplete at his death on 26 September 1945. Throughout the American years, then, Bartók's most consuming and personally most satisfying experiences lay in his folk-music scholarship.

These simple facts are but a scaffold which the last sixty years have clothed in most varied, sometimes absurd, and even lurid, interpretations. Three generations have now struggled with such highly charged questions as: Was Bartók a coward or a hero in leaving Hungary for the United States? How poor or sick really was he during his American years? Was he ungrateful to or neglected by the land which had taken him in? How much were his American compositions works of compromise with the forces of the American free market?

Barely had Bartók died before highly polarized answers started to emerge to these questions. In its obituary, the American journal *Listen* judged that 'The democratic world did not reward him for his courageous stand, nor for his musical mastery'.[1] As socialist realism swept newly Communist Hungary in the late 1940s this theme was amplified. While approving of the accessibility of Bartók's final works (but not the alienating 'formalism' of his middle period), Hungarian socialist realists condemned America's role in his final years. In 1950 Sándor Asztalos, for instance, graphically depicted Bartók as a victim of American 'millionaire dealers in war', and unrestrainedly exploited by rapacious concert bureaux: 'In cold autumnal rains, with a 39-degree fever, there stood one of the greatest figures in the history of new music, Béla Bartók, amid the asphalt jungle of America'.[2] Ten of Bartók's closer friends of American years were moved to collect together a volume of recollections to correct the 'extravagant and fanciful descriptions' (Menuhin's words) of Bartók's final years emanating from Hungary.[3] Meanwhile, the strident post-war dodecaphonist lobby, such as Boulez and Leibowitz, was finding Bartók guilty of betrayal of the spirit of modernism in his American-period works, particularly the highly popular Concerto for Orchestra.[4]

Amid such a babble of post-war accusations, which jumbled together aspects of life and works, a long legal battle commenced between Bartók's Hungarian and American estates which only succeeded in entrenching simplistic opposing interpretations of Bartók's final years. Even the description of Bartók's residency in the United States became full of implications. 'Exile', 'émigré' and 'emigrant' all stressed his status in relation to his homeland, Hungary. Technically, however, he entered the United States in late 1940 as a 'visitor', gained the additional status of 'enemy alien' between December 1941 and early 1945, and only became an American 'immigrant' in July 1945 after a day-long visit to Canada. Late in the war Bartók described himself as a 'voluntary refugee',[5] which is probably the most broadly appropriate term, given its stress upon his self-determined 'flight' from Hungary and its recognition of America as his place of self-chosen 'refuge'.

These post-war battles over the interpretation of Bartók's final years are not merely of historical interest, for they remain deeply embedded in the Bartók literature to this day. *Baker's Biographical Dictionary of Musicians* in its 1992 edition tells readers that Bartók's American problems were 'largely due to his uncompromising character',[6] while Tibor Tallián in 1995 blames the Philistines of the American press, who were unable to appreciate Bartók's worth as composer or pianist.[7] The pianist Andor Földes has recently resurrected the image of Bartók dying virtually unknown and destitute in America, having exchanged his Budapest 'palace' for a New York 'hut'.[8]

The musical world's reception of Bartók's final years is, then, far from settled. In the following paragraphs I probe this five-year period and the magnificent brouhaha which it has engendered against six criteria. The first three are more public concerns of ideology, morality and professional life. The second series, of family life, health and finances, is normally considered to rest more in the domain of private life.

Ideology

Underpinning so much of the commentary arising during the cold war was this question: where was Bartók to be situated amid the matrix of Communism, Nazism, nationalism and capitalistic democracy? As with his compatriot Ernő Dohnányi, Bartók had sometimes been inconsistent –

sometimes just naive – in his political stances. He was claimable for Communism, for instance, because of his membership of the Music Directorate under Béla Kun's short-lived Communist government in 1919, for nationalism because of his early anti-Habsburg sentiments and sometime chauvinistic statements, and for capitalistic democracy because of his decision to take refuge in America. Bartók was certainly no Nazi, yet was equally not the stalwart figure of resistance beloved of the biographies. Until 1937 he sought performing engagements in Nazi Germany, and even after the outbreak of the Second World War he undertook a concert tour of fascist Italy. On the other hand, he had spoken up for Toscanini when he was attacked by Italian fascists in 1931, and called for 'the protection of the integrity and autonomy of the arts'.[9] As a League of Nations committee member he espoused from the early 1930s a 'brotherhood of man' philosophy, which reflected his pluralist attitude to compositional sources as well. To see him as an anti-Nazi crusader forced to carry the flickering beacon of Hungarian humanity to the New World is, however, fanciful and overlooks the more prosaic and self-interested reasons for his departure.

In America Bartók moved largely in émigré Hungarian circles, with their fierce political currents. There he was sometimes a useful figurehead for its more wily operators, as in 1942 when he naively fronted for the patriotic movement 'For an independent Hungary'.[10] From his American correspondence, too, Bartók's ideological stance is less than clear. While recognizing the twin dangers to Hungary of Germany and Russia,[11] he was neither nostalgic for pre-war Hungary (where he had been less than welcome to right-wing officialdom) nor hoped, as did some nationalists, for the restoration of pre-1914 Greater Hungary. Yet, he could not convince himself of the advantages of émigré life in the New World. According to his friend Tibor Serly, Bartók believed 'My Europe . . . is finished forever. Russia – meaning Communism – offers security at the price of Liberty. America – meaning Democracy – provides freedom to starve'.[12] In short, in his final years Bartók had no coherent solution to the world's, or Hungary's, then predicaments. This made him an ideal target for misinterpretation and manipulation. At war's end ideology offered him no simple answers as to where to go and what to do. He did not want to stay in America, but did not feel secure about returning to Hungary. Death saved him from making that decision.

Morality

The emergence of an 'American guilt' theory has been traced back by Benjamin Suchoff to the winter of 1942–43.[13] It was during that winter that Bartók's means of daily support first came seriously into question. America was supposedly 'guilty' because of its inappropriate treatment of a man of Bartók's creative stature during his first years in the country, through only providing him with a low-level academic position on six-monthly renewal, through not offering lucrative performance engagements, through its indifference to the personal sacrifice he had made in abandoning his homeland and the personal strains he had experienced with the temporary loss of his luggage and, later, the anxieties of bringing his younger son, Peter, to America. It seemed, too – and certainly seemed to Bartók – that the propagation of his music had been ignored by the cartel of leading American concert agents (Bartók's concert agents at Boosey & Hawkes were, unfortunately, mere novices in the American performance world) and had been 'sabotaged' by the American Federation of Musicians through its stranglehold over the north American orchestras and its ability to exploit the unclear 'visitor' employment status of Bartók and his wife. While America was concerned with the refugees from those countries invaded by the Axis forces, it was less concerned with the plight of the citizens fleeing voluntarily from those demonized countries as Hungary was considered in 1941, which had bound themselves in with the Axis cause and were still in attacking rather than defensive postures.[14] By 1943, with Bartók seriously ill and hospitalized, a number of institutions and individuals did (according to the 'guilt' theory, all too belatedly) rally round. Harvard University and then the American Society of Composers, Authors and Publishers (ASCAP) took over the costs of his medical care and long-term recuperation. Hungarian friends – Viktor Bator, Szigeti, Eugene Ormandy – and Goodman, among others, campaigned for financial support. Publishers and distributors looked for ways of increasing his royalty payments and advances. After 1943, as the health and finances sections below show, Bartók's position did become more secure and his income more predictable. The 'guilt' theory had, meanwhile, gained a life of its own.

America's 'guilt' still lurks in the literature, especially that of Hungarian provenance. It finds a perfect parallel in Bartók's own attitude to the death of his cats while in the care of a New York dog and cat hospital in the late summer of 1942.[15] Two apparently healthy cats (although the veterinarian claimed they were already underfed and ill) mysteriously died while the Bartóks were away. Who was to blame? Clearly, the hospital. So, too, with the intelligentsia of Hungary's view of Bartók's death. He left the country apparently healthy, and, when the smoke of war cleared, he was dead. Who was to blame? America, of course, which must have been negligent in its care of him. But such a perception misses two important points: that most Americans could not fathom how dwelling in their 'land of opportunity' could be considered a hardship, especially when one looked at what was happening in the rest of the world at this time; that (as Bartók's wife Ditta, at least, had readily perceived) there is no America, but rather millions of Americans going about their own 'business'. The European conception of the 'state' and its responsibility for the doing of good works was but tenuously held in 1940s federal America. Witness even the difficulties for President Franklin D. Roosevelt in bringing about a national response to the Depression or to the moral dilemma posed by Nazi Germany.

One fifty-five-word American report – a mention of Bartók in the 'Milestones' column of *Time* magazine[16] – summarized for many of European sensibility America's crassness and moral irresponsibility towards this Hungarian genius. Sandwiched between an advertisement for an Argoflex camera and a 'Sunday Nite Chef griddle', the cheery article addressed the passing of this 'prolific Hungarian composer of piquant, sometimes cacophonous orchestral and chamber music', a 'radical modernist', whose only mentioned work was not his recently much-acclaimed Concerto for Orchestra, nor even the Menuhin-commissioned Sonata for Solo Violin, but *Contrasts* (undoubtedly because of its commissioning by someone then *really* famous in popular culture, Benny Goodman). For the Austrian-born composer Ernst Krenek, the report was almost as shocking as Bartók's death, for it treated a composer of 'immortal' attributes as just another piece of American 'business'.[17] Bartók was a 'milestone', and not included in the 'Music' section, because in dying he did not use his musical powers as composer or performer. His death was of minor social, not musical, significance. Krenek speculated that it was only because of his connection with Goodman that Bartók had gained a mention at all.[18] Where Krenek saw a moral question, most Americans just saw the normal operation of a consumerist society.

Professional life

In America Bartók set out to continue the professional life which he had pursued in Hungary for the last forty years: folk-music study, performance, composition, teaching. By 1940, teaching was his least concern, and he rejected early offers of professorships in composition at leading American conservatories. Given the overriding reason why he moved to America – to carry out ethnomusicological work – he was professionally most productive there. Most of the folk-music studies which he completed in America did not readily find a publisher although, by 1976, all had been published. As interest in these studies was slender then – as now – his priorities could be considered to have been unfortunate. They led Bartók, for instance, to forgo composing opportunities during the summer of 1944 so as to polish the text of his *Serbo-Croatian Folk Songs* volume. Similarly, his fallow compositional period of 1941–42 was not just the result of lack of inspiration, personal depression and illness, as many biographies suggest, but also a natural consequence of his prioritization of folk-music work and performance above composition. Unsure of how long he had to work on the Parry materials, and thoroughly enjoying the excellent recordings, equipment and intricacies of the music, Bartók was determined to make as much progress as possible. He did not, accordingly, write as many compositions in his final years as the musical world would now have liked, for that world has, quite rightly, rated his compositional activity as more marked by genius than his folk-music researches or his piano playing.

The sense of incompletion and want in the compositions of Bartók's final years is only heightened because he did not manage to see any of these works into print, so all, to greater or lesser extent, evidence the editorial, if not quasi-compositional, hand of others. Indeed, he only heard two of these works in live performance. In most Bartók biographies, however, because of a primary interest in 'the man and his music', the ethnomusicological activities in America gain only incidental mention. In such biographies his American years can easily appear professionally unfulfilled, especially when his death-bed comment about having to leave 'with his suitcase full'[19] is prominently featured. By way of correction, it would be fairer to say that Bartók did not compose more in America because other self-determined priorities deprived him of the necessary time. This was not a new circumstance for Bartók. He was not a generally prolific composer, and his output of substantial new compositions for 1941–45 is not significantly less than that for 1931–35 or 1921–25.

Bartók's heart was not in performance. Except for a short period after his graduation and a peak period of activity in 1927–29, it probably never had been. By the time he settled in America, performance was, to his mind, a twinned vehicle for supplementary earnings and propagating his own music (not necessarily easily compatible aims). Even in Hungary the audience for Bartók's own compositions was limited. In an America drifting towards war, it was close to non-existent. Although Bartók and his wife did try to broaden their repertory a little during their American years,[20] they never managed to break into the mainstream of American concert life. An additional liability was that a certain old-fashioned scholasticism of approach was interpreted by American audiences as mere dreariness.

While the issues of public life and its interpretation are undoubtedly important, Bartók's life during his American years was increasingly dominated by private and personal concerns. By early 1943 his health had forced him, for the first time since 1906, to become entirely self-employed.

The day-to-day flow of life was one increasingly centred around the home, and matters of health and material well-being.

Family life

The Bartóks' life in America did not begin auspiciously, and never much improved. Their baggage from Hungary – weighing over 300 kilograms – was lost, for three months. Their first flat proved noisy and inhospitable. The insecure situation of their teenage son, Peter, worried them constantly, until he finally arrived in the United States in April 1942. For much of 1941 they toyed with the idea of returning to Hungary, but as the war in Eastern Europe intensified that became less of an option. From December 1941, with America's entry into the war, all communication with friends and family in Hungary was severed. In New York there was a new language for Ditta Bartók to learn, and for both of them there were new customs, new food and the need to adjust to the American fixation, at least as Ditta saw it, on 'money, money, money'.[21] Ditta Bartók found it impossible to gain regular employment; even occasional piano students proved elusive. Once Bartók could no longer work regularly, relations between husband and wife came under additional strain. Bartók was depressed at his illness; his wife suffered from long-term self-doubt and personal insecurities, not directly related to his condition, that eventually led to her own hospitalization.[22] The couple lived apart for many months from late 1943, and then in the second half of 1944 came together again in very cramped and noisy quarters in central Manhattan. Although their personal relations do appear to have improved in the final year of Bartók's life, 1945 brought its own anxieties about which of their friends and relatives had survived the siege of Budapest, whether Bartók's folk-music collections there had remained intact, and concerns for his two sons caught on different sides of the war, one in the Hungarian[23] and one in the United States forces. The sense of constant anxiety in the Bartóks' private life during their American years is not unrealistically conveyed in Agatha Fassett's novel *The Naked Face of Genius*.[24]

Health

'Here one *must* always feel fine and excellent even if dying.' So moaned Bartók to his former piano student Wilhelmine Creel in 1941,[25] even before serious illness had been diagnosed. This necessity for a positive public face irked Bartók, for he never felt well during his years in America and seemed incapable of telling 'white lies'. Before leaving Budapest, in

August–October 1940, he had undertaken expensive but unsuccessful treatments at the rheumatics ward of the Gellért Baths because of persistent problems with his right shoulder. His son has even dated the signs of his father's mortal disease as far back as 1924, when he had first suffered from such shoulder pains.[26] In 1941, while on vacation in Vermont, he had problems moving his left shoulder, leading to X-ray treatment when he returned to New York. By April 1942 his leukaemia had been tentatively diagnosed, although the exact nature of the disease appears to have been held back from Bartók. His health only became critical in late February 1943, shortly after he had started presenting lectures at Harvard University. He was hospitalized – his weight had dropped to an alarming 40 kilograms – and intensive investigations of his condition were undertaken.[27] Hence, through the mediation of Hungarian friends, ASCAP took over management of his case, and in the following two-and-a-half years reportedly spent about $16,000 on his medical care and several periods of recuperation at Saranac Lake, New York, and Asheville, North Carolina. That care included use of the new 'wonder drug', penicillin, for pneumonia which Bartók contracted in March 1945. Family members and friends thought that Bartók's disease had been cured, although Ditta Bartók appears to have learned about its temporary retardation early in 1945, and Peter Bartók only after he had returned from armed service in August 1945. An account of one of Bartók's doctors, Israel Rappaport, makes it clear that his medical advisers were under no such illusion:

> In the spring of 1944 the symptoms of leukaemia were first observed. But initially they were able to fight the disease with drugs and blood transfusions. Later, however, its pace began to quicken and it started to become painful. Whereas in 1944 6,000–8,000 white blood cells were detected in Bartók's blood, in 1945 100,000 were found, and in September 1945 250,000 – which heralded his end.[28]

What is now clear is that Bartók was ill during the entirety of his American years with progressive stages of blood disorders. His condition first became life-threatening in early 1943, leading to Ernő Balogh's justifiable conclusion that the intervention of ASCAP 'prolonged Bartók's life by two and a half years, during which time he created the four final great masterworks of his life'.[29]

Finances

Central to many accounts of Bartók's American sojourn is the spectre of poverty. A review of his financial documents, as far as they have been available, suggests that at no stage did his after-tax income fall below $3,000 per annum.[30] (In 1940 the average full-time American wage, across all industries, was $1,315; by 1945 it was $2,205.[31]) Naturally, wages and costs were considerably higher in New York City than the American average. Bartók also had the disadvantages of insubstantial savings and an inability to access his Hungarian pension entitlements.

The sources of Bartók's income changed radically with the crisis in his health of early 1943. Prior to that time his main income sources were his research salary, net performance income and royalties (on his publications, performances of his music and mechanical royalties).[32] Throughout this earlier period, however, Bartók remained financially anxious. His concert income was drying up – he took part in only four concerts in 1942, compared with twenty-one in 1941 – and his research position at Columbia University required frequent applications for renewal. Moreover, in early 1942, with the United States already at war with Hungary, Bartók had to pay some $900 to expedite his younger son's trans-Atlantic journey. After February 1943 he gained no further income from concerts, nor was he able to draw a regular salary, hence his most acute anxiety at this time about his financial future. The prospect of vast medical bills only exacerbated his concern. Yet, Bartók's stated gross (pre-tax) income for 1943[33] was finally $4,296.68, consisting of

Concert appearance	$444 (Bartók and his wife)
Total royalties	$1,157
Lecture fees	$400 (Harvard University)
Commission	$1,000 (Koussevitzky Foundation)
Forward salary payment	$1,285.68 (Columbia University)
Article fee	$10
Total:	$4,296.68

Of this income, the considerable majority arose through initiatives of Bartók's friends – the forward salary payment through Columbia's Douglas Moore, the Koussevitzky commission of Concerto for Orchestra through Joseph Szigeti and Fritz Reiner, and $646.65 of the royalties through grossly inflated sales figures of Bartók recordings. Further benefits came to Bartók in March 1943 through an award of $500 hastily arranged for Bartók by Douglas Moore through the National Institute of Arts and Letters. As well, all but $400 of medical and dental costs of the Bartóks were picked up in 1943 by either Harvard University or ASCAP.

The year 1944 saw a major correction in Bartók's royalty payments, which had been reduced since his arrival in America by British exchange restrictions and his inability to access most European royalties.[34] His gross income for 1944 was:

Royalties	$2,239.42
Commission fees	$1,000 ($500 New York Ballet Theatre; $500 Menuhin)
Article fees	$55
Residual salary payment	$191.08 (Columbia University)
Total:	$3,485.50

As access to royalties increased, and his main publisher Boosey & Hawkes provided advances on new works, these payments became Bartók's main source of income. His own preliminary estimate of gross income for 1945 was $3,611, of which all but $80 came from royalties and advances.[35]

With hindsight it is possible to say that the claims of poverty were exaggerated. Yet as life is lived forwards, rather than backwards, Bartók's anxieties – and with them, a widespread impression of destitution – are easily understandable. Until 1944, and the freeing up of his royalties, he could not be sure that any line of income would remain in six months' time. Moreover, had ASCAP not assumed his health costs – which eventually amounted to almost the entire after-tax earnings of his American years – he would certainly have been unable to afford the quality of care that kept him alive, and artistically productive, until September 1945. A greater sense of financial calm did emerge during 1944, not because of an increase in income, but because the prospect of regular income allowed the ever-pessimistic Bartók to budget with some confidence for the future. Had he lived a few years longer and enjoyed the surge of post-war acclaim of his compositions, his royalties would have ensured a lifestyle of some affluence.

During his American years Bartók's circumstance was not easy. He was never fully healthy, only rarely felt financially secure, and experienced a private life often fraught with anxieties. For whatever reasons, he did not adapt well to urban American life. However, his professional achievements, despite the downturn in his performing career, were impressive. The decisive factor which had persuaded him to come to the United States in late 1940 had been a body of folk-music transcriptions, and his folk-music output during his final five years was enormous. Composition was, as in most of his life, an occasional activity. There was a long fallow period in 1941–42, but there had been earlier 'quiet' compositional times, in 1913–14, 1924–25 and 1932–34, during each of which Bartók had wondered if he had become an 'ex-composer'. Yet, once his health and financial well-being had been taken in hand, he produced four works of major stature, the popularity of which has not been dented by early claims of 'compromise'.

A 1945 survey of fifteen leading American-resident composers showed that these composers rarely expected to live by their compositions: 'the royalties which I receive [would not] be sufficient to keep me at an existence level', reported Stravinsky; 'my income from published works and from performance fees is less than a third of my income', commented Schoenberg.[36] Surprisingly, then, by 1945 Bartók *was* living almost entirely on royalties and publishers' advances. None the less, because of earlier travails, as well as the end-of-war timing and the tragic circumstances of his death, Bartók's case became a *cause célèbre*.

13 Bartók reception in cold war Europe

DANIELLE FOSLER-LUSSIER

On 26 September 1945, Béla Bartók died in New York City, more than 4,000 miles from home. Since he had left Hungary and entered voluntary exile in 1940, war-torn Europe had heard little of his music. As the war ended, though, nations began to rebuild or reform their concert programmes. Composers searched for new stylistic directions that would make sense to them, and implicit in their questions about new music was a desire to assess the value of recent musical styles, including Bartók's. As his last works received their European premieres in 1946 and 1947, it also became possible to evaluate his career as a historical whole, and to see in its changing course a path that could either be followed or rejected. The political turmoil of the early post-war years ensured that these musical questions carried political significance; as we shall see, musical and political judgements about Bartók's music continued to be as inseparable after his death as they were during his lifetime. In particular, growing antagonism between Soviet and American zones of influence in Europe meant that the musical aesthetics of the two regions diverged sharply, and this division left a deep impression on responses to Bartók's music after the war.

The charge of 'compromise'

Perhaps the most influential essay on Bartók from the early post-war years is René Leibowitz's notorious 'Béla Bartók, or the Possibility of Compromise in Contemporary Music'.[1] Leibowitz (1913–72) wrote the article as part of a polemical exchange with his fellow Parisian critic Boris de Schloezer. Both critics were themselves émigrés – Leibowitz was born in Poland, and Schloezer (1881–1969) was Russian by birth – and both were more sensitive than their peers to Bartók's status as a Central European 'outsider' in West European musical culture. Nonetheless, their attitudes towards Bartók's music, and towards the future of new music more generally, exhibited strikingly contrasting ideals.

Leibowitz's perspective stemmed from his reading of the critical works of Jean-Paul Sartre and other writers whose post-war thinking embodied a dramatic reaction to their wartime experiences of German-occupied France and the reactionary Vichy regime. As a sweeping series of 'purification trials' passed judgement on whether individuals had acted morally or not during the war, Sartre theorized that to write was itself a political act, and that the writer had a special responsibility to engage himself in the issues of the day. Though Sartre believed that music's obligation differed from literature's because it made less specific reference to events or objects in the world, Leibowitz altered and extended Sartre's ideas in applying them to an interpretation of Bartók's career and his music.[2] In terms reminiscent of what Tony Judt has called the 'Resistance syndrome', Leibowitz argued that Bartók's music was tinged with moral weakness: he found in Bartók's music 'an element of compromise and a lack of purity which are, to say the least, disquieting.'[3] His critique of Bartók reflects the same concern with moral virtue and manly courage that dominated public discourse in Paris during the purification trials.

The moral weakness in question here was Bartók's decision not to embrace the technique of composing with twelve tones advocated by Arnold Schoenberg and his disciples, among whom Leibowitz counted himself. In Leibowitz's view, the composer has a moral obligation to further the historical development of music by writing in a more 'advanced' style than his predecessors. According to Leibowitz, Bartók had achieved a bold and radical new chromatic language in certain of his works, particularly the two Sonatas for Violin and Piano (1921 and 1922); and in others, such as the Third and Fourth String Quartets (1927 and 1928), he sometimes used sophisticated techniques of inversion and variation similar to those favoured by the Schoenberg school. But although Bartók's style had progressed towards greater formal coherence and complexity up until the middle of his career, said Leibowitz, he had failed to take the final step away from tonality that the history of music required of him:

> The lucidity evinced in his Fourth Quartet led him definitively to the threshold of a new world before which he could not shrink without failing to honour his commitments. But Bartók did not seem to be fully conscious of these commitments and in the end he did not honour them. Instead of persisting in the forward movement which his last work called for, instead of crossing over the threshold he had just reached into that half-discerned world which can only be approached in the state of anguish that accompanies absolute liberty and its implied responsibilities, instead of all this, Bartók chose a less praiseworthy path, which was the *path of compromise*.[4]

As far as Leibowitz was concerned, all Bartók's works after the Fourth Quartet (1928) were tinged with compromise, the late works such as the Second Violin Concerto (1938), the Sixth Quartet (1939) and the Concerto for Orchestra (1943) most of all. Because Bartók had pursued a different course, composing tonal music throughout his career, Leibowitz felt that he had aimed for popularity and success rather than for the abstract development of musical style – a self-serving rather than a selfless choice. His critique thus embodies an inseparable fusion of style-critical judgements about the quality of Bartók's music and moral judgements about the composer's character. Leibowitz's politically charged moral certitude about musical style appealed to some and appalled others: in retrospect it seems a striking embodiment of the Manichean thinking of the times.

Boris de Schloezer soon responded to Leibowitz's arguments with measured scepticism. Unaffiliated with the Sartre circle, Schloezer felt no urgency to ally himself with their political stance; and as a musician whose aesthetic loyalties had been eclectic throughout his career, he was in a position to express a less stringently partisan point of view. First and foremost, Schloezer challenged Leibowitz's idea that a composer's work should be judged primarily according to the composer's place in a historical lineage. He also criticized Leibowitz's view that Bartók's music had contributed nothing to the historical development of twentieth-century music. Drawing a sharp distinction in value between historically influential composers and composers who leave no school or method behind, wrote Schloezer, leaves out what may be the most important issue of all: the aesthetic value of the music. For Schloezer, the interest in the particularities of the individual work of music superseded the need to designate one composer or method as central; he refused to assign his musical loyalties on the basis of historical criteria.

Equally important to Schloezer's defence of Bartók was his emphasis on artistic freedom. Schloezer argued that even though Bartók had not subscribed to any single compositional method and had left no organized school of followers, his musical decisions were justified because they expressed his own artistic logic.[5] Objecting vigorously to Leibowitz's reasoning, Schloezer asked:

> What then must a contemporary of Schoenberg do if his taste and his sensibility, his imagination and his conception of music, cannot accommodate themselves to the serial technique, and if he finds no need to make use of the 'chromatic total'? Should he keep silence? . . . Bartók, so we are told, is not free, since he has confused freedom with caprice and contingency, since he has claimed to do as he pleased without first finding out whether what he pleased would fit in with history, and since he has refused to be always quite consistent with himself, or logical to the death, as Schoenberg has been.[6]

Schloezer's emphasis on the individual's artistic freedom, like Leibowitz's on commitment, resonated with dominant currents of late 1940s French intellectual life. It had become apparent that the Soviet Union and the new East European states were abrogating personal and artistic freedoms in order to consolidate socialist power; therefore, French intellectuals who sympathized with Marxist ideals had to decide whether the sacrifice of such freedoms was morally justifiable.[7] To Schloezer and other like-minded critics, such a trade-off seemed philosophically untenable, and the ideal of artistic freedom became one of their central concerns.

The question of popularity

Leibowitz's harsh rhetoric was surely inspired at least in part by resentment of Bartók's widespread and growing popularity with audiences and critics, especially as compared to that of Schoenberg. In October 1947 French critic Bernard Gavoty reported that Bartók's music enjoyed great success with French audiences: Bartók was 'the man of the hour, the fashionable composer'.[8] His colleague Claude Rostand gushed, 'the music of Bartók ennobles all of music. And the contemporary world will soon be proud to be able to say, "We lived in the time of Bartók".'[9] In West Germany, too, Bartók's music – in particular his accessible late works such as the Concerto for Orchestra and the Third Piano Concerto, which were still new to European audiences – played a significant role in concert programmes all over the country.

   Some German critics found in Bartók's music, with its focus on new sounds couched in older forms, a vibrant renewal of the German symphonic tradition. Composer and critic Herbert Eimert (1897–1972), for example, pointed out that while the form of Bartók's Violin Concerto (1938) corresponded closely to traditional models, the sound of the piece seemed fresh and new to audiences:

> As simple as this form is, though, for the concert-goer it is not easily comprehensible, because the abundance of novelties of every other kind than formal overwhelms the often-perplexed listener. And it confirms that creative radicality and conservatism are related manifestations of character as soon as they come together within the scope of a strong personality. With a vicarious power of which only a few from each nation are capable, Bartók penetrated to the essential layer of folk music. As if from hidden springs or craters this ancient material wells up and washes around the rigid frame of symphonic form.[10]

Citing Bartók's affinity with German traditions, Kurt Zimmerreimer emphasized that Bartók's music was one of the most fruitful models for new German music to follow: 'What Bartók can teach us', he wrote, 'is the precise filling out of the smallest form with all its possibilities, the equal attention to home, school, and concert [musics], and finally the synthesis of openness and conscience, that were once a part of the German tradition'.[11] These critics admired Bartók's music because it seemed to indicate a viable path for their own strivings towards new musical styles – a path that reflected both their own sense of tradition and their desire for innovation.

Some German musical thinkers, though, questioned the value of Bartók's music as a model for the future. This was particularly evident among members of the new musical elite that had begun to take shape at the International Summer Courses for New Music established in the city of Darmstadt, within the American-occupied zone of West Germany. Just as some French intellectuals kept an eye on developments to the East, West German thinking, too, reacted strongly to the political events that were redrawing the map of Europe.[12] In February 1948, for instance, the Central Committee of the Soviet Communist Party published a resolution on music that chastised several important Soviet composers for paying too much attention to modernist technical innovations, including atonality, and not striving enough towards a music that could be embraced by the public.[13] The resolution was publicized widely and became controversial in musical circles across Europe; participants at the Darmstadt summer courses in 1948 and 1949 debated its validity intensely.[14]

In a 1948 Darmstadt lecture entitled 'Cultural Crisis and New Music', Hans Mayer articulated a position strongly influenced by the Soviet resolution, but also differing from it in its conclusions. Like Andrei Zhdanov (1896–1948), the architect of the Soviet resolution, Mayer believed that new music had to communicate intimately with its audiences by reflecting the needs and aspirations of the society around it – but like his contemporary, Theodor W. Adorno, who had developed an elaborate sociological theory supporting avant-garde music, Mayer believed that Schoenberg's music was the most appropriate form of expression for the post-war world.[15] Edwin Kuntz, a reporter who reviewed the summer courses, found Mayer's stance contradictory. He agreed with Mayer that music should be accessible to the public, but disagreed with his position on Schoenberg. Kuntz believed that the most recent works of Bartók and others more aptly addressed the public's musical needs:

> [Unlike Schoenberg], Hindemith and Stravinsky, and not least the tremendously strong Béla Bartók – who has been achieving ever-greater significance – have unmistakably turned towards society. Alfred Weber prophesied the sure demise of the elite if it continues to pursue esoteric goals instead of decidedly devoting itself to the task that is more important than any other: helping the masses in the development towards humanity

[*Menschwerdung*] which alone can unite them with the elite. It is as if
Hindemith, Stravinsky, and Bartók had at last understood precisely this.
Bartók's glorious Concerto for Orchestra (1943), Stravinsky's rich
Symphony in Three Movements (1945) and his delightful Concerto for
Strings in D (1946) – all works that one would like to hear in all the
symphony programs of the coming winter – are persuasive examples, to say
nothing of Hindemith.[16]

In Kuntz's opinion Bartók's Concerto for Orchestra was the best work performed at the summer music festival that year precisely because it succeeded in connecting with the public.[17]

Hermann Scherchen (1891–1966), a central figure at the summer
courses, felt differently. In an essay evaluating 'The Current Situation of
Modern Music', he described the Soviet demand for a turn towards the
public as a step backward for musical style. He felt that modern music's
difficulty was essential to its nature: were it not for socialist interference, he
asserted, 'no first-rate composer would ever go back to a "more natural",
more easily understandable means of expression'.[18] Scherchen's words
echo Adorno's response to Zhdanov's resolution; Adorno wrote that
although the resolution was correct in noting that modern music's relationship to society was not without contradictions, 'this does not justify
the screwing back of music by fiat to an earlier, cruder level'.[19] For these
staunch proponents of the avant-garde, the Soviet resolution meant a
threat to the modernist styles 'mandated by history', and they responded to
it with considerable agitation.

Since Bartók's music had already been singled out by several critics as a
paragon of accessibility, it is not surprising that in Scherchen's diatribe
against Marxist interference he also echoed Leibowitz's accusation that
Bartók's music was compromised:

> A number of leading composers have belatedly made concessions in their
> creative work: it is enough to compare Bartók's *Mandarin* and his Third
> Piano Concerto, or the first and second harmonizations of Hindemith's
> *Marienlieder*, or Milhaud's *Les Choéphores* and *Introduction et Marche
> funèbre*, or Stravinsky's *Les Noces* and the Concerto for Strings, or
> Shostakovich's Third and Ninth Symphonies, to see of what this
> compromise consists: in stretching the boundaries of classical harmony to
> the utmost and even beyond, but still ensuring for oneself a tonal alibi. The
> twelve-tone composers alone did not shirk the task that art assigns to every
> truly creative artist: consciously to develop new, finer capabilities in the
> human being.[20]

The inclusion of Shostakovich in this list is striking: though he composed
both the Third and Ninth Symphonies in the Soviet Union, the Third
reflected the relative freedom of the 1920s, whereas by the time of the

Ninth (1945) Shostakovich had endured years of oppressive state intervention. Although Bartók was not subject to artistic controls of the same nature, Scherchen interpreted the accessible sound of his music as if it had retroactively been tainted by the mere existence of such controls. In the new, politically charged context of cold war politics, accessible music sounded compromised to many Western composers because of the Soviet demand for such music – it was the very sound of the forced, the false, the distorted. To these composers, it seemed urgent that their arsenal of compositional techniques provide systematic means of preventing such compromises.

Largely as a result of these new ethical standards for listening, and despite the popularity of Bartók's music among audiences, many West European composers quickly learned to regard his music as irrelevant to their musical future. Erich Doflein remarked after giving lectures on Bartók at the 1950 Darmstadt summer courses that Bartók had begun to be regarded as a 'classic' very soon after completing his last composition:

> I had gone to Darmstadt with the intention of speaking out in favour of the work and the personality of a revolutionary and bold new composer. I left Darmstadt with the feeling that I had supported a classic. At that time they began to speak of the 'classics of new music'. This resulted not only from the experience of the completion of [his] life's work, but also from comparison with the more advanced style of the youngest generation, especially of the young Italians with whom Scherchen acquainted us.[21]

The West European emphasis on innovation, in response to East European calls for greater accessibility, only accelerated the process by which Bartók's music ceased to be relevant as 'new music'. By attaining the dubious status of a 'classic', Bartók's work no longer had real currency for many of the composers who participated in Darmstadt's musical activities.

Hungarian hopes

Meanwhile, when Bartók's last works made their way back from America to the new and initially democratic Hungarian republic, they met with a mixed reception similar to the responses they evoked in France and Germany.[22] Bartók's music had never been popular with a large proportion of Hungary's concert-goers; his following consisted mainly of composers, critics and artists from other disciplines who valued his music for its modernity as well as for its Hungarian qualities. At the Hungarian premiere of the Concerto for Orchestra on 22 April 1947, it became clear that the style of the work was not at all what Bartók's devotees had expected:

whether it was better or worse was a matter of debate. Composer Endre Szervánszky remarked that '[t]here were as many opinions as there were people! One saw the selling out of the spirit of modern music. Quite a few appraised the work's easy accessibility as chasing after success, as giving in to the dollar, and there were some who explained the multiplicity of styles in the Concerto as the exhaustion of Bartók's creativity'.[23] Szervánszky's comment enumerates some of the most prominent concerns Hungarian musicians voiced after hearing the Concerto's premiere: although they hardly believed it possible, they wondered if Bartók had made stylistic concessions in response to financial or social pressures.[24] Critics registered similar unease after the Hungarian premiere of the Third Piano Concerto in November of the same year.[25] Their concerns about the possibility of compromise were thus not altogether different from Leibowitz's, though they were framed in terms more sympathetic to Bartók.

In the success of the Concerto for Orchestra Szervánszky and other Communist critics saw the possibility of rebuilding the connection between artists and society. Although some Communists expressed doubts about conservative elements of the Concerto's style, most embraced the work as a harbinger of progress towards a socialist, folk-oriented music. Even after the Central Committee of the Soviet Communist Party published its resolution condemning musical modernism in 1948, many optimistic Hungarian Communists remained convinced that Bartók's music could remain central to their repertoire. While Szervánszky feared from the start that the resolution would be applied harshly to Bartók, several Communist musicians analysed Bartók's music and found it largely in tune with the Soviet demands. Lajos Vargyas (1914–), for instance, argued that Bartók's music differed fundamentally from the Soviet music criticized in the resolution. Since Bartók's music already featured folksong and respected classical forms, Vargyas asserted, it fulfilled the resolution's criteria perfectly and thus stood apart from the West European traditions of Schoenberg and Stravinsky reviled by the Soviet Central Committee.[26] A few, including composer András Mihály (1917–93), even began to hope that Hungarian music – not Soviet music – would form the basis of a new socialist art music.[27]

Hungarian realities

As the Hungarian Workers' (Communist) Party consolidated its Soviet-style control over Hungarian political and cultural life, however, such hopes were dashed. Beginning in early 1949, the Party commissioned lectures about Bartók's music that would attack his modernist works more and more stridently. Soviet composers visiting Hungary also indicated that many of Bartók's works could not possibly find a place in the musical life of a socialist nation: they chose to focus not on the relatively innocuous Concerto for Orchestra, but rather on *The Miraculous Mandarin*, which they regarded as clearly inappropriate for the uplifting of the masses due to its expressionist style and sexual themes. In February 1950, furthermore, Hungarian critic Géza Losonczy published an article in the Party newspaper *Free Folk* urging the removal of Bartók's stage works from the repertoire of the Opera House. Losonczy suggested that all the composer's music had been contaminated by Western decadence:

> Let there be no misunderstanding: we consider Béla Bartók to be *one of the greatest musical geniuses*, and we rank his art among the most precious treasures of Hungarian musical culture . . . It is, however, not possible to turn one's eye away from the fact that in Béla Bartók's art deep traces were left by the decadence and formalism of bourgeois music. Béla Bartók's genius was nourished not only by the pure sources of Hungarian folk music, but also by the bourgeois, decaying art of his time. Bartók's entire oeuvre carries with it the signs of this unceasing struggle that was carried on in him between the positive inspiration of the Hungarian folk music tradition and Western bourgeois decadence.[28]

Losonczy's article, published at the behest of the Hungarian government's Ministry of People's Culture, established something close to a Party line: while the Party still paid lip service to Bartók as a great man, it also wished to suppress many of his works.

By August 1950, as the fifth anniversary of Bartók's death approached, Hungarian Radio had developed an official list of banned works. In a letter to the chief of the Party's influential division of Agitation and Propaganda, Radio employee György Pollner reported:

> The Radio does not play the following Bartók works, since the bourgeois influence can be felt most strongly in them:
>   A. Stage works
>   *The Miraculous Mandarin*
>   B. Concert works
>   Piano Concerto No. 1
>   Concerto for Two Pianos, Percussion and Orchestra
>   Piano Concerto No. 2
>   C. Chamber works
>   String Quartet No. 3
>   String Quartet No. 4
>   String Quartet No. 5
>   Violin–piano Sonata No. 1
>   Violin–piano Sonata No. 2
>   Piano Sonata

    D. Piano works
        3 Etudes Op. 18
        Out of Doors
    E. Vocal works
        5 Songs on poems by Endre Ady[29]

This list seems to have represented the policy of the moment rather than a definitive or comprehensive survey. Despite the Radio's claim that during the commemoration of the fifth anniversary of Bartók's death in September 1950 listeners would find 'practically every outstanding work of his on the programme', many more works were omitted than this list would suggest, including *Music for Strings, Percussion and Celesta, Bluebeard's Castle, The Wooden Prince, Cantata profana, Allegro barbaro, Contrasts*, the Piano Suite Op. 14, the Second Quartet, the Rhapsodies for violin and orchestra, and most of the song settings.[30] By contrast, some of Bartók's later and more accessible works, particularly the Violin Concerto (1938), the Divertimento, the Concerto for Orchestra, the Third Piano Concerto, and the Sonata for Solo Violin, were heard very frequently throughout the early 1950s.

    Though Pollner's list is sketchy – including, for instance, the Concerto for Two Pianos and Percussion but not the Sonata on which it was based – examination of the blacklisted works reveals some of the Party's criteria for the ban. As Leibowitz had noted, for example, Bartók sometimes deliberately exploited the entire chromatic scale in the Sonatas for Violin and Piano as well as in the second of the Three Etudes Op. 18 (1918). This stylistic feature would not have endeared them to Schoenberg's socialist critics.[31] Likewise, several of the other pieces on the list, most notably the Piano Sonata and the First and Second Piano Concertos, bear some of the hallmarks of Stravinsky's mechanistic style, an equally problematic marker of modernism.[32] The presence or absence of folksong as an easily perceptible organizing device surely made a difference as well. Thus, the audible presence of folksong in Bartók's Eight Improvisations on Hungarian Peasant Songs Op. 20 (1920) for piano saved it from the ban, whereas the stylistically similar but significantly less folk-like *Out of Doors* suite was blacklisted. The ban on Bartók's 'unacceptable' works held sway at the Radio for the next five years.

The two Bartóks

The dearth of Bartók performances in Budapest did not go unnoticed in the West. In August 1950, the United States government's Voice of America radio programme began broadcasting the news that Bartók's music had been banned in Hungary on its East European programmes. This blatant propaganda tactic inspired sharply worded responses from Hungarian critics, who rejected foreign claims on the composer. Endre Székely cried hypocrisy:

> 'The Voice of America', which at one time viewed with indifference the incredible privation Bartók suffered during his stay in America, and which at that time did not even conceive of the idea of easing the sick composer's serious financial worries, today screams to the world that Bartók belongs to the American capitalists.[33]

Ferenc Szabó's account likewise questioned whether 'America's shamelessly lying voice' had any right to state that 'Bartók's work is organically close to their "Western" pseudoculture'.[34]

The Hungarian government seems to have perceived the American broadcast as a serious threat: most of the articles and speeches published around September 1950 featured overt attempts to reclaim Bartók as a specifically Hungarian composer and to emphasize socialist aspects of his music. As a memorial plaque was placed at Bartók's former residence on Budapest's Szilágyi Dezső Square, Miklós Csillag explained in a rousing speech that the US government's broadcasts were merely transparent propaganda attempts and proclaimed that Hungary would continue to embrace Bartók as its own:

> The favourite method of oppressors the world over – and the Hungary of the feudal lords was no exception to this – is to try to falsify and use for their own ends the best of humanity and of progress, if they cannot hide them from the people . . . And a similar attempt is now in progress in the imperialist West with Bartók. Those who . . . want to sharpen the terror of destruction, crush the freedom of peoples, threaten the lives of millions and the culture of humanity with new wars – they have no claim on Bartók or on his tradition! Bartók is ours! With his entire life's work, with his decisively formulated stand, he is on our side, and on our side he fights for peace and for the better future of humanity.[35]

Csillag did not, however, attempt to refute the basic claim of the Voice of America broadcast: that Bartók's music had in fact been banned in Hungary.

In a similarly polarized article, published in a special Bartók issue of the Hungarian *New Music Review*, Mihály sought to distinguish as cleanly as possible the Hungarian (and socialist) view of Bartók from the West European (and capitalist) view, taking Leibowitz's 1947 article as characteristic of the latter. Mihály responded to Leibowitz's remarks as if to a personal challenge, rebutting his arguments with sarcastic rebukes. Mihály gloated, for instance, that Leibowitz feared Bartók's good influence on West European composers because Bartók presented an attractive alternative to the traditions of Schoenberg and Stravinsky:

> For [Leibowitz], Bartók means the destruction of the revolution of modern
> music, a reactionary compromise from which the young generation of
> composers must be sheltered. It interests us, therefore, primarily because he
> asserts that our Bartók is a banner in the West for those young composers
> who have had enough of the two impoverished paths of bourgeois music . . .
> [and] who are seeking a fundamentally new path.[36]

Mihály continued by drawing a distinction between 'our' (Hungarian)
Bartók and the West's, pointing out that since Leibowitz chose only a few
works to praise, the West's Bartók was a scanty one compared to the East's,
which consisted of a rich assortment of folksong settings as well as the
master's most recent works. On this basis, Mihály asserted that Leibowitz
did not have a true connection with Bartók:

> We are justified in bringing up the question: does someone who accepts four
> works and a couple of movements out of [Bartók's] enormous life-work and
> dismisses the rest in the manner described above have anything to do with
> Bartók? The answer is unequivocal. Leibowitz has nothing to do with our
> great master and here I use the word 'our' not only as a Hungarian musician,
> but in the name of the progressive musicians of the world as well.[37]

Mihály thus claimed for Hungarians and for socialist peoples more generally a special kind of access to Bartók's music that was denied to Leibowitz
and other West European advocates of musical modernism. He further
emphasized the superiority of folklorism over modernism, explaining that
the Hungarians' Bartók was not interested in what Mihály called the
empty, meaningless 'formulae' that characterized the Western compositional tradition of the twentieth century, but rather in folklore, which
Mihály felt represented a vital connection to the Hungarian populace.

Mihály was well aware that the Hungarian picture of Bartók forms a
mirror image of Leibowitz's, a striking example of the post-war divergence
of East and West. 'Let us switch the signs', he wrote, 'as when the mathe-
matical formula is multiplied by negative one, and before us stands the
picture of Bartók that we love'.[38] Mihály's 'multiplication by negative one'
attests to the conscious attempt to overthrow or deny 'Western' musical
values at every turn and to assert in their places the opposite but corresponding socialist values. Mihály's formulations, like those of his colleagues, effectively divided Bartók into two: the populist, Eastern Bartók of
the late works and the folksong settings directly opposed the bourgeois,
modernist Bartók whose works Leibowitz praised.

Some in the West consciously perpetuated this mirror-image thinking
as well. In a 1953 article entitled 'The Two Bartóks', American critic Arthur
Berger (1912–) explained that Bartók's most obviously folkloric scores
(such as *For Children*) and his accessible works (such as *Contrasts*) lack the
interest that his modernist works (such as the Sonata for Solo Violin)

provide. Although Berger's choice of representative works differs from
that of Leibowitz or Mihály – it is noteworthy that some critics on both
sides acknowledged Bartók's accessible and technically sophisticated late
Violin Sonata – the value judgement remains similar in effect, and its root
causes are not unrelated. 'The difference between this folk vein and
Bartók's most profound and provocative style', Berger explained, 'goes far
beyond being simply one of mood or content. It is more like the difference
between a 'Hit Parade' song and a Bach fugue'.[39] Berger thus responded
with the least enthusiasm to works with folk-like or popular idioms – the
same idioms cultivated in Eastern Europe – and with praise for Bartók's
most clearly modernist achievements, considered in Eastern Europe to be
too difficult for the masses. Berger, like Mihály, engaged in a kind of 'multiplication by negative one', dividing the good Bartók from the bad according to the populist-versus-modernist split that characterized so much
music criticism in the early 1950s.

   In effect, then, the early cold war years tore Bartók's oeuvre in two.
Because his music defied easy categorization, it was accepted in its entirety
nowhere. Instead, it became a proving ground where critics and composers could test and define their own values by advocating or reviling certain
elements of his style. Bartók's critics and his adherents were all committed
partisans of new music, but each had also pledged himself to a very specific
vision of the path new music must take – towards or away from the public
– and what stylistic means should be used to achieve the necessary effects.
The intensely competitive culture of the cold war ensured that the East and
the West constantly scrutinized one another, each side distinguishing itself
and its cultural values from the other's as sharply as possible. As the whole
of Europe was divided into two, so too were musical values, and so too was
Bartók's life-work – for the music that was praised in the East was pilloried
in the West, and the works elevated in France as the pinnacle of
magnificent complexity were banned in Hungary.

14 Analytical responses to Bartók's music: pitch organization

IVAN F. WALDBAUER

Diverse analytical methods based upon pitch organization in Bartók's music are, with a single exception, products of the second half of the century. To see them and their differences in perspective, it will be well to summarize first what happened generally in the earlier half of the century and after that to outline briefly the particular circumstances facing the Bartók analyst. During the first two decades of the century it was the new sounds of all avant-garde music that provoked the most immediate and sharpest response from critics, but naturally enough, discourse about the music itself was conducted largely along aesthetic rather than technical lines. A shift occurs in the 1920s, the landmark being Schoenberg's development of his twelve-tone method and the debates surrounding it.[1] During the next two or three decades, the literature fairly bristles with technical discussions: pantonality, atonality, bitonality, polytonality and pandiatonicism are some of the terms that date back to this period; even Bartók, a notorious non-participant in these discussions, weighs in with the term polymodality.[2] A second landmark is produced in Paul Hindemith's *The Craft of Musical Composition*, perhaps the first comprehensive theory of pitch organization of twentieth-century music.[3] This tradition-oriented theory, largely dismissive of Schoenbergian assumptions, was influential for a while, but eventually fell into neglect, exactly in proportion to the ascendancy of Schoenberg's ideas and their ramifications. The latter came to be the principal force in the thinking of most analysts during the second half of the century, especially in America.

Although Hindemith's theory did not engender any significant literature concerning Bartók's music, the questions underlying that theory remain valid. Where did Bartók's new sounds originate? How do they work? To what extent are they a negation, to what extent an outgrowth, of traditional common practice? These are still the questions at the centre of theories about Bartók to which Schoenbergian thinking alone can provide only limited answers. This is perhaps the principal reason why pitch theories about Bartók's music were relatively slow to develop, but there are at least three others equally potent. First is, of course, Bartók's already noted reluctance to discuss his own music. He was indifferent to theory in general, and professed outright hatred of preconceived theories.[4] He willingly discoursed at length upon folklore, but when it came to folklore influence on his own music, he treated even that subject mostly in general terms. His only detailed and protracted utterance on matters technical, the Harvard Lectures (that contain the discussion of polymodality), is unique. A second reason is his self-avowed eclecticism. As a consequence of his openness to all influences, in equal measure from folk and art music and from old and new music, his oeuvre is extremely diverse from both a stylistic and a technical viewpoint. To many analysts only a case-by-case approach seems possible, with the wider applicability of any given method always in doubt.[5] And last but not least, all analysts must face the daunting task of mastering all the folklores that guided Bartók, for they affected all aspects of his music, even his most abstract and seemingly folklore-free compositions.

It is not surprising under these circumstances that a large proportion of Bartók analyses are individual efforts directed towards individual works. Rather it is a cause for wonder that between 1930 and 1992 no fewer than six different pitch theories directed towards the entire Bartók oeuvre, or a representative portion of it, have appeared.[6] In Bartók's music pitch organization keeps generating a level of controversy that makes it advisable to restrict the present survey to this one aspect of his music. However, since pitch organization is but one component of style, other technical aspects form the background to the discussions that follow. They are: formal procedures, including Bartók's beloved symmetrical arch form; the gradual emergence rather than straightforward statement of themes in many of the larger forms; the role of contrapuntal artifices in shaping forms large and small; continuous and progressive variation techniques; the refusal to bring back materials in their previously stated form; various types of motivic transformation, including the systematic use of vertical interval extension and contraction; free permutations of pitch order within motivic entities; and finally the kind of monothematicism that results from the above.

The present survey will touch upon these matters only rarely. Its goal is to report on theories of pitch organization and on the origins of their divergences. It will briefly outline the historical position of the two earliest theorists, Edwin von der Null and Ernő Lendvai, and identify in some detail their basic assumptions. Then it will trace the emergence of ideas that have proved most influential from about mid-century to the present. Inevitably, the choice of contributions to be discussed is highly selective. Many excellent and important analytical efforts had to be excluded if they contained no new insights concerning pitch organization, or if such insights, however promising, found no followers to date.

The importance of Null's monograph on Bartók's piano music from 1908 to 1926 is threefold. All through the process of writing his book, Null was in touch with Bartók;[7] he is the originator of the idea that Bartók's 'extended tonality' is, despite appearances, an evolutionary outgrowth of traditional common practice, that is to say, tonal, diatonic and triadic; and he is the first to formulate the concept of what we now call polymodal chromaticism as one of the technical features that render both triadic base and diatonicism 'latent'. The concept rests on the observation that in many shorter and longer passages Bartók uses all the notes of all diatonic modes based upon the same tonic in close proximity or sometimes simultaneously. The term polymodal chromaticism was expanded and detailed later by Bartók himself (see note 2), who presents it as a folklore-inspired extension of the traditional practice manifested in the simultaneous use of both the raised and natural forms of the sixth and seventh degrees of the melodic minor mode. Despite many good insights in matters of formal and melodic procedures, Null's harmonic analyses tend to exhaust themselves in chord-by-chord details of dubious relevance. As János Kárpáti remarks, Null's awkwardness in dealing with harmony 'is due chiefly to his effort to force the phenomena of Bartók's musical language, even though with praiseworthy freedom, into the Procrustean bed of earlier functional music. . . . He accepts the new but explains it from the point of view of the old'.[8] To paraphrase Stephen Jay Gould, Null shows a 'better style of hearing' but does not combine it with 'new ways of thinking'.[9]

Ernő Lendvai, the other early Bartók analyst, began publishing in 1947 and produced the first formulation of his theory in 1955.[10] As influential as his writings were for some years, for today's reader his historical position may be even more interesting. At the time he began expounding his theories, even music analysis was pervaded by ideology of one kind or another. The field Lendvai entered was politically charged. Relevant to his position were two particular contentions, one professed by the then ruling Hungarian Communist Party intent upon enforcing the infamous Zhdanovian doctrines, the other by representatives of the Schoenberg camp. In 1949 the Communists split the Bartók oeuvre down the middle. The part they claimed for themselves was the one which appeared to them to have both folklore connections and popular appeal. They asserted that these works were on the historically correct path of evolution. The other part they effectively put on the index as formalist and modernist – the two Sonatas for Violin and Piano and the Third and Fourth String Quartets among others – and as deviations from the correct (read Marxist) line. By contrast, René Leibowitz, the French composer and Adorno-inspired spokesman for the Schoenberg school, embraced precisely these modernist works in a 1947 article and denounced the others.[11] His view is also shaped by Hegelian determinism but of a different stripe, for he believed that these modernist works were on the true and inevitable path of evolution in that they approximate 'total chromaticism', while the folklore-based works as well as the later works reflect Bartók's naivety. They represent a pernicious compromise, not to be followed by the young. It is clear today that neither side had a very good idea of how folklore was absorbed in Bartók's music and also that Leibowitz reacts to the immense upsurge of Bartók's popularity in the post-war years. For his part, and to his credit, Lendvai brushes aside both the split mandated by the Communists – this must have taken some courage – and the inevitability of the Leibowitzian line of evolution. It is unfortunate, however, that Lendvai's writing is tainted by ideology and by notions of evolution almost as much as those of his adversaries. At least it would seem so from the words he uses to draw the line separating Bartók's 'twelve-note system' (as discovered through Lendvai's axis system) from Schoenberg's twelve-tone music. 'Schoenberg', he writes, 'annihilates and dissolves tonality whereas Bartók incorporates the principles of harmonic thinking in a perfect synthesis'.[12]

Lendvai's theory is not so much an analytical tool but rather an altogether new set of assumptions designed to bring together under a single umbrella a plethora of diverse Bartókian procedures. Since the theory was enormously influential for quite some time, with some aspects of it still currently in use, it must be considered here in some detail. It can be divided into three interlocking parts: the axis system and its counterpart in the 'acoustic scale'; the operations of the golden section and the Fibonacci series; and certain chord and scale models arrived at through the first two parts. Part 1, the axis system, argues that Bartók extends the regular alternation of the S(ubdominant)–T(onic)–D(ominant) functions through the entire chromatic aggregate. Figure 14.1 shows that, assuming C as tonic, every third pitch in the circle of fifths has the same function.

The lines within the circle connect notes of the same function with each other and thus represent the three axes of T, D and S. Lendvai emphasizes that a given axis should not be thought of as one diminished seventh chord, but rather as discrete individual notes each embodying a particular function. The axis system he derives from the circle of fifths is the basis of what he calls Bartók's 'chromatic style'. Lendvai points out that the axis system has a complement to it, the basis of Bartók's 'diatonic style', which he calls the 'acoustic scale'. This he derives (not entirely accurately) from the overtone system, and it is the sequence of T(one)–T–T–S(emitone)–T–S–T (e.g., C–D–E–F♯–G–A–B♭–C).[13] Both aspects of this first part of Lendvai's theory are purely speculative. His proposed concept for the tonic, subdominant and dominant functions is at variance with common usage and shows only his penchant for 'new ways of thinking'. Despite the emphasis on the truly important Bartókian interval of the tritone, the system has very little explicatory value in practical analysis, and it is probably for this reason that even those who follow Lendvai's other ideas tend to sidestep both the axis system and the acoustic scale.[14]

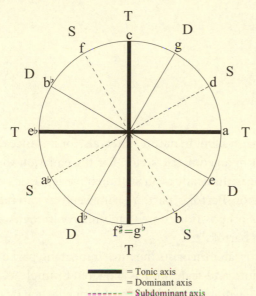

━━━━━━━ = Tonic axis
───────── = Dominant axis
- - - - - - = Subdominant axis

Figure 14.1 The circle of fifths with Lendvai's three axes.

Part 2 of Lendvai's theory concentrates on the golden section and the Fibonacci series. The golden section divides a given distance so that the ratio of the longer section to the shorter section equals the ratio of the whole distance to the longer section. If the distance is 1, the two segments are approximated by the irrational numbers 0.618 . . . and 0.382 . . ., respectively. In the Fibonacci series of integer numbers, each member is the sum of the two preceding members: 1–1–2–3–5–8–13–21–34–55–89–etc. The higher we go in the series, the closer the ratio of two consecutive numbers approximates the golden section: $2 \div 3 = 0.666$ . . .; $3 \div 5 = 0.6$; $5 \div 8 = 0.625$; . . . $55 \div 89 = 0.61797$ . . . etc. Fibonacci proportions are conspicuously frequent among natural phenomena: for instance, the arrangement of seeds in a sunflower or in certain pine cones is governed by them. Lendvai claims that in Bartók's chromatic style they determine both formal proportions (multifariously from the smallest to the largest scale) and pitch relations. If the distance between important pitches (initial and final notes of phrases, lowest and highest pitches within phrases, etc.) is counted in terms of intervals, and then these intervals are *equated* with the numbers 1 for minor seconds, 2 for major seconds, and so forth, Fibonacci numbers are seen by Lendvai as controlling factors in longer or shorter stretches of Bartók's music. Thus, according to Lendvai, the characteristic pentatonic formation shown in Example 14.1 (see p. 220) can be regarded as one of nature's characteristic formations, and as such one of the foundation stones of Bartók's chromatic style.

We may note that equating numbers with intervals (as distinct from the legitimate procedure of *labelling* intervals by numbers) cannot be a 'natural phenomenon', a property Lendvai insists is the basis of Bartók's

Example 14.1 Pentatony generated
by Fibonacci numbers

entire compositional system. In nature, intervals, for instance those of the chromatic scale, form a geometric series. For the equation to work they must be reduced logarithmically to an arithmetic series. This would imply conscious purpose on Bartók's part, a claim Lendvai carefully refrains from making and a proposition more than unlikely in the face of everything known about Bartók.[15]

The third, and for later theorists the most important, part of Lendvai's theory concerns chord and scale models shown in Example 14.2. Lendvai argues that a given harmonic function is best defined when it is combined with its own dominant. A radical application of his precept is the sounding of all pitches of one axis, say, the tonic axis in the key of C, C–E♭–F♯–A, together with the pitches of the dominant axis, C♯–E–G–B♭. The result is Lendvai's α chord, followed in the example by those segments of it in which both the T and D layers are present. The α chord gains additional justification for Lendvai by being built out of combinations of the Fibonacci intervals 2, 3, 2 + 3 = 5, and 3 + 5 = 8. A further application of Fibonacci intervals is seen by Lendvai in his 1:2, 1:3 and 1:5 models of Example 14.2b. It may be noted that the α chord and the 1:2 model are the same, called the octatonic scale by later analysts. The 1:3 model combines two overlapping γ chords or major-minor triads, the latter already identified by Nüll as one of the all-important polymodal chords in Bartók's music. And the 1:5 model, both as two perfect fourths a minor second apart and as two tritones a minor second or a perfect fourth apart, is what most later theorists refer to as the doubly symmetrical Z cell. Indeed, whatever the validity of Lendvai's explanations for the origins of these entities, all are well-observed Bartókian thumb prints; all later Bartók analysts must deal with them, and Lendvai deserves credit for isolating them.

Nüll's discovery of polymodal chromaticism and Lendvai's somewhat dubious endeavour to invoke the tonic–subdominant–dominant cycle slightly veil the stark contrast between these two approaches, which is the workability of a traditional theoretical framework versus its rejection in favour of an entirely novel framework. A succinct assessment of the situation can be found in Milton Babbitt's much-cited 1949 essay on Bartók's

Example 14.2

(a) Lendvai's α chord and its segments as explained in Lendvai, *Béla Bartók: An Analysis of his Music*, pp. 42–66, and in figure 37, p. 44

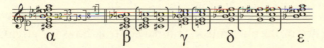

(b) Lendvai's 1:2, 1:3, and 1:5 models

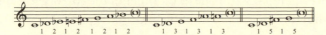

String Quartets.[16] To summarize Babbitt's argument, it is that Bartók achieves in his music an 'assimilated balance' between precompositional 'generalized functional tonal relationships' and 'unique internally defined relationships', the term used by Babbitt for what others call atonal or non-tonal, or simply abstract relationships. Bartók is too sophisticated to assign 'discrete regions of control' to either one of the two organizational principles. Rather they operate in such a way that their 'relationship is revealed through virtually non-perceptible phases of change in [their] relative autonomy'. The result is that 'easily perceived reiterations of thematic elements' that would bring with them unwanted functional connotations give way to constant mutations, and as a consequence, functionality becomes 'highly attenuated'.

To illustrate what he calls internally defined relationships, Babbitt turns to the Fourth Quartet, that is to say, to the work universally recognized as the one in which Bartók comes closest to atonality. It is probably for this reason that so many later writers also choose it for analysis. Babbitt identifies the primary motif of the piece, bar 7, cello – this is actually the linear form of George Perle's X cell (see pp. 223 and 224) – and traces its metamorphoses to show that 'rather than functioning as a fixed unit that is acted upon, [it] can itself act as a generator . . . creating . . . continuous phases of association'[17] with some analogy to tonal implications. To show that 'the harmonic region is revealed through polyphonic unfolding'[18] rather than by single harmonic events, he uses the whole-tone tetrachord Bb–C–D–E accompanying the above motif. In itself this tetrachord is a 'harmonically indefinite unit',[19] but its transposition by a whole step, that is, by the interval of its own constituent elements, at the end of the exposition creates a relationship that is perceived by Babbitt as analogous to a dominant–tonic progression. Let us note that Babbitt considers these events not actually tonal events, merely as analogous to tonal events.

Short as it is, Babbitt's essay is enormously important both from the historical and the analytical viewpoint. Historically, his term 'assimilated balance' is wholly devoid of any ideological content or value judgement, quite in contrast to Leibowitz's 'compromise'. Babbitt's value-free attitude is what so many analysts have been striving to adopt ever since, more so perhaps in America than elsewhere. As for the analytical specifics, the coexistence in Bartók's music of tonal control, however attenuated, with abstract techniques independent of precompositional tonal functionality enjoys general acceptance. The differences arising among analyses is a difference of emphasis on one or the other of the two organizational principles – but then that is also the difference that separates one work from the next in the Bartók oeuvre.

Six sophisticated Bartók studies that appeared during the decade following Babbitt's essay may be cited to show that analytical approaches tend indeed to divide according to whether their primary interest lies in following up one or the other of the dual properties diagnosed by Babbitt. The Schenkerians Felix Salzer (1952) and Roy Travis (1959) concentrate on tonal motion directed along more or less traditional lines, while George Perle (1955), Colin Mason (1957), Leo Treitler (1959), and Allen Forte (1960) focus on abstract techniques.[20] The latter group often employs terminology from Schoenbergian twelve-tone theory, and the word 'serial' is actually present in the titles of Mason and Forte. It will be convenient to begin with the discoveries of Perle and Treitler, since they form the basis of the important later theory of Elliott Antokoletz.

Discussions concerning inversional symmetry by Perle and his successors are more easily followed when two simple technical facts are kept in mind. All symmetrical formations have two axes of symmetry a tritone apart; and such axes are formed either by a single pitch or by a semitonal dyad (not to be confused with Lendvai's axes of symmetry). Thus the tetrachord A–C–E–G has D as its axis, inverted as E–G–A–C it has G♯ (= A♭) as its axis; similarly, the tetrachord E♮–G–C–E♭ has the A–B♭ dyad as its axis; inverted as C–E♭–E♮–G it has the E♭–E♮ dyad as its axis. The axis may or may not be present in a given symmetrical formation.

Perle's thesis is that Bartók's technique of having stable axis tones operating as tonal centres took many years to develop, and that the fully fledged form of the technique first appeared in the Fourth Quartet of 1928. Before turning to that work, however, he demonstrates a particularly clear-cut application of the technique at the end of the Fifth Quartet (1934) and contrasts this with an earlier stage of development in the Second Quartet (1915–17). Bartók himself has identified B♭ and E♮ as tonic and dominant in the two outer movements of the Fifth Quartet, and what Perle demonstrates is that the last sixty-six bars of the work revolve symmetrically around two pairs of axes, E♭–E♮ plus A–B♭ and E♮ plus B♭.[21] He relates the various vertical and linear events to these axes and shows that all were developed in the earlier course of the movement, where symmetries also play a role, and concludes that in these sixty-six bars 'every musical event anticipates and requires a single unharmonized b♭ for its ultimate resolution, an effect which Bartók achieves by means which are *entirely independent of traditional modal or tonal procedures*'.[22] This is not the case in the Second Quartet, where Perle sees symmetrical formations functioning as purely textural elements. For our purposes the most important part of Perle's essay is his discovery of two symmetrical four-note sets and their operations in the Fourth Quartet. He calls them X and Y, of which X is C–C♯–D–E♭, that is, the vertical form of Babbitt's 'primary motif', and Y is B♭–C–D–E, that is, the chord first heard as the accompaniment of the linear form of X. Leo Treitler adds to these a third set Z, that is, G♯–C♯–D–G♮ (Lendvai's 1:5 model in Ex. 14.2b, above). As Elliott Antokoletz will eventually carry investigations of these three sets a little further, one of his figures is borrowed here to show the interrelations of these three sets and some of their operations, see Figure 14.2, below.

To avoid possible confusion in the further course of this survey, a point only implied in the foregoing discussion of Babbitt, Perle and Treitler must be made explicit. In their technical discourse all three writers address internally (i.e., contextually) defined musical relationships exclusively. All three invoke analogies between these abstract procedures and tonal ones, but these are only analogies, and are not to be taken for any kind of tonal reality. When Perle writes in his 1955 essay that Bartók's symmetrical formations form 'only an incidental aspect of his compositional means' and later extols the Sixth Quartet 'as a remarkable symbiosis of traditional harmonic functions and those abstract and constructivist elements that had played an increasingly important role in the Second through the Fifth Quartet', he helps the reader to keep his or her perspective.[23] Treitler is the only one to use and define the term tonic in the Fourth Quartet, but both his context and his definition show that he means something radically different from what the term connotes in the common practice tradition. According to him, procedures in the Fourth Quartet are entirely independent of traditional procedures (just as Perle says about the end of the Fifth Quartet). Nevertheless, he identifies the C–E third as acting in the role of tonic. In his view, however, this sound is found at most important junctures of the piece as a static reference point, it has no role in generating structure.

It should not surprise us that the Schenkerian, Roy Travis, does not agree with Treitler, as we shall see presently. Travis states the basic premise of his and Salzer's Schenkerian (and generally tonal) approach as follows: 'Music is tonal when its motion unfolds through time a particular tone,

EXPOSITION

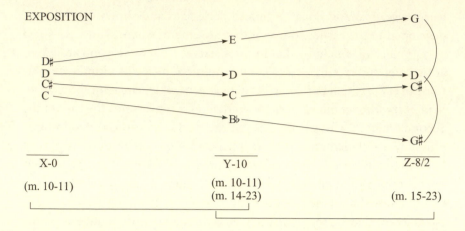

DEVELOPMENT

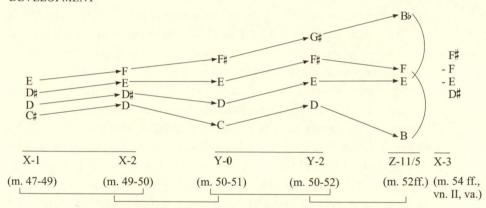

Figure 14.2 String Quartet No. 4, I, X–Y–Z progressions in exposition, bars 10–23, and development, bars 49 ff. The numbers following the set names X, Y and Z indicate the lowest pitch in each set by integer notation, in which C = 0, C♯ = 1, D = 2, etc. (After Elliott Antokoletz, *The Music of Béla Bartók*, p. 118)

interval, or chord'.[24] He posits the concept of 'tonic sonority' and explains: 'There is no reason why a major or minor third, a 7th chord, a 4th chord, a polychord, or any conceivable combination of tones appropriate to the composer's artistic purpose cannot become the tonic sonority of a tonal music. It is only necessary that the combination be capable of definition in terms of structure which is susceptible to vital and expressive prolongation.'[25] He illustrates this liberalized concept of tonal motion directed towards recognizable goals by three examples: the first nine bars of Stravinsky's *The Rite of Spring* and two complete pieces from Bartók's *Mikrokosmos*, Nos. 133 and 124. For the first and third of these, the latter of which 'does seem completely devoid of [traditional] harmonic influence', he produces unorthodox but convincing Schenkerian graphs. Rather amusingly, he reverses the analytical process for No. 133, 'Syncopations', casting it into the form of a compositional exercise. He identifies G–B–D–E♭–F♯ as the characteristic tonic sonority; then makes up prolongations for each chord of the characteristic sonority in a full I–IV–V–I progression, using models for these prolongations from a nineteenth-century piece. The exercise completed, he compares the made-up graph with the actual graph of the actual piece and finds them identical. He expressly disclaims any notion that Bartók would have in any conscious way worked in this manner, but he believes the result shows 'that reports of the death of the tonic–dominant system are greatly exaggerated'.[26]

The reader who would like to gain a fuller understanding of Travis's method would do well to turn to the graphs and to the analysis in his 1970 essay 'Tonal Coherence in the First Movement of Bartók's Fourth String Quartet'.[27] Unfortunately, in the present survey space disallows even a summary of Travis's sophisticated tonal analysis. A few salient features can, however, provide a basis of comparison with points made by the three scholars previously discussed. Travis identifies the very first chord of the piece, C–E–F♯, as its tonic sonority and explains the events of the movement in terms of a network of neighbour-chord motions around this sonority. He also recognizes the importance of the X, Y and Z cells, but in his reading the B♭–C–D–E position of Y (cf. Fig. 14.2) rather than being the first occurrence of the cell is a neighbour of the tonic sonority and as such, it is the 'contrast level' on which further thematic entities of the exposition unfold. Its transposition back to the C level at bar 50 is thus a return to the tonic, signalling the start of the development section. To be sure, Travis's analytical framework and his concept of prolongation are controversial; the user of his method must constantly look out for the dangers of arbitrariness.[28] Nevertheless, in the opinion of the present writer, Travis's good ear saves him from the danger. The advantages of a graph constructed along the lines suggested by Travis are twofold. It is invaluable as a descriptive tool even on those occasions when it fails to satisfy Schenkerian orthodoxy as an explicatory tool of all musical details. More important, its capacity to deal with a piece of any size in its entirety outweighs its liabilities.

All these analysts, as well as many others who follow them during the subsequent decades, work within the framework of intrinsic musical relationships, either 'abstract' or 'tonal', established by Babbitt. Even when their emphases are weighted towards one side, they are all keenly aware of the other. This is as true of the two Americans, Jonathan W. Bernard and Wallace Berry, who further explore Bartókian symmetries, as it is of the more tonally oriented work of two British scholars, Arnold Whittall and

David Gow. From his examination of the first two Quartets Gow actually develops the concept of 'emerging tonality'.[29] There is, however, another group of scholars who can, despite shared assumptions, be distinguished from the above by their greater interest in folklore influence. In their view folklore, rather than being extrinsic to the musical relationships discussed by the others, significantly modifies the perception of these relationships. Not surprisingly, Hungarian musicologists constitute the majority of this group, but substantial contributions come also from two German scholars, Erich Kapst and Peter Petersen (the latter being the author of one of the six important book-length studies) from the Finn Ilkka Oramo, and from the Belgian Yves Lenoir.[30] Let the work of János Kárpáti serve as a window through which to observe the guiding ideas of this group.

The portion of Kárpáti's work that is of paramount interest to the present survey was first formulated in 1967 and reappears with just a few refinements in subsequent works. It is Part 1 of his 1994 study, *Bartók's Chamber Music* (pp. 21–235), serving as a historical and theoretical framework to the analyses of Part 2. The greatest strength of Kárpáti's approach is its sober and pragmatic quality. He presents his findings in the form of an array of well-supported observations, discusses their relevance, and firmly resists making them the basis of any monistic system (either Bartók's or his own) *à la* Lendvai. His three chapters of greatest analytical consequence are 'The Folk Music Influence', '"Polymodal Chromaticism"', and 'Tonality and Polytonality – The Phenomenon of Mistuning'.[31]

The chapter on folk-music influence should be required reading for any Bartók scholar, not just those interested in analysing his music. In it, Kárpáti links an immense variety of Bartókian melodic turns to an equally immense variety of folklore models and demonstrates the harmonic ramifications of the latter as well as characteristic Bartókian modifications of them. For example, Kárpáti shows the Arabic model for the theme in the Fourth Quartet[32] (bars 14–29) in which Treitler's Z cell evolves (the pure form of the Z cell is first played by the first violin in bar 22; cf. Fig. 14.2, above; see also the beginning of the passage in Ex. 10.8a, p. 161 above). Particularly helpful is his discussion of both anhemitonic and hemitonic pentatony in various folklores and their role in Bartók's music.[33] His chapter on polymodal chromaticism is perhaps the most comprehensive short treatment of the subject to date and a welcome corrective to misapprehensions that arose after 1966, in the wake of John Vinton's partial publication of Bartók's comments on the subject.[34] In his final theoretical chapter Kárpáti breaks new ground. In the phenomenon of mistuning he identifies a hitherto unrecognized source of Bartókian chromaticism and shows it to be both a part of Bartók's practice throughout his creative life and a constant factor in his melodic and tonal-harmonic thinking. The

Example 14.3

(a) String Quartet No. 5, I, bars 4–6

(b) Imaginary model for the above proposed by
Kárpáti, in *Bartók's Chamber Music*, p. 197

phenomenon may be best explained with reference to one of Kárpáti's many examples reproduced here in Example 14.3.

Kárpáti notices that the theme in Example 14.3a sounds as if it were the distorted version of the theme in Example 14.3b. Specifically, the second half of the Bartók theme (from E♮, the second crotchet in bar 5) gives the impression as if it were sounding a semitone lower than expected after what was heard in bar 4, that is, as if it were played on a mistuned string. The many examples marshalled by Kárpáti for this phenomenon show that most of such distortions affect the traditional perfect fifth–octave framework, either stretching it or contracting it as is the case in our example. Kárpáti's insight receives a degree of authentication from those of his examples in which normal and mistuned forms of the same tune appear side by side. More important from the analytical viewpoint is that the practice is transferred from the horizontal to the vertical plane, mostly by mistuned imitations and mistuned accompaniments but also by other polyphonic means. The result is various types of bitonality and polytonality. Normally, such bitonal or polytonal passages represent only a momentary modification of the expected perfect fifth–octave framework, not a nullification of it.[35]

There are two more analytical methods to be discussed in this survey, one a continuation of the work on inversional symmetries begun by George Perle, the other based on the set theory of Allen Forte. The interests of Elliott Antokoletz of the Perle school are perhaps more heavily weighted on the abstract side of the Babbittian dichotomy. He is, of course, aware of the other side, but the subtitle of his 1984 book, *The Music of Béla Bartók: A Study of Tonality and Progression in Twentieth-Century Music*, is misleading. Tonality refers here to pitch priorities brought about by axes of symmetry, not to those brought about by traditional functionality. There may be some analogy between the two, but they are not the same. The gist of Antokoletz's argument is stated in his preface:

[O]ne senses in Bartók's total output an all-encompassing system of pitch
relations . . . Certain fundamental principles are related to a larger system
that has been referred to by George Perle as 'twelve-tone tonality' . . . [P]itch
relations in Bartók's music are primarily based on the principle of *equal
subdivision* of the octave into the total complex of interval cycles. The
fundamental concept underlying this equal-division system is that of
symmetry.[36]

Compared with his predecessors, Antokoletz greatly extends the
concept of symmetry. In addition to actual linear and vertical symmetries
he recognizes potential forms of these, that is, formations not in themselves symmetrical but being capable of being so rearranged. Further, he
recognizes what he calls 'gapped' structures, when the context so requires
or permits. Thus, Travis's tonic sonority in the Fourth Quartet, C–E–F♯,
can be considered a gapped form of Perle's Y cell. The term interval cycle
refers to subdividing the octave by a series of identical intervals. There are
thus a single cycle of semitones, two different cycles of whole tones, and so
forth, up to six cycles of tritones.[37] All these divisions and any of their segments are necessarily symmetrical. Further, there are many symmetrical
formations that are not themselves segments of one or the other of the
interval cycles but can be defined as combinations of two such cycles (e.g.,
the Z cell, the octatonic scale, Lendvai's 1:3 model, among others). By
tracing the generative relations of axes and interval cycles, and their interactions with non-symmetrical structures, Antokoletz also greatly expands
the scope of axis operations. Ultimately he is able to demonstrate that at
least in certain cases axes are capable of creating both the sense and sub-
stance of tonality (in his sense of the term) as well as those of progression
and modulation.

These are but the barest outlines of the system expounded by
Antokoletz. It derives a degree of authority from his circumspect tracing of
the emergence of its components (including the modification of folklore
models) in a succession of Bartók compositions from the Bagatelles of
1908 to the Fourth Quartet of 1928, the final stage of the entire development. Thereafter, as Antokoletz sees it, the system remains a constant
factor in Bartók's output, but it shares the role of establishing modal
centres with more traditional means. We may note that greatly as
Antokoletz extends the applicability of symmetry in the Bartók oeuvre, he
does not claim that phenomena of symmetry account for all other phenomena within that oeuvre.[38]

Before beginning the survey of the work by scholars who employ
Forte's set theory, it seems advisable to review briefly the principal tenets
of that theory. A set is a collection of pitches determined by its fixed
ascending (or descending) interval content. It retains its identity through

any of its transpositions, inversions, spacing and voicing. A set may be related in various ways to other sets, the simplest and most important of these relations being those to its own subsets and those to larger sets of which it itself is a subset. To follow the linear and vertical behaviour of a given set in a given composition and its interactions with other elements (rhythm, register, other significant sets) is to reveal something about how the piece works, sometimes even how the composer worked. The success of the method, as with the success of any method, depends on the good ear and the good judgement of the analyst. In set theory the critical factor is segmentation, that is, the identification of the truly meaningful set.

In 1981 Richard S. Parks and James Woodward were the first two scholars to apply set theory to Bartók, the former providing additional interest in his reading of 'Fourths' (*Mikrokosmos*, No. 131) because it offers comparison with the reading of Antokoletz.[39] In addition there are two exceptionally lucid and perceptive essays by Richard Cohn who states in so many words that a general theory of Bartók's music is 'not, by any means, a guaranteed prospect'.[40] He shows that despite the presence of tonal centricity, 'examination of several traits characteristic of Bartók's compositional idiom may be effectively carried out without appealing to tonal considerations'.[41] With his concept of transpositional combination he constructs a convincing analytical model for much music and many passages in Bartók's output. He combines a demonstration of this model with a critique of Antokoletz (and Perle) and shows that in many instances transpositional combinations are more perceptible and yield better local or structural determinants than inversional symmetry, even when the latter is also present. It is important, however, that Cohn sees no reason to make an absolute choice between these two models, for he believes Bartók may have kept returning to certain structures precisely because 'they could reflect both inversional and transpositional relations'.[42]

Cohn's view concerning the need for pluralism and his scepticism as to the possibility of an all-encompassing theory of all Bartók's music is shared by Paul Wilson in *The Music of Béla Bartók*. This study is the last book-length contribution to Bartók analysis to date. One of its themes is a most thorough examination of the applicability of set theory. The most decisive of the book's many virtues is the principle of structural overlay. Briefly, this means that several possibly disparate structural strands unfold simultaneously in the course of a single composition, and these strands may possibly but not necessarily interact with each other. Of course, they intersect, but the operations of a given strand are always independent from those of the others. One of the more easily followed occurrences of structural overlay in Wilson's analyses is the unfolding of the minor second + minor third + minor third set within the total context of the first movement of Bartók's

1926 Piano Sonata.[43] Wilson's carefully reasoned theoretical framework that precedes his analyses touches upon all conceivable parameters relevant to Bartók's pitch organization. Among these are much debated issues like harmonic function, hierarchies, or relative structural weight and also novel details, for instance 'projected sets' and 'privileged patterns'.[44] But it is the linking together of these and other issues through the concept of structural overlay that enables Wilson to produce that *rara avis* in purely theoretical writing, the comprehensive analysis of large and complex movements in their entirety.

The foregoing survey of pitch theories applicable to Bartók's music offers a threefold moral. First, the Bartók analyst must approach his or her subject by several routes. It is not enough to follow up just one 'tonal' and one 'abstract' possibility; determinations need to be made as to which of several competing methods designed to deal with abstract procedures is best justified by context. Second, since none of the recent analytical methods addresses the tonal-functional side of the Babbittian dichotomy, those who believe that no analysis of a given Bartók work is complete without an assessment of Bartók's use of, or reliance on, tonal-functional forces must forge ahead on their own as best they can. The point acquires some significance when we consider the many writers who have made important contributions to the Bartók literature with little or no recourse to the methods discussed in the foregoing, proceeding instead along more or less traditional lines. Students of this persuasion may look favourably upon Wilson's principle of structural overlay, as this allows simultaneous consideration of several disparate structural elements. Third, pitch organization, however important, is only one of the components relevant to style. Systematic music theory could make its contribution to some others – the neglected subject of temporal organization in twentieth-century music comes to mind – but even when it does, true style interpretation remains the domain not of music analysis but of the inspired musician, whether analyst, historian, composer or performer.

15 Bartók at the piano: lessons from the composer's sound recordings

VERA LAMPERT

In his essay on the authorial performance tradition, Hermann Danuser distinguishes four means through which composers can transmit their ideas of the interpretation of their works: 'first by performance instructions given in the text of the work, second, by their conception of performance communicated orally or in writing, third, by the realization of "exemplary" performances, and fourth, by fixing the authorial performance on a recording medium in the twentieth century'.[1]

Bartók utilized all these opportunities to convey his ideas of the performance of his music throughout his career. He edited his compositions carefully with an abundance of descriptive expressions and signs, indicating tempo and character, phrasing, dynamic shading, articulation and accents, their combinations, sometimes introducing novel signs for special effects. To further define the character of the composition, he indicated the tempo and tempo changes with metronome markings, and from the 1930s, he also started to provide the expected time to perform the work in the score at the end of each composition or individual movement.

Most of the elements of Western musical notation, however, are only approximations and need interpretation. There are conventions that the composer may take for granted but these might become forgotten in time. For this reason, any clarification about musical notations by a composer represents inestimable value. However, even armed with the systematic explanations of the performing signs Bartók employed in his instructional editions of classical music, there remain uncertainties in the interpretation of the score since certain nuances cannot be noted in a practical way without becoming too complicated and obscuring basic elements of the composition. Having spent countless hours transcribing folk music from field recordings, then revising transcriptions to include more details and particularities, Bartók was too well aware of the limitations of recording a live performance on paper. A more effective way to transmit musical interpretation was by teaching which, for him, meant first of all demonstration. The time and scope of a teaching activity is limited, however, and since Bartók was reluctant to teach his own music, only a few of his students could consult him about its details.

Nothing can reveal a composer's ideas as faithfully as his or her own performance. Most composers actively partake in the performances of their work in different capacities, depending on their abilities as performers. Bartók was one of those composers who were also first-rate pianists. One can get an idea of his pianistic abilities and accomplishments by considering his repertoire: he played about a dozen monumental Liszt compositions, including the B minor Sonata, the E♭ major Piano Concerto, *Totentanz, Concerto Pathétique, Spanish Rhapsody* and *La campanella*, this notwithstanding his own large-scale piano music, for example the Second Piano Concerto. Stephen Bishop-Kovacevich, who won the Edison award for his recording of this last piece in 1970, declared that he never played anything as technically difficult and he almost paralysed his hands while learning it.[2] Bartók played the Second Piano Concerto several times, admirably, as an unfortunately fragmentary and technically inferior recording of one of his broadcast performances also testifies.

More than his technical accomplishments, however, his unique interpretation was universally admired. His piano teacher at the Academy, István Thomán, maintained that 'of contemporary pianists, Busoni and Bartók most closely approached the sovereignty of Liszt'.[3] Although Bartók did not become a celebrated travelling virtuoso, he made concert tours from the early 1920s regularly. Sometimes he complained that these trips were a burden to him. Nevertheless, he continued to play until the end of his life, not only for financial reasons but, as he once wrote to his mother, because he felt that the propagation of his music was mainly his responsibility.[4]

Research into the performing style of the past centuries must content itself with hypothetical results, since it has to do without the ultimate verification – the composer's own performance – of the validity of its painstaking reconstruction. With the advent of sound-recording technology it is now possible for composers to leave to posterity not only the written form of their work but the music as it sounds itself. Bartók recognized the importance of perpetuating composers' performances of their own music:

> It is a well-known fact that our notation records on music paper, more or less inadequately, the idea of the composer; hence the existence of contrivances with which one can record precisely every intention and idea of the composer is indeed of great importance ... [The gramophone] offers the possibility for composers to pass on to the world their compositions not only as musical scores but in the form of their personal appearance or in a presentation which conforms to their ideas ... [D]eficiencies [– lack of certain overtones, extreme dynamic intensities and the dimensional quality of sound –] might impair the full aesthetic enjoyment of the reproduction, but such deficiencies mean very little to the scientific researcher in comparison with those infinite,

minute nuances which cannot be expressed notationally, yet can be immortalized in their totality on gramophone records.[5]

Despite the advance in technology Bartók blamed recording companies for forgoing their historical calling to record composers' performances for easy profit making: '[while they are quick to record] music hall ditties, song hits, and the like ... [t]hey miss many recordings that later will be unproducible, because the composer will no longer be alive'.[6] He himself gladly performed in the recording studio whenever the opportunity – not too often, unfortunately – presented itself. He also wanted to propagate his 'authentic performances', referring to them in his printed scores.[7] There are about ten hours of recorded music preserving his playing for posterity. Somewhat more than four hours of this is music by other composers (Bach, Scarlatti, Mozart, Beethoven, Chopin, Brahms, Liszt, Debussy and Kodály). The larger part, however – almost six hours of music – contains Bartók playing his own compositions. Those who were fortunate to hear him in person insist that his recordings cannot do justice to the extraordinary impression of his playing. Nevertheless, there is a growing camp of musicians and music lovers who never had a chance to hear him perform live, yet are convinced, on the basis of his sound recordings, that he is the best performer of his own music.

During Bartók's lifetime the technology of sound recording went through rapid development and his playing was recorded in various media. Bartók himself made the first recordings of his playing – a present to his friend Kodály's wedding in August 1910 – with the phonograph he used from 1906 to collect folk music.[8] Four more pieces followed in 1912 and one in 1915: six cylinders altogether (about fifteen minutes of music). This technology, which Bartók still used for recording folk music as late as 1936, was far from ideal for recording art music. A cylinder could contain only two-and-a-half minutes of music, and was easily damaged by use and storage. Nevertheless, these phonograph recordings have special value, as László Somfai points out, since they are 'very fresh' performances, made 'no more than four years later than the date of the composition, thus the interpretations have not become a matter of routine following frequent public performance'.[9]

Another recording technology used around the turn of the century was the paper roll to be played on a mechanical piano. In Bartók's words:

> This method of recording permanently fixes the tempo, the rhythm, and even the pedalling ... [The] advantages over the phonograph or gramophone are that misplays can be corrected on the reel and the instrument is not distorted when it is played. On the other hand, it is not able to produce the extreme dynamic levels: a true *pianissimo* or a great *fortissimo*.[10]

We know of two occasions when Bartók's playing was recorded for the mechanical piano: in 1922 in Paris (by Pleyela) and in 1928 in New York (by Welte-Licencee Inc.). Only the four rolls of the latter session survive: two complete compositions and parts of two other works, about eighteen minutes of music altogether.

Ten years after Edison invented the phonograph, a new recording technology appeared which used shellac discs instead of wax cylinders and had the advantage of a better sound; above all, it was more durable and easier to mass produce than the cylinder. It could play also somewhat longer (four-and-a-half minutes), although the recording technology, collecting the sound through a horn similar to the phonograph, made it difficult and almost impossible to record larger ensembles. No acoustic recording of this kind was made of Bartók's playing. However, the subsequent introduction of electrical recording technology in 1925 greatly improved the quality of sound recordings. The majority of the recordings of Bartók's performances – about two hours of solo piano music and one hour of chamber music – was done in this medium, between 1928 and 1945.

Bartók was engaged for studio recordings by four companies on seven occasions: His Master's Voice made the first series of recordings with him in Budapest, in December 1928, then in November 1929. During his 1930 visit to London, the British branch of Columbia made recordings of his playing. After a hiatus of five years, in 1936, the company Patria recorded Bartók in Budapest. The last studio recordings in Europe were made in 1939 by British Columbia again, in London. During his American visit in 1940, Bartók had a six-day recording session with Columbia, and, finally, Continental made recordings with him, probably in 1941. These studio performances are much closer to a live performance than such performances are today when sophisticated recording techniques allow extensive editing and correction of mistakes by combining different takes. During the early years of recordings a few takes were made of which the best one was released (there are two compositions which survived in two takes by Bartók). Or, if no takes were satisfactory, the performer simply did not approve the release of the recording (as in the case of the four Scarlatti Sonatas, published by Peter Bartók after his father's death).

The remaining recordings of Bartók's playing (about two-and-a-half hours) were made of live performances: the 1940 recital in the Library of Congress with Joseph Szigeti and four live broadcast recitals (Frankfurt Radio, 1932; Hilversum Radio, 1935; CBS New York, 1940; and New Jersey 'Kossuth' Radio, 1945). Finally, the Hungarian phonoamateur István Makai recorded off-the-air about three hours of music from broadcast recitals between 1936 and 1939 in Budapest. The sound quality of this material, mainly on X-ray foils discarded by hospitals, is rather poor and many of the pieces are incomplete and fragmentary, due to the fact that Makai was working with a single turntable until 1939. Yet, it contains invaluable examples of how Bartók played Bach, Mozart, Chopin and Brahms, in addition to unique recordings of two of his large-scale compositions: the Rhapsody for piano and orchestra Op. 1 and the Second Piano Concerto.

While most of the commercially produced recordings and some live recordings have been released on long-playing records between 1949 and 1972, much of the material, namely the phonograph recordings, some broadcast recordings and the whole Makai-material, remained unknown until the centennial year of Bartók's birth when the whole body of his surviving recorded playing was released by Hungaroton.[11] In the 1990s this material was digitized and republished, with some additions and corrections, in compact disc format.[12] Besides the twenty-two compositions by nine composers, which give an excellent overview of how Bartók approached the music of the past two centuries, twenty-nine of his own works are represented in the collection: fourteen full compositions (six for solo piano, six chamber music works, and two for voice and piano), including such important compositions as *Allegro barbaro*, Suite Op. 14, Second Violin Sonata, *Contrasts*, and Sonata for Two Pianos and Percussion; and one or more movements from thirteen compositions (eighty-five movements altogether), with an almost complete Improvisations Op. 20 and generous selections from the series *For Children* and *Mikrokosmos*. Compositions recorded twice, three or four times deserve special attention, especially if they contain consistent alterations compared to the written music, in which case there is reason to argue that the changes are not accidental and could be considered as variant versions of the composition.[13]

One can only regret that Bartók never had the chance to record some of his large-scale works: the Piano Sonata, *Out of Doors*, First Piano Concerto or First Violin Sonata, thus somewhat turning the scale of the recorded material in favour of the folksong arrangements. (A piece often featured on Bartók's recitals, the second movement of *Out of Doors* – 'The Night's Music' – was probably omitted from the last recording sessions with Continental only because it would not fit on a 78 rpm record in his performance: he gave the duration of the piece as five minutes several times in his correspondence.) Despite these serious gaps, the number of the recorded works is significant and provides valuable lessons about the composer's performance of his own music.

One reviewer hails the collection of recordings as 'a veritable textbook of how Bartók's music should be played'.[14] Investigation of this precious material began with Somfai's path-breaking studies about the different performances of *Allegro barbaro*, 'Evening in Transylvania' and about Bartók's performing style in general.[15] However, since the complete edition of Bartók's performances appeared in 1981 there has been a surge in critical analysis of the composer's performing style. Several unpublished American and German dissertations of the past fifteen years systematically compare and evaluate the deviations in his playing from the written music, in terms of notes, rhythm, articulation and dynamics, including comparative analyses of other performers. Among them Hayo Nörenberg's work stands out with its new method using computer technology to present the nuances of Bartók's rhythmic playing in easily perceivable diagrams. It also draws upon the analysis of folk recordings in order to investigate their influence on his performance.[16]

In one way or another these examinations all reach the same principal conclusion: that Bartók's interpretation of his works deviates greatly from the written music. There are occasional changes of pitch, whole bars added or left out, especially in repetitive, transitory sections, and dynamics and articulation may also differ. But the most conspicuous divergence between the scores and the playing is found in tempo and rhythm. Bartók generally plays significantly faster than the suggested tempo; furthermore, his tempo is not strict but oscillates throughout a piece. His rhythm is also at variance with the notated rhythms and is subject to frequent subtle modifications.

The ideal of flexible tempo and rhythm originates in the Romantic composers. According to contemporary accounts, Beethoven's playing 'was free of all constraint in respect to the beat';[17] Brahms despised metronome markings: 'I have never believed that my blood and a mechanical instrument go very well together',[18] and Liszt maintained that 'time and rhythm must be adapted to and identified with the melody, the harmony, the accent and the poetry . . .'.[19] Wagner also considered '*modification* of tempo . . . a *sine qua non*'.[20] This ideal was carried over to the turn of the century, when freedom of performance was considered the true sign of artistic maturity. Significantly, after one of the first sensational appearances of the pianist Bartók, still a student of the Academy, the only criticism he pondered was that he did not play with enough freedom.[21] Later, however, it was exactly the flexibility and freedom of his performances that was emphasised as the most memorable aspect of his playing in the recollections of his contemporaries. Andor Földes, who recorded Bartók's complete piano music in the 1950s, remembered 'his almost uncanny sense of rhythm – combined with a wonderful flexibility that characterised perhaps more than anything his playing'.[22] Otto Klemperer, the conductor of one of the first performances of the Second Piano Concerto, describing Bartók, the performer, had the same opinion: 'He was a wonderful pianist and musician. The beauty of his tone, the energy and the lightness of his playing were unforgettable. It was almost painfully beautiful. He played with great freedom, that was what was so wonderful'.[23]

Recent scholarship dealing with the history of performance practice pays increasing attention to early sound recordings, allowing us to consider Bartók's performing style from a wider perspective. Comparing hundreds of recordings made earlier in the century with later ones, it is now possible not only to conclude that musicians recording in the early 1900s preserved the performing style of the late nineteenth century, which then gradually changed as the twentieth century wore on, but also to describe the differences of the two styles in great detail and to detect how the transformation evolved.[24] Coming from a school cultivating Liszt's legacy, Bartók's playing virtually epitomizes the characteristics of the late Romantic performing style. For this reason the musicologist Richard Taruskin has recently chosen the recording by Bartók and his wife of Mozart's Sonata for two Pianos (K. 488) in order to contrast a typical Romantic performance with the controlled and exact one of Mozart's C minor Fugue (K. 426) by the most influential proponent of the new, objective performing style, Igor Stravinsky, and his son, Soulima.[25]

In the Bartóks' Mozart recording most of the typical features of the late nineteenth-century performing style are present. Flexibility permeates every level: there is no strict adherence to the tempo throughout the movements; rather, the tendency is to press ahead in loud or energetic passages (in the first movement for example, following the second theme, from bar 49), and to pass over hurriedly at relatively unimportant transitional sections (as at bar 25, before the second theme). Conversely, at lyrical moments, at the appearance of a new theme or important event the tempo is relaxed, sometimes drastically (as at bar 33); an even more striking example is the first movement of Beethoven's 'Kreutzer' Sonata where Bartók and Szigeti reduce the tempo at the second theme by one third of the tempo of the previous transitional section. Another typical feature is the brisk tempo of fast movements: in general, maximum tempi were much faster in earlier performances than those later in the century – one has to think only of the breathtaking speed of Bartók's Scarlatti Sonata recordings.

Flexibility was also present at the more local level of the late Romantic performance. Steadiness of the pulse was regarded as unnatural, because if 'the elastic give-and-take of movement is resisted, the performance is characterised by a certain lifelessness and affects the listener as being spiritless'.[26] Phrases were executed with subtle hastening and lingering, traditionally called 'rubato', the extent of which depended on the character of the music. Important notes were highlighted not only with dynamic stress or touch but also with slightly lengthened value, also called agogic accent. These are such universally applied devices of Bartók's playing that the examples are virtually countless; their variety ranges from the barely noticeable (as in the lyrical second theme in the Mozart Sonata) to the playful and dance-like (such as the 'Passepied' in Bach's G major Partita) to the dragging, painful rubato in Liszt's *Weinen, Klagen* variations. Also regarded effective, especially in slow melodies, was to delay the melody and to start a little after the accompaniment (as in Bartók's only Chopin recording, the Nocturne Op. 27 No. 1) or to break chords for emphasis and bring out clashes within a harmony (as in the slow introduction or in the second movement of the 'Kreutzer' Sonata). In patterns of long and short notes, short notes were shortened and long notes elongated which lent a certain lightness and vitality to the texture: particularly captivating examples can be found in bars 13, 16, 31 and 33 in one of Bartók's Scarlatti recordings (K. 427) or in the Brahms *Capriccio* (Op. 76 No. 2). All these devices appear in Bartók's recordings of his own music, the mercurial tempi, serving to emphasize structure, rubato phrasing, agogic accents, rolled chords and supple rhythm alike.

In addition to the Romantic rubato, Bartók adopted another type of free performance which has its origin in folk music. Some ancient layers of East European folk music preserved a declamatory style which Bartók, comparing it with Gregorian chant, or the recitative in Western art music, called *parlando rubato*. As he explained in one of his several descriptions, in *parlando rubato* performance 'the quavers of the original schema are often lengthened or shortened, reasonably and at times unreasonably. This method of performance frequently has all the characters of extemporization'.[27] Besides several original folksongs, one can find an abundance of melodies in Bartók's music fashioned after these particular types of folksong. Usually notated in equal note values – except maybe the first and last two notes of each line which are frequently longer in folk performance – Bartók executed them freely, as if narrating some unwritten text. The opposite of *parlando rubato* in Bartók's folk music nomenclature is *tempo giusto* but in his performance even that type is far from being metronomic and contains many fine modifications of the notated rhythm.

Freedom to go beyond the written score not only results in a wonderfully spontaneous performance but also allows more variety and individuality. Although Bartók's playing demonstrates general characteristics of late nineteenth-century performance practice, it was also uniquely his own. Critics noted the intensity and irresistible drive of his playing, his infallible sense of proportion and capability of evoking the monumental quality of compositions. He could produce extraordinary effects on the instrument and according to one of his contemporaries 'in his movements, his stretchings and sudden starts there was something of the panther, pre-dacious and fearful'.[28] Yet he did not favour harsh colours. His performance of his *par excellence* percussive piano piece, 'Tambourine' (from Nine Little Piano Pieces) owes its excitement to biting accents and subtle rhythmic and dynamic shading, rather than mere percussive touch. Reviewers of his recordings are enthralled by the wide range of his interpretative power and find the application of late nineteenth-century liberties in his playing always 'superlatively musical'.[29]

For various reasons – one of the most important among them the preva-lence of sound recording – the ideal of performance greatly changed by the second half of the twentieth century. Clarity, balance and control became major objectives, resulting in the curtailment of many spontaneous effects from the performance. Tempi are steadier, and their range within and between movements has narrowed. Rhythms are executed more exactly, and in general, performers adhere more literally to the written text than did Bartók's generation. Even Bartók's own students, who had countless opportunities to hear him play or demonstrate the way he interpreted his own music, have restrained themselves from emulating his style of playing, regarding it as something unusual or highly personal. György Sándor, for one, characterizes the composer's style with great insight: '[he] would take the most incredible liberties when interpreting his own and other composers' works in order to bring out the structure and essence of the music'[30] – implying at the same time that Sándor would not allow these liberties for himself.

Some of the liberties Bartók took in his performances occasionally resulted in more than deviation from marked dynamics, rhythm, articula-tion and even shortened or lengthened phrases. At the beginning of his pianistic career he complained that 'not a single one of my appearances of major significance occurs without ... minute unintentional changes'.[31] For this reason, wherever he could, he played from music. But not even that saved him from straying from the written music now and again. Agatha Fassett recalls such an event – the first American performance of the Concerto for Two Pianos, Percussion and Orchestra (Bartók's 1940 arrangement of the Sonata for Two Pianos and Percussion) – during which a wrong note played by the timpanist gave a sudden idea to Bartók who could not resist pursuing it, even at the risk of upsetting the performance.[32]

Incidents like this were unplanned and came about as a result of sudden inspiration. Sometimes, however, Bartók chose to deviate from the score, regarding certain sections of the written text as something not fixed but malleable during each performance: he recommended to Sándor, for example, to make the ostinato repetitions of *Allegro barbaro* before bar 101 'a few bars longer so that [there would be] enough time to reduce the dynamic level to the required quadruple piano'.[33] Yet on both his recordings Bartók plays one bar less of this ostinato section.[34] Another student, Mária Comensoli, recalls her astonishment at Bartók's comment when she first played him 'The Night's Music' from *Out of Doors*: 'Are you playing exactly the same number of ornaments that imitate the noises of the night and at exactly the same place where I indicated them? This does not have to be taken so seriously, you can place them anywhere and play of them as many as you like.'[35]

Conscious of the uniqueness of each performance, Bartók realized that no single interpretation, even his own, could be the only ideal representation of a work. In this respect, he was well aware of one major pitfall of the recorded sound:

> music recorded by machines hardens into something stationary . . .
> [whereas], the composer himself, when he is the performer of his own
> composition, does not always perform his work in exactly the same way.
> Why? Because he lives; because perpetual variability is a trait of a living
> creature's character. Therefore, even if one succeeded in perfectly preserving
> with a perfect process a composer's works according to his own idea at a
> given moment, it would not be advisable to listen to these compositions
> perpetually like that. Because it would cover the composition with boredom.
> Because it is conceivable that the composer himself would have performed
> his compositions better or less well at some other time . . .[36]

The belief in 'perpetual variability' predisposed Bartók, as other composers, to be rather tolerant of different interpretations of his music. For example, Debussy's reaction, after hearing George Copeland play *Reflets dans l'eau*, was that although he felt the piece differently, 'Copeland must go on playing it as he, Copeland, felt it'.[37] More recently Elliott Carter even went so far as to say about the performances of one of his pieces that 'whichever one I'm hearing always seems the best'.[38] Recollections about Shostakovich indicate that he trusted the instincts of performers in choosing their own tempi.[39] Similarly, when Bartók was asked about the meaning of the duration he gave at the end of his pieces, he explained: 'It isn't as if I said: "this *must* take six minutes, twenty-two seconds", but I simply go on record that when *I* play it the duration is six minutes, twenty-two seconds'.[40] Andor Földes once played the Sonatina for Bartók who said: 'very interesting . . . It's not quite the way I play it – I think of it as a more naïf piece – you play it more virtuoso-like – but I really don't mind it . . .'.[41]

Naturally, Bartók criticized unprepared or otherwise inadequate performances, and there is at least one report according to which he tried to discourage a harsh, hammering interpretation, remarking ironically

'Please don't play it in such a "Bartókian" manner . . .'.[42] More characteristically, however, he did not volunteer explanations to performers seeking his opinion. If pressed, he spoke in general terms, such as 'I imagined this a little faster'.[43] Otherwise he spoke highly of many performances of his music. He found Egisto Tango's *Wooden Prince* 'perfect',[44] Tossy Spivakovsky's rendition of the Violin Concerto No. 2 and Sergei Koussevitzky's Concerto for Orchestra 'excellent',[45] Yehudi Menuhin's performance of the Violin Concerto No. 2 'marvelous' and his world premiere of the Sonata for Solo Violin 'wonderful'.[46] Speaking of Menuhin, he said: 'when there is a real great artist, then the composer's advice and help is not necessary, the performer finds his way quite well alone'.[47]

These performers, of course, were not only exceptional artists but his own contemporaries, and either had a chance to consult him or at least seemed to share most of his own interpretative ideals. The fundamental changes of these ideals since Bartók's death have left their mark on the performances of his music. While they might be true to the written text, they have become too tightly controlled and angular, missing some of the essential characteristics of the music. Sandra P. Rosenblum writes in her essay on rubato performance, that the '1980s seem to have brought an awareness of the need for better balance between literal observance of the score and consideration of period and composers' styles'.[48] There is no better way to learn about a composer's style than from his or her own performance. Naturally, it is not mere imitation that one would expect from such a study, but to make the most of the opportunity to gain a deeper understanding of how the musical logic worked for the composer, to evaluate current tendencies of interpretation, to discover and correct differences which are not in harmony with the composer's legacy, and to look afresh on forgotten practices of vital importance to the music. There can be surprisingly beneficial results from studying a composer's recordings, as Paul Griffiths claims in a recent *New York Times* article. He recalls the case of Elgar's recordings, made in the twenties and thirties which, re-released some thirty years later, sounded revelatory since they were so refreshingly different from the way Elgar's music was interpreted at the time. By now, according to this reviewer at least, the 'lessons [of Elgar's recordings] have been learned, especially by the latest generation of British conductors, who seem to have listened to them hard and well'.[49]

Bartók's recordings may yet induce a similar rejuvenation. Since his sound recordings have become widely available, critics have started measuring new recordings against the Bartókian ideal and have welcomed the endeavour to emulate some of the most important features – eminently the rhythmic aspects – of his performance. Comparative analysis shows that the rhythm in the interpretation of Zoltán Kocsis, one of the editors of the complete Bartók sound-recording collection who gets much praise for his recordings, comes closest to that of the composer.[50]

No one could foresee the proliferation of sound recordings of Bartók's music after the post-war decades. As technology became more sophisticated and the recording industry expanded with every improvement, the number of recordings of Bartók's works also increased in great proportions. In the 1940s Szigeti still complained that Bartók was under-represented in record catalogues,[51] but after this tentative start the number of the recordings of Bartók's music soared and reached one hundred by the late 1950s. Bartók became one of the most frequently recorded twentieth-century composers, a position he holds even now, with a listing of nearly five hundred entries under his name in recent Schwann catalogues.[52] Some of Bartók's compositions were popular choices for sound recordings from the beginning (the Concerto for Orchestra, an all-time favourite, is now represented in the catalogue with thirty-five different recordings), some others gained popularity later on (as the Second Piano Concerto around 1970). At present, practically every Bartók work is available commercially, including the easiest learning material and even some of the youthful works unpublished in the composer's lifetime.

Perhaps Bartók would be pleased with most of these recordings; he would certainly speak enthusiastically about the greatest renditions of many of his works. But no doubt there would be cases when he would rather turn on some of his treasured folk recordings – as he used to when he wanted to demonstrate to his chamber music partners and students how the original tunes arranged in his compositions sounded. Or he would just sit down at the piano to show his own differing interpretation. Sadly, only very little is available from the recorded folk music collected or transcribed by Bartók.[53] But his piano playing can and should be listened to by everyone interested in studying or performing Bartók's music. Not only is it a stunning listening experience both musically and technically but it also reveals special insights into his music.

Notes

1 The political and cultural climate in Hungary at the turn of the twentieth century

1 See Tibor Tallián, *Béla Bartók: The Man and His Work*, trans. Gyula Gulyás, trans. rev. Paul Merrick (Budapest: Corvina, 1988), pp. 24 and 57 for further details.

2 Berkeley: University of California Press, 1998. Additionally, Frigyesi's dissertation, 'Béla Bartók and Hungarian Nationalism: The Development of Bartók's Social and Political Ideas at the Turn of the Century (1899–1903)', Ph.D. diss., University of Pennsylvania (1989), explores Bartók's ideological origins, especially his extreme nationalism of these years and its relationship to the symphonic poem *Kossuth*.

3 See Tibor Frank, 'Hungary and the Dual Monarchy, 1867–1890', in *A History of Hungary*, ed. Peter F. Sugar, Péter Hanák and Tibor Frank (Bloomington: Indiana University Press, 1990), pp. 252–61, and Géza Jeszenszky, 'Hungary through World War I and the End of the Dual Monarchy', *ibid.*, p. 270.

4 Ethnic minorities were referred to as 'nationalities' (in contrast to the Magyar 'nation'). Many writers of the day commented on the strangeness of this locution.

5 The counties referred to here and in subsequent chapters are the specific regions into which Hungary was divided prior to the First World War.

6 A powerful selection of Ady's voluminous journalistic writings appears in English translation as *The Explosive Country: A Selection of Articles and Studies, 1898–1916*, ed. Erzsébet Vezér (Budapest: Corvina, 1977). Judit Frigyesi also discusses Ady's vigorous journalistic advocacy for the poor and criticism of racism and chauvinism in *Béla Bartók and Turn-of-the-Century Budapest*, pp. 171–72.

7 Jeszenszky, 'Hungary through World War I', p. 282.

8 Frank, 'Hungary and the Dual Monarchy', pp. 258–60.

9 Mary Gluck, *Lukács and His Generation: 1900–1918* (Cambridge, Mass.: Harvard University Press, 1985), pp. 45–46.

10 Jeszenszky, 'Hungary through World War I', p. 275.

11 Gluck, *Lukács and His Generation*, p. 48, quoting Balázs' diary.

12 John Lukacs, *Budapest 1900: A Historical Portrait of a City and Its Culture* (New York: Weidenfeld and Nicolson, 1988), pp. 71, 187.

13 Gyula Laurencic, *The Millennium of Hungary and the National Exhibition: A Collection of Photographic Views of the most interesting parts of the country, of towns and art-treasures of Hungary, as also of the most noteworthy objects in the Exhibition* (Budapest: William Kunosy and Son, 1896), p. 96.

14 *Ibid.*, p. 79.

15 *Ibid.*, p. 32.

16 Jeszenszky, 'Hungary through World War I', p. 269. The *ispán* was the top county administrator; in rural areas he could rule almost as a feudal lord, even in the early twentieth century.

17 Ernő Baloghy, *A Magyar Kultúra és a Nemzetiségek* [Hungarian Culture and the Nationalities] (Budapest: Deutsch Zsigmond és Társa Könyvkereskedése, 1908), pp. 40–41. One choice quote: 'There is no Serb culture in Hungary, nor could there be'. *Ibid.*, p. 159. This and other translations are by the present author unless otherwise noted.

18 *Ibid.*, pp. 204–05.

19 This 1911 lecture/article was reprinted in A. Komlós (ed.), *Ignotus válogatott írásai* [Ignotus's Collected Writings] (Budapest: Szépirodalmi Könyvkiadó, 1977), pp. 650–68.

20 From the review entitled 'A magyar kultúra és a nemzetiségek', reprinted in Baloghy, *A Magyar Kultúra*, pp. 615–19.

21 Excerpt. The entire poem is collected in József Láng and Pál Schweitzer (eds.), *Ady Endre Összes Versei* [Endre Ady's Collected Poems] (Budapest: Szépirodalmi Könyvkiadó, 1977), pp. 181–82. The translation for the first two stanzas was adapted from that appearing in Oszkár Jászi, *Homage to Danubia*, trans. G. Litván (Lanham, Md.: Rowman and Littlefield Publishers, Inc., 1995), p. 195.

22 Tallián, *Béla Bartók*, pp. 7–10.

23 *Ibid.*, p. 10.

24 *Ibid.*, p. 21.

25 Frigyesi, 'Hungarian Nationalism', p. 85.

26 Halsey Stevens, *The Life and Music of Béla Bartók*, 3rd edn, ed. M. Gillies (Oxford: Clarendon Press, 1993), pp. 9–10.

27 Frigyesi, 'Hungarian Nationalism', pp. 30, 86.

28 This quote from Kodály, 'Confession', p. 210, cited in Frigyesi, 'Hungarian Nationalism', p. 45.

Frigyesi also discusses the complex issue of German and German-speaking Jewish intellectuals in Budapest culture in considerable depth.

29 Frigyesi, 'Hungarian Nationalism', pp. 30–35, discusses Bartók's relationships with Jewish concert-goers and salon guests in depth, with the relevant quotes from his letters. Bartók first went to Gruber's salon in 1901 (*ibid.*, p. 70) and they became close friends.

30 *Ibid.*, pp. 85–89.

31 Frigyesi, 'Hungarian Nationalism', discusses in detail the development of Bartók's most nationalist years and the context of *Kossuth*. For more on its reception and on the reception of subsequent pieces, see David E. Schneider's essay, chapter 11, in this volume.

32 'The cost [of publication] was borne by the composers and the few subscribers they had managed to cajole ... Five hundred copies were published – which took thirty years to sell out'. Tallián, *Béla Bartók*, p. 58.

33 *Ibid.*, p. 59.

34 From Bartók's letter of 6 September 1907, published in János Demény (ed.), *Béla Bartók Letters* (London: Faber & Faber, 1971), p. 76. (Translation adapted from Demény.)

35 *Ibid.*, p. 83.

36 Quoted in Frigyesi, *Béla Bartók and Turn-of-the-Century Budapest*, p. 156.

37 *Ibid.*, p. 154; original emphasis.

38 *Ibid.*, pp. 154–55.

39 *Ibid.*, p. 171; see also pp. 157–71.

40 *Ibid.*, p. 178.

41 *Ibid.*, p. 177.

42 *Ibid.*, p. 171; see also pp. 177–85.

43 Gluck, *Lukács and His Generation*, p. 15.

44 Rezső Alberti, 'A Rózsavölgyi és Társa cég története 1908-tól 1949-ig' [The History of the Rózsavölgyi Publishing House, from 1908 to 1949], *Magyar zenetörténeti tanulmányok* 3. *Mosonyi Mihály és Bartók Béla emlékére* [Essays in the History of Hungarian Music, vol. 3. In Memory of Mihály Mosonyi and Béla Bartók], ed. Ferenc Bónis (Budapest: Zeneműkiadó, 1973), p. 192.

45 The present author's work on UMZE is part of a forthcoming dissertation, part of which was presented at the 1997 American Musicological Society Annual Meeting in a paper entitled 'Reconciling Modernism and Nationalism: Béla Bartók and the New Hungarian Music Society'.

46 Letter to Emma Gruber, 25 November 1906, quoted in Tallián, *Béla Bartók*, p. 55.

47 Translation adapted from 'On Hungarian Music' (1911), in *Béla Bartók Essays*, ed. Benjamin Suchoff (London: Faber & Faber, 1976 repr. Lincoln, Nebr., and London: University of Nebraska Press, 1992), p. 302.

2 Bartók and folk music

1 Zoltán Kodály, 'Magyar zenei folklore 110 év előtt' [One Hundred and Ten Years of Hungarian Musical Folklore], *Visszatekintés* [Retrospection] (Budapest: Zeneműkiadó, 1964), vol. 2, pp. 155–83.

2 For a critical review of these publications see Béla Bartók, *Hungarian Folk Music*, trans. M. D. Calvocoressi (Oxford: Oxford University Press, 1931), p. 5; reprinted as *The Hungarian Folk Song*, ed. Benjamin Suchoff (Albany: State University of New York Press, 1981), p. 5.

3 Bálint Sárosi, *Gypsy Music* (Budapest: Corvina, 1971), pp. 85–119.

4 Bence Szabolcsi, *A Concise History of Hungarian Music* (Budapest: Corvina, 1964) contains a consideration of the rise of *verbunkos* in chapter 6.

5 See Zoltán Kodály, *Folk Music of Hungary*, trans. Ronald Tempest and Cynthia Jolly (London: Barrie and Rockliff, 1960), pp. 14–15.

6 József Ujfalussy (ed.), *Bartók breviárium* (*levelek, írások, dokumentumok*) [Bartók breviary (correspondence, essays and documents)] (Budapest: Zeneműkiadó, 1958), p. 12. All translations are by the present author unless otherwise stated.

7 See John Lukacs, *Budapest 1900: A Historical Portrait of a City and Its Culture* (New York: Weidenfeld and Nicolson, 1988), pp. 116–17.

8 Béla Bartók Jr. and Adrienne Gombocz-Konkoly (eds.), *Bartók Béla családi levelei* [Béla Bartók's Family Letters] (Budapest: Zeneműkiadó, 1981), p. 110; letter of 8 September 1903.

9 Kodály in one of his caustic remarks characterizes Bartók's *Kossuth* symphony as 'the declaration of Hungarian independence in German language', in János Demény, 'Bartók Béla tanulóévei és romantikus korszaka (1899–1905)' [Béla Bartók's Student Years and Romantic Period (1899–1905)], *Zenetudományi tanulmányok* [Studies in Musicology] (hereafter *Zt*), ed. Bence Szabolcsi and Dénes Bartha, 2 (Budapest: Akadémiai Kiadó, 1954), p. 367.

10 See András Szőllősy (ed.) *Bartók Béla összegyűjtött írásai I* [Béla Bartók's Collected Writings I] (Budapest: Zeneműkiadó, 1967), p. 9. Another translation appears in Benjamin Suchoff (ed.), *Béla Bartók Essays* (London: Faber & Faber, 1976; repr. Lincoln, Nebr., and London: University of Nebraska Press, 1992), p. 409.

11 *Bartók Béla családi levelei*, p. 123; 26 December 1904.

12 'Bartók the Folklorist', in *The Selected Writings of Zoltán Kodály*, ed. Ferenc Bónis, trans. L. Halápy and F. MacNicol (London: Boosey and Hawkes, 1964), p. 102.

13 The counties referred to are the specific

regions into which Hungary was divided prior to the First World War.

14 See Denijs Dille, 'Bartók und die Volksmusik', *Documenta Bartókiana* 4 (1970), pp. 70–129.

15 'Magyarország parasztzenéje' [Peasant Music of Hungary], *Bartók Béla összegyűjtött írásai I*, ed. Szőllősy, p. 354.

16 *Ibid.*, p. 355.

17 *Bartók Béla családi levelei*, p. 182; 5 July, 1907.

18 János Demény, 'Bartók Béla művészi kibontakozásának évei I: találkozás a népzenével (1906–1914)' [The Years of Béla Bartók's Artistic Evolution I: Encounter with Folk Music (1906–1914)], *Zt* 3 (1955), p. 322.

19 *Bartók Béla családi levelei*, p. 187; 4 February 1909.

20 'Bartók the Folklorist', p. 104.

21 Lajos Vargyas, *Hungarian Ballads and the European Ballad Tradition* (Budapest: Akadémiai Kiadó, 1983).

22 *Bartók Béla családi levelei*, p. 163; 21 August 1906.

23 János Demény (ed.), *Bartók Béla levelei* [Béla Bartók Letters] (Budapest: Zeneműkiadó, 1976), 14 August 1909.

24 Bartók Béla Jr., *Apám életének krónikája* [Chronicle of my Father's Life] (Budapest: Zeneműkiadó, 1981); János Demény, 'Bartók Béla tanulóévei és romantikus korszaka (1899–1905)', *Zt* 2 (1954), pp. 323–487; 'Bartók Béla művészi kibontakozásának évei I: találkozás a népzenével (1906–1914)', *Zt* 3 (1955), pp. 286–459; and 'Bartók Béla művészi kibontakozásának évei II: Bartók Béla megjelenése az európai zeneéletben (1914–1926)' [The Years of Bartók's Artistic Evolution II: Bartók's Appearance in European Musical Life (1914–1926)], *Zt* 7 (1959), pp. 7–425.

25 See Bartók's essay 'Arab Folk Music from the Biskra District', *Béla Bartók: Studies in Ethnomusicology*, ed. Benjamin Suchoff (Lincoln, Nebr. and London: University of Nebraska Press, 1997), pp. 29–77.

26 See *Turkish Folk Music from Asia Minor*, ed. Benjamin Suchoff with Afterword by Kurt Reinhard (Princeton: Princeton University Press, 1976).

27 Quoted in Stephen Erdely, *Music of Southslavic Epics from Bihac Region of Bosnia* (New York: Garland Publishing Co., 1995), p. 6.

28 *Bartók Béla összegyűjtött írásai I*, ed. Szőllősy, p. 582. Another translation appears in *Béla Bartók Essays*, ed. Suchoff, p. 10.

29 Ilmari Krohn, 'Welche ist die beste Methode, um Volks – und volksmässige Lieder nach ihrer melodischen Beschaffenheit lexikalisch zu ordnen', *Sammelbände der Internationalen Musikgesellschaft* 4 (1902–03), pp. 643–60.

30 Béla Bartók and Zoltán Kodály, 'Az uj egyetemes népdalgyűjtemény tervezete' [Plan of the Universal Collection of Hungarian Folksongs], *Ethnographia* 24 (1913), pp. 313–16. See also Stephen Erdely, *Methods and Principles of Hungarian Ethnomusicology*, Indiana University Publications, Uralic and Altaic Series, 52 (The Hague: Mouton & Co., 1965), p. 45.

31 Béla Bartók, *Die Melodien der Rumänischen Colinde* (Vienna: Universal Edition, 1935), p. VII.

32 *Cântece poporale romaneşti din comitatul Bihor (Ungaria)* (Bucharest: Academia Română, 1913); also Suchoff (ed.), *Béla Bartók: Studies in Ethnomusicology*, pp. 1–24.

33 Denijs Dille (ed.), *Béla Bartók: Ethnomusicologische Schriften Faksimile-Nachdrucke* (Mainz: B. Schott's Söhne, 1966), vol. 2.

34 (Vienna: Universal Edition, 1935).

35 *The Hungarian Folk Song*, ed. Benjamin Suchoff (Albany: State University of New York Press, 1981). Originally published in English as *Hungarian Folk Music* (Oxford: Oxford University Press, 1931).

36 Since Bartók devised his classification system some of the tunes have been reclassified into Class A, others were identified as alien or borrowed forms.

37 Suchoff (ed.), *Béla Bartók: Studies in Ethnomusicology*, pp. 174–241.

38 József Ujfalussy, *Béla Bartók* (Budapest: Corvina, 1971), p. 301.

39 *Ibid.*, p. 280.

40 *Ibid.*, p. 301.

41 Details of each of these volumes can be found in the Bibliography.

3 Bartók's orchestral music and the modern world

1 In *Bartók and His World*, ed. Peter Laki (Princeton: Princeton University Press, 1995), p. 52.

2 'Harvard Lectures' (1943), in *Béla Bartók Essays*, ed. Benjamin Suchoff (London: Faber & Faber, 1976 repr. Lincoln, Nebr., and London: University of Nebraska Press, 1992), p. 354.

3 'Modernity', in *The Concise Encyclopedia of Western Philosophy and Philosophers*, ed. Jonathan Rée and James Opie Urmson (London: Routledge, 1989). See also Judit Frigyesi, *Béla Bartók and Turn-of-the-Century Budapest* (Berkeley: University of California Press, 1998) and Christopher Butler, *Early Modernism: Literature, Music and Painting in Europe 1900–1916* (Oxford: Oxford University Press, 1994).

4 That he appeared to move away from an 'advanced' and even supposedly formalist approach in the twenties and thirties to an overtly populist one in his later works, particularly those written in America, was taken to be indicative of his compromise, cowardice and reaction by critics supportive to the modernist cause such as René Leibowitz. See chapter 11, pp. 187–88, chapter 13, pp. 202–05 and chapter 14, pp. 217–18 for an evaluation of such criticisms.

5 'Mechanical Music' (1937) in *Béla Bartók Essays*, ed. Suchoff, p. 292. (My adaptation of the original translation.)

6 Andrew Chester, 'Second Thoughts on a Rock Aesthetic: The Band', *New Left Review* 62 (1970), pp. 75–82.

7 Hans Keller, 'The State of the Symphony: Not only Maxwell Davies (1978)', in *Hans Keller: Essays on Music*, ed. Christopher Wintle (Cambridge: Cambridge University Press, 1994), pp. 108–09. Keller's emphasis.

8 On the title page of the Boosey & Hawkes miniature score, the dates 2 April 1903 – 18 August 1903 appear. However, János Demény suggests in his note to a letter dated 1 April 1903 that Bartók had already started on the composition. János Demény (ed.), *Béla Bartók Letters*, trans. Péter Balabán and István Farkas, trans. rev. Elizabeth West and Colin Mason (Budapest: Corvina, 1971), p. 373.

9 From Denijs Dille's introduction to the Boosey and Hawkes pocket score of *Kossuth*.

10 The song is discussed in my paper 'Bartók and the Encoding of Hungarian National Identity' (unpublished).

11 Demény (ed.), *Béla Bartók Letters*, p. 28. My emphasis.

12 There are only two possible transpositions of the whole-tone scale.

13 Bence Szabolcsi, *A Concise History of Hungarian Music* (Budapest: Corvina, 1964) contains a consideration of the rise of *verbunkos* in chapter 6.

14 See Jonathan Bellman, *The Style Hongrois in the Music of Western Europe* (Boston: Northeastern University Press, 1993).

15 'Strauss: *Sinfonia Domestica*' in *Béla Bartók Essays*, ed. Suchoff, pp. 437–45.

16 Demény (ed.), *Béla Bartók Letters*, p. 132; 10 December 1915.

17 Malcolm Gillies, review of David Cooper, *Bartók: Concerto for Orchestra*, in *Music Analysis*, 17/1 (1998), p. 94. In 'Two Orchestral Suites', *The Bartók Companion*, Malcolm Gillies (London: Faber & Faber, 1993), p. 457.

18 Theodor W. Adorno, 'Béla Bartóks Tanzsuite', in *Gesammelte Schriften* 18, ed. Rolf Teidemann and Klaus Schultz (Frankfurt: Suhrkamp Verlag, 1984), pp. 279–81.

19 Francis Korbay, *Hungarian Melodies* (London and Leipzig: Stanley Lucas, Weber, Pitt and Hatzfeld Ltd., 1893), No. 18, p. 72.

20 Frigyesi, *Béla Bartók and Turn-of-the-Century Budapest*, p. 248.

21 In fact, Bartók described the work as a serenade on a postcard sent to Etelka Freund on 17 August 1907, noting that the fourth movement remained to be orchestrated.

22 The word *puszta* has a range of meanings including barren, bleak and desert. It may be that Bartók was recalling the Hungarian plain, or that he was thinking of Gerlice puszta, the village, now in Slovakia.

23 'The Folk Songs of Hungary' (1928), in *Béla Bartók Essays*, ed. Suchoff, p. 335.

24 Demény (ed.), *Béla Bartók Letters*, p. 105.

25 *Ibid.*, p. 66; 10 September 1906. The songs (ten with accompaniments by Bartók, ten by Kodály) were published as *Magyar Népdalok* in 1906.

26 Demény (ed.), *Béla Bartók Letters*, p. 382.

27 'The Influence of Debussy and Ravel in Hungary' (1938), in *Béla Bartók Essays*, ed. Suchoff, p. 518.

28 'Hungarian Peasant Music' (1920), in *Béla Bartók Essays*, ed. Suchoff, p. 306. A major division in folk-music performance style, according to Bartók, was between *tempo giusto* (strict time) and *parlando rubato* (free and speech-like).

29 'The Relation of Folk Song to the Development of the Art Music of Our Time' (1921), in *Béla Bartók Essays*, ed. Suchoff, p. 322.

30 Demény (ed.), *Béla Bartók Letters*, p. 202.

31 Bill Ashcroft, Gareth Griffiths and Helen Tiffin, *The Empire Writes Back: Theory and Practice in Post-Colonial Literature* (London: Routledge, 1989), p. 158.

32 See Malcolm Gillies, 'Dance Suite', in *The Bartók Companion*, ed. Gillies, pp. 487–97.

33 See David Cooper, *Béla Bartók: Concerto for Orchestra* (Cambridge: Cambridge University Press, 1996).

34 'Béla Bartók's Opinion on the Technical, Aesthetic and Spiritual Orientation of Contemporary Music' (1938), in *Béla Bartók Essays*, ed. Suchoff, p. 516.

35 Hermann Hesse, *Musik, Betrachtungen, Gedichte, Rezensionen und Briefe* (Frankfurt am Main: Suhrkamp, 1985), p. 215, diary entry of 15 May 1955, translated for the present author by Peter Franklin.

4 The stage works: portraits of loneliness

1 Bartók's revisions to the ending of the opera from 1911 to 1918 are outlined in chapter 5 of Carl Leafstedt, *Inside Bluebeard's Castle: Music and Drama in Béla Bartók's Opera* (New York: Oxford University Press, 1999), pp. 125–58.

2 These descriptions are taken from reminiscences recorded in Malcolm Gillies (ed.), *Bartók Remembered* (London: Faber & Faber, 1990).

3 Cited in Judit Frigyesi, *Béla Bartók and Turn-of-the-Century Budapest* (Berkeley: University of California Press, 1998), p. 110.

4 Both essays may be found in Árpád Kadarkay (ed.), *The Lukács Reader* (Oxford: Blackwell, 1995).

5 Bartók to his mother, 10 September 1905. In János Demény (ed.), *Béla Bartók Letters* (London: Faber & Faber, 1971), p. 53.

6 The manuscript with this inscription is in the collection of Peter Bartók, Homosassa, Florida.

7 Balázs, notes on the text, *c.* 1915. The playwright's discussion of the *Bluebeard* drama is translated in Leafstedt, *Inside Bluebeard's Castle*, pp. 201–03.

8 An elaboration on the F♯–C opposition and its symbolic meaning may be found in Frigyesi, *Turn-of-the-Century Budapest*, pp. 253–76; see also Leafstedt, *Inside Bluebeard's Castle*, pp. 58–61.

9 Tibor Tallián, *Béla Bartók: The Man and His Work*, trans. Gyula Gulyás, trans. rev. Paul Merrick (Budapest: Corvina, 1988), p. 78.

10 Béla Bartók, 'On *Duke Bluebeard's Castle*' (1918), in *Béla Bartók Essays*, ed. Benjamin Suchoff (London: Faber & Faber, 1976 repr. Lincoln, Nebr., and London: University of Nebraska Press, 1992), p. 407.

11 Balázs, diary entry, 5 September 1906. Published in Anna Fabri (ed.), *Béla Balázs Napló*, vol. 1 (Budapest: Magvető, 1982), p. 339.

12 For more on Balázs, see, in English, Jozsef Zsuffa's fine biography *Béla Balázs: The Man and the Artist* (Berkeley and Los Angeles: University of California Press, 1987). On his relationship with Bartók, see Leafstedt, *Inside Bluebeard's Castle*, pp. 13–32.

13 Cited in Frigyesi, *Turn-of-the-Century Budapest*, p. 202.

14 Balázs, notes on the text, *c.* 1915. See Leafstedt, *Inside Bluebeard's Castle*, p. 202.

15 Béla Bartók, 'About *The Wooden Prince*' (1917), in *Béla Bartók Essays*, ed. Suchoff, p. 406.

16 Frigyesi, *Turn-of-the-Century Budapest*, p. 213.

17 *Ibid.*, p. 279.

18 Balázs, *The Wooden Prince*, in English National Opera Guide 44 (London: John Calder; New York: Riverrun Press, 1991), *The Stage Works of Béla Bartók*, ed. John Nicholas, p. 76. All quotations from the present paragraph are taken from this source.

19 Cited in György Kroó, 'Pantomime: The Miraculous Mandarin', in *The Bartók Companion*, ed. Malcolm Gillies (London: Faber & Faber, 1993), p. 373.

20 *Ibid.*

21 The full chronology of the work is presented in Vera Lampert, '*The Miraculous Mandarin*: Melchior Lengyel, His Pantomime, and His Connections to Béla Bartók', in *Béla Bartók and His World*, ed. Peter Laki (Princeton: Princeton University Press, 1995), pp. 149–71.

22 Translated in Ferenc Bonis, '"The Miraculous Mandarin": The Birth and Vicissitudes of a Masterpiece', in *The Stage Works of Béla Bartók*, ed. Nicholas, p. 87.

23 György Kroó, *A Guide to Bartók* (Budapest: Corvina, 1974), p. 100.

24 Cited in Vera Lampert, '*The Miraculous Mandarin*', in *Béla Bartók and His World*, ed. Laki, p. 156.

5 Vocal music: inspiration and ideology

I would like to express my thanks to László Somfai and László Vikárius for their assistance at the Budapest Bartók Archive where I researched this article over the Christmas period 1998, and to the Research Fund of the Royal Academy of Music, London, which financed my trip there. I should also like to thank László Somfai for his valuable comments on an early draft, on the strength of which I was able to improve this chapter considerably.

1 'Hungarian Peasant Music' (1920), in *Béla Bartók Essays*, ed. Benjamin Suchoff (London: Faber & Faber, 1976 repr. Lincoln, Nebr., and London: University of Nebraska Press, 1992), p. 306.

2 József Ujfalussy, *Béla Bartók*, trans. Ruth Pataki (Budapest: Corvina, 1971), p. 330.

3 Published in translation in 'Hungarian Folksongs', in Zoltán Kodály, *The Selected Writings of Zoltán Kodály*, trans. L. Halápy and F. MacNicol (London: Boosey and Hawkes, 1964), p. 9. My italics.

4 His other attempt was the unpublished Two Romanian Folksongs for female choir (*c.* 1909).

5 Regrettably the manuscript cannot be reproduced here for copyright reasons.

6 A new version of the eighth song is written on American paper.

7 John Lukacs, *Budapest 1900: A Historical Portrait of a City and its Culture* (New York: Weidenfeld and Nicolson, 1988), p. 164.

8 The piano parts of these songs are very bland, but the performances were evidently brought to life by the outstanding *diseuses* of the period; contemporary accounts are uniformly impressed by their vividness.

9 As reproduced in Vera Lampert, 'Quellenkatalog der Volksliedbearbeitungen

von Bartók', *Documenta Bartókiana* 6 (1981), pp. 109–10.

10 Bartók made an arrangement of the last three songs of *Village Scenes* for four or eight women's voices and orchestra in 1926 which highlights the similarity.

11 Lampert, 'Works for Solo Voice with Piano', in *The Bartók Companion,* ed. Malcolm Gillies (London: Faber & Faber, 1993), p. 398, quoting from 'The Influence of Peasant Music on Modern Music' (1931), in *Béla Bartók Essays,* ed. Suchoff, p. 342.

12 'The Relation between Contemporary Hungarian Art Music and Folk Music' (1941), in *Béla Bartók Essays,* ed. Suchoff, p. 352.

13 The Hungarian version of both essays also uses the word 'mottó': Tibor Tallián (ed.), *Bartók Béla Írásai* [The Writings of Béla Bartók] (Budapest: Zeneműkiadó, 1989), vol. 1, pp. 142 and 159.

14 See Paul Wilson, 'Approaching Atonality: Studies and Improvisations', in *The Bartók Companion,* ed. Gillies, pp. 167–91.

15 *Ibid.,* p. 168.

16 Bartók made orchestral arrangements of the accompaniments to five of these songs, known as Five Hungarian Folksongs for voice and orchestra (1933). His choice cuts across the divisions of Twenty Hungarian Folksongs: he selected two from the second volume and three from the third. The work remains in manuscript.

17 See also László Somfai, 'Experimenting with Folkmusic-Based Concert Sets: Béla Bartók's Arrangements Reconsidered', *Melos* 12–13, *Special Issue on Bartók* (Spring–Summer 1995), pp. 66–76.

18 Lampert, 'Works for Solo Voice' describes this aspect of the work very well.

19 This crisis is discussed by Tibor Tallián in *Béla Bartók: The Man and His Work,* trans. Gyula Gulyás, trans. rev. Paul Merrick (Budapest: Corvina, 1988), p. 157.

20 *Ibid.,* pp. 158–59.

21 László Vikárius, 'Béla Bartók's *Cantata Profana*', *Studia musicologica* 35/1 (1993), p. 261.

22 Miklós Szabó, 'Choral Works', in *The Bartók Companion,* ed. Gillies, p. 418.

23 See György Kroó, '*Cantata profana*', in *The Bartók Companion,* ed. Gillies, p. 427.

24 Unpublished letter to Universal Edition, quoted in Tallián, *Béla Bartók,* p. 162.

25 Vikárius, 'Béla Bartók's *Cantata Profana*', p. 263.

26 Kroó, '*Cantata profana*', p. 434.

27 The similarities are pointed out in Vikárius, 'Béla Bartók's *Cantata Profana*', pp. 276–82.

28 *Ibid.,* p. 289.

29 In 1945, the year he died, Bartók began *Goat Song (The Husband's Lament)* for voice and

piano on a Ruthenian melody and Three Ukrainian Folksongs, for voice and piano, but they remain unfinished.

30 MS gyűjtőfüzet [Collecting Book] M.Vi, fol. 5r; MS *támlap* [Proof] Bartók-Rend C-II 602e.

31 Bartók's own reference on the first score, published by Magyar Kórus.

32 Bartók provided seven of the choruses with orchestral accompaniments in Seven Choruses with orchestra (1937–41).

33 See Szabó, 'Kodály széljegyzetei Bartók Kórusműveihez' [Kodály's Marginal Notes to Bartók's Choral Works], *Muzsika* (September 1995), vol. 1, pp. 27–33, and (October 1995), vol. 2, pp. 16–22.

34 *Ibid.,* vol. 1, p. 27.

35 Jegyezetek [Notes] to Hungarian Folksongs (Budapest: Editio Musica, 1938). My translation.

36 All these performances are preserved on *Bartók at the Piano,* Hungaroton HCD 12326–31.

6 Piano music: teaching pieces and folksong arrangements

1 'Contemporary Music in Piano Teaching' (1940), *Béla Bartók Essays,* ed. Benjamin Suchoff (London: Faber & Faber, 1976 repr. Lincoln, Nebr., and London: University of Nebraska Press, 1992), p. 426.

2 Malcolm Gillies (ed.), *Bartók Remembered* (London: Faber & Faber, 1990), p. 45.

3 György Sándor, private interview, 17 April 1994.

4 'About István Thomán' (1927), in *Béla Bartók Essays,* ed. Suchoff, p. 489.

5 Gillies (ed.), *Bartók Remembered,* p. 45.

6 'About István Thomán' (1927), in *Béla Bartók Essays,* ed. Suchoff, p. 490.

7 'About the "Piano" Problem (Answer to a Questionnaire)' (1927), in *Béla Bartók Essays,* ed. Suchoff, p. 288.

8 Sándor Reschofsky, unpublished letter to Benjamin Suchoff.

9 *Béla Bartók Essays,* ed. Suchoff, p. 432.

10 See *Bartók at the Piano: 1920–1945, Centenary Edition of Bartók's Records,* vol. I (Hungaraton HCD 12326–33: 1981).

11 See Benjamin Suchoff, *Guide to Bartók's Mikrokosmos* (New York: Da Capo Press, 1983), p. 14, for a discussion of 'percussive' and 'non-percussive' touches.

12 *Bartók at the Piano* (Hungaroton).

13 János Demény (ed.), *Bartók Béla Briefe* (Budapest: Corvina, 1973), p. 64.

14 Halsey Stevens, *The Life and Music of Béla Bartók,* 3rd edn, ed. Malcolm Gillies (Oxford: Clarendon Press, 1993), p. 35.

15 'The Relationship Between Contemporary

Hungarian Art Music and Folk Music' (1941), in *Béla Bartók Essays*, ed. Suchoff, p. 349.
16 *Ibid.*, p. 351.
17 *Ibid.*, pp. 351–2.
18 'On Hungarian Music' (1911), in *Béla Bartók Essays*, ed. Suchoff, p. 301.
19 Béla Bartók and Zoltán Kodály, Hungarian Folksongs for Voice and Piano (Budapest: Editio Musica, 1950).
20 'Harvard Lectures' (1943), in *Béla Bartók Essays*, ed. Suchoff, p. 375.

7 Piano music: recital repertoire and chamber music
1 Igor Stravinsky, *Poetics of Music in the Form of Six Lessons*, trans. A. Knodel and I. Dahl (New York: Vintage Books, 1956), p. 129, and Stravinsky, *An Autobiography* (New York: The Norton Library, 1962), p. 75.
2 Halsey Stevens, *The Life and Music of Béla Bartók*, 3rd edn, ed. Malcolm Gillies (Oxford: Clarendon Press, 1993), p. 9.
3 My own teacher, the late Harold Craxton, said more than once, and as if on good authority, that Dohnányi was jealous of Bartók, four years the younger and embarking on a parallel career as composer/pianist, and that he actively encouraged the latter's folksong collecting forays into the countryside in order from time to time to remove him from the concert scene in Budapest. Little good it did him, for he could not then have guessed that Bartók's ethnomusicological efforts were to repay him a hundredfold; without them, his development of an idiosyncratically Hungarian style might well have been forestalled by the increasingly seductive influence of colleagues down the road in Vienna.
4 Stevens, *Life and Music*, pp. 335 and 68.
5 Constant Lambert, *Music Ho!* (London: Penguin Books, 1948), p. 126.
6 Oddly, Nos. 5–8 of the Nine Little Pieces were omitted from the Hawkes and Son contract of 1938, an anomaly which persists to this day; they are still published by Universal Edition.

8 The Piano Concertos and Sonata for Two Pianos and Percussion
1 Reproduced in Bruno Ernst, *The Magic Mirror of M. C. Escher* (New York: Ballantine, 1976), p. 76.
2 'About the Sonata for Two Pianos and Percussion' (1938), in *Béla Bartók Essays*, ed. Benjamin Suchoff (London: Faber & Faber, 1976 repr. Lincoln, Nebr., and London: University of Nebraska Press, 1992), pp. 417–18.
3 'Rhapsody for Piano and Orchestra (Op. 1)' (1910), in *Béla Bartók Essays*, ed. Suchoff, pp. 404–5; 'About the Sonata for Two Pianos and Percussion' (1938), in *ibid.*, pp. 417–18;

'Analysis of the Second Concerto for Piano and Orchestra' (1939), in *ibid.*, pp. 419–23.
4 'Harvard Lectures' (1943), in *Béla Bartók Essays*, ed. Suchoff, p. 376.
5 László Somfai, *Béla Bartók: Composition, Concepts, and Autograph Sources* (Berkeley: University of California Press, 1996), p. 11.
6 Tibor Tallián, *Béla Bartók: The Man and His Work*, trans. Gyula Gulyás, trans. rev. Paul Merrick (Budapest: Corvina, 1988), p. 140.
7 Ernő Lendvai, *Béla Bartók: An Analysis of His Music* (London: Kahn and Averill, 1971), pp. 1–16. See chapter 14 in this volume for a summary and critique of Lendvai's analytical technique.
8 'Analysis of the Second Concerto for Piano and Orchestra' (1939), in *Béla Bartók Essays*, ed. Suchoff, p. 419.
9 It has also been argued that all the thematic material is derived from a common source: see Frank Michael, 'Analytische Anmerkungen zu Bartóks 2. Klavierkonzert', *Studia musicologica* 24 (1983), pp. 425–37.
10 Lendvai, *Analysis*, pp. 4, 5–7, 18–26, 36–38, 45, 65–66, 69–72, 75–76, 91–92, 95, 96; this information is effectively summed up in Roy Howat, 'Masterworks (II): Sonata for Two Pianos and Percussion', in *The Bartók Companion*, ed. Malcolm Gillies (London: Faber & Faber, 1993), pp. 315–30.
11 See John A. Meyer, 'Beethoven and Bartók: A Structural Parallel', *Music Review* 31 (1970), pp. 315–21.
12 Maria Anna Harley, '*Natura naturans, natura naturata* and Bartók's Nature Music Idiom', *Studia musicologica* 36 (1995), pp. 329–49.
13 See Bence Szabolcsi, 'Man and Nature in Bartók's World', in *Bartók Studies*, ed. Todd Crow (Detroit: Information Coordinators, 1976), pp. 63–75; Harley, '*Natura naturans*'; Jószef Ujfalussy, *Béla Bartók*, trans. Ruth Pataki (Budapest: Corvina, 1971), pp. 232–37.
14 While much of Agatha Fassett's description seems rather romanticized, there is no reason to doubt the many reports therein of his exceptional hearing: *Béla Bartók's Last Years: The Naked Face of Genius* (London: Gollancz, 1958), pp. 25, 38, 90, 101–05.
15 See Meyer, 'Beethoven and Bartók'.
16 Somfai, *Béla Bartók*, p. 110.
17 *Ibid.*, pp. 54–55.
18 'About the "Piano" Problem (Answer to a Questionnaire)' (1927), in *Béla Bartók Essays*, ed. Suchoff, p. 288.
19 'The So-called Bulgarian Rhythm' (1938), in *Béla Bartók Essays*, ed. Suchoff, pp. 40–49. His own performance of Bulgarian rhythm, with the last quaver of the bar clipped almost in half, is best exemplified by the recording of Six

Dances in Bulgarian Rhythm No. 2 (*Mikrokosmos*, No. 149) on Hungaroton HCD 12329, track 5.

20 Judit Frigyesi, 'Between Rubato and Rigid Rhythm: A Particular Type of Rhythmical Asymmetry as Reflected in Bartók's Writings on Folk Music', *Studia musicologica* 24 (1983), pp. 334–36.

21 'The So-called Bulgarian Rhythm' (1938), in *Béla Bartók Essays*, ed. Suchoff, p. 48.

22 See Vera Lampert's chapter in this volume on Bartók's recordings.

23 The Sonata is on Hungaroton HCD 12331, track 1–3; the Rhapsody, on Hungaroton HCD 12336, track 1; and the Second Concerto, on Hungaroton HCD 12335, track 1.

9 Violin works and the Viola Concerto

1 *Béla Bartók and Turn-of-the-Century Budapest* (Berkeley: University of California Press, 1998), pp. 216–29.

2 Bence Szabolcsi, 'Bartók Béla élete' [The Life of Béla Bartók]. English translation in Ferenc Bónis (ed.), *Béla Bartók: His Life in Pictures*, 2nd edn (Budapest: Corvina, 1964), p. 62.

3 See 'About the "Piano" Problem (Answer to a Questionnaire)' (1927), in *Béla Bartók Essays*, ed. Benjamin Suchoff (London: Faber & Faber, 1976 repr. Lincoln, Nebr., and London: University of Nebraska Press, 1992), p. 288, as well as chapters 6, 7 and 8 in this volume, especially pp. 94, 115–116 and 128.

4 First by Denijs Dille in the first and second volumes of *Documenta Bartókiana* (1964–65), later printed by Editio Musica Budapest.

5 There is a fragment of a two-page Andante in F♯ major (Bartók Archives, Budapest) that probably dates from around the time of the 1903 Sonata which could possibly be an alternative slow movement.

6 'The Influence of Peasant Music on Modern Music' (1931), *Béla Bartók Essays*, ed. Suchoff, p. 344. For Bartók's often-quoted discussion of the three levels of folk-music assimilation, see *ibid.*, pp. 340–44.

7 János Kárpáti, *Bartók's Chamber Music*, trans. Fred MacNicol and Mária Steiner, trans. rev. Paul Merrick (New York: Pendragon Press, 1994), pp. 289–320; Paul Wilson, 'Violin Sonatas', in *The Bartók Companion*, ed. Malcolm Gillies (London: Faber & Faber, 1993), pp. 243–56.

8 Kárpáti, *Bartók's Chamber Music*, p. 294.

9 See Joseph Macleod, *The Sisters d'Aranyi* (London: George Allen and Unwin Ltd., 1969), p. 139.

10 Kárpáti, *Bartók's Chamber Music*, p. 300.

11 The lecture 'Béla Bartók. Second Sonata for Violin and Piano', originally a radio broadcast, was published by Editio Musica Budapest in *A*

hét zeneműve [The Masterpiece of the Week] No. 4 (1977), pp. 44–55.

12 See, for example, 'Some Problems of Folk Music Research in Eastern Europe' (1960), in *Béla Bartók Essays*, ed. Suchoff, pp. 173–92 (esp. pp. 181–83).

13 Somfai, *A hét zeneműve*; Kárpáti, *Bartók's Chamber Music*, pp. 304–05, 316.

14 'Final Chamber Works', in *The Bartók Companion*, ed. Gillies, pp. 341–44.

15 The letter is printed as a preface to the Menuhin edition.

16 See his letter to Menuhin dated 21 April 1944, quoted in György Kroó, *A Guide to Bartók* (Budapest: Corvina, 1974), p. 234.

17 The microtonal version was first published – with notational symbols borrowed from Witold Lutosławski – in Peter Petersen, 'Bartóks Sonata für Violine solo. Ein Appell an die Hüter der Autographen', *Musik-Konzepte 22: Béla Bartók* (Munich: Edition text und kritik, 1981), pp. 55–68 (see esp. 64–68). Peter Bartók published an Urtext edition (London: Boosey & Hawkes, 1994).

18 Joseph Szigeti, *With Strings Attached* (New York: Knopf, 1967), p. 128. Some of the reconstructions of the folk originals of the Rhapsodies can be heard on an excellent CD recorded by the Jánosi Ensemble: *Rhapsody: Liszt and Bartók Sources*, Hungaroton Classic HCD 18191 (1995).

19 The originals are listed in Vera Lampert, 'Quellenkatalog der Volksliedbearbeitungen von Bartók', *Documenta Bartókiana* 6 (1981), pp. 15–149.

20 The Ruthenians are Ukrainians residing in the Carpathian mountains; the county where this particular melody was collected, Máramaros, was part of Hungary until 1918. Today, it is in Romania and is known as Maramureş.

21 Claude Kenneson, *Székely and Bartók: The Story of a Friendship* (Portland: Amadeus Press, 1994), p. 115.

22 László Somfai, *Béla Bartók: Composition, Concepts, and Autograph Sources* (Berkeley: University of California Press, 1996), p. 201.

23 *Ibid.*

24 Günter Weiss-Aigner, 'The "Lost" Violin Concerto', in *The Bartók Companion*, ed. Gillies, p. 469.

25 It should be noted that the second portrait, which is a 'grotesque' distortion of the first, is actually an orchestrated piano piece – Bagatelle Op. 6 No.14, 'Ma mie que danse'.

26 The term 'polymodal chromaticism' is discussed in chapter 14 of this volume. The concept was used by Bartók in his 'Harvard Lectures' (1943) (see *Béla Bartók Essays*, ed. Suchoff, p. 367) and has been further elaborated

upon in Kárpáti, *Bartók's Chamber Music*, pp. 169–85. The mixing of modes discussed by Kárpáti involves pitch alterations similar to those that would turn Ex. 9.7a into 9.7b.

27 See Denijs Dille, 'Angaben zum Violinkonzert 1907, den *Deux Portraits*, dem Quartett Op. 7 und den Zwei rumänischen Tänzen', *Documenta Bartókiana* 2 (1965), p. 92. See also János Kárpáti, 'A Typical *Jugendstil* Composition: Bartók's String Quartet No. 1', *The Hungarian Quarterly* 36 (Spring 1995), pp. 130–40, esp. 134.

28 Weiss-Aigner, 'The "Lost" Violin Concerto', p. 475.

29 See Lampert, 'Second Violin Concerto', in *The Bartók Companion*, ed. Gillies, pp. 515–25. The sources were examined in Joseph Nagy, 'Béla Bartók's Violin Concerto No.2: An Analysis of the Creative and Compositional Process Through a Study of the Manuscripts', Ph.D. diss., City University of New York (1992).

30 I developed this thesis in an unpublished lecture delivered at the International Bartók Festival in Szombathely, Hungary, in 1993.

31 In his lecture delivered at the Annual Congress of the American Musicological Society in Boston, 1998.

32 Suchoff (ed.), *The Hungarian Folk Song* (Albany: State University of New York Press, 1981), p. 299, No. 299*b*.

33 'Strategics of Variation in the Second Movement of Bartók's Violin Concerto 1937–38', *Studia musicologica* 19 (1977), pp. 161–202.

34 See in particular Sándor Kovács, 'Reexamining the Bartók/Serly Viola Concerto', *Studia musicologica* 23 (1981), pp. 295–322, and *idem*, 'Formprobleme beim Violakonzert von Bartók/Serly', *Studia musicologica* 24 (1982), pp. 381–91. A recent panel discussion on the various versions of the Viola Concerto took place at the 1997 International Viola Congress in Austin, Texas. The proceedings were published in the *Journal of the International Viola Society* 2 (1998).

35 The study of the Viola Concerto is now greatly facilitated by the publication of the original source: Béla Bartók, *Viola Concerto: Facsimile Edition of the Autograph Draft*, with a Commentary by László Somfai; fair transcription of the draft with notes prepared by Nelson Dellamaggiore. Bartók Records, 1995.

36 Bartók's original plan to write a four-movement concerto, with a scherzo in second place, was abandoned or, at any rate, does not seem to be reflected in the extant sketches. In his article 'Formprobleme' Kovács has speculated about a possible five-part plan to the Concerto (first movement – Scherzo – Adagio – Scherzo – finale) but this is entirely

hypothetical. The existing draft seems to be for a work in the traditional three-movement concerto format (with or without ritornelli linking the movements – another bone of contention).

37 See Bartók, *Viola Concerto: Facsimile Edition*, p. 52, third system.

38 Sándor Kovács, 'The Final Concertos', in *The Bartók Companion*, ed. Gillies, p. 552.

10 The String Quartets and works for chamber orchestra

1 Also known on tour as the Hungarian String Quartet, the group was formed by the violinist Imre Waldbauer in 1910, expressly to perform the new quartets of Bartók and Kodály.

2 János Kárpáti, *Bartók's Chamber Music*, trans. Fred MacNicol and Mária Steiner, trans. rev. Paul Merrick (New York: Pendragon Press, 1994), p. 129.

3 'The Folk Songs of Hungary' (1928), in *Béla Bartók Essays*, ed. Benjamin Suchoff (London: Faber & Faber, 1976 repr. Lincoln, Nebr., and London: University of Nebraska Press, 1992), p. 336. For a comparison of Bartók's use of the seventh chord as a closing consonance see David Cooper's discussion of the Suite No. 2 for orchestra, Op. 4 (1905–07) in chapter 3 of this volume.

4 'The Folk Songs of Hungary' (1928) in *Béla Bartók Essays*, ed. Suchoff, p. 336.

5 *Ibid.*, p. 338.

6 *Ibid.*

7 Halsey Stevens, *The Life and Music of Béla Bartók*, 3rd edn, ed. Malcolm Gillies (Oxford: Clarendon Press, 1993), p. 178.

8 Bartók describes his introduction to Schoenberg's music in 1912 through one of his piano students in his essay, 'Arnold Schoenberg's Music in Hungary' (1920), in *Béla Bartók Essays*, ed. Suchoff, p. 467.

9 David E. Schneider explores this relationship in his essay, 'Bartók and Stravinsky: Respect, Competition, Influence, and the Hungarian Reaction to Modernism in the 1920s', in *Bartók and His World*, ed. Peter Laki (Princeton: Princeton University Press, 1995), pp. 172–99.

10 *Béla Bartók Essays*, ed. Suchoff, pp. 369–70.

11 'The Problem of the New Music', *ibid.*, pp. 455, 457.

12 Stevens, *The Life and Music*, p. 67.

13 *Béla Bartók Essays*, ed. Suchoff, p. 459.

14 'Structure of the Fourth String Quartet' (1930?), *ibid.*, p. 412.

15 Stevens, *The Life and Music*, p. 190.

16 Details of the structure of this movement are discussed by the present author in 'Bartók's String Quartet No. 4, Third Movement: A New Interpretative Approach', *Music Analysis* 19/3 (2000), pp. 353–82.

17 László Somfai, *Béla Bartók: Composition, Concepts, and Autograph Sources* (Berkeley: University of California Press, 1996), p. 272.
18 'The Influence of Peasant Music on Modern Music' (1931), in *Béla Bartók Essays*, ed. Suchoff, pp. 343, 344.
19 Judit Frigyesi, *Béla Bartók and Turn-of-the-Century Budapest* (Berkeley: University of California Press, 1998), p. 267.
20 'Rumanian Folk Music' (1931), in *Béla Bartók Essays*, ed. Suchoff, p. 115.
21 'Structure of the Fourth String Quartet' (1930?) in *ibid*, pp. 412–13.
22 *Béla Bartók Essays*, ed. Suchoff, pp. 345–47.
23 See David E. Schneider, 'Bartók and Stravinsky'.
24 'Analysis for the Fifth String Quartet' (1935), in *Béla Bartók Essays*, ed. Suchoff, p. 414.
25 Benjamin Suchoff, 'Structure and Concept in Bartók's Sixth String Quartet', *Tempo* 83 (Winter 1967–68), pp. 2–11.
26 Kárpáti, *Bartók's Chamber Music*, p. 161.
27 'Structure of *Music for String Instruments*' (1937), in *Béla Bartók Essays*, ed. Suchoff, p. 416.
28 *Ibid.*, p. 381.
29 Somfai, *Béla Bartók: Composition, Concepts, and Autograph Sources*, p. 21.

11 Hungarian nationalism and the reception of Bartók's music, 1904–1940
1 Mrs Béla Bartók to Mrs Gyula Baranyai, 4 April 1904; János Demény (ed.), *Béla Bartók Letters*, trans. Péter Balabán and István Farkas, trans. rev. Elizabeth West and Colin Mason (London: Faber & Faber, 1971), p. 40.
2 'Béla Bartók', *Zenevilág* (19 January 1904), quoted in János Demény, 'Bartók Béla tanulóévei és romantikus korszaka (1899–1905)' [Béla Bartók's Student Years and Romantic Period (1899–1905)], *Zenetudományi tanulmányok* [Studies in Musicology] (hereafter *Zt*), ed. Bence Szabolcsi and Dénes Bartha, 2 (Budapest: Akadémiai Kiadó, 1954), p. 412. All translations are mine unless otherwise specified.
3 [Andor Merkler], 'A filharmonikusok mai hangversenye' [Today's Philharmonic Concert], *Magyarország* [Hungary] (14 January 1904), in János Demény, 'Zeitgenössische Kritiken über die Erstaufführungen der Kossuth-Symphonie von Béla Bartók (Budapest, 13. Januar 1904 – Manchester, 19. Februar 1904)', *Documenta Bartókiana* (hereafter *DB*) 1 (1964), p. 31.
4 Pongrácz Kacsóh, 'Bartók Béla', *Zenevilág* (19 January 1904), quoted in *DB* 1 (1964), p. 58.
5 On Bartók's competition with Dohnányi see László Vikárius, *Modell és inspiráció Bartók zenei gondolkodásában* [Model and Inspiration

in Bartók's Musical Thinking] (Pécs: Jelenkor Kiadó, 1999), pp. 82–90.
6 Aurél Kern, *Budapesti Hírlap* (14 January 1904), quoted in *DB* 1 (1964), pp. 32–33.
7 'A filharmonikusok mai hangversenye', *Magyarország* (14 January 1904), quoted in *DB* 1 (1964), p. 31.
8 For a summary of the English reception of *Kossuth* see Malcolm Gillies, *Bartók in Britain* (Oxford: Oxford University Press, 1989), pp. 6–8.
9 Tibor Tallián, *Béla Bartók: The Man and His Work*, trans. Gyula Gulyás, trans. rev. Paul Merrick (Budapest: Corvina, 1988), p. 42.
10 Emil Haraszti, *Budapesti Hírlap* (27 February 1913), quoted in János Demény, 'Bartók Béla művészi kibontakozásának évei I: találkozás a népzenével (1906–1914)' [The Years of Béla Bartók's Artistic Evolution I: Encounter with Folk Music (1906–1914)], *Zt* 3 (1955), p. 425.
11 *Ibid.*
12 *Ibid.*
13 For reviews of the performance, most of which describe the audience's reaction, see Demény, 'Bartók Béla művészi kibontakozásának évei I', pp. 425–28.
14 My discussion of the social implications of 'gypsy music' in Hungary is indebted to Judit Frigyesi, *Béla Bartók and Turn-of-the-Century Budapest* (Berkeley: University of California Press, 1998), pp. 55–60.
15 Gyula Fodor, *A Hét* [The Week] (20 May 1917), quoted in János Demény, 'Bartók Béla művészi kibontakozásának évei II: Bartók megjelenése az európai zeneéletben (1914–1926)' [The Years of Bartók's Artistic Evolution II: Bartók's Appearance in European Musical Life (1914–1926)], *Zt* 7 (1959), p. 38.
16 An exception is István Gajáry's review for *Az Ujság* [The News] (13 May 1917), quoted in *Zt* 7 (1959), p. 48.
17 *Pesti Hírlap* (13 May 1917), quoted in *Zt* 7 (1959), p. 45. See also Peter Laki, 'The Gallows and the Altar: Poetic Criticism and Critical Poetry about Bartók in Hungary', in *Bartók and His World*, ed. Peter Laki (Princeton: Princeton University Press, 1995), pp. 82–83.
18 *Zenei Szemle* [Musical Review] 1/4 (1917), quoted in *Zt* 7 (1959), pp. 34–35.
19 'Jegyzetek a filharmonikusok idei műsorához' [Notes on this Year's Philharmonic Programme], *Nyugat* (1 March 1923), in *Zenei írások a Nyugatban* [Musical Writings in the Nyugat], ed. János Breuer (Budapest: Zeneműkiadó, 1978), pp. 196–99.
20 János Hammerschlag, *Pester Lloyd* (13 May 1917), quoted in *Zt* 7 (1959), p. 46.
21 Aladár Tóth, 'Bartók Béla

zongoraversenyműve a hétfői filharmonikus hangversenyén' [Béla Bartók's Piano Concerto on the Philharmonic's Monday Concert], *Pesti Napló* [Pest Journal] (20 March 1928), quoted in János Demény, 'Bartók Béla pályája delelőjén: teremtő évek – világhódító alkotások (1927–1940)' [Béla Bartók at the Height of his Career – Creative Years – World-Conquering Works (1927–1940)], *Zt* 10 (1962), p. 270.

22 'Béla Bartók: Piano Concerto – On the Occasion of its Premiere 1 July 1927', *Melos* 6/6 (June 1927), pp. 256–57. Quoted in *Zt* 10 (1962), p. 218.

23 Theodor W. Adorno, 'Das fünfte Fest der Internationalen Gesellschaft für Neue Musik in Frankfurt a. M.', *Die Musik* 19/12 (September 1927), p. 881.

24 *Nieuwe Rotterdamische Courant* (9 November 1928), quoted in *Zt* 10 (1962), p. 291.

25 'Bartók bemutató' [Bartók Premiere], *Budapesti Hírlap* (20 March 1928), quoted in *Zt* 10 (1962), p. 272.

26 Bartók performed publicly in Budapest on 5 May 1930 and not again until 12 January 1934 when he accompanied Imre Waldbauer in a recital at the Music Academy. During this time he did perform occasionally for the Hungarian Radio.

27 Bartók to Joseph Szigeti, 10 August 1935; János Demény (ed.), *Bartók Béla levelei* [Béla Bartók Letters] (Budapest: Zeneműkiadó, 1976), p. 506.

28 *The Miraculous Mandarin* was not staged in Hungary until 1945.

29 Sándor Jemnitz, 'Bartók Béla és Magyarország', *Népszava* [People's Word] (25 March 1931), quoted in *Zt* 10 (1962), pp. 398–99.

30 Montague Smith, 'Active Society', *The Evening Citizen* (1 March 1932), quoted in *Zt* 10 (1962), p. 422.

31 Bartók to Ioan Buşiţia, 20 December 1931; Demény (ed.), *Béla Bartók Letters*, pp. 220–21.

32 Bartók to Walter Frey, 28 April 1934; Demény (ed.), *Bartók Béla levelei*, p. 479.

33 Aladár Tóth, 'A Fából faragott királyfi: Bartók táncjátéka az *Operaházban*' [*The Wooden Prince*: Bartók's Pantomime at the Opera], *Pesti Napló* (31 January 1935), quoted in *Zt* 10 (1962), pp. 496–97.

34 'Bartók új műveinek bemutatása az éneklő ifjúság hangversenyén' [Premiere of Bartók's New Works at the Concert of the Singing Youth], *Pesti Napló* (8 May 1937), quoted in *Zt* 10 (1962), pp. 611–12.

35 'A népművelési Bizottság Bartók-estje' [Bartók Concert (organized) by the Committee for Adult Education], *Pesti Napló* (11 December 1936), quoted in *Zt* 10 (1962), p. 581.

36 See the reviews by L. M. G. Arntzenius, Herman Rutters and Lou van Strien in *Zt* 10 (1962), pp. 699–701.

37 See chapter 13 in this volume by Danielle Fosler-Lussier, especially pp. 202–05.

38 Béla Bangha, 'Tollheggyel' [With the Tip of a Pen], *Magyar Kultúra* [Hungarian Culture] 24 (5–20 July 1937), quoted in *Zt* 10 (1962), p. 615.

39 'Bartók Béla és B. Pásztory Ditta' [Béla Bartók and Ditta Pásztory B(artók)], *Népszava* (9 October 1940), quoted in *Zt* 10 (1962), p. 726.

40 Eric Hirsch, 'Pure Sources, Pure Souls: Folk Nationalism and Folk Music in Hungary in the 1930s', Ph.D. diss., University of California at Berkeley (1995), especially pp. 1–8 and 62–73.

12 Bartók in America

1 [Kurt List], 'Measure for Measure', *Listen* (November 1945), p. 18.

2 Sándor Asztalos, 'Bartók a mienk' [Bartók is Ours], *Új zenei szemle* [New Music Review] 1/4 (September 1950), p. 31.

3 Vilmos Juhász (ed.), *Bartók's Years in America* (Washington DC: Occidental Press, 1981), Preface, originally produced in mimeographed form in 1956.

4 See, for instance, Leibowitz, 'Béla Bartók ou la possibilité du compromis dans la musique contemporaine', *Les temps modernes* 2/25 (1947), pp. 705–34.

5 'My Activities During the War' (1945), in *Béla Bartók Essays*, ed. Benjamin Suchoff (London: Faber & Faber, 1976 repr. Lincoln, Nebr., and London: University of Nebraska Press, 1992), p. 434.

6 'Bartók', 8th edn (New York: Schirmer Books, 1992), p. 116.

7 'Bartók's Reception in America', in *Bartók and His World*, ed. Peter Laki (Princeton: Princeton University Press, 1995), pp. 101–18.

8 *Erinnerungen* (Berlin: Limes, 1993), p. 106.

9 János Demény (ed.), *Béla Bartók Letters*, trans. Péter Balabán and István Farkas, trans. rev. Elizabeth West and Colin Mason (London: Faber & Faber, 1971), p. 208.

10 See, further, Yves Lenoir, *Folklore et transcendance dans l'œuvre américaine de Béla Bartók (1940–1945)* (Louvain-la-Neuve: Collège Erasme, 1986), pp. 101–02.

11 Some early Hungarian editions of Bartók's letters excised his most critical comments about the Soviet Union, resulting in persistent misquotations in the Bartók literature.

12 Quoted in typescript, 'Béla Bartók: An Intimate Biography', New York Public Library, Research Libraries collection.

13 'Bartók in America', *Musical Times* 117 (1976), p. 123.

14 See, for instance, the elaborate 'New York at War' march of 13 June 1942 (pamphlet, *The*

Plan of Demonstration issued by the Mayor's Committee for Mobilization) with its equation of 'refugees' with those fleeing 'conquered countries'.

15 See draft letters, dated 16 September and 7 October 1942, to the Zoo Dog and Cat Hospital (Bartók Archives, Budapest).

16 8 October 1945, p. 74.

17 See *Exploring Music: Essays by Ernst Krenek*, trans. Margaret Shenfield and Geoffrey Skelton (London: Calder & Boyars, 1966), p. 231.

18 The journalistic reporting of Bartók's death was repeated for the other half-dozen unfortunates featured in the 'Milestones' column. In fact, Bartók's treatment erred on the more sober side. Dr Smith Ely Jelliffe was summarized as a 'belligerent Freudian' neuropsychiatrist, while Mrs Jacob Leander Loose's only claim to fame in later years was showering 'Washington society with champagne and Sunshine biscuits'.

19 As, for instance, quoted in Tibor Tallián, *Béla Bartók: The Man and his Work*, trans. Gyula Gulyás, trans. rev. Paul Merrick (Budapest: Corvina, 1988), p. 238.

20 See Tibor Tallián, *Bartók fogadtatása Amerikában, 1940–1945* [Bartók's Reception in America 1940–1945] (Budapest: Zeneműkiadó, 1988) for Bartók's concert programmes, and Malcolm Gillies, 'Bartók's Last Concert?', *Music and Letters* 78 (1997), pp. 92–100, for Bartók's later performance plans.

21 Yves Lenoir, 'Vie et œuvre de Béla Bartók aux Etats-Unis d'Amérique (1940–1945)', diss., Université Catholique de Louvain (1976), vol. 3, p. 54.

22 See, for instance, Lenoir, 'Vie et œuvre', vol. 3, pp. 153–54.

23 See Béla Bartók Jr., *Az öt földrész: Ahogy én láttam 186 utazásomon* [The Five Continents: As I Have Seen Them on My 186 Journeys] (Budapest: Püski, 1992), pp. 22–43.

24 London: Victor Gollancz, 1958.

25 Letter, 17 October 1941; Demény (ed.), *Béla Bartók Letters*, p. 317.

26 Béla Bartók Jr., 'Béla Bartók's Diseases', *Studia musicologica* 23 (1981), pp. 434, 438, 441.

27 See Vera Lampert, 'Bartók at Harvard University', *Studia musicologica* 35 (1993–94), pp. 134–48.

28 Quoted in Malcolm Gillies, *Bartók Remembered* (London: Faber & Faber, 1990), p. 195.

29 Quoted in *ibid.*, p. 196.

30 Rough estimates of Bartók's after-tax income during his American years are US$5,000 (1941), perhaps $3,300 (1942), $3,500 (1943), $3,000 (1944), and Bartók's own estimate of $3,158 for 1945. These estimates,

and the more detailed information provided below, are extrapolated from loose pages found among Bartók's collected correspondence (Peter Bartók's collection, Homosassa, Florida). By contrast, Bartók's own yearly salary at the Hungarian Academy of Sciences in 1940 was 8,640 pengős, approximately US$1,500 at nominal exchange rates. To this, must be added a variety of royalties, private-lesson fees, and significant undeclared foreign-earned income.

31 *The National Income and Product Accounts of the United States, 1929–74: Statistical Tables* (Washington DC: Department of Commerce, 1977), p. 211.

32 Respectively, $3,000, $2,233, and $721.20 in 1941. Bartók's concert income was often hard-won. A circuit of seven concerts between 14 February (Monticello College) and 10 March 1941 (Kansas City) brought in $1,185 in fees, but involved expenses of $1,040 (transport, accommodation, agent's commission), leaving a still taxable $145.

33 Before taxes, personal exemptions, costs for medical and dental care, and allowable deductions were taken into consideration.

34 See, further, Malcolm Gillies, 'Bartók and Boosey & Hawkes: The American Years', *Tempo* 205 (July 1998), pp. 8–11.

35 Estimate of 10 March 1945.

36 [Kurt List], 'Music Composition: Life Work or Side-Line?' *Listen* (June 1945), pp. 5, 6. Bartók, too, was invited to contribute to this survey, but declined.

13 Bartók reception in cold war Europe

Research for this article was supported in part by a grant from the International Research and Exchanges Board (IREX), with funds provided by the National Endowment for the Humanities and the United States Department of State under the Title VIII program; by the American Council of Learned Societies; by the American Musicological Society; and by the University of California, Berkeley. None of these organizations is responsible for the views expressed.

1 René Leibowitz, 'Béla Bartók, ou la possibilité du compromis dans la musique contemporaine', *Les Temps modernes* 3/25 (October 1947), pp. 705–34. Leibowitz's article was also published in English as 'Béla Bartók, or the Possibility of Compromise in Contemporary Music', in *Transition Forty-Eight* 3 (1948), pp. 92–123. My citations are from the English version.

2 See Jean-Paul Sartre, *What is Literature?* trans. Bernard Frechtman (New York: Harper and Row, 1965), pp. 1–2.

3 Leibowitz, 'Béla Bartók, or the Possibility of Compromise', p. 99. See Tony Judt, *Past Imperfect: French Intellectuals, 1944–1956* (Berkeley: University of California Press, 1992), pp. 45–74.

4 Leibowitz, 'Béla Bartók, or the Possibility of Compromise', p. 112.

5 See Ivan F. Waldbauer's chapter in this volume for a discussion of the importance of systematic categorization in the analytical reception of Bartók's music. I would like to thank Professor Waldbauer for sharing his essay with me prior to its publication.

6 Boris de Schloezer, 'Béla Bartók (History vs. Esthetics)', *Transition Forty-Eight* 3 (1948), p. 126.

7 See Judt, *Past Imperfect*, pp. 101–50; Ariane Chebel d'Appollonia, *Histoire politique des intellectuels en France, 1944–1954* (Brussels: Editions Complexe, 1991), esp. vol. 1, pp. 135–69, and vol. 2, pp. 55–105; Maurice Merleau-Ponty, *Humanism and Terror: An Essay on the Communist Problem*, trans. John O'Neill (Boston: Beacon Press, 1969).

8 Bernard Gavoty, 'Bericht aus Paris: Die letzten Werke von Béla Bartók', *Melos* 14/2 (October 1947), pp. 343–44.

9 Claude Rostand, 'Béla Bartók: Chemins et contrastes du musicien', *Contrepoints* 3 (March–April 1946), p. 31.

10 Herbert Eimert, 'Das Violinkonzert von Bartók', *Melos* 14/12 (October 1947), p. 335.

11 Kurt Zimmerreimer, 'Der Stil Béla Bartóks', *Musica* (Kassel) 1/5–6 (September–December 1947), p. 266.

12 On American music policy in West Germany, see especially 'Negotiating Cultural Allies', chapter 1 of Amy Beal, 'Patronage and Reception History of American Experimental Music in West Germany, 1945–1986', Ph.D. diss., University of Michigan (1999). I would like to thank Dr Beal for sharing this chapter with me in advance of its publication.

13 The resolution, aimed at Vano Muradeli, also mentioned Shostakovich and Prokofiev, among others. 'Ob opere "Velikaya druzhba" V. Muradeli, Postanovleniye TsK VKP(b) ot 10 fevralya 1948 g.' [On the Opera 'The Great Friendship' by V. Muradeli, issued by the Central Committee of the Communist [Bolshevik] Party of the Soviet Union on 10 February 1948], *Sovyetskaya Muzyka* [Soviet Music] 1 (1948), pp. 3–8; trans. George S. Counts and Nucia Lodge, *The Country of the Blind: The Soviet System of Mind Control* (Boston: Houghton Mifflin, 1949). This translation has been reprinted in Andrey Olkhovsky, *Music Under the Soviets: The Agony of an Art* (New York: Frederick A. Praeger for the Research Program on the USSR, 1955), pp. 280–85.

14 See Inge Kovács's excellent article, 'Die Ferienkurse als Schauplatz der Ost-West Konfrontation', in *Im Zenit der Moderne: Die Internationalen Ferienkurse für Neue Musik Darmstadt, 1946–1966*, ed. Gianmario Borio and Hermann Danuser (Freiburg im Breisgau: Rombach Verlag, 1997), vol. 1, pp. 116–39.

15 Hans Mayer, 'Kulturkrise und Neue Musik', *Melos* 15/8–9 (August–September 1948), pp. 218–23, and 10 (October 1948), pp. 276–79.

16 Edwin Kuntz, 'Zwischen Hindemith und Schönberg', *Rhein-Neckar-Zeitung* (6 August 1948), p. 2.

17 Bartók's Sixth String Quartet and his Sonatina for Piano were also performed at the Darmstadt summer courses that year.

18 Hermann Scherchen, 'Die gegenwärtige Situation der modernen Musik', *Melos* 16/10 (October 1949), p. 258.

19 Theodor W. Adorno, 'Die gegängelte Musik: Bemerkungen über die Musikpolitik der Ostblockstaaten' (Frankfurt: Verlag Eremiten-Presse, 1954). This essay has been reprinted in Adorno, *Gesammelte Schriften* 14, ed. Rolf Tiedemann (Frankfurt: Suhrkamp Verlag, 1973), pp. 51–66.

20 Scherchen, 'Die gegenwärtige Situation der modernen Musik', pp. 258–59. For a discussion of the accessible style of Milhaud's *Introduction et Marche funèbre* and its political ramifications, see Leslie Sprout, 'Muse of the *Révolution française* or the *Révolution nationale?* 1936–1944', *repercussions* 5/1–2 (Spring–Fall 1996), pp. 73–89.

21 Erich Doflein, 'Gleichgewicht von Geben und Nehmen', in *Musique pure dans un siècle sale: New Music Darmstadt 1950–1960*, compiled by Friedrich Hommel and Wilhelm Schlüter (Darmstadt: Internationales Musikinstitut, 1987) (unpaginated).

22 The post-war Hungarian reception of Bartók's music is explored in greater depth in the author's dissertation, entitled 'The Transition to Communism and the Legacy of Béla Bartók in Hungary, 1945–1956', Ph.D. diss., University of California, Berkeley (1999).

23 Endre Szervánszky, 'Bartók-bemutató' [Bartók Premiere], *Szabad Nép* [Free Folk] (25 April 1947), p. 4.

24 See also critiques by István Péterfi, 'Muzsika – Bartók Béla Concertója' [Music: Béla Bartók's Concerto], *Szabadság* [Freedom] (27 April 1947), p. 4; and József Ujfalussy, 'Zene' [Music], *Új Szántás* [New Ploughing] 1/5 (May 1947), pp. 302–03.

25 See József Ujfalussy, 'Zene', *Új Szántás* 1/11

(November 1947), pp. 662–63; and Endre Gaál, 'Bartók emlékest bemutatóval' [Evening in Bartók's Memory, with a Premiere], *Magyar Nemzet* [Hungarian Nation] (3 October 1947), p. 3.

26 See Lajos Vargyas, 'Zene és közösség' [Music and Community], *Válasz* [Reply] 7 (1948), p. 338.

27 See András Mihály, 'Harc a formalizmus ellen' [Battle against Formalism], *Fórum* 3/3 (March 1948), p. 238.

28 Géza Losonczy, 'Az Operaház legyen a népé!' [Let the Opera House be the People's!], *Szabad Nép* [Free Folk] (5 February 1950), p. 10.

29 György Pollner, letter to Jenő Széll, 9 August 1950. Magyar Országos Levéltár (Hungarian National Archives) 276/89/386, p. 37.

30 *Magyar Rádió Újság* [Hungarian Radio News] (18–24 September 1950).

31 For a discussion of similarities between Bartók's and Schoenberg's music, see János Kárpáti, *Bartók's Chamber Music*, trans. Fred MacNicol and Mária Steiner, trans. rev. Paul Merrick (New York: Pendragon Press, 1994), pp. 36–62.

32 See David E. Schneider, 'Expression in the Time of Objectivity: Nationalism and Modernity in Five Concertos of Béla Bartók', Ph.D. diss., University of California, Berkeley (1997), pp. 46–122.

33 Endre Székely, 'Előre Bartók Béla szellemében a nép kulturális felemelkedéséért!' [Forward in the Spirit of Béla Bartók for the Cultural Advancement of the People!], *Éneklő Nép* [Singing Folk] 3/ 9 (September 1950), p. 2.

34 Ferenc Szabó, 'Bartók nem alkuszik' [Bartók Does Not Compromise], *Új Zenei Szemle* [New Music Review] 1/4 (September 1950), p. 5.

35 Miklós Csillag, 'Csillag Miklós beszéde a Bartók-emléktábla leleplezésénél' [Miklós Csillag's Speech at the Placing of the Bartók Memorial Plaque], *Új Zenei Szemle* 1/5 (October 1950), p. 23.

36 Mihály, 'Válasz egy Bartók-kritikának' [Response to a Bartók-Critique], *Új Zenei Szemle* 1/4 (September 1950), p. 49.

37 *Ibid.*, p. 51.

38 *Ibid.*, p. 55.

39 Arthur Berger, 'The Two Bartóks', *The Saturday Review* (29 August 1953), p. 53.

14 Analytical responses to Bartók's music: pitch organization

1 Discussed in detail by Gregory Dubinsky in 'The Dissemination of Twelve-Tone Composition, 1921–1945', Ph.D. dissertation in progress, University of California, Berkeley. I

would like to thank Mr Dubinsky for making available the typescript of the first chapter.

2 'Harvard Lectures' (1943), in *Béla Bartók Essays*, ed. Benjamin Suchoff (London: Faber & Faber, 1976 repr. Lincoln, Nebr., and London: University of Nebraska Press, 1992), pp. 364–71 and 376–83.

3 Trans. Otto Ortmann (New York: Associated Music Publishers, Inc., 1941–42; rev. 1945).

4 'Harvard Lectures' (1943), in *Béla Bartók Essays*, ed. Suchoff, p. 376. For another personal statement by Bartók, confirming his somewhat negative attitude towards theory, see his interview with Denijs Dille, originally in *La Sirène* I, No. 1 ([March] 1937). János Demény gives a Hungarian translation of it in 'Bartók Béla pályjája deleőjén: teremtő évek – világhódító alkotások (1927–1940)' [Béla Bartók at the Height of his Career – Creative Years – World-Conquering Works (1927–1940)], *Zenetudomanyi tanulmanyok* [Studies in Musicology] 10 (1962), pp. 599–600. An English translation of the latter is to be found in David Schneider 'Expression in the Time of Objectivity: Nationality and Modernity in Five Concertos by Béla Bartók', Ph.D. diss., University of California, Berkeley (1997), pp. 324–26.

5 V. Kofi Agawu discusses this problem in some detail in 'Analytical Issues Raised by Bartók's Improvisations for Piano, Op. 20', *Journal of Musicological Research* 5 (1984), pp. 131–63; see also Malcolm Gillies, 'Bartók Analysis and Authenticity', *Studia musicologica* 36 (1995), pp. 319–27.

6 Edwin von der Nüll, 1930; Ernő Lendvai, 1955 (also 1971 and 1983); János Kárpáti, 1967 (and 1991); Peter Petersen, 1971; Elliott Antokoletz, 1984; and Paul Wilson, 1992. Details of these works are listed in the Bibliography.

7 Nüll's thirteen letters to Bartók, housed in the Budapest Bartók Archives, indicate that Bartók has responded to his questions in detail. Bartók's letters have not been recovered.

8 Kárpáti, *Bartók's Chamber Music*, trans. Fred MacNicol and Mária Steiner, trans. rev. Paul Merrick (New York: Pendragon Press, 1994), p. 187. For examples and somewhat more detailed discussion of Nüll's monograph see Ivan Waldbauer, 'Theorists' Views on Bartók from Edwin von der Nüll to Paul Wilson', *Studia musicologica* 37 (1996), pp. 93–121.

9 Stephen Jay Gould, 'Writing on the Margins', *Natural History* 107/9 (November 1998), pp. 16–20, considers the marriage of 'new ways of thinking with better styles of seeing' as the condition of all fundamental scientific discoveries.

10 Ernő Lendvai, *Bartók stilusa a 'szonáta két zongorára és ütőhangszerekre' és a 'Zene húros-ütőhangszerekre és celestára' tükrében* [Bartók's Style as Seen in the Sonata for Two Pianos and Percussion and in the Music for Strings, Percussion and Celesta] (Budapest: Zeneműkiadó, 1955). Two accounts of this theory are available to the English reader, Ernő Lendvai, *Béla Bartók: An Analysis of his Music* (London: Kahn and Averill, 1971, rev. edn 1979) and his perhaps more detailed *The Workshop of Bartók and Kodály* (Budapest: Editio Musica, 1983).

11 René Leibowitz, 'Béla Bartók, ou la possibilité du compromis dans la musique contemporaine', *Les Temps modernes* 3/24 (October 1947), pp. 705–34. See also chapter 13 in this volume. A detailed discussion of the entire controversy, including Leibowitz's critique and one Hungarian response to it, is to be found in the chapter '"Bartók is Ours", the Sundering of Bartók's Legacy', in Danielle Fosler-Lussier, 'The Transition to Communism and the Legacy of Béla Bartók in Hungary, 1945–1956', Ph.D. diss., University of California, Berkeley (1999). Hungarian readers may also consult János Breuer, 'Bartók Béla Pere' [The Trial of Béla Bartók] in his *Bartók és Kodály* (Budapest: Magvető Könyvkiadó, 1978), pp. 108–38.

12 Lendvai, *Béla Bartók: An Analysis of his Music*, p. 16.

13 This scale has been identified as a folk mode particularly frequent in Romanian folk music.

14 A thorough critique of Lendvai's axis system is found in Paul Wilson, *The Music of Béla Bartók* (New Haven: Yale University Press, 1992), pp. 6–8 and 203–08.

15 An important predecessor to Lendvai's theory is J. H. Douglas Webster, 'Golden-Mean Form in Music', *Music and Letters* 31 (1950), pp. 238–48. Tibor and Peter J. Bachmann, 'An Analysis of Béla Bartók's Music through Fibonnacci Numbers and the Golden Mean', *Musical Quarterly* 65 (1979), pp. 72–82, follow in Lendvai's footsteps. Without accepting Lendvai's theory Perle (in 'The String Quartets of Béla Bartók', in *A Musical Offering: Essays in Honor of Martin Bernstein*, ed. Claire Brook and E. H. Clinkscale [New York: Pendragon Press, 1977], pp. 193–210) counsels against rejecting it out of hand on statistical grounds. Finally Roy Howat criticizes it in both 'Bartók, Lendvai and the Principles of Proportional Analysis', *Musical Analysis* 2 (1983), pp. 65–95 and in 'Masterwork (II): Sonata for Two Pianos and Percussion', in *The Bartók Companion*, ed. Malcolm Gillies (London: Faber & Faber, 1993), pp. 315–30.

16 Milton Babbitt, 'The String Quartets of Bartók', *Musical Quarterly* 35 (1949), pp. 377–85.

17 *Ibid.*, p. 378.

18 *Ibid.*, p. 380.

19 *Ibid.*, p. 380.

20 Details of these references can be found in the Bibliography.

21 Concerning some reservations as to the unequivocal dominant role of E♭ see Ivan Waldbauer, 'Polymodal Chromaticism and Tonal Plan in the First of Bartók's Six Dances in Bulgarian Rhythm', *Studia musicologica* 32 (1990), pp. 241–62.

22 George Perle, 'Symmetrical Formations in the String Quartets of Béla Bartók', *Music Review* 16 (1955), p. 305. Emphasis added.

23 Perle, 'Symmetrical Formations', p. 312, and Perle 'The String Quartets', p. 208.

24 Travis, 'Towards a New Concept of Tonality?' *Journal of Music Theory* 3 (1959), p. 261.

25 *Ibid.*, p. 263. Space precludes a credible summary of the rationale of Salzer's influential analytical technique and its differences from that of Travis. The reader is referred to more detailed descriptions of their work cited in the Bibliography.

26 *Ibid.*, p. 281.

27 *Music Forum* 2 (1970), pp. 298–371.

28 Two thoughtful critiques are in James Baker, 'Schenkerian Analysis and Post-Tonal Music', in *Aspects of Schenkerian Theory*, ed. David Beach (New Haven and London: Yale University Press, 1983), pp. 153–86, and in Joseph N. Straus, 'The Problem of Prolongation in Post-Tonal Music', *Journal of Music Theory* 31 (1987), pp. 1–21; both are more concerned with the Schenkerian method as such than with what Travis has to say about Bartók in particular. In the essay 'Post-Tonal Voice Leading', in *Models of Musical Analysis: Early Twentieth Century*, ed. Jonathan Dunsby (Oxford: Blackwell, 1993), pp. 20–41, Baker himself produced a Schenker graph of the second movement of Bartók's Suite Op. 14. To the best knowledge of the present writer, this is the only orthodox Schenkerian analysis of any Bartók music to date.

29 'Tonality and Structure in Bartók's First Two String Quartets', *Music Review* 32 (August–November 1973), pp. 259–71.

30 With the exception of Kárpáti, the Hungarian scholars, rather than producing new theories, merely make use of music theory in their analyses. For the contributions of László Dobszay, Sándor Kovács, László Somfai, Bence Szabolcsi, Tibor Tallián, József Ujfalussy and András Wilheim, as well as those of Kapst, Lenoir and Oramo, the reader is referred to

Elliott Antokoletz, *Béla Bartók: A Guide to Research*, 2nd edn (New York: Garland Publications, 1997).

31 Kárpáti, *Bartók's Chamber Music*, pp. 81–127, 169–183, and 185–235, respectively.

32 *Ibid.*, p. 102.

33 *Ibid.*, pp. 107–20.

34 John Vinton, 'Bartók on his Own Music', *Journal of the American Musicological Society* 19 (1968), pp. 232–43.

35 Bartók expressed his views on the theoretical and practical impossibility of bitonality and polytonality in the 'Harvard Lectures' (1943), in *Béla Bartók Essays*, ed. Suchoff, p. 366.

36 Antokoletz, *The Music of Béla Bartók*, p. XII. His emphases.

37 Antokoletz, *ibid.*, p. 68, lists all interval cycles. In this and subsequent discussions of interval cycles he draws on Perle, *Twelve-Tone Tonality* (Berkeley and Los Angeles: University of California Press, 1977) and *idem*, 'Berg's Master Array of the Interval Cycles', *Musical Quarterly* 63 (1977), pp. 1–30.

38 The reader intent upon getting better acquainted with the theory of Antokoletz is advised to begin with his three articles in *The Bartók Companion.*, ed. Malcolm Gillies: '"At last something truly new": Bagatelles', pp. 110–23; 'The Middle-period String Quartets', pp. 257–77; 'Concerto for Orchestra', pp. 526–37; as well as 'Organic Development and Interval Cycles', *Studia musicologica* 36 (1995), pp. 249–61 before facing the technical complexities of Antokoletz, *The Music of Béla Bartók*.

39 Richard S. Parks, 'Harmonic Resources in Bartók's "Fourths"', *Journal of Music Theory* 25 (1981), pp. 245–74; James E. Woodward, 'Understanding Bartók's Bagatelle, Op. 6/9,' *Indiana Theory Review* 4 (1981), pp. 11–32. Park's analysis may be compared with Antokoletz, *The Music of Béla Bartók*, p. 198.

40 Richard Cohn, 'Inversional Symmetry and Transpositional Combination in Bartók', *Music Theory Spectrum* 10 (1988), p. 42.

41 Cohn, 'Bartók's Octatonic Strategies: A Motivic Approach', *Journal of the American Musicological Society* (1991), p. 264.

42 Cohn, 'Inversional Symmetry', p. 42.

43 Wilson, *The Music of Béla Bartók*, pp. 55–71. This aspect of Wilson's analysis is summarized without recourse to the specialized terminology and symbols of set theory in Waldbauer, 'Theorists' Views', pp.111–12 and *passim*.

44 These terms refer to widely separated but prominently exposed pitches eventually congealing into sets, and to easily recognized

patterns from the pre-compositional resource, e.g., bass progression by the circle of fifths, in Wilson, *The Music of Béla Bartók*, pp. 23–24 and 39–41, respectively.

15 Bartók at the piano: lessons from the composer's sound recordings

1 Hermann Danuser, 'Auktoriale Aufführungstradition', in *Atti del XIV Congresso della Società Internazionale di Musicologia 1987*, ed. Angelo Pompilio *et al.*, *III: Free Papers* (Turin: E.D.T. Edizioni di Torino, 1990), p. 332. Translation mine.

2 David Dubal, *Reflections From the Keyboard* (New York: Summit Books, 1984), pp. 73–74.

3 Quoted in Hamish Milne, *Bartók: His Life and Times* (Tunbridge Wells: Midas Books, 1982), p. 67.

4 Béla Bartók Jr. and Adrienne Gombocz-Konkoly (eds.), *Bartók Béla családi levelei* [Béla Bartók's Family Letters] (Budapest: Zeneműkiadó, 1981), p. 415.

5 'Mechanical Music' (1937), in *Béla Bartók Essays*, ed. Benjamin Suchoff (London: Faber & Faber, 1976 repr. Lincoln, Nebr., and London: University of Nebraska Press, 1992), pp. 298 and 292.

6 *Ibid.*, p. 293.

7 László Somfai, *Béla Bartók: Composition, Concepts, and Autograph Sources* (Berkeley: University of California Press, 1996), p. 279.

8 The following summary of Bartók's recordings is based on the accompanying material to László Somfai *et al.* (eds.), *Centenary Edition of Bartók's Records*, vol. 1: *Bartók at the Piano 1920–1945* (LPX 12326–33) and vol. 2: *Bartók Record Archives 1912–1944* (LPX 12334–38) (Budapest: Hungaroton, 1981).

9 Somfai *et al.* (eds.), *Centenary Edition*, vol. 2, p. 20 of booklet.

10 'Mechanical Music' (1937), in *Béla Bartók Essays*, ed. Suchoff, pp. 291–92.

11 See note 8.

12 *Bartók at the Piano 1920–1945* (Budapest: Hungaroton, 1991; HCD 12326–31) and *Bartók Recordings from Private Collections* (Budapest: Hungaroton Classic, 1995; HCD 12334–37).

13 Somfai, *Béla Bartók: Composition, Concepts*, pp. 283–85.

14 Philip Hart, in *Fanfare* 5/3 (1982), 67.

15 Somfai, *Béla Bartók: Composition, Concepts*, p. 264.

16 Nörenberg, 'Béla Bartók als volksmusikalisch informierter Interpret eigener Werke', diss., Universität Hamburg (1998).

17 Quoted in Robert Philip, *Early Recordings*

and Musical Style: Changing Tastes in Instrumental Performance, 1900–1950 (Cambridge: Cambridge University Press, 1992), p. 219.

18 *Ibid.*, p. 218.

19 *Ibid.*

20 *Ibid.*, p. 8.

21 Bartók Jr and Gombocz-Konkoly (eds.), *Családi levelek*, pp. 66–67.

22 Andor Földes, 'Béla Bartók', *Tempo* 43 (1957), p. 23.

23 Malcolm Gillies, *Bartók Remembered* (London: Faber & Faber, 1990), p. 98.

24 See in particular Robert Philip's work cited above in note 17 and Robert S. Winter, 'Orthodoxies, Paradoxes, and Contradictions: Performance Practices in Nineteenth-Century Piano Music', in *Nineteenth-Century Piano Music*, ed. R. Larry Todd (New York: Schirmer, 1990), pp. 16–54.

25 Richard Taruskin, *Text and Act: Essays on Music and Performance* (Oxford: Oxford University Press, 1995), p. 131.

26 Achille Rivarde, *The Violin and its Technique* (London: Macmillan, 1921), p. 44. Quoted in Philip, *Early Recordings*, p. 37.

27 Béla Bartók, *The Hungarian Folksong*, ed. Benjamin Suchoff (Albany: State University of New York Press, 1981), p. 14. (Originally published in English as *Hungarian Folk Music* (London: Oxford University Press, 1931.)

28 From Bence Szabolcsi's recollections in Gillies, *Bartók Remembered*, p. 88.

29 Richard Hudson, *Stolen Time: The History of Tempo Rubato* (Oxford: Clarendon Press, 1994), p. 376.

30 György Sándor, 'Versatility as a Stylistic Principle – The Piano Music of Béla Bartók', programme notes to *Béla Bartók Solo Piano Works*, vol. 4 (New York: Sony Classical, 1995), p. 6.

31 Letter to István Thomán, after 18 February 1905. Quoted in Tibor Tallián, *Béla Bartók: The Man and His Work*, trans. Gyula Gulyás, trans. rev. Paul Merrick (Budapest: Corvina, 1988), p. 44.

32 Agatha Fassett, *Béla Bartók's Last Years: The Naked Face of Genius* (London: Gollancz, 1958), pp. 261–62.

33 György Sándor, 'Versatility as a Stylistic Principle', p. 6.

34 Somfai, *Béla Bartók: Composition, Concepts*, pp. 283–85.

35 Ferenc Bónis (ed.), *Így láttuk Bartókot* [As We Saw Bartók] (Budapest: Püski, 1995), p. 148. Translation mine.

36 'Mechanical Music', in *Béla Bartók Essays*, ed. Suchoff, p. 298.

37 Quoted in Taruskin, *Text and Act*, p. 54.

38 *Ibid.*

39 Elizabeth Wilson, *Shostakovich: A Life Remembered* (Princeton: Princeton University Press, 1994), p. 453.

40 Joseph Szigeti, *With Strings Attached*, 2nd edn (New York: Alfred A. Knopf, 1967), p. 129.

41 Földes, 'Béla Bartók', p. 23.

42 *Ibid.*, p. 24.

43 From the recollections of Antal Doráti, in Bónis, *Így láttuk Bartókot*, p. 84. Translation mine.

44 Quoted in the 'Autobiography' (1921), in *Béla Bartók Essays*, ed. Suchoff, p. 411.

45 Letter to Wilhelmine Creel, 17 December 1943, quoted in Tallián, *Béla Bartók*, p. 229; and letter to Wilhelmine Creel, 17 December 1944, quoted in János Demény (ed.) *Béla Bartók Letters*, trans. Péter Balabán and István Farkas, trans. rev. Elizabeth West and Colin Mason (London: Faber & Faber, 1971), p. 342, respectively.

46 Letter to C. P. Wood, 27 November 1943, quoted in Demény (ed.), *Béla Bartók Letters*, p. 329; and letter to Wilhelmine Creel, 17 December 1944, *ibid.*, p. 342, respectively.

47 Letter to Wilhelmine Creel, 17 December 1943, quoted in Tallián, *Béla Bartók*, p. 229.

48 Rosenblum, 'The Uses of *Rubato* in Music, Eighteenth to Twentieth Centuries', *Performance Practice Review* 7 (1994), p. 53.

49 Griffiths, 'Uncorking Elgar's Essence: Five Critics Savor the Bouquet', *New York Times* (22 January 1999), p. E4.

50 Nörenberg, 'Béla Bartók', pp. 88–90.

51 Szigeti, *With Strings Attached*, pp. 338–39.

52 Vera Lampert, 'Bartók's Music on Record: An Index of Popularity', *Studia musicologica* 36 (1995), pp. 393–412.

53 See László Somfai (ed.), *Magyar népzenei hanglemezek Bartók Béla bejegyzéseivel* [Hungarian folk music: gramophone records with Béla Bartók's transcriptions] (Budapest: Hungaroton, 1981) LPX 18058–60, and Bálint Sárosi (ed.), *Magyar népzene Bartók Béla fonográf-felvételeiből* [Hungarian folk music: phonograph cylinders collected by Béla Bartók] (Budapest: Hungaroton, 1981) LPX 18069.

Select bibliography

Béla Bartók's writings

Bartók, Béla Jr., and Adrienne Gombocz-Konkoly (eds.), *Bartók Béla családi levelei* [Béla Bartók's Family Letters] (Budapest: Zeneműkiadó, 1981).

Demény, János (ed.), *Bartók Béla levelei* [Béla Bartók Letters] (Budapest: Magyar Művészeti Tanács, 1948–71); 5th edn (Budapest: Zeneműkiadó, 1976).
Béla Bartók Letters, trans. Péter Balabán and István Farkas, trans. rev. Elizabeth West and Colin Mason (London: Faber & Faber, 1971).
Bartók Béla Briefe (Budapest: Corvina, 1973).

Suchoff, Benjamin (ed.), *Béla Bartók Essays* (London: Faber & Faber, 1976; repr. Lincoln, Nebr., and London: University of Nebraska Press, 1992).

Szőllősy, András (ed.), *Bartók Béla összegyűjtött írásai I* [Béla Bartók's Collected Writings I] Budapest: Zeneműkiadó, 1967).

Tallián, Tibor (ed.), *Bartók Béla Írásai* [The Writings of Béla Bartók], vols. 1 and 5 (Budapest: Zeneműkiadó, 1989 and 1990).

Ujfalussy, József (ed.), *Bartók breviárium (levelek, írások, dokumentumok)* [Bartók breviary (correspondence, essays and documents)] (Budapest: Zeneműkiadó, 1958).

Folk-music studies

Bartók, Béla, and Zoltán Kodály (eds.), *Erdélyi magyar népdalok* [Transylvanian Hungarian Folksongs] (Budapest: A Népies Irodalmi Társaság, 1923; repr. Budapest: Állami Könyvterjesztő Vállalat, 1987).

Bartók, Béla, and Albert B. Lord, *Serbo-Croatian Folk Song* (New York: Columbia University Press, 1951); later published as vol. 1 in Suchoff, Benjamin (ed.), *Yugoslav Folk Music* (Albany: State University of New York Press, 1978), 4 vols.

Dille, Denijs (ed.), *Béla Bartók: Ethnomusicologische Schriften Faksimile-Nachdrucke* (Mainz: B. Schott's Söhne, 1965–68), 4 vols.

Dobszay, László, and Janka Szendrei (eds.), *Catalogue of Hungarian Folksong Types* (Budapest: Institute for Musicology of the Hungarian Academy of Sciences, 1992).

Elscheková, Alica, Oskár Elschek and Jozef Kresánek (eds.), *Slovenské ľudové piesne/Slowakische Volkslieder* (Bratislava: Academia Scientiarum Slovaca, 1959 and 1970), 2 vols.

Kovács, Sándor, and Ferenc Sebő, *Magyar népdalok: Egyetemes gyűjtemény I* [Hungarian Folksongs: Universal Collection I] (Budapest: Akadémiai Kiadó, 1991).

Suchoff, Benjamin (ed.), *Romanian Folk Music* (The Hague: Martinus Nijhoff, 1967–75), 5 vols.

Turkish Folk Music from Asia Minor (Princeton: Princeton University Press, 1976).

Yugoslav Folk Music (Albany: State University of New York Press, 1978), 4 vols.

The Hungarian Folk Song (Albany: State University of New York Press, 1981). Originally published in English as *Hungarian Folk Music* (Oxford: Oxford University Press, 1931).

Béla Bartók: Studies in Ethnomusicology (Lincoln, Nebr., and London: University of Nebraska Press, 1997).

Secondary sources

Agawu, V. Kofi, 'Analytical Issues Raised by Bartók's Improvisations for Piano, Op. 20', *Journal of Musicological Research* 5 (1984), pp. 131–63.

Antokoletz, Elliott, *The Music of Béla Bartók: A Study of Tonality and Progression in Twentieth-Century Music* (Berkeley: University of California Press, 1984).

'Organic Development and Interval Cycles', *Studia musicologica* 36 (1995), pp. 249–61.

Béla Bartók: A Guide to Research, 2nd edn (New York: Garland Publications, 1997).

Babbitt, Milton, 'The String Quartets of Bartók', *Musical Quarterly* 35 (1949), pp. 377–85.

Bachmann, Tibor, and Peter J., 'An Analysis of Béla Bartók's Music through Fibonnacci Numbers and the Golden Mean', *Musical Quarterly* 65 (1979), pp. 72–82.

Baker, James, 'Schenkerian Analysis and Post-Tonal Music', in *Aspects of Schenkerian Theory*, ed. David Beach (New Haven and London: Yale University Press, 1983), pp. 153–86.

Baloghy, Ernő, *A Magyar Kultúra és a Nemzetiségek* [Hungarian Culture and the Nationalities] (Budapest: Deutsch Zsigmond és Társa Könyvkereskedése, 1908).

Bartók, Béla, Jr., 'Béla Bartók's Diseases', *Studia musicologica* 23 (1981), pp. 427–41.

Bellman, Jonathan, *The Style Hongrois in the Music of Western Europe* (Boston: Northeastern University Press, 1993).

Berger, Arthur, 'The Two Bartóks', *The Saturday Review* (29 August 1953), pp. 52–53.

Bernard, Jonathan W., 'Space and Symmetry in Bartók', *Journal of Music Theory* 30/2 (Fall 1986), pp. 185–201.

Berry, Wallace, 'Symmetrical Interval Sets and Derivative Pitch Materials in Bartók's String Quartet No. 3', *Perspectives of New Music* 18 (1979–80), pp. 287–379.

Bónis, Ferenc (ed.), *Béla Bartók: His Life in Pictures*, 2nd edn (Budapest: Corvina, 1964).

Így láttuk Bartókot [As We Saw Bartók] (Budapest: Püski, 1995).

The Selected Writings of Zoltán Kodály, trans. L. Halápy and F. MacNicol (London: Boosey and Hawkes, 1964).

Borio, Gianmario and Hermann Danuser (eds.), *Im Zenit der Moderne: Die Internationalen Ferienkurse für Neue Musik Darmstadt, 1946–1966* (Freiburg im Breisgau: Rombach Verlag, 1997).

Cohn, Richard, 'Inversional Symmetry and Transpositional Combination in
    Bartók', *Music Theory Spectrum* 10 (1988), pp. 19–42.
    'Bartók's Octatonic Strategies: A Motivic Approach', *Journal of the American
    Musicological Society* 54 (1991), pp. 262–300.

Cooper, David, *Béla Bartók: Concerto for Orchestra* (Cambridge: Cambridge
    University Press, 1996).

Crow, Todd (ed.), *Bartók Studies* (Detroit: Information Coordinators, 1976).

Demény, János, 'Bartók Béla tanulóévei és romantikus korszaka (1899–1905)' [Béla
    Bartók's Student Years and Romantic Period], *Zenetudományi tanulmányok*
    [Studies in Musicology], ed. Bence Szabolcsi and Dénes Bartha, 2 (1954), pp.
    323–489.

    'Bartók Béla művészi kibontakozásának évei I: találkozás a népzenével
    (1906–1914)' [The Years of Béla Bartók's Artistic Evolution I: Encounter with
    Folk Music (1906–1914)], *Zenetudományi tanulmányok*, ed. Bence Szabolcsi and
    Dénes Bartha, 3 (1955), pp. 286–459.

    'Bartók Béla művészi kibontakozásának évei II: Bartók megjelenése az európai
    zeneéletben (1914–1926)' [The Years of Bartók's Artistic Evolution II: Bartók's
    Appearance in European Musical Life (1914–1926)], *Zenetudományi
    tanulmányok*, ed. Bence Szabolcsi and Dénes Bartha, 7 (1959), pp. 5–425.

    'Bartók Béla pályája delelőjén: teremtő évek – világhódító alkotások (1927–1940)'
    [Béla Bartók at the Height of his Career – Creative Years – World-Conquering
    Works (1927–1940)], *Zenetudományi tanulmányok*, ed. Bence Szabolcsi and
    Dénes Bartha, 10 (1962), pp. 189–727.

    'Zeitgenössische Kritiken über die erstauffuhrüngen der Kossuth-Symphonie von
    Béla Bartók (Budapest, 13. January 1904 – Manchester, 19. Februar. 1904)',
    Documenta Bartókiana 1 (1964), pp. 30–62.

Dille, Denijs, 'Angaben zum Violinkonzert 1907, den *Deux Portraits*, dem Quartett
    Op. 7 und den Zwei rumänischen Tänzen', *Documenta Bartókiana* 2 (1965), pp.
    92–102.

Dubal, David, *Reflections From the Keyboard* (New York: Summit Books, 1984).

Dunsby, Jonathan (ed.), *Models of Musical Analysis: Early Twentieth Century*
    (Oxford: Blackwell, 1993).

Eimert, Herbert, 'Das Violinkonzert von Bartók', *Melos* 14/12 (October 1947), pp.
    335–37.

Éri, Gyöngyi, and Zsuzsa Jobbágyi (eds.), *A Golden Age: Art and Society in Hungary
    1896–1914* (Budapest: Corvina, 1989).

Fassett, Agatha, *Béla Bartók's Last Years: The Naked Face of Genius* (London:
    Gollancz, 1958).

Földes, Andor, 'Béla Bartók', *Tempo* 43 (1957), pp. 22–24.

Forte, Allen, 'Bartók's "Serial" Composition', *Musical Quarterly* 40 (1960), pp.
    233–45.

Frigyesi, Judit, 'Between Rubato and Rigid Rhythm: A Particular Type of
    Rhythmical Asymmetry as Reflected in Bartók's Writings on Folk Music', *Studia
    musicologica* 24 (1983), pp. 327–37.

    'Béla Bartók and the Concept of Nation and "Volk"', *Musical Quarterly* 78/2
    (1994), pp. 255–87.

Béla Bartók and Turn-of-the-Century Budapest (Berkeley: University of California Press, 1998).

Gillies, Malcolm, *Notation and Tonal Structure in Bartók's Later Works* (New York: Garland, 1989).

Bartók in Britain (Oxford: Oxford University Press, 1989).

Bartók Remembered (London: Faber & Faber, 1990).

'Bartók Analysis and Authenticity', *Studia musicologica* 36 (1995), pp. 319–27.

'Bartók and Boosey & Hawkes: The American Years', *Tempo* 205 (July 1998), pp. 8–11.

'Bartók's Last Concert?' *Music and Letters* 78 (1997), pp. 92–100.

Gillies, Malcolm (ed.), *The Bartók Companion* (London: Faber & Faber, 1993).

Gluck, Mary, *Lukács and His Generation: 1900–1918* (Cambridge, Mass.: Harvard University Press, 1985).

Gow, David, 'Tonality and Structure in Bartók's First Two String Quartets', *Music Review* 32 (August–November 1973), pp. 259–71.

Howat, Roy, 'Bartók, Lendvai and the Principles of Proportional Analysis', *Musical Analysis* 2 (1983), pp. 69–95.

Kadarkay, Árpád (ed.), *The Lukács Reader* (Oxford: Blackwell, 1995).

Kárpáti, János, *Bartók's String Quartets*, trans. Fred MacNicol (Budapest: Corvina, 1975). (The Hungarian original was published in 1967.)

Bartók's Chamber Music, trans. Fred MacNicol and Mária Steiner; trans. rev. Paul Merrick (New York: Pendragon Press, 1994).

'A Typical *Jugendstil* Composition: Bartók's String Quartet No. 1', *The Hungarian Quarterly* 36 (Spring 1995), pp. 130–40.

Kenneson, Claude, *Székely and Bartók: The Story of a Friendship* (Portland: Amadeus Press, 1994).

Korbay, Francis, *Hungarian Melodies* (London and Leipzig: Stanley Lucas, Weber, Pitt and Hatzfeld Ltd., 1893).

Kovács, Sándor, 'Reexamining the Bartók/Serly Viola Concerto', *Studia musicologica* 23 (1981), pp. 295–322.

'Formprobleme beim Violakonzert von Bartók/Serly', *Studia musicologica* 24 (1982), pp. 381–91.

Krenek, Ernst, *Exploring Music: Essays by Ernst Krenek*, trans. Margaret Shenfield and Geoffrey Skelton (London: Calder & Boyars, 1966).

Kroó, György, *A Guide to Bartók* (Budapest: Corvina, 1974).

Laki, Peter (ed.), *Béla Bartók and His World* (Princeton: Princeton University Press, 1995).

Lampert, Vera, 'Quellenkatalog der Volksliedbearbeitungen von Bartók', *Documenta Bartókiana* 6 (1981), pp. 15–149.

'Bartók at Harvard University', *Studia musicologica* 35 (1993–94), pp. 113–54.

'Bartók's Music on Record: An Index of Popularity', *Studia musicologica* 36 (1995), pp. 393–412.

Leafstedt, Carl, *Inside Bluebeard's Castle: Music and Drama in Béla Bartók's Opera* (New York: Oxford University Press, 1999).

Leibowitz, René, 'Béla Bartók, ou la possibilité du compromis dans la musique contemporaine', *Les Temps modernes* 3/25 (October 1947), pp. 705–34.

Published in English as 'Béla Bartók, or the Possibility of Compromise in Contemporary Music' in *Transition Forty-Eight* 3 (1948), pp. 92–123.

Lendvai, Ernő, *Bartók stilusa a 'szonáta két zongorára és ütőhangszerekre' és a 'Zene húros-ütőhangszerekre és celestára' tükrében* [Bartók's Style as Seen in the Sonata for Two Pianos and Percussion and in the Music for Strings, Percussion and Celesta] (Budapest: Zeneműkiadó, 1955).

Béla Bartók: An Analysis of his Music (London: Kahn and Averill, 1971; rev. edn 1979).

The Workshop of Bartók and Kodály (Budapest: Editio Musica, 1983).

'The Limits of Musical Analysis', *The New Hungarian Quarterly* 26/97 (Spring 1985), pp. 201–07.

Lukacs, John, *Budapest 1900: A Historical Portrait of a City and Its Culture* (New York: Weidenfeld and Nicolson, 1988).

Macleod, Joseph, *The Sisters d'Aranyi* (London: George Allen and Unwin Ltd., 1969).

Mason, Colin, 'An Essay in Analysis: Tonality, Symmetry, and Latent Serialism in Bartók's Fourth Quartet', *Music Review* 18 (1957), pp. 189–201.

Mayer, Hans, 'Kulturkrise und Neue Musik', *Melos* 15/8–9 (August–September 1948), pp. 218–23, and 10 (October 1948), pp. 276–79.

Meyer, John A., 'Beethoven and Bartók: A Structural Parallel', *Music Review* 31 (1970), pp. 315–21.

Michael, Frank, 'Analytische Anmerkungen zu Bartók's 2. Klavierkonzert', *Studia musicologica* 24 (1983), pp. 425–37.

Mihály, András, 'Harc a formalizmus ellen' [Battle against Formalism], *Fórum* 3/3 (March 1948), pp. 236–38.

Milne, Hamish, *Bartók: His Life and Times* (Tunbridge Wells: Midas Books, 1982).

Nüll, Edwin von der, *Béla Bartók: Ein Beitrag zur Morphologie der neuen Musik* (Halle and Saale: Mitteldeutsche Verlags-Aktiongesellschaft, 1930).

Olkhovsky, Andrey, *Music Under the Soviets: The Agony of an Art* (New York: Frederick A. Praeger for the Research Program on the USSR, 1955).

Parks, Richard S., 'Harmonic Resources in Bartók's "Fourths"', *Journal of Music Theory* 25 (1981), pp. 245–74.

Perle, George, 'Symmetrical Formations in the String Quartets of Béla Bartók', *Music Review* 16 (1955), pp. 300–12.

'The String Quartets of Béla Bartók', in *A Musical Offering: Essays in Honor of Martin Bernstein*, ed. Claire Brook and E. H. Clinkscale (New York: Pendragon Press, 1977), pp. 193–210.

Petersen, Peter, *Die Tonalität im Instrumental-Schaffen von Béla Bartók* (Hamburg: Karl Dieter Wagner, 1971).

Philip, Robert, *Early Recordings and Musical Style: Changing Tastes in Instrumental Performance, 1900–1950* (Cambridge: Cambridge University Press, 1992).

Salzer, Felix, *Structural Hearing: Tonal Coherence in Music*, 2nd edn (New York: Dover, 1962) (first edn 1952).

Scherchen, Hermann, 'Die gegenwärtige Situation der modernen Musik', *Melos* 16/10 (October 1949), pp. 257–59.

de Schloezer, Boris, 'Béla Bartók (History vs. Esthetics)', *Transition Forty-Eight* 3 (1948), pp. 123–28.

Somfai, László, 'Béla Bartók. Second Sonata for Violin and Piano', *A hét zeneműve*
  [The Masterpiece of the Week] 4 (Budapest: Editio Musica, 1977), pp. 44–55.
  'Strategics of Variation in the Second Movement of Bartók's Violin Concerto
  1937–38', *Studia musicologica* 19 (1977), pp. 161–202.
  Béla Bartók: Composition, Concepts, and Autograph Sources (Berkeley: University
  of California Press, 1996).
Stevens, Halsey, *The Life and Music of Béla Bartók*, 3rd edn, ed. Malcolm Gillies
  (Oxford: Clarendon Press, 1993).
Straus, Joseph N., 'The Problem of Prolongation in Post-Tonal Music', *Journal of
  Music Theory* 31 (1987), pp. 1–21.
Stravinsky, Igor, *Poetics of Music in the Form of Six Lessons,* trans. A. Knodel and I.
  Dahl (New York: Vintage Books, 1956).
  An Autobiography (New York: The Norton Library, 1962).
Sugar, Peter F., Péter Hanák and Tibor Frank (eds.), *A History of Hungary*
  (Bloomington: Indiana University Press, 1990).
Szabolcsi, Bence, *A Concise History of Hungarian Music* (Budapest: Corvina, 1964).
Szigeti, Joseph, *With Strings Attached*, 2nd edn (New York: Alfred A. Knopf, 1967).
Tallián, Tibor, *Béla Bartók: The Man and his Work*, trans. Gyula Gulyás, trans. rev.
  Paul Merrick (Budapest: Corvina, 1988).
  Bartók fogadtatása Amerikában, 1940–1945 [Bartók's Reception in America
  1940–1945] (Budapest: Zeneműkiadó, 1988).
Taruskin, Richard, *Text and Act: Essays on Music and Performance* (Oxford: Oxford
  University Press, 1995).
Travis, Roy, 'Towards a New Concept of Tonality?' *Journal of Music Theory* 3 (1959),
  pp. 257–84.
  'Tonal Coherence in the First Movement of Bartók's Fourth String Quartet', *Music
  Forum* 2 (1970), pp. 298–371.
Treitler, Leo, 'Harmonic Procedures in the Fourth Quartet of Béla Bartók', *Journal of
  Music Theory* 3 (1959), pp. 292–98.
Ujfalussy, József, *Béla Bartók*, trans. Ruth Pataki (Budapest: Corvina, 1971).
Vikárius, László, 'Béla Bartók's *Cantata Profana*', *Studia musicologica* 35/1–1 (1993),
  pp. 249–301.
  Modell és inspirátió Bartók zenei gondolkodásában [Model and Inspiration in
  Bartók's Musical Thinking] (Pécs: Jelenkor Kiadó, 1999).
Waldbauer, Ivan, 'Polymodal Chromaticism and Tonal Plan in the First of Bartók's
  Six Dances in Bulgarian Rhythm', *Studia musicologica* 32 (1990), pp. 241–62.
  'Theorists' Views on Bartók from Edwin von der Nüll to Paul Wilson', *Studia
  musicologica* 37 (1996), pp. 93–121.
Whittall, Arnold, 'Bartók's Second String Quartet', *Music Review* 32 (1971), pp.
  265–70.
  Music Since the First World War (New York: St Martin's Press, 1977).
Wilson, Paul, *The Music of Béla Bartók* (New Haven: Yale University Press, 1992).
Zimmerreimer, Kurt, 'Der Stil Béla Bartóks', *Musica* (Kassel) 1/5–6
  (September–December 1947), pp. 262–66.
Zsuffa, Jozsef, *Béla Balázs: The Man and the Artist* (Berkeley and Los Angeles:
  University of California Press, 1987).

Index